The Orientation of Future Cinema

Technology, Aesthetics, Spectacle

BRUCE ISAACS

B L O O M S B U R Y

LONDON • NEW DELHI • NEW YORK • SYDNEY

Bloomsbury Academic

An imprint of Bloomsbury Publishing Plc

175 Fifth Avenue	50 Bedford Square
New York	London
NY 10010	WC1B 3DP
USA	UK

www.bloomsbury.com

First published 2013

Library of Congress Cataloging-in-Publication Data
Isaacs, Bruce.
The orientation of future cinema : technology, aesthetics, spectacle / by Bruce Isaacs.
p. cm.
ISBN 978-1-4411-8422-1 (hardcover : alk. paper) 1. Motion picture industry–Technological innovations. 2. Motion pictures–Aesthetics. 3. Digital media–Influence. I. Title.
PN1995.9.T43I83 2013
791.4301–dc23
2012033532
ISBN 9781441184221
2012045678

ISBN: HB: 978-1-4411-8422-1

Typeset by Fakenham Prepress Solutions, Fakenham, Norfolk NR21 8NN
Printed and bound in the United States of America

Contents

PART THREE On the Characteristics of Future Cinema 237

Acknowledgements

This book benefited enormously from financial support from the University of Sydney. The School of Letters, Art and Media provided two annual grants that contributed to research and writing. I also received a research grant from the United States Studies Centre that enabled me to undertake research in Los Angeles and San Francisco in early 2012.

I'm very fortunate to work with a number of great people, who help to make my job as a film academic a source of genuine pleasure. I wish to make special mention of the constant support and encouragement over a number of years of David Kelly, Peter Marks, Judith Keene and Jennifer Milam. These people, in one way or another, have been instrumental in the development of my career, my thinking on cinema and art, and my own place in the evolving role of arts-based scholarship.

I am deeply grateful for the generosity of Sam Cosentino and Jenny Ward, who were instrumental in getting me 'connected' with key practitioners in the studio system. I thank Steve Ross at USC, who put me in touch with Tad Marburg, who in turn put me in touch with key production personnel in Los Angeles and San Francisco. I especially wish to thank Rick Sayre at Pixar, who was generous with his time, but also interested in what I had to say. I got to spend an afternoon with Richard King, a key sound designer and editor at Warner Bros. – Richard's insights into the contemporary studio system were illuminating. John Lee, second editor on *The Dark Knight Rises*, provided the kind of insight into large-scale studio production that is hard to get at second or third hand. Philip Lelyveld and Bryan Gonzales at the Entertainment Technology Center at USC provided up-to-date and insightful commentary on contemporary 3-D image (and sound, yes, 3-D *sound*) technology. Katie Gallof at Continuum Press has been an absolute pleasure to work with on this project. She brought a fantastic presence to the professional side of things.

I wish to thank my family, who are keen film enthusiasts. A great deal of my thinking in this book filters through my twin brother, Herschel, whose experience of cinema accompanied, and continues to accompany, my own. Last, I wish to thank Rebecca Goldsworthy, my wife, who has supported every aspect of my fascination with cinema. Every thought in

ACKNOWLEDGEMENTS

this book is bounced off of her first, revised, and invariably enriched. I thank her for everything she has brought to this book, and to our lives together.

PART ONE

The age of late cinema

1

On cinematic experience

Early and late cinema

Screen, film, spectator; image, movement, and time; representation and the problem of 'realism', or the relation of image to referent; signification and narrative; technology and art: the form and vocabulary in which these questions are posed has changed continuously in the history of film theory as a series of conflictual debates. Yet the basic set of concepts has remained remarkably constant.[1]

One of the earliest experiences of moving images was an encounter with a train arriving at a station. The spectacle of Lumière's train (*L'Arrivée d'un Train à La Ciotat* [*Arrival of a Train at a Station*], 1895) assaulted the senses of an unsuspecting audience who had merely gathered in a café, as they had so many times before, to see what the fuss was about.[2] The train was, as Tom Gunning has suggested, a shock to the spectator.[3] The object of fascination was not a mechanical form, not the instrument of modern industrialized life, but an image on a screen. It was this image in movement that enthralled the 'naïve' spectator. And yet now, after a century of viewing cinema, of living life through the screen, that early encounter seems so far distant as to be almost incomprehensible. What must that moment have been like, to see actual life

---

[1] D. N. Rodowick, *The Virtual Life of Film* (Cambridge, MA: Harvard University Press, 2007), 188.
[2] Auguste and Louis Lumière, *L'Arrivée d'un Train à La Ciotat* (*Arrival of a Train at a Station*, 1895), YouTube Video (0:50sec.), http://www.youtube.com/watch?v=1dgLEDdFddk [accessed 14 March 2011]. For a lively account of the formation of early cinema, see Kristin Thompson and David Bordwell, *Film History: An Introduction* (New York: McGraw-Hill Education, 2010), 3–21.
[3] Tom Gunning, 'An Aesthetic of Astonishment: Early Film and the (In)Credulous Spectator', in *Viewing Positions: Ways of Seeing Film*, ed. Linda Williams (New Brunswick, NJ: Rutgers University Press, 1995), 115. While Gunning rejects the mythology of 'initial terror' that inflects a great deal of the theory of early cinema spectatorship, he acknowledges that 'there is no question that a reaction of astonishment and even a type of terror accompanied early projections' (116).

transfigured in a moving image? How would the spectator have made sense of such a spectacle?

This chapter reflects on how cinema manifests in individual and collective minds, from Lumière's early moving images to what I call the age of late cinema, in which new technologies, new cinematic spaces, the new material of cinematic life, transforms the old medium into something equally astonishing.[4] I begin by revisiting some of the sacred positions brought to bear on a century of meditation on the medium: on its claims to aesthetic brilliance, philosophical truth, or more humbly, to represent that which we already experience in our sensory lives – the image of the world. Surely this is where we begin each time we enter the darkened space of the theatre, or sit in front of our laptops – the cinema gives us back the life we experience through our senses.

However, cinema could never maintain a century-long life as merely representation. For the image to be of any real value, it must be greater than, merely, the image of the world. As Bazin suggests, the question of experiencing the world through cinema, which is perhaps the fundamental question that drives its spectators to the theatre, is a psychological one.[5] Cinema represents an obsessive tendency to experience the world in a certain way. In an engaging meditation on cinema's effect, Sean Cubitt declares: 'I want to know what cinema does. If it causes no effect, however ornery or belated, cinema doesn't do anything, and there is left only the question of what it is or, more exactly, what it fails to be. Cinema does something, and what it does matters.'[6] Cubitt's charge here is to return to the essence of cinema – the matter that makes it what it is. But what it *is*, for Cubitt, is determined by what kind of transformation it effects. His position is thus a savvy confrontation with the long history of cinema that traces its being, its ontological presence, without also illuminating its purpose. How else might a spectator explain an obsession with cinema, but as a radically *new* image of the world? Why else would we seek it out?

In this chapter, I wish to charge the spectator (and reader) with the self-same shock of the image Gunning identifies in Lumière's early film

---

[4] For an account of cinema's transformation from early to late, and its concomitant transformation of private and public sphere engagement, see Miriam Hansen, 'Early Cinema, Late Cinema: Permutations of the Public Sphere', *Screen* 34, no. 3 (1993), 197–210.

[5] André Bazin, 'The Myth of Total Cinema', in *What is Cinema? Volume 1*, trans. Hugh Gray (Berkeley and Los Angeles: University of California Press, 1967). Bazin's reading of the trajectory of the image toward a 'total cinema' implies a psychological and active engagement with that image rather than a passive absorption of the perfect illusion of the real. See also André Bazin, 'The Ontology of the Photographic Image', in *What is Cinema? Volume 1*, trans. Hugh Gray (Berkeley and Los Angeles: University of California Press, 1967), 7. The image of the real, for Bazin, is necessarily ambiguous.

[6] Sean Cubitt, *The Cinema Effect* (Cambridge, MA: MIT Press, 2004), 1.

– images that, spellbinding then, materialize now as grainy, degraded, flawed, and for this lack of pixilated brilliance, all but inaccessible. Take a moment to stream a YouTube clip of Lumière's *L'Arrivée d'un Train en Gare de La Ciotat* (Arrival of a Train at a Station, 1895). Experience the banality of this black and white image, that was once new and pristine, but is now degraded in digital form. To my students, and perhaps to the majority of contemporary cinema spectators, this image is lifeless. But if cinema is to maintain its life for the foreseeable future, if it is to invigorate an image of the world growing ever distant from the celluloid century of the medium, the image must continue to manifest as astonishment, as novelty object. This must be its overarching effect: to astonish, to fascinate, to engage, to overwhelm the senses, to transform the internally, psychologically animated lives of its spectators.

Old and new technologies of the image

Lumière's celluloid image, and the celluloid image of the greater part of the life of cinema, was a product of technological opportunity. At a point of origin in the late nineteenth century, with the image so strikingly new to the world, equally fascinating and disconcerting for the early spectator was the technological object that gave the image in movement its unnatural life – the *Cinématographe* (figure 1.1).

This small square box rested on tripod legs (though it could easily be held and carried) and cranked out, quite literally, its moving image of the world. The device permitted the observer to 'capture' the world – a speeding locomotive, or women leaving a factory, a baby being fed, a comedic routine involving a garden hose, later royal parades and commemorations, exotic wonders of the Far East, even races at Flemington, Melbourne.[7] These worlds, once present and past in the same instant to our sensory perception, and irrecoverable outside of the still life of a photograph, were brought back in the fullness of their movement – a train that was now a projectile, bursting into a station that had materialized in the quaint interior of a Parisian café (Salon Indien du Grand Café).

The fascination of early cinema was equally a fascination with the technology of a new world, a mechanism that belonged to industrial modernity alongside the motorcar and the airplane. Much of Lumière's most interesting early cinema depicts industrial processes, such as a train arriving at a station, or workers exiting a factory. In an account of the origins of the

---

[7] Thompson and Bordwell, *Film History*, 12–13.

FIGURE 1.1 *Early Cinema's Apparatus: the* Cinématographe.

Cinématographe, Bordwell depicts the early presence of the camera as a novelty mechanism, and Lumière and his coterie of cinematographers as fiercely protective of the secret of their new technology. Other pioneers of varying kinds, including Méliès, attempted to purchase the *Cinématographe* from the Lumières without success. Even when travelling the world, spanning the continents of Europe and North America in the first year (1895–96), and much of the rest of the world by 1897, Lumière's cinematographers kept their technology to themselves.[8]

Cinema was a technological object then, a product of an industrial modernity, and its long history has seen an evolution of that technological form. The screened image engages our senses, certainly. We are moved, or in currently fashionable language, *affected* by its potentiality on the screen. But the technology that once gave life to moving images, and arrested the world's attention with its seemingly magical properties, is equally present in the material of current cinematic life. The technology of the life of the image remains a profound presence in the most immediate, unadorned, uncon-cocted cinema. The most determinedly and self-consciously realist cinema, the early Dogme films for example, present a technological image, an image born of a uniquely technological effect. To return to Cubitt, surely the quest for the purpose of cinema must engage the image as a material that springs, at the end of a long itinerary, not from the actual physical world, or from the world of the senses, or indeed from the internal world of the imagination – but from a mechanical contraption.

I'm sitting at the present moment in my office surveying the product of new technology: YouTube and its technological shell, an iMac (27" wides-creen display) with its assorted paraphernalia of image production and reception. On screen, I have a stream of film, streaming in the present an

---

[8] For an account of the creation and industrial development of early cinema in France, see Richard Abel, *The Ciné Goes to Town: French Cinema 1896–1914* (Berkeley and Los Angeles: University of California Press, 1994), 10–18.

image from December 1895, when Lumière first captured a group of women exiting a factory: *La Sortie des usines Lumière à Lyon* [*Workers Leaving the Lumière Factory in Lyon*, 1895].[9] The clip stream is 38 seconds in duration. Cubitt makes ingenious use of this simple tract of film (though, of course, it's no longer film, a notion I will attempt to project to its radical end), but here, on YouTube, with the image moving in awkward, spasmodic sections, I wish to merely stop it in its natural motion. The natural life of this image in 1895 was as an image in motion – as what Bazin terms, in another context, the image of inherent continuity;[10] I address this section of film as a continuous flow of place and people in time. But now, on my iMac screen, this inherent continuity of motion, this movement, has been stilled. I have the YouTube clip on pause, bringing what was a natural progression of early cinema to the more artificial still-life digital rendering. You may wish to call up this image on your own screen. The pause is arbitrary, at 17 seconds; the postures of the bodies are natural, though their stillness is a contrivance of the technology at my fingertips.

Stilled this way, Lumière's image takes on a new and unintended life of its own. My contemplation of the women stilled has altered either my perception of them or the ontology of the streamed image. Stilling the progression, I change in some essential way the image as object. The women now seem constrained by the boundaries of the image; off-screen space, so alive to the potential of the image in movement, is absent here.[11] I *read* the image as a still, I am subjected to the perceptual and psychological properties of a static image. I am prevented from contemplating the possibilities of the 'beyond of the image' because that duration is absent. The photographic image is not only dissimilar from the moving image, but is made out of the *absence of movement*.[12] But should I click my mouse and again animate the image,

---

[9] Auguste and Louis Lumière, *La Sortie des usines Lumière à Lyon* [*Workers Leaving the Lumière Factory in Lyon*], YouTube Video (1:50sec.), http://www.youtube.com/watch?v=BO0EkMKfgJI [accessed 14 March 2011].

[10] André Bazin, 'The Evolution of the Language of Cinema', in *What is Cinema? Volume 1*, trans. Hugh Gray (Berkeley and Los Angeles: University of California Press, 1967), 37.

[11] For an influential discussion of the image 'beyond the frame', see Stanley Cavell, *The World Viewed: Reflections on the Ontology of Film* (Cambridge, MA: Harvard University Press, 1979), 24–5.

[12] Gilles Deleuze, *Cinema 1: The Movement Image*, trans. Hugh Tomlinson and Barbara Habberjam (Minneapolis: University of Minnesota Press, 2009), 2–3. Deleuze distinguishes between cinema's movement that is 'in the apparatus' and the still image as a discretized unit, the 'photogram'. For Deleuze, the image in movement presents a particular effect and affect: 'in short, cinema does not give us an image to which movement is added, it immediately gives us a movement-image.' For a discussion of the photograph's 'immanent storytelling' that 'project[s] the images into the past and into the future', see Damian Sutton, *Photography, Cinema, Memory: The Crystal Image of Time* (Minneapolis: University of Minnesota Press, 2009), 143.

its life becomes a cinema of motion and continuity. And again, in motion, I sense that this is how it *must* be experienced – in motion and continuity. The distinction between the still life of Lumière's factory (something like a tableau) and a moving image, a daily ritual of leaving a factory, is a function of the technology (once a *Cinématographe*, now a more complex image production apparatus) that has captured an image of the world.

Critical to our consideration of the meaning of the cinematic image is its life through movement. Certainly Lumière could have stilled the image in 1895. But why would he want to? Why would a new filmmaker (in its earliest incarnation, the filmmaker was something like the classical explorer, bent on discovering a new world),[13] a pioneer of the moving image, wish to still it? Rather, he would play with the coordinates of natural time. Early filmmakers, notably Méliès, but also Lumière, sped up the image progression, or slowed it down. It was not for some time that the image fixed to a transparent narrative context, and even then it maintained the novelty of this new way of capturing the world, playing with its coordinates of space and time, speeding up and slowing down life's internal rhythms, manifesting as a trick effect.[14] The moving image, Lumière discovered, could provide a caricatured 'trace of the real', and this is how he used his new technology. It would be some time before cinema would find its natural, narrative speed, which perhaps constitutes the grounding of narrative realism.[15]

The upshot of this imagining of the image in the past and present is to return cinema to a question of materiality, both the material of its construction, its technology, and the materiality of its purpose, how it translates to spectators as a part of their lives – cinema's overarching and essential use-value. Lumière's women exiting a factory are bodies in motion. This is the essential matter of their being, of what I've called their cinematic life. I disagree that progression and continuity is merely one possibility of this cinematic image.[16] Of course I could alter this continuity, I could make this motion discontinuous. Lumière could have rendered these women before a factory as a photograph. But in the age of the *Cinématographe*, why would

---

[13] For an engaging account of Robert Flaherty as explorer, see Eric Barnouw, *Documentary: A History of the Non-Fiction Film* (New York: Oxford University Press, 1993), 34–51.

[14] See Barry Salt, *Film Style and Technology: History and Analysis*, 2nd edition (London: Starword, 1992), 34–6.

[15] Musser locates early cinema's narrativization in the travel film, which sought to produce the experience of movement, a 'perception which was initially disorienting, then pleasurable'. See Charles Musser, 'The Travel Genre in 1903–1904: Moving Towards Fictional Narrative', in *Early Cinema: Space, Frame, Narrative*, ed. Thomas Elsaesser (London: BFI, 2010), 128.

[16] For this position, see Cubitt, *Cinema Effect*, 35–41. For a persuasive reading of Lumière's early cinema as structured narrative form, see Marshall Deutelbaum, 'Structural Patterning in the Lumière Films', *Wide Angle* 3, no. 1 (1979).

he want to? Why would the spectator of industrial modernity and its new technology of seeing wish to see the world in such an archaic, stately, way? Industrialization craved movement, freneticism and intensity. No, the stilled image – or the image of discontinuity – is an aberration in Lumière.

And yet, there is nothing aberrant about the stilled moving-image on a computer screen. The still is like a screen itself. In fact, a simple click and save and scroll through a Tools menu, and Lumière's photographic image of women exiting a factory transforms into my very own wallpaper, inscribed with the signature of my own spectatorship. The image, no longer the property of the technology of the new modernity, becomes personalized in the postmodern, virtual space of the computer screen. On my screen the still image acquires another life altogether. This object, streamed through YouTube but stilled for the moment, takes on a renewed life *as a still image*. This new life stems from, among other things, how I make use of it through the technology of the image. And if this is the case for early cinema and its contemporary presence on an array of office screens, how else might cinema be made use of? This is the currency of the image in contemporary use: as technology, as technological object. It is the process of digitization that reinvigorates celluloid, streaming the past in renewed form, and displaying it as an image discrete from movement or stasis; streamed on YouTube, the early celluloid image in movement becomes a discretized object. To concur with Joseph Natoli, we experience this new technology, and its image, differently, as a different mode of fascination.[17]

Image as itinerary: The image of reality and the synthetic image

What is on screen is not reality but its precipitate, its tracing, its remains which, like the mummy, may allow us to conjure the presence of something fuller, the phantom of that paradoxically more solid reality that hovers spectrally around, behind, or before the screen.[18]

I use the term itinerary to talk about the cinematic image because in its essential material, the screened image is a pathway. It makes little sense as an end in itself. My engagement with cinema is founded upon a desire to

---

[17] Joseph Natoli, *Memory's Orbit: Film and Culture 1999–2000* (Albany: SUNY Press, 2003), 32.
[18] Dudley Andrew, *What Cinema Is!: Bazin's Quest and its Charge* (Malden, MA: Wiley-Blackwell, 2010), 41.

understand further, and more deeply, the condition of life. Cinema, as has been told to us by countless theorists, notably Cavell, but also Eisenstein, Bazin and others, is not *life*.[19] We perceive the world differently to the world we perceive screened back to us. And if we entertain the notion of the autonomous apparatus of cinema, cinema *itself* perceives the world differently.[20] The camera sees something that lies outside of the perceptual coordinates of our senses, visual and aural. When Dziga Vertov roams the city with a camera in *Man With a Movie Camera* (1929), he perceives with a cinematic-eye, an artificial visual perception. This new perception in Soviet cinema is also the product of montage, and montage *is* cinema, to paraphrase Eisenstein.[21] Hitchcock's subjective shot in *Psycho* (1960) – for example, Norman Bates (Anthony Perkins) spying on Marion Crane (Janet Leigh) – is a conflation of various conflicted subjectivities. There is something voyeuristically fascinating and unsettling in inhabiting the subjective space of Norman, yet we are neither Norman, nor categorically ourselves, but a cinematic subject beyond the instrument of a simplistic identification. In the legendary shot of Arbogast's murder, we survey the falling body through a complex movement on a matte background as the body 'falls' down the stairs. Clearly, as spectators subjected to the gaze of Norman (who as Mother presumably views Arbogast's fall after stabbing him), we cannot equate our common visual perception with the cinematic perspective offered by Hitchcock (figure 1.2). That shot, that perception of life, is intrinsic to cinema's creation of the image. Hitchcock's other great cinematic image is the famous '*Vertigo* shot',[22] which in some sense signifies Scottie's (James Stewart) sensation of vertigo, but provides only the barest trace of the perceptual experience of vertigo for the spectator suffering from that condition.

The remarkable achievement of cinematic vision, from its earliest manifestation, is to render a new image of the world. This is cinema's overarching purpose: to render the world as a creative movement beyond the perception of life. Yet in spite of the fundamental gap between reality and the cinema, we must accept that cinema presents life back to the spectator – this is, in my theory of the cinematic image, a point of origin. Without this itinerary, what purpose can the cinema image hope to serve? Without a tacit acceptance

---

[19] Cavell, *The World Viewed*, 16–19. Cavell's critical point, working through Bazin, is that 'film awakens as much as it enfolds you' (17).

[20] On cinema's autonomy, see Daniel Frampton, *Filmosophy* (London: Wallflower Press, 2006), 5–11. For Frampton, cinema manifests the capacity to think the formation of the world and experience.

[21] Sergei Eisenstein, 'The Cinematographic Principle and the Ideogram', in *Film Form: Essays in Film Theory*, ed. and trans. Jay Leyda (New York: Harvest, 1977), 28.

[22] For a discussion of this shot between Truffaut and Hitchcock, see François Truffaut, *Hitchcock* (London: Paladin, 1986), 372–4.

FIGURE 1.2 *Hitchcock's cinematic subjectivity:* Psycho *(1960).*

of this position, of this fundamental relation between the real and its image counterpart, cinema becomes an esoteric object playing on screens oblivious to the spectator. Like the quantum particle, the cinematic image materializes through perception; this is its meaning, its itinerary and its point of coming into being. And that subjective perception, regardless of how normative or perverse it might be, searches for the indexical qualities of the image.[23]

But there is also something else at stake in thinking through the itinerary of the image. Cinema cannot merely be about personal, individual experience. What would be the purpose of experiencing cinema in isolation? Cinema maintains as a popular and pervasive art form. A film like *Avatar* (2009) matters for any number of reasons, but first it matters because it was viewed – and re-viewed – by a global audience of tens of millions of spectators. It has registered as a cultural and aesthetic object of enormous significance.[24] Thus, while cinema gains its material from the world (its essential itinerary), the world also takes its meaning from cinema. Žižek is no doubt correct in reading the virtual image of 9/11 as a *cinematic* image.[25] This is at times Baudrillard's position on American studio productions, the world as image-fantasy: 'The war as entrenchment, as technological and psychedelic fantasy, the war as a succession of special effects, the war become film even before

---

[23] Cavell is again instructive here: 'Apart from the wish for selfhood … I do not understand the value of art.' See Cavell, *The World Viewed*, 22.

[24] I'm pleased to note Cavell's very similar, and romantic, reflection in prompting a contemplation of cinema's importance: 'Rich and poor, those who care about no (other) art and those who live in the promise of art, those whose pride is education and those whose pride is power or practicality – all care about movies.' See Cavell, *The World Viewed*, 4–5.

[25] Slavoj Žižek, 'Passions of the Real, Passions of Semblance', in Slavoj Žižek, *Welcome to the Desert of the Real!: Five Essays on 11 September and Related Dates* (London: Verso, 2002), 11–16.

being filmed.'[26] Baudrillard is instructive here, but against his determined pessimism, cinema can also enrich the experience of the real, and provide the aesthetic material for communication between the subjects who inhabit that space. The itineraries of the cinematic image thus not only present a way of 'getting back to the world', but establish vital links between spectators and otherwise isolated subjective experiences.

I am calling this relationship between the image of the world and cinema's image an *itinerary*, and I perceive, speaking generally, two image itineraries that govern a great deal of thinking, writing, production, and theoretical discourse in cinema: a realist image, and a synthetic (artificial) image. As much as an aesthetic of realism and an aesthetic of artifice converge, and even share common stylistic traits, I would argue that the conventional distinction between an aesthetic of reality and an aesthetic of artifice maintains in production practice, scholarship and mainstream critical commentary. The distinction maintains in production as contemporary filmmakers seek the image of the real, and seek to recreate the rhythms of actual life on the screen through new technologies. We see this in Lars von Trier's spectacular images in *Melancholia* (2011), powerfully inscribed with the mark of the real, with von Trier's unique brand of dogmatic realism. In *Michael Clayton* (2007), the studio genre film partakes of a realist image itinerary: in the final sequence, Clayton (George Clooney) is isolated in a contemplative space, animated by an image wholly unconventional in a Hollywood thriller. The character appears to inhabit the moving image in much the same way that Antonio Ricci (Lamberto Maggiorani) inhabits the space of the city in De Sica's *Ladri di Biciclette* (*The Bicycle Thieves*, 1948).

Most importantly, perhaps, the distinction between a realist and synthetic image maintains in contemporary cinema spectatorship, as audiences continue to cling to a distinction between an image of the world as it is perceived, and an image of the world as it is fantasized. In an age in which the film spectator is media (rather than cinema) savvy, we perceive the competing registers of the realist and synthetic image almost intuitively. The spectator reads the synthetic image through visual and audio cues. The non-diegetic musical cue that accompanies an opening sequence in *The Lord of the Rings: The Fellowship of the Ring* (2001) alerts the spectator to its synthetic image itinerary. The astonishing synthetic movement of the camera in the opening sequence of *The Dark Knight* (2008) signifies a particular aesthetic register (figures 1.3–1.6).

Cameras seeking to present the real simply cannot move this way, with such disregard for the itineraries of common perception. Such synthetic

---

[26] Jean Baudrillard, *Simulacra and Simulation*, trans. Sheila Faria Glaser (Detroit: University of Michigan Press, 1994), 59.

FIGURES 1.3–6 *Synthetic movement and subjectivity:* The Dark Knight *(2008).*

movements in Nolan (but equally in the majority of contemporary cinema spectacles) are orchestrated as a montage of astonishment, animated by a synthetic construction of frame composition, movement, diegetic and non-diegetic sound, and genre signification: in short, synthetic gestures that seek an image 'more than' the image of our perception. The most resonant synthetic image in contemporary mainstream cinema is perhaps a production logo: the metonymic image of Spielberg's Amblin Entertainment, a graphic rendering that displays the figures of Elliott (Henry Thomas) and E.T. moving across the face of the moon.[27]

Both the realist image and the synthetic image configure pathways between the screened image of cinema and the image derived through our perceptual experience of the world. 'Synthetic', in my usage, is not a pejorative term, as is implied in the use of 'plastic' to describe the image of classical montage. The synthetic image is engaged in a reflection on the real, yet it partakes of a different aesthetic register than the image of reality. The synthetic image is no less engaged with the pursuit of an affective cinematic experience. There is no hierarchical relationship between a realist image and a synthetic image such that the realist image, or cinematic realism *per se*, is deemed to provide a more authentic experience of the world. Simply because

---

[27] Buckland offers an astute analysis of the transformation of Spielberg's 'brand image' from Amblin's archetypal register of emotion (which Buckland calls 'the impossible fantasy effect') to the emblematic sentimentalism of the Dreamworks logo. See Warren Buckland, *Directed by Steven Spielberg: Poetics of the Contemporary Hollywood Blockbuster* (New York: Continuum Press, 2006), 23–5.

Spielberg's *E.T.: The Extra-Terrestrial* (1982) or Nolan's *The Dark Knight* partake of the register of the synthetic image does not in some way negate these texts, and such modes of cinema, as meaningful experience, as authentic engagement.[28]

The register of the synthetic image is most obviously visible in Hollywood's classical studio aesthetic, in which the image is the outcome of a carefully formulated and systematized master-shot technique, continuity cinematographic and editing strategies, regulated production practices from story development to distribution and exhibition, and the overarching textual framework of classical genre.[29] While there are anomalies in the system (notably Welles, and most visibly in *Citizen Kane's* [1941] expressive deep focus cinematography), a great deal of Hollywood's output during the classical era exemplifies a compositional aesthetic founded on a synthetic image. The synthetic image constitutes the aesthetic material of the unique genius of Hollywood's industrial system. While some convincing argument has been made to problematize an aesthetic distinction between a classical and post-classical Hollywood,[30] the synthetic image is clearly visible in Hollywood production from the height of its classical studio era to contemporary production practices. Is Hollywood's 'invisibility of style' not merely the aesthetic system that organized its production of synthetic images? The final sequence in *Casablanca* (1942), in which Rick (Humphrey Bogart) and Ilsa (Ingrid Bergman) part ways, is a marvel of synthetic image strategies: mechanistic shot reverse-shot relations, camera movement for emphasis, forced framing, non-diegetic musical accompaniment for emotional effect, soft focus on the woman to maintain the ephemerality and unattainability of the female image, etc. (figures 1.7–1.11). Yet in spite of the highly orchestrated

---

[28] Gunning presents an intriguing and ambitious revision of cinema's essential effect. For Gunning, more important than indexicality is cinema's capacity to display *movement*. Through movement, cinemas of reality and fantasy display the world to equal and codependent effect. See Tom Gunning, 'Moving Away from the Index: Cinema and the Impression of Reality', *differences: A Journal of Feminist Cultural Studies* 18, no. 1 (2007), 45–6.

[29] For a comprehensive overview of Hollywood's stylistic practices during the classical era, see David Bordwell, Janet Staiger, and Kristin Thompson, *The Classical Hollywood Cinema: Film Style and Mode of Production to 1960* (New York: Columbia University Press, 1985). See especially Chapter One, 'An Excessively Obvious Cinema'. For a detailed analysis of shot composition and editing styles, see Robert Ray, *A Certain Tendency of the Hollywood Cinema: 1930–1980* (Princeton, NJ: Princeton University Press, 1985).

[30] For two excellent collections charting the industrial and aesthetic form of a 'New Hollywood', see *The New American Cinema*, ed. Jon Lewis (Durham: Duke University Press, 1998), and *The Last Great American Picture Show: New Hollywood Cinema in the 1970s*, ed. Thomas Elsaesser, Alexander Horwath, and Noel King (Amsterdam: Amsterdam University Press, 2004). Both collections, while illustrating points of distinction between a classical and a new Hollywood, also provide subtle analyses of continuity in modes of production and industry formation.

composition, movement and continuity inherent in the sequence, the spectator's engagement with the emotional lives of Rick and Ilsa is personal, deeply reflective, and profoundly *real*.

In contrast with the synthetic image of Hollywood, the image of reality is conventionally situated within a modernist or post-classical, independent and national context. This is why for Deleuze the realist image inaugurates a crisis in a classical aesthetic, in which the image of action (and agency) fractures into so many 'any-instant[s]-whatever'.[31] For Bordwell, the post-classical art film is distinguished by its disposition toward realism and narrative ambiguity.[32] Of course, in the great complexity of the cinema industry, particularly after 1948 and the collapse of complete studio ownership of the film product, the distinction is not neat. Hitchcock is clearly interested in a mode of psychological realism that transgresses an ideological norm, yet his aesthetic, in even the most experimental films – *Vertigo* (1958); *Psycho* (1960); *The Birds* (1963) – is rendered in classical compositional terms. Sam Fuller's idiosyncratic productions of the 1960s, notably *Shock Corridor* (1963) and *The Naked Kiss* (1964), partake of a classical studio aesthetic while engaging in social, psychological and, to an extent, aesthetic realisms.

The image of reality, in Bazin, is often described in terms of its revelation of the real, the capacity of the image to provide access to the flow of reality. Realism is not merely a question of social, political and cultural truth, but is also a measure of the aesthetic material of the image. Cinematic realism is crafted out of the mechanics of the medium: space and time, unfolding on screen, are crafted out of the instruments of the camera, of actual physical space, of the paraphernalia of production. These instruments are put to use by the filmmaker in orchestrating an aesthetic of reality: 'it is by way of its poetry that the realism of De Sica takes on its meaning, for in art, at the source of all realism, there is an aesthetic paradox that must be resolved.'[33] But more than a question of materiality, there is the inference in Bazin that a realist image must be *desired* by the filmmaker. The cinema of Murnau, Flaherty, Stroheim desired the aesthetic register of reality even in producing the image through highly orchestrated montage.[34] Welles and Renoir use long shots and space in depth, and such strategies for Bazin are built on a realist imperative that is at once aesthetic and ethical. For Deleuze, post-classical cinema inscribes

---

[31] Gilles Deleuze, *Cinema 2: The Time-Image*, trans. Hugh Tomlinson and Robert Galeta (Minneapolis: University of Minnesota Press, 2009), 1–24.
[32] David Bordwell, 'The Art Cinema as a Mode of Film Practice', *Film Criticism* 4, no. 1 (1979), 57–9.
[33] André Bazin, 'De Sica: *Metteur en Scène*', in *Vittorio De Sica: Contemporary Perspectives*, ed. Howard Curle and Stephen Snyder (Toronto: University of Toronto Press, 2000), 65.
[34] Bazin, 'The Evolution of the Language of Cinema', 27–8.

FIGURES 1.7–11 *Hollywood's 'invisible style'*: Casablanca *(1942).*

realism in images of inaction, stasis or contemplation.[35] Space opens itself to the flow of the image's inherent reality. We can see this ethical imperative toward an image of reality in a great deal of digital production of the last ten years. The advent of digital technology, particularly in various world cinemas, has seen a return to alternative aesthetics, realism, political cinema, and strategies of vérité. While the digital scanner and printer enabled an unprecedented expansion in synthetic image technologies and aesthetic strategies,

---

[35] Deleuze, *Cinema 2*, 6–7.

the digitally produced image, as Rombes astutely argues, returns the image to its inherent reality.[36] The desire to manifest the world through the cinema image, even in the technology of digital production, remains, in current practice, a matter of an ethical position.[37]

If we address the cinematic image in terms of a foundational *ethic*, a desire for a realistic or synthetic image, Eisenstein's montage (conventionally a synthetic image) is not necessarily in conflict with Bazin's image of reality. The image that arises out of conflict through montage is of course different from the image that reveals the inherent continuity of the real (Bazin's deep focus/depth of field image in Welles, or later in Rossellini and De Sica). But the engagement for the spectator is with an image itinerary that strives to create a vision of the world. In this way also, Welles's image in depth in *Citizen Kane* is not necessarily an image of reality. Deep focus, because it is not the indexical equivalent of perceptual reality, partakes both of what Bazin perceived to be an image of reality *and* the register of the synthetic image. In fact, couldn't we say that realism is not purely the manifestation of the realist image, and its uniquely spatial and temporal relations (Bazin), but the manifestation of an ethical *desire* of the film to configure reality? Could we not adequately describe cinematic realism as the aesthetic system through which the image manifests an ethical commitment to reality? The ethical material of cinema was also critical to Eisenstein, for whom cinema mattered as the image of political consciousness. This is Eisenstein's plastic image, the most explicitly articulated synthetic image in early cinema, with which Tarkovsky would take issue.[38] And yet, for all its plasticity, Eisenstein's montage, at every step, in his practice and writing on cinema, manifests the ethical life of an image that seeks to 'get back to the world'.

The image of reality and the synthetic image in concert

Rossellini's *Roma, Città Aperta* (*Open City*, 1945) partakes of a dual register of the image, the realist image and the synthetic image, but manifests the

---

[36] Nicholas Rombes, *Cinema in the Digital Age* (London: Wallflower Press, 2009), 81–2.

[37] See Lucia Nagib, *World Cinema and the Ethics of Realism* (New York: Continuum Press), 27. Tarkovsky approaches a similar position, albeit through a particularly poetic, almost mystical, sensibility. See Andrey Tarkovsky, *Sculpting in Time: Reflections on the Cinema*, trans. Kitty Hunter-Blair (London: Faber, 1989), 27: 'Masterpieces are born of the artist's struggle to express his ethical ideals.'

[38] Tarkovsky, *Sculpting in Time*, 114–21.

unique aesthetic and ethical imperative toward cinematic realism. In the following analysis, I focus on the famous sequence in which Pina (Anna Magnani) is gunned down in a street. While the sequence is interspersed with several cuts, I argue that it maintains an internal unity, a coherent ethical and aesthetic life.

The section of film depicting Pina's death comprises one of the critical points of origin of the Neorealist image as it is defined by Bazin, and later, Bondanella: 'Rossellini's *Rome, Open City* represents the landmark film of this group [the films associated with the Neorealist tradition, 1945–51]. It so completely reflected the moral and psychological atmosphere of this moment that it alerted both the public and the critics to a new direction in Italian film.'[39] But unlike Bondanella and a great deal of analysis of Neorealist cinema, Bazin emphasizes the aestheticization of the *image*, valorizing Rossellini's realist image over and above the historical context of the story. In a letter to Guido Aristarco, editor-in-chief of *Cinema Nuovo*, Bazin writes: 'one does have the right to reject the moral or spiritual postulate that is increasingly evident in his [Rossellini's] work, but even so to reject this would not imply rejection of the aesthetic framework within which this message is manifest.'[40] This aesthetic framework is what makes Rossellini's vision distinctly Neorealist. The Neorealist aesthetic in this sequence presents a convergence of synthetic image and shot relation (montage) *and* a realist image of depth and duration. Further, I argue that it is precisely the relationship between an image of reality and the synthetic image that provides a distinctive Neorealist aesthetic that reflects upon, and yet moves beyond, the deep focus/depth of field cinematography Bazin identifies in Welles and Renoir. Deleuze is thus correct to attribute a special status of the image to De Sica's *Umberto D* (1952), and Neorealism more generally, that moves beyond an earlier, less critically reflexive image of cinematic realism.

The sequence presents a simple narrative section of the film [55:47–57:03]:[41] Pina runs after a truck of German soldiers that will take Francesco (Francesco Grandjacquet) to prison. Before she can reach the truck, she is shot and falls in the street. Don Pietro (Aldo Fabrizi) arrives and cradles her fallen body.

This astonishing moment in the history of cinema presents an aesthetically complex awakening of the realist imperative within the cinematic image.

[39] Peter Bondanella, *Italian Cinema: From Neorealism to the Present* (New York: Continuum Press, 2001), 37.

[40] André Bazin, 'In Defense of Rossellini: a Letter to Guido Aristarco, Editor-in-Chief of Cinema Nuovo', in *What is Cinema? Volume 2*, trans. Hugh Gray (Berkeley and Los Angeles: University of California Press, 2004), 97.

[41] Time-code references are to Disc One (*Rome Open City*), *Roberto Rossellini's War Trilogy* (*Rome Open City/Paisan/Germany Year Zero*) [DVD] (The Criterion Collection, 2010).

Rossellini's film is both realistic in its subject matter, and melodramatic. To this end, Keating offers a very convincing reading of the 'fictional worlds' of Rossellini's film.[42] Immediately preceding Pina's death, Rossellini engages Don Pietro in a comedic routine involving an ailing old man. At the conclusion of the routine, a dented pan serves as a punch line, a sign for the audience to laugh. This is a contrivance of screwball comedy in a film of great tragedy. And because of the synthetic rhythms of the comedic preface, Pina's pursuit of the truck and her ensuing death presents a deliberate transformation into one of the most elegant examples of a realist film aesthetic. The camera initially holds in medium shot over a group of assembled women [55:47]. After a brief confrontation between Pina and a soldier, the film cuts to an image in long shot of Francesco escorted to the truck. In a simple shot reverse-shot, Rossellini cuts back to Pina, who calls out 'Francesco!', thereby constructing the point of view relation. This is a synthetic construction of the proximity of the two figures in the sequence (figures 1.12–1.13).

A series of shots depicts the respective struggles of Pina and Francesco to escape their captors and reunite. The image then cuts on movement as Pina breaks free from the hold of the soldier and runs through a narrow alley separating her from the truck.

It is here that Rossellini's sequence attains a new complexity and sophistication through integrating shots in depth/duration and synthetic compositional structures. As Pina runs into the alley, the camera holds on her retreating figure. The shot is held until she exits and we receive the required reverse-shot to maintain continuity, a synthetic cue. The ensuing depth of the shot encompassing Pina's retreating figure – the alley in deep background, as well as the duration of the image – is critical to the realist imperative of this movement. Depth of field here manifests Bazin's inherent continuity of the real. In the final moment of the shot before the cut, Pina's figure is minuscule in proportion to the figures in foreground (figure 1.14).

Rossellini is interested here in the continuity and physicality of space. While the duration of the shot is critical, the enormity of this tragedy is rendered principally through spatial composition.

At 56:25, the reverse-shot for continuity returns to the conventional shot reverse-shot synchronicity between Pina and Francesco, establishing point of view, the spectator's emotional engagement with the unfolding drama, and the necessary proximity between the two protagonists. But here again Rossellini fractures the synthetic shot reverse-shot. He locates Pina in an extreme long shot. The distance between the spectator and the image is perceptually lengthened through the geography of the space: the street

---

FIGURES 1.12–13 *A synthetic construction of proximity: shot reverse-shot between Pina and Francesco:* Open City *(1945).*

FIGURE 1.14 *Orchestrated depth of field in Italian Neorealism:* Open City *(1945).*

running vertically into deep background; a lone soldier next to a motorcycle at screen right; an assemblage of bystanders in geometric rows. This geometry of the space is foundational to a perception of the image of reality (figures 1.15–1.16).

Rossellini maintains this shot in depth. The spectator anticipates a series of cuts, mirroring the play of shot reverse-shot immediately preceding this movement. But it is here that Rossellini effectively effaces the synthetic image from the movement. A series of cuts display Pina from the front and in profile, from a multiplicity of perspectives. But these cuts are deliberately random images displaying Pina's movement. The speed of these cuts – extreme long shot of Pina; medium profile shot of Pina in flight; a reaction shot of Don Pietro obscuring the child's view; the return to extreme long shot of Pina as she is gunned down [56:39–56:45] – render each a random cinematic image in movement (figures 1.17–1.19).

The effect is not unlike that of a series of still images connected through succession, each autonomous and animated individually. Such randomly

FIGURES 1.15–19 *Aesthetic realism through depth of field, duration and montage:* Open City *(1945).*

assembled cuts recall the paradoxical realism through movement one feels in watching something like Chris Marker's still images in *La Jetée* (1962). The cuts prior to Pina's death function almost as still images, autonomous objects moving beyond the flow of the synthetic (melodramatic) narrative and the synthetic compositional structure of shot reverse-shot relations. The cuts do not construe continuity or forge a synthetic emotional connection between Pina and the spectator, but rather *display* Pina from a series of perspectives. Could we not say, precisely as Bazin does of the continuity of reality in *Citizen Kane*, that these cuts, randomized, presenting an image of Pina in movement, offer the space in its full capacity as physical space, as realist space? And further, that here a multiple perspective montage serves a similar purpose to a long shot in extreme depth in Welles – or Rossellini, for that matter? Essentially, I am suggesting that montage in Rossellini's sequence is no less an aesthetic image of the real than depth cinematography and duration. Here Rossellini's impulse to cut the image is built of that same impulse to maintain continuity in Bazin's image of reality. Montage inscribed this way is still, to follow the reasoning of Nagib, an ethical imperative toward cinematic realism.

Rossellini's sequence concludes with one of the monumental images of aesthetic realism in cinema's history: Pina is gunned down. The sound of the bullet, occurring before the image returns to Pina, is random; the spectator cannot isolate the ontological source of the sound. Pina's death occurs in the background of a cinematic space. The death, unobserved, is critical to Rossellini's ethical and political imperative. The lasting image of Pina's death manifests in the spectator's mind in long shot, as the truck recedes. The shot of Pina falling as the truck reverts from her body surely constitutes one of the clear points of origin of the documentary image in cinema history; the unstable image resembles the immediacy, the uncontrived spontaneity, of the image of life as it manifests in cinema. This is not to describe Rossellini's shot as 'documentary', but to suggest that his image of reality partakes of the documentary's imperative to capture life 'unawares'.[43] For the moment that encompasses Pina's movement in the street and her fall, the character is unaware of her presence within the diegetic space of the narrative. Fittingly, the flight and death of the heroine – a melodramatic trope in a classical studio aesthetic – is composed entirely in long and medium shot. Rossellini resists the allure of the close-up, even as Don Pietro, at Pina's side, mourns her death.

The legacy of Rossellini's aesthetic of realism is well acknowledged. This is a trajectory of the image that frames the history of cinematic form, and which continues to provide a vital point of contact between cinema and the world spectators inhabit and experience. The tension between an image of reality and a synthetic image continues to inform production, reception and theoretical discourse. A critical approach to any engagement with the image of late cinema and its technological apparatus is to reconcile the realist and non-realist itineraries of the image. Such a reconciliation is not only a necessary revision of a formal distinction that has informed a great deal of reflection on film, but provides a platform from which the spectator might engage with the digital image – essentially a synthetic object – as *real*, as

---

[43] For an analysis of Vertov's philosophy of cinematic perception and revelation, see Vlada Petric, 'Dziga Vertov as Theorist', *Cinema Journal* 18, no. 1 (1978), 29–44.

made of the same material of reality that gives life to Rossellini's Neorealist spaces. In this way, we might perceive the continuation of an ethical realism in the cinema of figures as diverse as Alfonso Cuarón, Steven Soderberg, or Michael Haneke. Cuarón's virtuoso long shot that constitutes the major movement of the opening sequence of *Children of Men* (2006) makes Rossellini's Neorealist aesthetic contemporary. What was the object reality of a space in *Open City* becomes a synthesis of actual and virtual reality in *Children of Men*. Rossellini's image is imprinted on celluloid; Cuarón's image is a digital composition.[44] Rossellini's camera is fastened to a tripod as it is moved; Cuarón's camera is hand-held. Rossellini's camera traces the movement of Pina for the entirety of its duration; Cuarón's camera has the capacity to leave the action entirely, to literally cast its gaze across the physical space – the autonomous camera of cinema's modernity. For both Rossellini and Cuarón, depth cinematography and the shot in duration is critical to experiencing the field within the film as 'real'. Yet each cinema achieves an elegant interaction of synthetic and realist image strategies. Rossellini's realism *is* melodramatic. Cuarón's realism through shot duration is manufactured; it is a synthetic image, a virtual movement. Does it bother us that Cuarón did not compose the sequence in a single shot, as Welles did for the bravura opening of *Touch of Evil* (1958), or Altman for the opening sequence shot of *The Player* (1992)? Does it bother us that indexical realism is always already a synthetic manifestation in digital production?

The itinerary of the image presents a pathway toward an image of the world. Such pathways are inscribed with compositions, movements and rhythms that create uniquely cinematic visions, and that invest the image with an aesthetic and ethical life. Whether the material of celluloid, or the virtual composition of the digital apparatus, the image of cinematic realism maintains, and must continue to maintain, as an aesthetic and ethical endeavour in the age of late cinema.

---

[44] I return to this notion at length in Part Two of the book, but composition through digital technology is nearer in spirit to the process of simulation, in which the synthesis of celluloid and digital material fuses into an imagistic whole. On the long take in *Children of Men,* Cuarón acknowledges: 'Sometimes it's more than what it looks like. The important thing is how you blend everything and how you keep the perception of a fluid cinematography.' The long take in *Children of Men* is thus more appropriately a synthetic simulation. See Peter DeBruge, 'Editors Cut on Tricky Sequences', Interview with Alfonso Cuarón, *Variety*, 16 February 2007, http://www.variety.com/article/VR1117959745?refcatid=13 [accessed 12 June 2010].

The digital image

Was there something more essential in film that was somehow absent even in lived experience? I wonder if new cinemas, new kinds of framing of the forgotten past, will have the same wonder as tactile, degraded, and perpetually degrading, film stock?[45]

You're talking about memories.
Deckard (Harrison Ford), *Blade Runner: Final Cut* (2007).

There seem to be two positions, diametrically opposed and naturally antagonistic, on the ontology of the new digital image of cinema.[46] Digitization came into the lexicon as a cinematic descriptor in the early 1990s. A decade later, Lucas had declared his production of *Star Wars Episode II: Attack of the Clones* (2002) an epochal cinematic event: the first film composed entirely of digital images. Lucas's experiment with the century-old medium of the moving image again beckoned the question: what was cinema in the age of digital reproduction? This is an old question cast in a new light, in a new material context: is the image created out of digital code *cinematic*?

In the mid–1940s, Bazin wrote about the unique material of the photographic image as a precursor to his complex ontology of the moving image of cinema. This question – 'what is cinema' – was a driving passion for Bazin, whether he specifically contemplated the realist image in Rossellini and De Sica, or montage aesthetics in Eisenstein. But this ontology of the film image in Bazin, implicitly or explicitly, accepted the tangible truth of celluloid. Cinema was made of hard matter. It was worked through a mechanical instrument and displayed a form based on physical properties. Celluloid could be composed into ordered sections, which, once cut, would form the itinerary of the moving image. This was the essence of the various schools of montage. Even the image of plasticity (Eisenstein's montage, to take an example), breaching continuity, was grounded in the objectivity of form and substance. While Eisenstein's montage was built out of the conflict of two images put together, that conflict was directly related to a mode of perceiving the actual world. This is also why the cinema of celluloid was cherished as an imprint of life, Tarkovsky's notion of 'sculpting in time'. Sculpting is to take a physical material and mould it to form. While Bazin does not address Vertov's

---

[45] Bruce Isaacs, 'Do Not Screen – Frames 1321–1332', http://donotscreen.net/ [accessed 19 June 2011].
[46] Rodowick, *The Virtual Life of Film*, 96–7.

work in *Man With a Movie Camera* in any great capacity,[47] Vertov is the natural compositor of the image in celluloid. Each cut of Vertov's film is like a blink, a closing and opening of the eye of the camera, and a renewal of its vision. All continuity, Vertov reminds us at every turn, is a matter of cutting, assembling, and gluing the physical stuff of cinema together.[48]

The theoretical positions on the digital image either speak of the radical newness of this image and its ontological transformation of the celluloid image; or they speak of the unremarkable verisimilitude of the digital image to the real, arguing that cinema remains a function of its resemblance to the physical world, regardless of how it is created or disseminated. Belton, writing in 2002, argues that 'digital projection as it exists today does not, in any way, transform the nature of the motion-picture experience. Audiences viewing digital projection will not experience the cinema differently, as those who heard sound, saw colour, or experienced widescreen and stereo sound for the first time did.'[49] Clearly Belton is correct here. The digital image (even if composed *and* exhibited digitally, a rarity in 2002 but increasingly common in contemporary cinema) bore its initial imprint of life in *direct relation* to the technology of celluloid that had preceded it. Digital, for all intents and purposes, was celluloid cinema reconstituted out of a new technology. Digital cinema looked like film. It moved with film's internal rhythms: 24 frames per second of film was perceptually equivalent to digital cinema's 25 frames per second (NTSC). Current digital technology can record at the film standard 24 frames per second, providing an increased indexical appearance of film quality. A great deal of digital cinema production at both high-end (*Star Wars Episode II*, *Cloverfield*, 2008) and lower-end (*Che*, 2008) is produced simply for the expedience of shooting and editing in digital form, which is more cost-effective than producing the same motion picture on film, scanning it digitally for editing, then printing again in film (if so desired). Digital technology, especially in its early phase of use and production, was thus not inherently a transformation in the 'nature' of the moving image, to use Belton's terminology. Unsurprisingly, the digital moving image continues to be called 'film' in a great deal of cinema commentary.

Yet in spite of the widespread acceptance of the digital image as built of the same material of the real as celluloid, there is something in this image

---

[47] Bazin acknowledges the impact of Vertov's Kino-eye philosophy on the evolution of Soviet cinema. See André Bazin, 'The Myth of Stalin in the Soviet Cinema', in *Bazin at Work: Major Essays and Reviews From the Forties and Fifties*, trans. Alain Piette and Bert Cardullo (London: Routledge, 1997), 24.

[48] For a reading of Vertov's 'Kino-eye' as a movement beyond assemblage, see Deleuze, *Cinema 1*, 81–4.

[49] John Belton, 'Digital Cinema: A False Revolution', *October* 100 (2002), 104.

that leaves a unique imprint on the mind of the spectator. Those familiar with the textures of film projected in theatres will note the unique image quality of digital production: high-end digital technology potentially provides a greater resolution than celluloid.[50] Light and colour qualities derive from the material of digital coding, and while such qualities resemble film form, digital technology is not an extension of film technology. Which is merely to suggest that, technologically speaking, film is not the point of inception, or the authentic original, of the digital image. There is not the hard assurance of form that celluloid provides in its material substance. The digital imprint is not the material trace of the real (that for Bazin was the essence of the moving image on celluloid), and yet it bears the aesthetic signature of reality. The digital image purveys the 'truth' of the world in image form, yet there is a subtle deviation, an ontological sidestep that renders digital cinema new and the disturbing obverse to its celluloid precursor: 'We confront something [the digital image] that looks like photography, and continues to serve many of its cultural functions. Yet a felt change is occurring, or perhaps has occurred, in our phenomenological relation with these images.'[51] This is a question not only of how cinema manifests reality, but again, of what cinema *is*. And digital cinema is clearly not film.

Five years after Belton wrote about the sameness of the experience of cinema in digital form, I attended one of two Sydney screenings of Ridley Scott's *Blade Runner: Final Cut*, a 25th anniversary commemoration of the film's first release in 1982. Commemoration was hardly an appropriate word to describe the redux of the original *Blade Runner*, superseded by the seminal *Blade Runner: Director's Cut* in 1991. In some circles, *Final Cut* was deemed a studio attempt to cash in on the legacy of *Blade Runner*. While not a box office success on first release, the director's cut of 1991 had attained a rare cult status and established a loyal audience in small theatre venues. In response to a call from devotees for a definitive (and final) version, Scott released *Final Cut* – exclusively in digital form. The original film print of 1982, refigured in the Director's Cut edition of 1991, was granted new life through digital projection. Theatres purchased a digital object, a *file*, which was

---

[50] I thank an editor and colleague, Anthony Cox, for current information on digital production and exhibition technology. While exhibition inevitably lags behind the technology of capture, the industry norm appears to be resting at 4k projection in the US, Europe and Australia. Image capture potential is projected at 28k (Red Camera), seven times the pixel density (and resolution) of a contemporary digital cinema screening. Luhrmann's *The Great Gatsby* (2013) was shot on a Red Epic at a 5k resolution, exceeding the current norm by some measure. I thank Matt Villa (editor) for information on the camera used for production on *The Great Gatsby*.

[51] Rodowick, *The Virtual Life of Film*, 98.

circulated through invisible global communication networks. Instantaneous circulation constituted the new mobility of the digital cinema text.

I have seen *Blade Runner* two or three times in small theatre settings (art-house cinemas) and countless times on video, DVD and Blu-Ray. I consider *Blade Runner: Director's Cut* a seminal film for its dystopian, post-humanist vision, and its allegory of the confrontation between humanity and technology. Re-viewing the film in 2007 in a renewed cut (an anachronism in the digital era), I could not but anticipate a confrontation between film and the relatively new technology of digital production. This was to be an experiment not only in the expansion of a classic text, but also in the reconstruction of the material object of cinema. A Sony executive introduced the film, explaining that what we were about to see had not been seen before, and certainly not in Australia. The executive was appropriately excited about the potential of the new technology. Sony was not interested in *Blade Runner per se*; rather, it was advertising a 4k digital projection system (now, five years later, common-place) that was mobile, broadly assimilable and global in its impact. The Orpheum Theatre in Sydney had permitted Sony to install the digital apparatus in the week preceding the first screening of *Final Cut*; trouble-shooting had taken two full days. The system would be uninstalled and shipped off at the conclusion of the second screening of the film the following evening.

My encounter with this reconstructed *Blade Runner*, a film I knew intimately in filmic (and analogue video) form, can only be described as unsettling. The authentic world of *Blade Runner* cohered in some sense in my memory of the film image. But now the resolution of the image of Batty's (Rutger Hauer) eyes, superimposed over the dystopian cityscape (which I also knew to be a subtle visual quotation of Coppola's opening shot of *Apocalypse Now* [1979], a great auteurist 70mm film), had sculpted Batty into something new. The image I now saw of Batty was something like a doppelganger of his prior filmic self. Scott's uncannily appropriate thematic of 'more human than human' seemed reconstituted in the digital image of Batty and the dystopian Los Angeles as 'more real than real'. The image was, and is on my Blu-Ray (which I have currently paused in front of me, screening on a 52" LCD Sony Bravia TV), of unfathomable resolution. Vangelis's glorious synthesized sounds had never sounded so authentic. In digital imaging, the city comes to life in flame, imbued with an unsettling and complex synth soundscape accentuated with a hard snare drum. The image opens in a panoramic shot, the lights now clearer, more acutely observed and distinct from each other. The shot recedes into a deep background. The space gradually swells through a slow, almost imperceptible camera move. There is a single cut that brings the image of the city nearer to the position of the spectator. In sound and vision, the image presents to its audience the wonder of something old and cherished suddenly imbued with new life. The image seems newly resolved.

Seated in the Orpheum, a veritable space of cinema's history, at least in an Australian context, I recall wondering how to make sense of this new image of *Blade Runner*, and what it might mean for a seminal (or cult) text to be remade this way. What would become of the archive of film and its filmed memories? I can't claim to share the unfathomable burden of Deckard's realization of his own replicancy at the end of the film; Deckard's reaction to the discovery of the origami object from his dreams is a whimsical smile, an acknowledgement not only of what he is, but of the trauma inherent in coming to that realization. But clearly Scott's experiment had been designed to confront the spectator with a digital object, and in so doing, to enable the spectator to confront the trauma of an object falling into the past and losing the memory of that past. If *Blade Runner* is fundamentally about the extinction of a human-organic self, the exhibition of *Final Cut* in 2007 was also about the threat of extinction of a technological form. That threat of the extinction of celluloid had been imprinted in the experience of the digital image.

The release of *Final Cut* provided an experience and allegorical rendering of the potential of new cinema. The digital image of film functioned as a distilled memory, a simulacral representation – both the trace of its prior filmic form and the newness of its digital life. There has been a great deal of work on the impact of this image, and Rodowick's *The Virtual Life of Film* seems to engage most deliberately with the relation between the digital image and the history of film form. This itinerary of the digital image as either continuous, or discontinuous and a rupture in the seam of film form, is critical to Rodowick's engagement. But while his acknowledgement of the changes inherent in the production and reception of the digital image is a critical advance on the debate, one again senses his unwillingness to confront directly the disturbance of this sensation. While he inventively accounts for the complexity of the affective and effective ontological properties of digital images, he presents film as an object possessed of unique aesthetic qualities that are absent in a digital image. The material of the celluloid image is, in Rodowick's memory-experience of it, different from the digital image. Celluloid is another mode of capturing the world. Celluloid creates the world differently, and out of different images. For Rodowick, this lack inherent in the digital image is a matter of time and duration:

As film disappears into an aesthetic universe constructed from digital intermediates and images combining computer synthesis and capture, and while I continue to feel engaged by many contemporary movies, I still have a deep sense, which is very hard to describe or qualify, of time lost. Ironically, since in 2007 most commercial films are still released to theatres on projected celluloid, reprinting to an analogical support seems not to be able to return to digital movies the experience of watching film.[52]

Here Rodowick betrays an essential commitment to the 'lost' past of film history – as personal and collective experience, reflection and memory. This is the kind of nostalgia Rombes identifies in the wake of film's evacuation, that attends the gradual effacement of the film object as experience: 'there is nostalgia not only for the content of these movies, but for their mediums, as well, which conjure boring, hot summer days of wandering around the city, taking in a movie to escape the heat in the dark.'[53] Rodowick cites the filmmaker Babette Mangolte, who asks: 'Why is it difficult for the digital image to communicate duration?'[54] For Mangolte, it is difficult for the filmmaker, now skilled in the digital image through necessity, to 'go back'. The difficulty of duration for Mangolte is a function of the tools required to produce the digital image. Digital images are produced from algorithms comprising the material of the image; the digital image is edited in time *code*, film in the physical properties *of* time: 'in film, two seconds is three feet and twenty seconds is thirty feet. There is no way to ignore duration when you physically manipulate the piece of film.'[55] Rodowick's claim follows this trajectory, emphasizing the unique characteristics (and inherent limitation) of the technology of digital production, which is by its nature an assemblage, a series of discrete intervals rather than duration.[56] I have seen many 'films' produced through digital processes. It constantly astonishes me when I discover some time after an initial screening that a film was digitally produced. Mel Gibson's *Apocalypto* (2006) is one such case, Greg Mclean's *Wolf Creek* (2005) is another, both films engaging the potentiality of the visual image of cinema. Granted, these are not films about time, providing

---

[52] Rodowick, *The Virtual Life of Film*, 164. For a discussion of the breach of time's indexicality in digital imaging, see Mary Ann Doane, 'The Indexical and the Concept of Medium Specificity', *differences: A Journal of Feminist Cultural Studies* 18, no. 1 (2007), 128–52 (esp. 142–4). For something of a rejoinder to the discourse of digital as destruction of analog indexicality, see Tom Gunning, 'Moving Away from the Index'. Gunning usefully reorients the analog/digital divide away from indexicality. The simplicity/commonsensicality of Gunning's position seems to be that we continue to *experience* the object through a digital image, even if that object is not necessarily 'present' in the image.

[53] Rombes, *Cinema in the Digital Age*, 20.

[54] Cited in Rodowick, *The Virtual Life of Film*, 163.

[55] Babette Mangolte, 'Afterward: A Matter of Time', in *Camera Obscura, Camera Lucida: Essays in Honor of Annette Michelson*, ed. Richard Allen and Malcolm Turvey (Amsterdam: Amsterdam University Press, 2003), 267.

[56] Rodowick, *The Virtual Life of Film*, 166.

a 'time experience',[57] yet neither are they films in which time is 'forgotten'.[58] How would Mangolte's (and Rodowick's) position account for low-end digital cinematography in independent filmmaking, now integral to global cinema production? How could this position address Christian Marclay's monumental meditation on time, *The Clock*? Marclay's text composed of film fragments is in every sense a digital assemblage. It is a *reconfiguration* of film, not classical montage, but a digitized montage composed of a history of pure images of time. Surely Marclay's exhibition presents a deeply *affective* relationship to time.[59]

In Rodowick's work, the digital image is ultimately a deterioration of the replete image of celluloid, and this deterioration represents the incapacity of the digital image to encode an experience of time. In the nostalgia of Rodowick's position, the profound experience of cinema is always a matter of time. A position that treats film as past (and thus the ontological presentiment of *pastness*) necessarily elevates it to an ideal, a cherished origin that accounted for the initial experiential life and power of the medium. Lumière's arrival of a train in 1895 could only be experienced *on film* – thus serving a nostalgic reflection on the past and coterminous negation of the present. But what it is, what digital cinema *is*, even if open to debate, constitutes part of that experience of the digital, that is not filmic and yet bears the trace of film form. Perhaps Dixon offers the much-needed corrective in his reading of digital spectacle: 'Firstly, we must embrace the future of cinema/video representation and reproduction, rather than seek to ignore and/or avoid it.'[60] Rodowick is correct to perceive something of a death through effacement of the real in the digital image. Yet this death is creative, enriching, and filled with aesthetic possibilities beyond the reckoning of the purely celluloid image.

This presence of the digital image, an image that is projected now as an epochal change in the history of moving image forms, is a question of affect as well as effect. The digital disturbance of the old register of the image in celluloid – first in mainstream studio production through Cameron's morphing shapes in *The Abyss* (1989) and *Terminator 2: Judgment Day* (1991), or Spielberg's digital dinosaur in *Jurassic Park* (1993) – is an integral element of its cinema effect. Digital cinema *unsettles* the celluloid material of cinema. This is a history of the medium of cinema imprinted on celluloid

---

[57] Mangolte, 'Afterward', 263.
[58] Mangolte, 'Afterward', 262.
[59] See Daniel Zalewski, 'The Hours: How Christian Marclay Created the Ultimate Digital Mosaic', The New Yorker, 12 March 2012, http://www.newyorker.com/reporting/2012/03/12/120312fa_fact_zalewski.
[60] Wheeler Winston Dixon, *The Transparency of Spectacle: Meditations on the Moving Image* (Albany, State University of New York Press, 1998), 8.

and potentially reconfigured through the presence of the digital apparatus: industrially, aesthetically, and culturally. For Rodowick, is the experience of film, of celluloid's materialized duration, effaced on digital Beta? Or DVD? Or Blu-Ray?

The digital image is a transformative material. This is its primary ontological imprint. The image is no longer merely indexical, nor representative. Rather, its materiality is the accumulation of the *memory* of celluloid, created and projected digitally as a stream of cinematic images of the past.[61] The digital image bears the effacement of celluloid; this mark of the digital as post-film is an essential component of what it is. And this is surely the revelation of Lumière's YouTube streamed image of women exiting a factory. What once was film is now remade, and while film maintains its form in reflection, it is permanently recast through digital sound and image production, editing and projection technologies. The question Rodowick asks of the capacity of the digital image to inscribe duration is more a matter of asking what duration is, why it is integral to *that* mode of experiencing the image, and why duration should be cast as the essence of cinematic experience *per se*. As we move ever farther into the digital spaces of cinema – its production and exhibition capacities, its unique image properties, its trajectories toward increased complexity in hybridization and convergence – cinema becomes a form of fluid and mobile media. Cinema experience takes on the experiential itineraries of screened media that are incompatible with – even unfathomable in – the age of celluloid cinema. In 2011, Park Chan-Wook released *Night Fishing*, a short film shot entirely with the iPhone 4. The radicalism of this gesture is not to create a new image resolution through digital technology (grainy, jerky, washed, lacking clarity in depth) but to make cinema mobile, which is another consideration entirely when talking about duration and the experience of cinematic time and space.

On the function of theory

What does philosophy value in art … Philosophy finds inspiration in art because there the will to create is brought to its highest powers.[62]

---

[61] For a fascinating discussion of digitality's index as incorporating celluloid's imprint, see Mary Ann Doane, 'Indexicality: Trace and Sign: Introduction', *differences: A Journal of Feminist Cultural Studies*, 18, no. 1 (2007), 1–6. Doane argues that 'the digital has not annihilated the logic of the photochemical, but incorporated it' (5).

[62] David Rodowick, 'An Elegy for Theory', *October* 122 (Fall, 2007), 105–6.

I offer the following discussion as a coda to Chapter One. I explore the place and use-value of film theory in more complex ways in the following chapter. But at this point, I want to be very clear in my reading of the creative potential of the cinema image. The discourse of film studies – its theoretical legacies and practice – is inadequate in accounting for the experience of film. This is the phenomenological gap between the world rendered in image and the world rendered in concept. I wouldn't know how to express the experience of cinema *in words*. Perhaps this is something personal, but I sense this inadequacy of theoretical discourse, and the disconcerting ephemerality of the cinematic object, to be a shared abjection. This was Tarkovsky's position, a filmmaker specially attuned to the capacities of the image:

> It is hard to imagine that a concept like *artistic image* could ever be expressed in a precise thesis, easily formulated and understandable. It is not possible, nor would one want it to be so. I can only say that the image stretches out into infinity, and leads to the absolute. And even what is known as the 'idea' of the image, many dimensional and with many meanings, cannot, in the very nature of things, be put into words.[63]

Perhaps the essence of philosophy brings to art its conceptual base, and this is the inspiration of art for philosophy. This is the continuing project of philosophy, to make the life of concepts and ideas useful and resonant. But concepts in philosophy ultimately manifest in words, and my experience of the words of the concepts of philosophy are rarely satisfactory when accounting for my experience of cinema. This basic incommensurability of the image and word is at the heart of Bazin's notion of a cinema of adaptation, which is more appropriately thought of as a cinema of transformation – a cinema that takes the essence of the novel, image in words, and makes it *cinematic*, makes it the stuff of pure cinema:

> The image – its plastic composition and the way it is set in time, because it is founded on a much higher degree of realism – has at its disposal more means of manipulating reality and of modifying it from within. The film-maker is no longer the competitor of the painter and the playwright, he is, at last, the equal of the novelist.[64]

For Bazin, the filmmaker achieves the apotheosis of the form – capturing the ephemerality of the perceptual world through the apparatus of cinema. This

---

[63] Tarkovsky, *Sculpting in Time*, 104.
[64] Bazin, 'The Evolution of the Language of Cinema', 39–40.

is why he anointed Welles the purveyor of new cinematic images, the artist of aesthetic realism. Welles transformed a text of words into a radically new world composed out of images. Intriguingly, Welles's *oeuvre* is an assemblage, in one way or another, of literary texts. In the late 1930s, Welles had invested in a production of Conrad's *Heart of Darkness*, which might have substituted for his other great novelistic text, *Citizen Kane*.

The arduous task of enunciating cinema in words and concepts falls to the critic and commentator, or the theorist, who has been bolstered in recent decades (perhaps beginning with Deleuze) by assurances of the compatibility of cinema and philosophy, or even more than compatibility, *symbiosis*. For Frampton, who projects Deleuze's formulation of cinema as philosophical concept to its natural end, cinema is a mode of *thinking* – divorced from either the diegetic subject/object relation or the non-diegetic subject/object relation.[65] For all of Frampton's excellent argument to the opposite, I can't help feeling that this is again cinema's life reduced to philosophy – reduced to a mode of explaining the world and its concepts, signs and effects. Frampton's argument seems to confirm Mullarky's position regarding the growth of cinema-philosophy in film studies: 'the circularity evident when philosophers do extol the thinking of film (or art in general) is not an easy obstacle to avoid.'[66] I confess to being intrigued by these various positions, and intersections of thought, experience, enunciation, and cinema. But there is something in my reflection on the experience of cinema, and my reflection on my perceptual and cognitive relationship to the world, that cannot be curtailed by the play of word and concept. And such words are performative. Words are not images; this is the essence of that bifurcation between literature and cinema Dudley Andrew observes:

> It is at this point that the specificity of these two signifying systems is at stake. Generally film is found to work from perception toward signification, from external facts to interior motivations … from the givenness of a world to a meaning of a story out of that world. Literary fiction works oppositely. It begins with signs (graphemes and words) building to propositions which attempt to develop perception.[67]

Andrew perceives a fundamental break of form, and a break in the reception of the perceptual world. Theory, it seems, seeks to suture this world of philosophical reflection through concept to the world of image-experience.

---

[65] Frampton, *Filmosophy*, 116–38.

[66] John Mullarky, *Philosophy and the Moving Image: Refractions of Reality* (London: Palgrave, 2009), xii.

[67] Dudley Andrew. *Concepts in Film Theory* (Oxford: Oxford University Press, 1984), 101.

How does the theorist describe (description is the treasured tool of the film theorist) the *material* of a shot in *Lawrence of Arabia* (1962), randomly, the moment in which the young Sherif Ali (Omar Sharif) materializes on the distant horizon? First, we would have to think outside of the accepted discourse of theoretical analysis founded on the unity of shot and the relation of one shot to the next. Why should we begin with the shot as foundation to an experience of cinema, as perhaps a semantic analysis of literary text begins with the clause? If we accept that cinema is not a language, at least not in the literary sense, why should we resort to the convenience of the shot to make meaning of cinema? What constitutes the shot, except the space between cuts, and this is surely only a convenient designation of the shot, which tells us almost nothing about the material incorporated in the screen in this duration, from this cut to the next, or about the aesthetic strategies that give life to the image (Lean's wide-angle lens encompassing the expanse of desert), or indeed, about the kind of technological innovation that enabled such an image. If we can begin to think beyond the shot as structural signification, perhaps we might move further toward realizing the essential experience of cinema, which lies beyond a series of grammatical relations encoding time. Cinema is not, purely, an experience of an image of time, though this image of time is certainly one of its seductive experiential possibilities.

Sherif Ali approaches a well in the distance of a long shot in Lean's *Lawrence of Arabia* (figures 1.20–1.22).

Shots of such length and visual precision in the early 1960s are common and unremarkable. Yet this is the shot, according to Spielberg, that set him on a filmmaking career; the legendary cut to the desert sunrise is quoted in *Schindler's List* (1993).[68] The shot is thus, inherently, 'beyond' the cinematic frame, the shot is a liminal object at its point of my experience of it; the shot is pushing against and beyond the boundaries of the frame. This shot, as particularity, is a marvel of cinematic technology, aesthetic virtuosity, and authorial signature. The shot swells in significatory potential, and ultimately the material of the shot will function as a metonym for the cinema of David Lean and the genre of the epic; further it will signify a post-colonial rendering of time, place and ideology in the Hollywood studio film.[69]

---

[68] 'A Conversation With Steven Spielberg', featurette in *Lawrence of Arabia* [DVD] – Collector's Edition (2-Disc Set), Sony Pictures, 2001.

[69] For an analysis of Lawrence's *Seven Pillars of Wisdom* as Orientalist discourse, see Edward Said, *Orientalism* (London: Penguin, 1991), 237–43. For a nuanced reading of the figuration of Lawrence in Lean's film, and a response to Said and the Said-inflected reading of the film by Ella Shohat, see Steven Charles Caton, *Lawrence of Arabia: A Film's Anthropology* (Berkeley: University of California Press, 1999), 172–99.

FIGURES 1.20–2 *Cinema's ephemeral image:* Lawrence of Arabia *(1962).*

All of these separate but interrelated materials of the image come together *at a point* – but this point is beyond our grasp, or it is permanently deferred. The point is not unlike the imaginary and undiscoverable point in the shot itself at which Ali's figure metamorphoses from insubstantiality (mirage) to substantiality (a body on horseback, approaching in long shot). The material of this image is thus both substantial (and substantive) and ephemeral. This movement that cannot be isolated, between form and formlessness, is a profound aspect of the material of the cinematic image. The mirage exists in our perceptual lives, but it materializes more forcefully in the cinema.

Reflecting on cinema and experiencing cinema are interrelated processes. My reflection on Lean's shot recalls a kaleidoscope of memories of this image, and its function in my own experience of Lean's cinema. One might even argue that experience is a mode of reflection, and that reflection is invariably a constituent of experience. But I seek to move beyond a clinical reading of the coordinates of a way of thinking about film, or accounting for its continued presence in our philosophical, psychological, existential (and, indeed, physical) lives. Such accounts invariably miss the essence of cinema. Thus: how does one *write* to encapsulate this experience? How does the theorist compose a reflective discourse on cinema without decomposing the material object *of* cinema?

Rodowick's 'An Elegy For Theory' springs forth, in part, from the various challenges posed to Grand Theory by Bordwell, Carroll and others. Much of this theory and its trajectory is examined in the volume, *Post Theory:*

Reconstruction Film Studies, edited by Bordwell and Carroll.[70] I agree with several of the criticisms of Grand Theory, the corpus of which is useful for a theoretical reflection on cinema, but is not explicitly engaged with the cinematic image as a mode of experience. Rodowick calls for a re-energizing not of theory (theory reads as Grand Theory) but of the natural filiation between ideas, thought and cinema.[71] This is a passionate attempt to return to a mode of cinema theory (his identification of the slippage between 'theory' and 'philosophy' in Deleuze[72] reveals something about that problematic relation in film studies discourse) *as philosophy*: 'bound up with our modes of existence and with our relations with others and to the world.'[73] For Rodowick, thinking, being, and the philosophy of cinema (not *about* cinema but *of* cinema) lie beyond the scientific domain of inscription – the word. This is an object that inheres in a plane of immanence and materializes in thought.

Cinema, in Rodowick's elegy for the ways we might think about this art form, is 'philosophical expression'.[74] But this elegiac expression of cinema has everything to do with cinema as philosophical ideal ('Cinema takes up where philosophy leaves off, as the preconceptual expression of the passage to another way of being'),[75] and little to do with cinema as *experience*. What does this conceptual model tell us about the lived experience of cinema? About the vitality of that experience? There is a distinction between experience and being. 'Where contemporary philosophy has reneged on its promise of moral perfectionism, film has responded.'[76] But which films? And for which subject? This is the theoretical reductionism inherent in a universal reflection on film as philosophy. Rodowick's subtle negotiation of the pitfall of Grand Theory (a necessary move) finds the same pitfall in conceptualizing cinema as a philosophical enterprise. Can the new edifice of cinema-philosophy encompass the object of cinema and its relationship to those who experience it, an individual and collective spectatorship?

Foundational to the project of cinema-philosophy, a cinematic thought that renders the world and subject anew, is the edifice of modernist, post-classical cinema. Modernist cinema presents the avant-garde periphery to the orthodoxy of studio produced narrative cinema, whether Hollywood's wish-fulfillment commodity and its assortment of culture industries, or Cinecittà's

---

[70] *Post-Theory: Reconstructing Film Studies*, ed. David Bordwell and Noël Carroll (Madison: University of Wisconsin Press, 1996).
[71] Rodowick, 'An Elegy for Theory', 103–4.
[72] Rodowick, 'An Elegy for Theory', 102.
[73] Rodowick, 'An Elegy for Theory', 105.
[74] Rodowick, 'An Elegy for Theory', 106.
[75] Rodowick, 'An Elegy for Theory', 107.
[76] Rodowick, 'An Elegy for Theory', 109.

cinema of the 'White Telephones', or France's 'Cinema of Quality'. Modernist cinema came out of the trauma of new experience. Modernist cinema enabled a philosophical cinema, a cinema about philosophical thought, and then, a cinema that was itself a philosophical mode. This is, for Deleuze, the foundation of the crisis that shifts cinema from the classical to the modernist: an enlivening of cinema's essential philosophical capacities. For Deleuze, the cinema that comes from the crisis in action and the culmination of the Second World War is exemplified in the Neorealist tradition, that lays the groundwork for images of time, that will be picked up and forcefully deployed in the work of Ozu, Antonioni, Godard, Bergman – each, in their own way, cinema-philosophers. To engage with the cinema of these modernists is to ask what their films *mean*. Cinema that functions as philosophical creation of the world thinks through new problems of space and time, and the crisis inherent in that changing relationship. This is why cinema-philosophy cherishes the cinema of the philosophical filmmakers, filmmakers who think, and rethink, the constituency of the physical, mental and philosophical world through cinema. This is why the cinema of the time-image is accorded a special status in cinema-philosophy even though the modernist cinema of the time-image is an exclusive and rarified object in the age of late cinema. Can one philosophize being through a cinema of spectacle, through the common-place experience of genre and its inevitable repetition, through the rollout of the Hollywood franchise aesthetic in the most dominant industrial setting in contemporary global production?

2

Theoretical trajectories in the age of late cinema: Time and space

The unfortunate burden of time

For a filmmaker, you could say that time is of the essence and is everywhere inscribed into film in a complex and metaphorical manner … Basically, a filmmaker constructs a 'sense of time' and a 'sense of place' in every film. The two are inextricably intertwined and meshed into the fabric of film itself, its projected image and playback sounds.[1]

Film's virtual life is sustained by its relationship with time. The powers of analogy are not those of representation or of a spatial mimesis, but rather of duration.[2]

I want to ask a very basic question about the experience of cinema: what is my relationship to the image of time? And how, and in what way, does time become a *thing in itself* when cinema is projected on a screen? Clearly, time is something we must think about when contemplating cinema. There are films that require an active contemplation of time; there are also films that provide an *experience* of time – of duration. Kubrick's *2001: A Space Odyssey* (1968), if it can be distilled into a thematic or experiential unity, is about time. As Capps argues, Kubrick's overture to the film presents not only an experience of the depths of unfathomable space, but the image of unfathomable time – the spectator experiences the enormity of a time beyond

---

[1] Mangolte, 262.
[2] Rodowick, *The Virtual Life of Film*, 73.

calculation, measurement, or form.[3] Kubrick's radical cut, from bone to spaceship, the objects synchronized through lyrical motion, is more explicitly a cut in time than a cut in space. Surely this is what Deleuze means by the pure image of time manifested in cinema. After cinema had been rigorously, exhaustively theorized as space, it became in Deleuze a pure symbol of time. The flow of time became duration, and time became an object detached from the sensory-motor faculties, and then from the itinerary of movement itself. First cinema's image was figural (space is figural) – and then abstract. A pure image of time, the image of duration, is not a representative image.

For theorists such as Cubitt, the 'turn to time' is a categorical reformation of the past and future orientation of cinema: 'Cinema thus does not represent time but originates it. At this foundational stage, then, we can no longer share Bazin's (1967) and Kracauer's (1960) proposals that cinema's destiny was the depiction.'[4] Here Cubitt, reflecting on the heavyweights of the ontology of the film image, presents an intriguing diversion. Bazin and Kracauer are simply inadequate for the contemplation of time in a post-classical phenomenological theory of cinema's effect. In Bazin and Kracauer, but certainly most clearly in Bazin, cinema's effect was to render the world in image form. Cinema was modernity's machine writing for the energy of experience. Whether or not it was a destiny of the work of art (as Bazin claims)[5] is immaterial; for Bazin, the *depiction* of the real constituted cinema's entrenched existential identity. For the Bazin adherent, for example, Dudley Andrew most recently and forcefully in *What Cinema Is*, Cubitt's turn away from this entrenched reality myth of the image is catastrophic.[6]

Time is, as Mangolte suggests, the basic material of cinema. It maps movement in the projector and on the screen. It inscribes flow through editing – images in *time code*. This is the common argument against cinema as, among other things, a compression *of time*.[7] This is something cinema does without a second thought: it takes the fullness of time and moulds it

---

[3] Emma Capps, *Time, Consciousness, and the Potential of Cinema*. Masters Dissertation, University of Sydney, 2011. For a seminal reading of *2001: A Space Odyssey*, see Annette Michelson, 'Bodies in Space: Film as Carnal Knowledge', *Artforum* 7, no. 6 (1969).

[4] Cubitt, *The Cinema Effect*, 35.

[5] See Bazin, 'The Myth of Total Cinema', 21. Bazin's famous declaration, 'In short, cinema has not yet been invented!' inscribes cinema with its unique image *telos*.

[6] See Andrew, *What Cinema Is*, xviii: 'I mean to advance quite a different idea of cinema, one that is in accord with the title neither of Cubitt's nor Manovich's texts: cinema is not, or has not always been, a primarily special effects medium.'

[7] For an overview of the discourse of cinema as perverse historical representation, see Hayden White, 'Historiography and Historiophoty', *The American Historical Review* 93, no. 5 (1988), 1193–9. See also Robert Rosenstone, 'History in Images/History in Words: Reflections on the Possibility of Really Putting History onto Film', *The American Historical Review* 93, no. 5 (1988), 1173–85.

to form, and in so doing, makes time into a new image. Bazin's celebration of the realist image was intimately connected to time's 'presence' within cinema. Deleuze's *Cinema 1* and *Cinema 2* build a theory of the presence of time within the moving image, which takes Bergson's several theses about time and movement and puts them against, and within, the image of cinema. In fact, I would argue that Deleuze's conceptual movement – which Elsaesser and Hagener call 'the single most important resource in film theory in the last two decades'[8] – is *toward time* as the object of cinematic experience:

> The movement-image has not disappeared, but now exists only as the *first dimension* [my emphasis] of an image that never stops growing in dimensions ... While the movement-image and its sensory-motor signs were in a relationship only with an indirect image *of* time (dependent on montage), the pure optical and sound image, its opsigns and sonsigns, are directly connected to a time-image which has subordinated movement. It is this reversal which means that time is no longer the measure of movement but movement is the perspective of time: it constitutes a whole cinema of time.[9]

I emphasize Deleuze's reading of the movement-image as a 'first dimension' because it seems to imply some evolutionary process in the cinematic image, a gradual though identifiable improvement of the image, from the basic coordinates of sensory-motor schema and movement (classical montage and continuity/classical narrative inscribed through the agency of a protagonist) to contemplation, stasis and time. This movement also inscribes an aesthetic shift from a classical cinema to independent cinemas of modernity, which appear in nascent form from the late 1940s in what Deleuze calls cinemas of 'crises' – Italian Neorealism, the French New Wave, early New German Cinema, etc.[10] I'd include something like the American independent productions of Maya Deren or John Cassavetes in this regard (Deleuze mentions Cassavetes in a similar vein, though without examining much of his work).[11]

---

[8] Thomas Elsaesser and Malte Hagener, *Film Theory: An Introduction Through the Senses* (New York: Routledge, 2010), 157.

[9] Deleuze, *Cinema 2*, 22.

[10] See Deleuze, *Cinema 2*, 33: 'The interval of movement was no longer that in relation to which the movement-image was specified as perception-image, at one end of the interval, as action-image at the other end, and as affection-image between the two, so as to constitute a sensory-motor whole. On the contrary the sensory-motor link was broken, and the interval of movement produced the appearance as such of *an image other than the movement-image* (original emphasis).'

[11] Cassavetes's landmark film, *Shadows* (1959), exemplifies the restlessness of an emerging aesthetic in which narrative fragments into temporal experiences, or sensations. *Shadows* in fact bears an uncanny resemblance to the destabilizing aesthetic of the French New Wave captured only a short time later in Godard's *À Bout de Souffle* (*Breathless*, 1959).

The crisis in movement provides the impetus for a cinema of the image of time in pure form. These several crises in the image are represented by the 'deliberate disturbances of narration in modern cinema'.[12]

Time, suggests Deleuze, is the manifestation of the *potentiality* of cinema. The cinema of the time-image is a cinema of maturity, complexity and aesthetic sophistication. We must contemplate the image of time to comprehend (though this is not exclusively an intellectual, nor strictly affective process in Deleuze) the cinema of Kubrick, or Antonioni – a filmmaker Deleuze accords special status in the promulgation of the image of time.[13] The crisis in the image of movement manifests as a restlessness, or tension, within the movement-image itself. There is still montage (how could cinema function without splitting time into discrete sections?), but now the flow of time across these sections is restless, or unsettled. In Antonioni's radical images, time materializes as a strange, unrecognizable thing, and we are shocked to discover our aversion to its effect. The pure image of time is initially unrecognizable; it registers as a change in the order of things. First, this image constitutes an intervention into narrative progression. But Deleuze, working through Antonioni, takes this much further. It is not merely a breach of narrative – such a breach would construe narrative as the natural cinematic form. Instead, it is the rendition of an entirely separate register – I have been using the word itinerary – of the image. What begins as an experience of narrative disturbance materializes as an entirely new form of image and experience. Gradually, in Antonioni, the spectator perceives, and comes to terms with, the material presence of the image of time. One such moment is striking in Antonioni's cinema, demonstrating the crisis in action, and the subtle, incremental separation of movement from time.

In the penultimate narrative segment of *Blow Up* (1966), the photographer searches for the body he has apparently photographed. While he has *seen* the body once, the previous night, he desires to photograph it now – the photograph takes on the substance of reality and reality the ephemeral nature of an image. This inversion of a basic ontological relationship between reality and its image is a philosophical notion at the core of several of Antonioni's films.[14] At 1:43:50,[15] the photographer approaches the tree in the park, camera in hand. Antonioni shoots the entire sequence to the diegetic sound

---

[12] Deleuze, *Cinema 2*, 26.

[13] Deleuze, *Cinema 2*, 23–4. Thus, 'Antonioni's art is like the intertwining of consequences, of temporal sequences and effects which flow from events out-of-field.'

[14] While *Blow Up* is the most explicit meditation on the subject, the ontological threat to the object manifests in subtle and not so subtle ways in *L'Avventura* (*The Adventure*, 1960), *La Notte* (1961), *Zabriskie Point* (1970) and *The Passenger* (1975).

[15] Time-code references are to *Blow Up* (DVD), Warner Home Video, 2004.

THEORETICAL TRAJECTORIES IN THE AGE OF LATE CINEMA

of the wind in the trees – though precisely whether this sound is diegetic or non-diegetic is unclear. Shots in depth and duration provide an odd sense of the immensity of the space; for Antonioni, the park is ontologically separate from the space of the city. As the photographer comes into shot, standing in the space in which he had previously seen the body (the body is now absent), the image cuts to a tighter shot on the photographer, and shifts slowly in through a perceptible zoom. His exhaustion, the outcome of the confrontation with his own ontological insubstantiality, is palpable. There is something here of Deleuze's body that 'contains the before and after, tiredness and waiting'.[16]

The intensity of the shot is captured in this gradual movement toward the photographer. The diegetic sound of the wind is brought up to immerse the photographer within the space. At this moment in the film, the park is a hermetically sealed space, an ontological insularity. It is thus fitting that Antonioni will render here a concrete image of time, requiring the spectator to contemplate time as an independent variable in cinema.[17] Recall Rossellini's use of shot reverse-shot as part of his realist aesthetic. The shot reverse-shot relation in Rossellini in no way undermines the ethical imperative toward the real in *Open City*. However, in *Blow Up*, Antonioni subtly disturbs the mechanism of shot reverse-shot as a mode of continuity. At 1:44:20, the image cuts to an overhead shot of the photographer crouched on the ground (figure 2.1). The sound of the trees rises, as if in crescendo to this movement, and the photographer raises his head to the sky (figure 2.2). What is he listening to? What has he heard? The image holds momentarily, then cuts to the standard point of view shot of the trees that are indeed swaying in the wind (figure 2.3). This is a simple point of view shot relation, establishing the photographer's gaze. While the photographer's eye-line does not move across the line of the camera (the standard camera move contriving point of view), the spectator is aware of her subject-identification with the photographer through the turn of the head, the eyes focused upward, and the cut to the shot of the trees. It is precisely here, within the concrete continuities of shot reverse-shot mechanics, that Antonioni installs a subtle optical image that grants a 'perspective of time'.[18] 'Perspective' is entirely appropriate as well because the image is a new *perspective*, configured temporally rather than spatially.

The (photographer's) point of view shot holds for several seconds. The spectator must anticipate the reverse-shot – a return to the photographer – that will complete the itinerary of the shot reverse-shot. But this image

[16] Deleuze, *Cinema 2*, 189.
[17] Rodowick, 'An Elegy for Theory', 105.
[18] Deleuze, *Cinema 2*, 22.

of the photographer no longer exists. The camera that holds on the trees (holding also the photographer's point of view) gradually pans across the sky, and down, to reveal the figure of the photographer, now standing rather than crouched, now some distance from where he had once been (figures 2.4–2.5). First, the spectator must account for this *movement*. How, and when, did the movement occur? Where did it originate? How was it effected? This is a question of a movement in space. But clearly, this movement was not 'recorded' by, or manifested in, some duration of time. In fact, that chain of progression, narrative flow, the very substance of movement, has been erased through a cut. What stands in for narration is a disturbance of movement, a manifestation of the inability of the protagonist to act, to effect change on the body and its surroundings. The image finally cuts to a long shot of the entrance/exit to the park (figure 2.6). Clearly, here, the photographer contemplates this spatial/temporal disturbance. And this disturbance is related directly to the conflation of time segments; the photographer is dislocated in space, but equally, in time. 'The direct time-image always gives us access to that Proustian dimension where people and things occupy a place in time which is incommensurable with the one they have in space.'[19] Is it outlandish to suggest that the photographer, an inhabitant of a *cinematic image*, is bewildered by a movement dislocated from narrative, from the ordered flow of time?

The image of time not only makes sense in this sequence in *Blow Up*, but is critical to a consideration of a modern cinema that manifests a disturbance in narrative progression. Antonioni's cut is a lacuna, but the space is the segment of time that is now autonomous, that has its own form within the film, and that affects the protagonist and spectator not as action and movement toward, but precisely away from, spatial and temporal resolution.

There is a more complex rendition of time in *The Passenger* (1975). Again Antonioni works against the shot as narrative segment. At 19:43,[20] the image opens on a spinning fan (symbolic of the simultaneity of stasis and movement), holds momentarily, then shifts downward to reveal David Locke (Jack Nicholson) (figures 2.7–2.8). We hear a knock at the door, followed by Locke's 'come in'; these sounds occur off-screen. A cut then reveals that we are listening to a tape recording (figure 2.9). Here Antonioni employs a similar device to that of the shot reverse-shot break, though the independent variable of time is more explicitly indicated in this sequence. The voices continue on the recording as Locke gets up and moves off camera. The camera moves left across the room and out onto the balcony, where it again picks up Locke (figures 2.10–2.13).

---

[19] Deleuze, *Cinema 2*, 39.

[20] Time-code references are to *The Passenger* (DVD), Sony Pictures Home Entertainment, 2006.

FIGURES 2.1–6 *A perspective of time:* Blow Up *(1966).*

These dual movements – that of the camera and Locke – occur in a single shot, yet the 'present' that was constituted by Locke seated at a table listening to a tape recording now encompasses the past. The figure of Locke on the balcony enacts the recorded (past) conversation *in the present*. This is not a flashback. Rather, for Antonioni, the image of the past within the present creates what Deleuze describes as an independent image of time. Antonioni's image here is particularly ingenious because it moves between image and sound, with the layer of diegetic sound played through the recording. As past and present collide forming one whole, so non-diegetic and diegetic film collide. Who speaks in this conversation? Who utters these words? And *when* are these words spoken? For Antonioni, these are not merely breaks in narrative, such as the conventional ellipses, or what Allison Ross describes as 'narrative discontinuity',[21] but, more radically, *non-narrative* film images.

---

[21] Allison Ross, 'Michelangelo Antonioni: The Aestheticization of Time and Experience in *The Passenger'*, in *Cinematic Thinking: Philosophical Approaches to the New Cinema*, ed. James Phillips (Stanford: Stanford University Press, 2008), 48.

FIGURES 2.7–13 *The image of the past within the present: Antonioni's time-image in* The Passenger *(1975).*

This examination of an image of time – with time's independence from movement – is to concur with Elsaesser and Hagener's position on Deleuze. I acknowledge the invention of this ontology of the image. I also agree that Deleuze's work opens up a particular mode of cinema in new ways that sustain close analysis of the text, and indeed, enrich a contemplation of story, character and theme. Antonioni's fracture of the classical shot reverse-shot in *Blow Up* has two key narrative functions: it provides a visual expression of the photographer's growing insubstantiality; and it establishes a conceptual link to the final sequence in which space and time are rendered immaterial. The photographer's vanishing in the final shot of the film leaves only a trace of a body that is no longer part of that space, and is dislocated from any subordinate itinerary of time. In *The Passenger*, Antonioni's collapse of the present into an independent image of time serves several critical narrative purposes. Ross indicates that such narrative disturbances work within the broader thematic of Locke's search for an identity.[22] In this way, a contemplation of time feels right in Antonioni – it feels *necessary* in a contemplation of *L'Avventura* (*The Adventure*, 1960), *La Notte* (*The Night*, 1961), *Blow Up* (1966), *Zabriskie Point* (1970) and *The Passenger* (1975). Deleuze's image of time thus provides a framework to think through Antonioni's modernist, and richly philosophical, cinema.

Deleuze argues that the image of time is not an endpoint. It is merely a kind of image, one that comes into cinema as cinema comes into modernity and undergoes the several crises of the mid-twentieth century: 'Something different happens in what is called modern cinema: not something more beautiful, more profound, or more true, but something different.'[23] Yet I would argue that the 'turn' to images of time in film studies discourse has resulted in just such a privileging of the image of time, and of the image of pure situations. If we perceive the image of time as coming into being within the cinema of modernity – which is also, essentially, an auteurist cinema of distinction, numbering De Sica, Antonioni, Godard, Resnais, Visconti, and earlier, via the auteur theory of Bazin and the *Cahiers* group, Renoir, Welles, Ozu in the fold – how can we not chart movement *toward time* as an evolutionary ideal, as the pursuit and attainment of the ideal of philosophical, aesthetic and cinematic modernity?[24] Against Deleuze's image of time, which is not especially 'beautiful', Rodowick writes of an image 'need[ing] to get beyond the "real" no less than beyond movement'.[25] Rodowick is here faithfully interpreting Deleuze, but this interpretation requires a teleological framework and a language that inscribes an evolutionary movement. 'The image must turn from exteriority or extensiveness in space toward a genesis in mental

---

[22] Ross, 'Michelangelo Antonioni', 48.

[23] Deleuze, *Cinema 2*, 40.

[24] See Sutton, *Photography, Cinema, Memory*, 40: 'Deleuze does not propose, in the movement-image and time-image, opposing systems of meaning or necessarily conflicting modes of representation but rather a single principle that flourishes in two alternate modes: the movement-image, which has its ontological basis in the movement within the cinema apparatus; and the time-image, which exploits any awareness of this reliance thus (arguably) leaving it behind.' While the time-image is thus not precisely antagonistic to the movement-image, the materialization of time effectively *dematerializes* movement, action, and the traversal of deterministic space.

[25] D. N. Rodowick, *Gilles Deleuze's Time Machine* (Durham, NC: Duke University Press, 1997), 79.

relations or time.'[26] And there is a further sleight of hand in Rodowick, in which what is *merely* an image becomes the essence of the image of cinema. This is not unlike Bazin's reading of the myth of cinema toward the aesthetic realization of reality. For Rodowick, the image of time is in effect the outcome of a process of becoming. Similarly projecting a possible 'future cinema' through Deleuze, Filser treats the endpoint of present cinema as the time-image: 'Now that cinema has discovered *its essence* [my emphasis] in the time-image, the evolutionary line from movement-image to time-image can hardly be continued beyond the latter.'[27]

This becoming is what the cinema of modernity – in Deleuze, in Rodowick, in Filser, in auteur cinema – requires, and furthermore, constitutes. Interpreting Deleuze, Sutton describes a cinema of the time-image 'being self-conscious, cinema saying it has grown up (or grown apart)'.[28] Rodowick and Filser effectively negate – or at least marginalize – the emphatic image of space and action in cinema that remains the foundational image of a classical Hollywood aesthetic. And here we see the ontological move, almost a sleight of hand, that has been played in a great part of the discourse of film-philosophy: to elevate the essential experience of cinema (cinema as medium) to a question of time, or more correctly, temporality, which implies the objectification of time as duration rather than the functionality of time as measurement. For Cubitt, cinema's evolution is to ever more sophisticated ways of perspectivizing time: 'slow motion, freeze-frame, steadicam, bullet-time: across three decades, cinema moves toward a spatialization of time.'[29] Which is to say that, in the purest form of cinematic experience, time is all there is.

Is there an alternative to time as the guiding itinerary (and evolutionary movement) of the cinematic image? I am not suggesting here a rejection of this image of time for some other image form, but a way of theorizing the image that presents alternative images of cinema that cohere within the wider play of image trajectories in cinema. This is to ask whether the perceived image progression from the movement-image to the time-image in Deleuzian theory is an appropriate conceptual and methodological model for all cinemas. Of course, there is an irony here. I am deliberately casting a cinema of space and movement through action as 'alternative cinema'. It seems to me that cinema that calls for an engagement with space, with geography, with the nuances of spatialized and historicized culture and

---

[26] Rodowick, *Gilles Deleuze's Time Machine*, 79.
[27] Barbara Filser, 'Gilles Deleuze and a Future Cinema: Cinema 1, Cinema 2, and Cinema 3?', in *Future Cinema: The Cinematic Imaginary After Film*, ed. Jeffrey Shaw and Peter Weibel (Cambridge, MA: MIT Press, 2003), 216.
[28] Sutton, 50.
[29] Cubitt, *The Cinema Effect*, 8.

identity, with a *spatialized aesthetics*, is incompatible with a Deleuzian mode of theory in which space, now no longer subordinating time, is subordinated by time. Time, in one way or another, becomes the loftier ideal. Against Antonioni's purely optical and sound situations – clearly evident in some of his greatest works – might we not also privilege the cinema of James Cameron, Clint Eastwood and Christopher Nolan? Could one read *The Unforgiven* (1992) or *True Lies* (1994) as cinemas *toward time*? Could one subdue Nolan's cinema to an image *of time* (*Memento* [2000]; *Inception* [2010])?[30] Outside of the Deleuzian image semiotic, from a Deleuzian perspective, the image of classical film theory, and to some extent, classical narrative cinema, ceases to function simply because the reification of time theory in film studies has also reified a particular film aesthetic.[31]

This is not an exaggeration of the claims, and presence, of time-theory in current film studies discourse. Describing the reception of Deleuze's film theory, Flaxman suggests that: 'Perhaps, finally, the audacity of "the cinema books" hit home: for while the complaints about the cinema books range across a spectrum of smaller concerns, the real sticking point remains the spectrum itself, the grandiose, even gaudy scope of the two volumes.'[32] The outcome of *Cinema 1* and *Cinema 2* is first a taxonomy, a 'colla[tion of] the various aspects of film forms and screen-generated concepts'.[33] This collation then builds the foundations of an 'autonomous cinematic consciousness';[34] and this consciousness is a matter of a direct perspective of, and engagement with, *time*. Deleuze put time into the physical, into the matter of cinema. Deleuze's notion that 'the greatness of Cassavetes's work is to have undone the story'[35] recalls Bazin's description of De Sica's accomplishment in *The Bicycle Thieves*: 'disappearance of the actor, disappearance of *mise en scène* … The very principle of *Ladri di Biciclette* is the disappearance of a story.'[36] In

---

[30] I note here Shaviro's recent fascinating discussion of Olivier Assayas's *Boarding Gate* (2007). For Shaviro, Assayas's cinema, and in particular *Boarding Gate*, demonstrates a 'crossing over' between the image of movement and the image of time. There is something provocative here in conceptualizing how the image of time might operate in a genre film such as *Boarding Gate*, and clearly Shaviro's position is necessary simply to identify the continued presence of movement and action in cinema: 'But Assayas suggests that, in the space of transnational capitalism, the break is never definitive, and the turn [from movement to time] is never completed.' See Steven Shaviro, *Post-Cinematic Affect* (New York: Zero Books, 2010), 60.

[31] For an account of the evolution of Deleuze's taxonomy of signs, see Filser, 214.

[32] Gregory Flaxman, 'Introduction', in *The Brain is the Screen: Deleuze and the Philosophy of Cinema*, ed. Gregory Flaxman (Minneapolis: University of Minnesota Press, 2000), 2.

[33] Felicity Colman, *Deleuze and Cinema: The Film Concepts* (Oxford: Berg, 2011), 1.

[34] Colman, *Deleuze and Cinema*, 1.

[35] Deleuze, *Cinema 2*, 192.

[36] André Bazin, 'Bicycle Thief', in *What is Cinema? Volume 2*, trans. Hugh Gray (Berkeley and Los Angeles: University of California Press, 1971), 58.

Deleuze, De Sica and Cassavetes put time into the image. Cassavetes's mode of performance 'put time into the body'.[37] De Sica's capturing of a movement through a city brought time into its own display.

Perhaps my criticism, not of Deleuze, but of how Deleuze has come to orient a kind of thinking on the cinematic image, is merely the same criticism levelled at a great deal of theory that privileges the European art tradition.[38] Martin-Jones suggests that Deleuze's at times dense and complicated texts are often criticized for being impenetrable, and too focused on auteur cinema. Impenetrability is not a terminology issue in Deleuze; rather, the reader of Deleuze submits to a necessarily paradigmatic analysis of cinema. I suspect that asking questions about the applicability of theory is more than simply asking what a theory says about cinema. It is to acknowledge that theory is a creative act, and that the image that gives life to time, in some sense, brings about a stasis, or decomposition, and then invisibility, of the image in space – the image in action – as it manifests as representative figure or significatory mechanism. What is it to talk about the meaning (or signification) of the spatial image, if such semiotic systems are outmoded? What is it to talk about the figure, the representative mode? While images of time, such as those in Kubrick or Antonioni, are visible examples of the image of modern cinema, I wonder if such a system of creating an experience of time is not merely one avenue, one creative approach to what cinema is, to what its fundamental building block, the image, can do? 'I know of two films that have succeeded in creating a time experience for the viewer by collapsing time as space and time as movement. The two films are *Wavelength* (Michael Snow, 1967) and *2001* (Stanley Kubrick, 1968).'[39] Mangolte presents the cinema of time distilled to two great texts that 'create a time experience'. What about the cinemas that fall short of the plenitude of the image of time? How might the spectator engage with the richness of images that project no 'presence of time', that are not built of the 'images and signs with the "monographs" of the great directors'?[40]

---

[37] Deleuze, *Cinema 2*, 192.

[38] David Martin-Jones, 'Demystifying Deleuze: French Philosophy Meets Contemporary U.S. Cinema', in *Film Theory and Contemporary Hollywood Movies*, ed. Warren Buckland (New York: Routledge, 2009), 214. For a discussion of the problematic relationship between Deleuzian theory and Deleuzian analyses within the academy, see Sutton, 25–31.

[39] Mangolte, 263.

[40] Deleuze, *Cinema 1*, x.

The potential distraction of time

Everything in film seems to be about time.[41]

In a substratum of theories of the cinematic image, the burden of time (that comes from 'putting time into the image') requires the presence of time – whether direct images (as we see in Antonioni) or some other metaphorical presence of time – in disparate modes of cinema. The time-image of Deleuze is often a broad-based, discursive, but also non-specific use-value of time. Cinema's theorizing as a critical, scholarly and cultural activity is thus elevated through a contemplation of time and its image. While there is no doubt great merit in the attempt to read time in the classical movement-image – the action film, or the science-fiction film, the romantic comedy, or the horror genre – one senses in such accounts the *burden of time* in artificially moulding the shape and effect of cinema and its history.

Lim's recent book charting non-chronological and asynchronous time as a way of moving beyond accepted chronological histories is a critical (and very useful) account of how cinema's multiple durations – present and past, and pastness within the flow of the image – construct and deconstruct actual social histories. Lim's work demonstrates how a reading through Bergson and Deleuze might be attached to a post-colonial examination of historicity within the Western hegemonic tradition.[42] However, taking a very different approach to the use-value of Deleuze (and Bergson), Martin-Jones begins his chapter in *Film Theory and Contemporary Hollywood Movies* by talking about the 'usefulness' of theory: 'this chapter unpacks Deleuze's film philosophy to demonstrate its usefulness for analyzing contemporary US cinema, both in its mainstream and alternative, independent form.'[43] Here the question of use-value is almost an apology to the bemused: why Deleuze and the rom-com? But why should Deleuze's usefulness have to be demonstrated? Shouldn't value be an effect of placing text and theory in a dialectical relationship, rather than choreographing a use-value itinerary inherent in the time-image? Martin-Jones's bold departure is to suggest that Deleuzian cinema-philosophy is applicable to 'US cinema' (presumably, the antithesis of European auteur cinema). His object for assessment is the romantic comedy, *Fifty First Dates* (2004). He then proceeds to read *Fifty First Dates* within

---

[41] Mangolte, 262.
[42] Bliss Cua Lim, *Translating Time: Cinema, the Fantastic, and Temporal Critique* (Durham: Duke University Press, 2009). For a lucid account of the freedoms inherent in the experience and acknowledgement of duration, see esp. Chapter 2.
[43] Martin-Jones, 214.

the genre of the Hollywood romantic comedy, tracing its lineage through the classical era, *It Happened One Night* (1934) and *Bringing Up Baby* (1938), both films inscribed with the narrative ethos of the classical era. Yet, for Martin-Jones, the classical male protagonist (always the agent of the romantic comedy) is 'drawn into a series of increasingly humorous comedic situations over which he is unable to assert any kind of authority through his own actions';[44] 'In this sense, these movement-images begin to display qualities normally found in the time-image.'[45] Turning to *Fifty First Dates*, Martin-Jones perceives a similar itinerary of the mainstream contemporary image, in which Lucy Whitmore (Drew Barrymore) suffers from short-term memory loss. The basic premise of this romantic comedy is that the male protagonist must reprise his courting of the woman from where he left off the previous night. Nolan's *Memento* offers a similar narrative premise, though it plays out within the context of a revisionist *noir* film.

There is potentially something interesting here about how contemporary cinema has manifested stories, characters and themes – a cinematic narrative form – that fractures continuity and indeed questions the formal properties of narrative itself. Trifonova offers such a reading of recent Hollywood cinema in which time 'is not a means to end but has become the end itself'.[46] Films of the 1990s and 2000s, for Trifonova, display a provocative interest in the various mechanisms around which time is unfolded, played out and reflected upon. While it is for me problematic (and revealing) that for Trifonova time's '*function* (my emphasis) now is to increase the level of ambiguity in the film, to conflate the present with the past, the real with the unreal'[47] (in what sense is the image of time functional?), what is clear in her reading is that 1990s and 2000s audiences are increasingly attracted to the presentation of a time out of narrative joint, nowhere better illustrated than in *The Matrix*'s famous bullet-time shot, in which the narrative pauses as an image of time is materialized on screen.[48]

My criticism of Martin-Jones and, to some extent, Trifonova's approach to recent American cinema, is in the loose appropriation of the time-image to any cinema that potentially problematizes narrative progression. I would argue, as does Deleuze and various commentators such as Filser and Rodowick, that the time-image is a product of a historical, and then aesthetic, crisis. While Deleuze's treatment of the time-image is limited in its examination of cinema's

44 Martin-Jones, 218.

45 Martin-Jones, 218.

46 Temenuga Trifonova, 'Time and Point of View in Contemporary Cinema', *CineAction* 58 (2002), 11.

47 Trifonova, 12.

48 Bruce Isaacs, *Toward a New Film Aesthetic* (New York: Continuum Press, 2008), 143–6.

production context, what is valuable is the elemental relationship between a creative perspectivizing of the world through a cinematic image, and a social, political, cultural and aesthetic objectivity of that world. Neorealism makes sense as a nascent time-image because it is also embedded within a specific historical context. The image of time makes no sense outside of a context within which the image of time is allowed to materialize – in the cinema cultures of Italy, France, Germany, and later, the United States. We sense the gradual intrusion of time in the images of *The Bicycle Thieves* (1948) as we sense a new cinematic image of social, political, cultural and existential despair in Italy's post-fascist modernity.

Yet the attempt to read Deleuze's time-image in the classical genre film (the studio romantic comedy) seems to me misguided. Such genre films provide the basic image of time subordinated to narrative progression; and narrative is inscribed almost exclusively as action in the classical cinema. Why would the spectator read the various interruptions of the classical protagonists' goals (how often are Philip Marlowe's or Sam Spade's 'goals' interrupted?) as anything but the creation of a complex series of obstacles to be encountered and overcome? These interruptions, in classical cinema and contemporary studio cinema, are the building blocks of cinematic narrative. Lucy Whitmore's short-term memory loss in *Fifty First Dates* is resolved, and the courtship successful and ideologically normalized. Martin-Jones acknowledges this tendency of the studio romantic comedy 'towards resolution, as is typical of the movement-image', yet argues that 'aspects of the time-image *invade* (my emphasis) the movement-image'.[49] This 'invasion' is the sticking point. The invasion of the movement-image, for Martin-Jones, is clearly not equivalent to Deleuze's crisis of the movement-image that gives rise to a direct image of time. Rather, 'mainstream cinemas [of the 1990s and 2000s] around the world have begun to produce films that are, broadly speaking, hybrids of Deleuze's two image categories'.[50] Hybridization implies a synthesis, a coming together and forming of something new. But the synthesis of movement and time is clearly not possible in Deleuze. In my reading of the time-image as the essence of cinema (Filser), the movement image must suffer a crisis, and it must subsequently, in the fullness of time, be vanquished by the time-image. Thus, the movement-image is in a perpetual state of becoming, to be effaced by the presence of the direct image of time when it intrudes upon the classical image itinerary of cinema.

The distraction of time, in a great deal of Deleuzian theory, is the outcome of an over-determination of the time-image in its application to classical narrative

---

[49] Martin-Jones, 219.
[50] Martin-Jones, 217.

modes of cinema. There is a necessary distinction between the time-image (Deleuze), a special sign within the orientation of the cinematic image, and a pervasive and astonishingly popular mode of cinema that engages *thematically* in new ways of thinking about narrative form. Film theory needs to rigorously conceptualize contemporary narrative to recognize the richness and complexity of classical progressive movement (narrative) rather than a direct image of time. This is why Buckland's 'Puzzle Film' is not a convenient label but a genuine attempt to theorize ways in which cinema reflects experience through invigorated narrative forms.[51] Nonlinear narrative in *Memento* or *Fight Club* (1999) does not in my opinion constitute a direct image of time, except in a broader, non-specific application, which might then be turned to any mode of cinema. If we are to read classical genre cinema as partaking of the itinerary of the time-image (whether Hawks's classical studio era romantic comedy or western, or a contemporary film such as *Groundhog Day* [1993]), the conceptual richness of this philosophical mode – indeed, cinema as a mode of creating consciousness – is diminished. I acknowledge that there is a series of films, which I would locate specifically as a genre movement from the mid- to late 1990s, that display time in more emphatic ways. Tarantino's revisionist framing in *Pulp Fiction* (1994),[52] Fincher's self-reflexive frame construction in *Fight Club*, are two such examples. But even so, I would wish to exhaust a corpus of new narrative theories[53] before identifying the presence of the direct image of time in these films. How does the image of time present in a film in which the resolution of action is 'already appointed'?[54]

Charlie Kaufman, *Eternal Sunshine of the Spotless Mind*, and cinema's spatialities

'Don't you wanna know what happened to me? This is important. There's a tiny door in my office, Maxine. It's a portal, and it takes you inside John

---

[51] See the edited collection, *Puzzle Films: Complex Storytelling in Contemporary Cinema*, ed. Warren Buckland (Chichester: Wiley-Blackwell, 2009).

[52] Bruce Isaacs, 'Nonlinear Narrative', in *New Punk Cinema*, ed. Nicholas Rombes (Edinburgh: Edinburgh University Press, 2005), 131–2.

[53] The work of Allan Cameron seems especially provocative in this regard. See, for example, Allan Cameron, 'Contingency, Order, and the Modular Narrative: *21 Grams and Irreversible*', *The Velvet Light Trap* 58 (2006), 65–78. Cameron attempts to formulate a framework through which to read modular narrative experimentation. While I ostensibly agree with Doane and Cubitt about the (primal) 'determinacy' of modular narratives (Cameron, 68–9), the framing of modularization in Cameron is a useful engagement with classical and post-classical narrative systems.

[54] Cubitt, *The Cinema Effect*, 240.

Malkovich. You see the world through John Malkovich's eyes, and then after about fifteen minutes you're spit out into a ditch on the side of the New Jersey turnpike … I had a piece of wood in my hand, Maxine. I don't have it anymore. Where is it? … Is it still in Malkovich's *head*?'
Craig Schwartz (John Cusack), *Being John Malkovich* (1999).

'I'm happy. I've never felt that before'.
Joel Barish (Jim Carrey), *Eternal Sunshine of the Spotless Mind* (2004).

I would like to conclude this chapter by contemplating the object of cinematic space. Against time, Sobchack grounds the experience of cinema through the 'historical space of situation', and this is, to my mind, a critical intervention into various phenomenological theories of cinema.[55] 'Space' is my point of entry into a broader and more ambitious notion of the cinematic image as an autonomous object, which constitutes the terrain of Chapter Three. I conclude that chapter with an analysis of the ontology of the film frame, which I argue is not a still, but a 'restless image'. More specifically here, I wish to offer a reading of Charlie Kaufman's *Eternal Sunshine of the Spotless Mind* as an image of space, and of kinds of spaces critical to an engaged experience of cinema. I would like to recast this film, often theorized as a film about time,[56] as a film about cinematic space that functions within, and sometimes outside of, the diegesis of the film. I wish to argue that while *Eternal Sunshine* conforms in several respects to a cinema about time – and potentially a direct image of time – the film also presents unique possibilities for contemplating subjectivity in space, subjective space, and the image of space itself as a presence through which to view and think cinematic experience.

Kaufman's cinema appears in the late 1990s as the natural extension of what Jim Hillier calls the 'American Independent'. The term describes the oddity of a studio production through a boutique label – for example, Miramax's Tarantino productions parented by the Disney Corporation, or New Line Cinema shifting beneath the aegis of Time-Warner in 1996. The Hollywood independent manifests this spirit of innovation we perceive in the independent American cinema of the late 1960s and early 1970s. Neither Miramax nor New Line Cinema are independent in the way that BBS or Corman's AIP was in the late 1960s, but for Hillier the creative drive toward alterity, fringe aesthetics and ideological deviance from the norm

---

[55] Vivian Sobchack, *The Address of the Eye: A Phenomenology of Film Experience* (Princeton: Princeton University Press, 1992), 31.
[56] See, for example. Jason Sperb, 'Internal *Sunshine*: Illuminating Being-Memory in *Eternal Sunshine of the Spotless Mind*', *Kriticos* 2 (2005).

is inscribed in the American Independent film of the 1990s and 2000s.[57] The location of *Being John Malkovich* on the fringe of American cinema is therefore important. Kaufman's cinema takes this innovative ethos as a point of origin, effectively pushing against the boundaries of a classical narrative structure, and against the prevailing ideologies of self and society that authorize such structures. In Kaufman, the classically perceiving and acting subject is immersed in a drama of contemplation. Craig Schwartz (*Being John Malkovich*) is the embodiment of Kaufman's late 1990s Hollywood existentialism. The predicament of postmodern man is to confront the fragility of the *physical* world, 'supernatural for want of a better word'. Kaufman seems to ask: what happens if there are unmapped spaces in the world, spaces that materialize, and open up, unpredictably?

In a sense, Kaufman's characters seem to do precisely what Deleuze suggests of the time-image cinema: they enter into another ontological mode of being. In *Eternal Sunshine*, Joel (Jim Carrey) and Clementine (Kate Winslet) are engaged in a process of meeting, breaking up, and meeting again. The film concludes on an apparently optimistic note, resolving the conflict at the core of the film. The characters set out to relive their experiences, to re-experience the time that has been lost. The spectator (and the protagonist) entertains the possibility to effect change, to alter the past. This is for Kaufman a conventional gesture of faith in the itinerary of his love story. This is all very ordinary, all very formulaic in contemporary genre cinema.

However, narrative resolution in *Eternal Sunshine*, and in Kaufman more generally, is rarely what it seems. The optimism of love offered and requited is undermined by the burden of Joel and Clementine's experience, renewed each time for each other but always merely the same for the spectator. A series of subtle jump cuts in the final sequence of the film (1:40:06–1:40:14)[58] reveals the eternal return of Joel and Clementine to a particular setting: the beach at Montauk in winter. In this closing shot (though merely the next iteration in the itinerary of eternal return), accompanied by Beck's 'Everybody's Gotta Learn Sometime', Joel and Clementine not only inhabit the beach at Montauk, but they are shown to return to it in perpetuity. They embark upon the same narrative journey each time *as if for the first time* (figures 2.14–2.17).

On first seeing *Eternal Sunshine* in a cinema in 2004, I was ebullient at the reconciliation of Joel and Clementine. The audacity to confront inevitability and discard it in the face of love! The film seemed tragic in its tone,

---

[57] Jim Hillier, 'Introduction', in *The New American Cinema*, ed. Jim Hillier (London: BFI, 2001).
[58] Time-code references are to *Eternal Sunshine of the Spotless Mind* [DVD], 2-Disc Collector's Edition, Roadshow Home Entertainment, 2004.

FIGURES 2.14–17 *The burden of eternal return: the beach at Montauk,* Eternal Sunshine of the Spotless Mind *(2004).*

in Kaufman's signature chic existentialism, or Gondry's strangely surrealist visuals. But here, in *Eternal Sunshine*, the cynicism of *Being John Malkovich* and *Adaptation* (2002) seemed, on a first viewing, absent. It was only several months later, re-viewing the film on DVD, that I noticed the series of jump cuts – the cuts I'd taken to be nothing more than Gondry's expressionistic montage. And it occurred to me then: how was I to make sense of this strangeness? How is the spectator to experience this love story if it concludes in an eternal return in which the lovers (and the spectator) can find no conclusive fulfillment?

The landscape of the beach at Montauk presents Kaufman's most evocative space of the consciousness of cinema, which opens up in the itinerary of the image in eternal return. The spectator must actively contemplate the disturbance of that space in this strange progression – its immersion in the present (filled with optimism) contains the fullness of the tragedy of the past. It is here, in Kaufman, or perhaps even more obviously in filmmakers such as David Lynch, that a cinema *as philosophical contemplation* seems most appropriate. There are other spaces in Kaufman that intrude into the traditional narrative frame – the space of the page in *Adaptation*, on which Charlie and Donald inscribe the material that moves the film. Who is Donald Kaufman? The death of Kaufman as author (the banishment from the set of *Being John Malkovich* is the most elegant metaphor I've yet encountered of Barthes's dead author) is also the creative life of a new author-figure, not God-like, but a cinematic sibling that comes to life only through writing. The portal in *Being*

John Malkovich is neither part of the physical space of the office nor the subjective interiority of Malkovich. It exists somewhere in between, and it is not purely a conduit, but a physical space in itself. 'I had a piece of wood in my hand, Maxine … Is it still in Malkovich's *head*?'

Kaufman's cinema creates these spaces between the real and the fantastic (or unconscious). Clearly we could not say this of a classical narrative cinema (not necessarily linear, but progressive and resolute in its form), which is why Nolan's *Memento* or *Inception* are remarkable puzzle films without presenting the radical ontological intrusion we see in Kaufman, Lynch, Fincher or Tarantino. Nolan's studio cinema 'resolves', collapsing all prior cinematic spaces into a narrative past. But Kaufman's spaces are ontological *presences*. They materialize in cinema, and can be visualized through the cinematic image, which is why Spike Jonze and Michel Gondry are such key collaborators in building Kaufman's images. How else can the spectator experience the disturbing movement of eternal return in *Eternal Sunshine*? How else can the spectator not only contemplate the burden of eternal return, but *see* it, spatially, in progression?

Next to Joel and Clementine's futile movement across the snow sits Milan Kundera's musing on the burden of eternal return: 'Let us therefore agree that the idea of eternal return implies a perspective from which things appear other than as we know them: they appear without the mitigating circumstance of their transitory nature.'[59] For Kundera, eternal return is a weight; it makes the loftiness of transitory moments *physical*, a burden. The eternal return on the beach at Montauk is equally a sensation. It is an 'affective space which punctures the past, present and future, but which also essentially remains outside all three planes'.[60] This is a cinematic space infused with the existential weight of being. We feel the abjection of the movement of Joel and Clementine that goes nowhere. Beck's 'Everybody's Gotta Learn Sometime' plays like diegetic sound, giving truth to Antonioni's impasse between diegetic and non-diegetic cinematic soundscapes. The image bears the weight of eternal return, but it also inscribes the actuality of space, and movement in that space, as cinematic experience. These are conscious and unconscious spaces of cinema, neither real nor precisely subjective imaginings.

In this analysis, I've treated Kaufman as a 'filmmaker'. Yet in these works I've referenced, he is credited only as screenwriter. This is a deliberate intervention on my part into a theory of the image that reads it only on the screen, through

---

[59] Milan Kundera, *The Unbearable Lightness of Being*, trans. Michael Henry Heim (London: Faber and Faber, 1984), 4.
[60] Sperb.

the mechanism of the camera. Kaufman's cinema originates on the page. His words animate the figures on screen that, otherwise, would be shapeless objects without affective life. The spaces I argue are charged with cinematic life on the screen – the beach at Montauk, the white space of Charlie's script pages in *Adaptation*, the portal in *Being John Malkovich* – materialize also on the page. Indeed, the image on screen cannot (and should not) be read apart from its literary imprint. This presence of the image beyond the screen is what film studies has failed to address for much of its history.[61] This is to argue in some sense for cinema, in its essence, as a cumulative movement displayed as progression; for moving images to establish continuity and flow, and for interruption – a direct image of time, for example – to enrich the whole. Perhaps the most important distinction in thinking through the potential of space in Kaufman is precisely to recast the auteur as writer, or inscriber. Deleuze's image of time is a function of duration, which is present in the apparatus of cinema. But the apparatus rarely extends to the literary precursor to the cinematic object. Kaufman's spatial exteriority is more precisely a function of *writing*. This is to say simply that screenwriters work with space, internalized and exteriorized. Space on the page – 'white space' marked with ink. Kaufman's excursions from linearity are thus a mode of spatializing narrative, of creating narrative arenas in which the past, present, and potential future collide and coalesce in interesting ways. Space in Kaufman is, critically, a literary signifier transposed to cinema, and enriched.

Conclusion

… and the glaze of the wax, and the curl of the braided wick, and the chipped rim of the mug that holds your yellow pencils, skewed all crazy, and the plied lives of the simplest surface, the slabbed butter melting on the crumbled bun, and the yellow of the yellow of the pencils, and you try to imagine the word on the screen becoming a thing in the world …[62]

I conclude this chapter by asking, simply, how the cinematic image gives life to the world. And how has this life manifested in the 'conflictual discourse'

---

[61] Here I differentiate between a material presence (screenplay, film print, digital file, etc.) and a significatory presence, or meaning. Of course, film studies has been enriched through the various cultural studies discourses that accounted for the 'exteriority' of the cinematic text – exemplary works include Manthia Diawara, 'Black Spectatorship: Problems of Identification and Resistance', *Screen* 29, no. 4 (1988), 66–79; and Fred Pfeil, 'From Pillar to Postmodern: Race, Class, and Gender in the Male Rampage Film', in *The New American Cinema*, ed. Jon Lewis (Durham: Duke University Press, 1998), 146–86.

[62] Don DeLillo, *Underworld* (London: Picador, 1998), 827.

of the discipline of film studies? Perhaps more importantly, how does cinema continue to be experienced, and internalized, as an experience of life, as a crystallization of our perception of the world? I have attempted to trace, like Cubitt, the 'effect' of the image. This effect is an inscription on a screen. But it is also something more than the screen, more than the movie theatre or multiplex, more than the cinematic text itself. DeLillo's monumental novel, *Underworld*, seeks to get underneath the surface of things, to find the affective material, 'the yellow of the yellow.' DeLillo's vision here, as in so much else he has written, takes the form of cinema. The literary sign, the word, is imbued with the life of an image in movement. Indeed, DeLillo's image in the excerpt above plays across the page as rhythmically as it plays across the screen of our internal vision. The notion of the essence of an image, beneath the substance itself, beneath the material, is something ephemeral in DeLillo. It's this literary register I wish to signal in shifting into the next chapter, which is a meditation on the potential of the cinematic image to attain an autonomous form. The trajectory of the image in cinematic history attests to the ever-increasing capacity of the image to become autonomous, to act for its own ends, and to demand from the spectator a contemplation of the image-in-itself. Without some notion of autonomy in the image, this image remains a constraint on the experience of cinema, shackled to some itinerary that serves a higher conceptual, aesthetic or philosophical purpose. Mullarky expresses such a profound capacity of cinema: 'there is more to film than any one transcendent theory ... can exhaust.'[63] The image can never be one thing. It cannot manifest some purely abstract trajectory, such as the movement toward a pure experience of time. In attaining autonomy, the cinematic image acquires the capacity to reflect the fullness of experience, and the fullest substance of our experience of life.

---

[63] Mullarky, 3.

3

The autonomous image of cinema

The image as object in reproduction

I will propose that film be seen instead as an immanent set of processes, specifically as a series of relational processes and hybrid contexts comprising the artists' and audience's psychologies, the cinematic 'raw data', the physical media of film, the varied forms of its exhibition, as well as all the theories relating themselves to these dimensions.[1]

Yet for all their contemporaneity, images have risen to a place of honor precisely after he [Walter Benjamin] unmoored them from their social privilege they enjoyed in the classical era.[2]

This chapter, and to some extent this book, is an attempt to come to terms with the unique power of images in our culture. But it is also an attempt to locate the site of this power, the place where the image gains clarity for the spectator. I take as my specific object of analysis the image of cinema, yet this image is now inevitably corrupted by the ubiquitous mediation of the world in image form. Such networks, as I attempted to show in Chapters One and Two, require new technologies, new ways of working with images, and ultimately inscribe new modes of image experience. At least we must acknowledge that, for whatever cinema *is*, in our current practice of it, it functions within a network of image systems, each implicated in the virtual construction of

---

[1] Mullarky, 10.
[2] Dudley Andrew, 'Introduction', in *The Image in Dispute: Art and Cinema in the Age of Photography*, ed. Dudley Andrew (Austin: University of Texas Press, 1997), 4.

our lives. The recent console game, *Red Dead Redemption*,[3] acknowledges the allure of cinema as mediated text. One encounters in *Red Dead's* first act (a term I would argue is applicable to gaming's reliance on conventional narration) the mediated image of cinema and its virtual inscription in a simulation of cinematic images. The image in cinema, television, gaming, and advertising feels as if it is a spatial and temporal accompaniment to the world, increasingly important as an object in itself, less a medium to a concrete field of the real than the real itself; why else would we seek out an image as an object in itself, as something to possess? DeLillo's mildly absurdist, though disconcerting, gesture to seek out the 'most photographed barn in America'[4] unsettles us because the object, in reproduction, presents the greatest allure. We are no longer interested in the image as some lesser representation of the real, but as a semblance of the life of the object itself. In cinema, this virtual life of images is particularly profound, and particularly alluring.

Benjamin, as Andrew observes, acknowledged the power of the image with some ambivalence. The image, for Benjamin, possessed the unique characteristics to intoxicate its spectator, to make the spectator, in a sense, into an image of itself (absorbing the spectator into the field of the artwork). The conventional privileging of the spectator over the image (the spectator who has the capacity to read the image makes the image into an object and thus masters its significatory potential) was lost when Benjamin announced the allure of the image of mechanical reproduction. Benjamin conceptualizes this ambivalence as distraction. Distraction prefigures the concern over the potential of the image to distract, subvert, and manipulate the masses; this concern was the foundation of Adorno's culture industry of modernity.[5] But the critical move for Benjamin, accounting for his importance in cultural studies and its engagement with cinema, is to recast the classical engagement with art ('concentration') as absorption. Absorption *by* art in the classical context is inverted in the age of mechanical reproduction; the distracted mass absorbs the work of art: 'Reception in a state of distraction, which is increasing noticeably in all fields of art and is symptomatic of profound changes in apperception, finds in the film its true means of exercise.'[6] The difficult work Benjamin does here is to conceptualize not only the profoundly new ways of thinking and engaging with the image as reproduced form, but to categorize

---

[3] *Red Dead Redemption* (Playstation 3/Xbox 360), Rockstar Games, 2010.

[4] Don DeLillo, *White Noise* (New York: Viking, 1985), Chapter Three.

[5] Theodor Adorno, 'Culture Industry Reconsidered', in *The Culture Industry: Selected Essays on Mass Culture*, ed. J. M. Bernstein (London: Routledge, 1991), 85–92.

[6] Walter Benjamin, 'The Work of Art in the Age of Mechanical Reproduction', in *Film Theory and Criticism: Introductory Readings*, ed. Leo Braudy and Marshall Cohen (Oxford: Oxford University Press, 2004), 809.

this engagement as something other than a classical ideal in which art gives the world back to its dutifully concentrating spectator. Distraction 'makes the cult value [of art] recede into the background', and creates new subjects of modernity who accept the image for its new potentialities. Any consideration of the allure of the image of cinema must take account of this absorption of the cinematic image (the networked image of reality) into the fabric of contemporary life.[7]

The image is now, several decades after the great heights attained by spectator theory, much more than signification. It finds a life of its own as an aesthetic object. The spectator theorists, and especially the feminist psychoanalytic theorists, made a great deal of Hitchcock in accounting for how cinema functioned on the spectator, how it impacted upon the screen of the spectator's psyche and sutured what was in the image-text to what was already present within the subject.[8] This was thinking through cinema as instrumental object. Yet even a brief encounter with Hitchcock's most complex meditation on the image of cinema – *Vertigo* (1958) – reveals the radical variability of the image in composition. The image in Hitchcock is revealed to be 'an immanent set of processes' in which the image and the spectator are implicated. In Scottie's first encounter with Madeleine, Hitchcock plays a convoluted series of subjective and pseudo-subjective shots to align the spectator's gaze with Scottie, and as Žižek argues, that which is more than Scottie, Scottie's *desire*.[9] While Žižek presents a convincing reading of precisely why Hitchcock renders 'more than the subjective', there is something fundamentally corrosive of the woman's image as stable signifier, as meaning. The classic conundrum of *Vertigo* concerns how the spectator is to account for the identity of the woman on the screen – for example, the moment in which Scottie turns from Madeleine, and she stands in profile as the red of the background dramatically saturates (figures 3.1–3.2). Who is this woman standing in profile? For Scottie, Kim Novak (the actress) here performs Madeleine. For the spectator

[7] For a more recent and radical attempt to theorize new art and media experience, see David Rodowick, *Reading the Figural, or, Philosophy After New Media* (Durham: Duke University Press, 2001), 43–4: 'Their [new digital media] invention, cultural form, and patterns of distribution and use are based on a set of concepts that recast the genealogy of visuality and the aesthetic in new contexts.' Recalling Benjamin in an earlier context, Rodowick asks: 'How can critical thought engage these new modes of expression and comprehend the forms of reading they have generated?' (46).

[8] For a useful overview and movement beyond a theory of 'suture and subjectivity', see George Butte, 'Suture and the Narration of Subjectivity in Film', *Poetics Today* 29, no. 2 (2008), 277–308. For the most famous example of the ideologizing of Hitchcock's spectator-subject, see Laura Mulvey, 'Visual Pleasure and Narrative Cinema', in *Feminism and Film Theory*, ed. Constance Penley (New York: Routledge, 1988), 64–7.

[9] Slavoj Žižek, '*Vertigo*: The Drama of a Deceived Platonist', *Hitchcock Annual* (2003–2004), 70–1.

unfamiliar with the film, Novak is concretely Madeleine as well. For Elster, the woman presented is Judy, an actress playing·the role of Madeleine. For the *familiar* spectator – for whom this viewing of *Vertigo* is a re-vision – the woman is Judy, and the spectator perceives that which Scottie does not, that the image of Madeleine is a creative act, a constructed ideal.

Yet my position is less confident that Hitchcock's image of woman should be read as *either* Judy or Madeleine, but that it is in fact an exemplary object-form of the ephemeral image of cinema. The woman that stands in relief from the background is more appropriately a synthetic composition of an ideal. Novak does not present Benjamin's classical ideal that was possessed of an aura, but the inauthentic image of a reproduction. The iteration of the form (Judy, Carlotta, Midge, Mrs. Gavin Elster, Madeleine), each new image presented, refigures the original and subdues its presence. The image of woman here attains an autonomous register – functioning as an aesthetic object quite separate from the story of Scottie's obsession with Madeleine. As William Rothman argues, the woman of *Vertigo* is a cinematic apparition.[10]

But there is more at stake in talking about this radical variability (and potential) of the image as reproduced. More than simply asking, what does this image *mean*, in *Vertigo* Hitchcock presses us to ask: what does this image *contain*? What is it possessed of? And further, what is the image of cinema possessed of, in its subtle association with the internal life of the spectator? If it is in fact more than meaning, more than signification, what is the nature of this engagement with the cinema image? Such questions revivify the enduring concerns of film theory, about film's relationship to the real (Bazin), or the import of the psychology of the spectator within the filmic text (Metz), or the nature of affect in thinking about the potential effect of cinema. Above and beyond these itineraries of the image, which I sought to explore in Chapters One and Two, I contend that we must think cinema and its image foundation as an aesthetic object, attentive to its own design and creative potential. This is not to reject the intrinsic relationship between the image and the world (or the world of perception); such engagements are what intoxicate the spectator. But it is to open up another ontological space for the image – to suggest that, even as the image of cinema composes the world and the spectator's experience of that world, it exhibits its own artificiality, its own aestheticized (reproduced) presence. Isn't this precisely what Bazin means by an 'aesthetic of reality'? This aestheticism – the ontological

---

[10] William Rothman, 'Vertigo: The Unknown Woman in Hitchcock', in *The 'I' of the Camera: Essays in Film Criticism, History and Aesthetics* (Cambridge: Cambridge University Press, 2004), 221–40. The object of Hitchcock's (and Scottie's) woman is an apparition, visible in its pure form in the moment in which the reproduction emerges, solid, ephemeral in its completion, from the bathroom.

FIGURES 3.1–2 *Hitchcock's apparition: Carlotta Valdes, Mrs. Gavin Elster, Midge, Judy, Madeleine:* Vertigo *(1958).*

presence of the image as reproduced form – is surely how the spectator must address cinema: as an experience of the world in reproduction. And in reproduction, the image can depart from the intrinsic nature of the world and be subjected to the itinerary of a purely cinematic movement.

The narrative image and the image-in-itself

Now, we all want the same thing. We have these images in our minds, and we want to get them onto the screen.[11]

There is a contest in film studies between thinking cinema as an assemblage of narrative images – images that serve to enclose and realize narrative form – and thinking cinema as an assemblage of images that function according to some other aesthetic imperative, that detach from the guiding impulse to tell stories, to reveal character, to inscribe narrative progression.

In a sense, perhaps, narrative takes the image closer to a perception of the world. This, more than anything else, accounts for the endurance of cinematic narrative within mainstream production contexts. Theorists such as Kristin Thompson, David Bordwell, or more recently Warren Buckland, work through cinema's complexity as a narrative form, and examine the spectator's cognitive engagement with this cinema. For Bordwell, this codification of experience within narrative is the essence of the classical Hollywood era, not specifically its industrial formation, but its aesthetic that overarches and gives meaning to studio production.[12] The itinerary of the narrative image provides not only a way of thinking cinema as a storied mechanism, but provides the

---

[11] James Cameron, 'Effects Scene: Technology and Magic', *Cinefex* 51 (1992), 5.

[12] See David Bordwell, *The Way Hollywood Tells It: Story and Style in Modern Movies* (Berkeley and Los Angeles: University of California Press, 2006). Bordwell traces the continuity of a studio aesthetic across several production eras and various industrial transformations. See esp. Chapter Two, 'Continuing Tradition, By Any Means Necessary'.

building blocks for a theory of psychological engagement with the image. In this way, Bordwell and other cognitive theorists are essentially construing cinema *as a narrative form*. Such a formulation has not only been influential, but is invaluable in accounting for the significance of cinema to a global mass culture.[13]

The 'image' in the words of James Cameron above, I would argue, is one such narrative image – animated by the intrinsic narrativization of human experience. Cameron's cinema partakes of the familiar structure of genre and its storied elements; while *The Terminator* (1984) and *The Abyss* are image experiments, their legacy to contemporary Hollywood and its spectatorship remains story. 'This is the great schizophrenia of filmmaking – balancing the palette of technical tools with the emotional and narrative goals of the film.'[14] I'll return to Cameron's intriguing association of the aesthetic with the techno-logical in Chapter Seven, but here I read Cameron's 'emotion' and 'narrative' as mutually dependent; he imports narrative as a foundation of the emotional register of cinema. What is 'in' the mind, and is thus formally composed – a problematic notion in itself – should manifest on the screen. The image-in-itself – what Deleuze would equate with a concept – is subsumed by the itinerary of the image as story element, or narrative movement. For Cameron, such a narrative imperative is intrinsic to the industrial and aesthetic demands of Hollywood. The revolutionary motion-capture virtuality of Pandora, built of the same sublimity Bukatman discovers in the special effects film as a discrete genre,[15] requires the formulaic and familiar narrative shell of *Avatar's* heroic mythological quest. Without this narrative framework through which to animate the image, *Avatar* would be an exercise in image production, which is rarely (and never in Cameron) what distinguishes the High Concept Hollywood film as commodity.[16] This is why George Lucas built Industrial Light and Magic to create the imagined universe of *Star Wars Episode IV: A New Hope* (1977),

---

[13] For a detailed examination of the movement of mass-articulated cinemas globally, see Charles R. Acland, *Screen Traffic: Movies, Multiplexes, and Global Culture* (Durham: Duke University Press, 2003).

[14] Cameron, 5.

[15] See Scott Bukatman, *Matters of Gravity: Special Effects and Supermen in the Twentieth Century* (Durham: Duke University Press, 2003), 93: 'The precise function of science fiction, in many ways, is to *create* the boundless and infinite stuff of sublime experience and thus to produce a sense of transcendence beyond human finitudes.'

[16] For a useful overview of the evolution of a 'High Concept' Hollywood aesthetic, see Justin Wyatt, *High Concept: Movies and Marketing in Hollywood* (Austin: University of Texas Press, 1994). I discuss High Concept American cinema at some length in Part Two of this book, signifi-cantly departing from Wyatt's emphasis on High Concept as a function of commoditization.

yet exhaustively mapped the narrative terrain of the franchise first, through Joseph Campbell's mytho-poetics in *Hero With a Thousand Faces*.[17]

While narrative remains a dominant aesthetic form in contemporary cinema, as Cubitt rightfully argues, it is merely one way to think through the itinerary of the cinematic image. Cubitt seems to work through Tom Gunning's influential examination of early cinema as attraction. Gunning engages this conflict between narrative and 'image as attraction' explicitly:

> The history of early cinema, like the history of cinema generally, has been written and theorized under the hegemony of narrative films. Early filmmakers like Smith, Méliès, and Porter have been studied primarily from the viewpoint of their contribution to film as a storytelling medium, particularly the evolution of narrative editing.[18]

Here the image of cinema – for example, Hitchcock's ephemeral image of woman in *Vertigo* or Cameron's motion-capture Na'vi warrior in *Avatar* – is not inherently narrative. Each has the potential to be more, to manifest some other aesthetic presence. For Cubitt, feature-length cinema's propensity toward narrative storytelling is a historical phenomenon; as it is in Gunning, the imbrication of narrative form is the product of the institutionalization and regulated production of cinema within an industrialized system.[19] Deleuze's movement toward time in cinema's modernity is surely an attempt to recast the myth of cinema (just as Bazin recast classical montage toward its realist successor) toward its non-narrative potential. For Deleuze, the pure image of time manifests outside of action, which is to say, outside of the animating action of classical narrative form.

Against the image of narrative, film theory has sought to describe a number of image itineraries, several of which I've discussed. Most provocative in contemporary film studies is perhaps Deleuze's image of time, the subject of Chapter Two. Notable also is the attempt to conceptualize a 'spectacle image', which Ndalianis reads as a neo-baroque aestheticism in contemporary cinema. This is a cinematic image in which 'reality and performance blur'.[20] Bazin's reading of the image as real, and Nagib's recent return to the

---

[17] Joseph Campbell, *The Hero With a Thousand Faces* (Princeton: Princeton University Press, 1968). For a seminal reading of the mytho-poetic framework of *Star Wars Episode IV*, see Andrew Gordon, '*Star Wars*: A Myth for our Time', *Literature/Film Quarterly* 6, no. 4 (1978), 314–26.

[18] Tom Gunning, 'The Cinema of Attractions: Early Film, Its Spectator and the Avant-Garde', in *Early Cinema: Space, Frame, Narrative*, ed. Thomas Elsaesser (London: BFI, 1990), 56.

[19] Gunning, 'The Cinema of Attractions', 56–7.

[20] Angela Ndalianis, *Neo-Baroque Aesthetics and Contemporary Entertainment* (Cambridge, MA: MIT Press, 2005), 195.

realist image from an ethical standpoint, attempt, in one way or another, to subvert the contrived modulation of cinema through narrative progression.[21] If narrative is a formal assemblage of events, ordered and temporalized,[22] it is, in Gunning or Cubitt, a constriction of the creative potential of the image.

A gesture toward thinking the cinematic image outside of (if not beyond) narrative, I would argue, is to address the image as an autonomous object – as a reproduced, and thus aestheticized, form. This image-form, or image-object, is what I will refer to as the image-in-itself.[23] On the one hand, this image gives up its status as authentic object, the originary form, having shifted into the mass domain through reproduction (Benjamin). Yet in doing so, the object becomes attentive to its status as reproduction. The image on display is no longer exclusively the image *of something*, but materializes as an exhibitionist object. In this sense, we can say that the image of Madeleine/Judy in Ernie's restaurant (*Vertigo*) *acts upon* the background of the shot, effectively saturating the red of the fabric on the wall. Hitchcock's saturation is an effect of the image, the suffusion of red motivated by the dramatic visual contrast between Madeleine/Judy's green dress and the red of the deep background of the shot. The red is more than merely Scottie's desire materializing as a symbolic image (this would be banal in Hitchcock), but exhibits the allure of the image-in-itself and its curious effect.

The image-in-itself is not purely denotational, nor purely representational. Rather, the image as object pushes beyond the significatory boundaries of the frame. It animates an aesthetic and affective movement, a combination

---

[21] For example, Nagib argues that, rather than 'anti-realism', 'discontinuous editing and a multi-layered, polyphonic soundtrack ... [allow] for the expression of the *contingent* [my emphasis] real'. See Nagib, 126. In Nagib's model, contingent realism represents a dramatic departure from illusionistic narrative.

[22] Kristin Thompson, *Storytelling in the New Hollywood: Understanding Classical Narrative Technique* (Cambridge, MA: Harvard University Press, 1999), 10.

[23] Here I wish to distinguish between an autonomous image – the image as art or experiential object – from the relatively recent trend toward thinking the image as *material* – as matter. Thus, the image-in-itself to which I refer is markedly different from Deleuze's (or Cubitt's) image, which is matter, which is material. I merely find the notion of an autonomous image-object functional for my purpose, which is to think through how the image of cinema works as an aesthetic object. The image-in-itself ascribes a status and register of engagement that moves outside the conventional reading of the image as signification (commonly fused with a mode of spectator-oriented theory), or reading the image as a literary (and narrativized) imprint, or reading the image as cultural manifestation. Of course, 'reading' is foundational to the analysis of cinema's image, and modalities of reading continue to contribute to cinema's significatory and affective life. Yet as Robert Ray has suggested, movies are often experienced as 'intermittent intensities (a face, a landscape, the fall of light across the room) that break free from the sometimes indifferent narratives that contain them'. See Robert Ray, *How a Film Theory Got Lost: And Other Mysteries in Cultural Studies* (Bloomington: Indiana University Press, 2001), 4.

of the 'visual, the auditory and the textual',[24] demonstrating a 'fascination with expanding spatial parameters'.[25] The image that attends to its status as an object for contemplation presents a 'series of views to an audience, fascinating because of their illusory power'.[26] Illusion here does not connote the fake, but the reproduction, the image that 'displays its visibility, willing to rupture a self-enclosed fictional world for the chance to solicit the attention of the spectator'.[27] Ndalianis astutely returns to Gunning here. If narrative presents the image with an anchor, a formal itinerary that constrains its capacity to exhibit itself, Gunning reveals the image of cinema, at the very point of the inception of the medium, as attentive to its own design, its aesthetic and affective register, and its unique potentiality to imagine the world aesthetically. This is an image that shocked the spectator not because of its resemblance to the world but because of the spectacular displacement of the world in a newly rendered moving image.

Contemporary cinema abounds with the image attentive to its aesthetic form. Such images function as an engagement with the senses that elicits the affective gasp, metaphorically if not literally, or the visceral charge presented in cinemas of the body, such as Scott's *Alien* (1979) or Cameron's *The Terminator*. As Tomasovic suggests, Gunning 'ventured to widen the concept's [cinema of attractions] reach by asserting that the attractions constitute a visual mode of address to the spectator not only in early cinema but also in other periods of film history'.[28] When Nolan's Parisian streetscape in *Inception* transforms before our eyes, we contemplate the image not of the city, not of a Paris we may have visited, but of *cinema* and its capacity to astonish the senses. In such moments, cinema's overarching narrative pauses in the spectator's contemplation – these are lacunae in our engagement with cinema's natural narrative flow – and gives life to the purely aesthetic register of an image in movement. Such images, whether of early or contemporary cinema, determinedly push past the boundaries of space and time that organize our perception in narrative continuity.

Cinema continues to imaginatively explore the image severed from its narrative flow. Indeed, I would argue that the cinematic image-in-itself presents the most aesthetically complex and discursive mode of image production in contemporary cinema. This is not to marginalize the cinema of narrative. But it is to carve out a space for a cinema, whether of the

---

[24] Ndalianis, 5.

[25] Ndalianis, 27.

[26] Ndalianis, 230.

[27] Ndalianis, 230.

[28] Dick Tomasovic, 'The Hollywood Cobweb: New Laws of Attraction', in *The Cinema of Attractions Reloaded*, ed. Wanda Strauven (Amsterdam: Amsterdam University Press, 2006), 311.

avant-garde or mainstream, that exhibits the art of the *image*, and requires a contemplative engagement with this image as a synthesis of technology and aesthetic design. The much discussed bullet-time shot of the Wachowskis's *The Matrix* demands to be read as an image attentive to its capacity to exhibit itself.[29] John Gaeta, the special effects artist on *The Matrix*, revels in simulated cinema's capacity to makeover the real, to take the image in life and alter its itinerary. To this end, bullet-time is perhaps the image of attraction perfected in the age of late cinema. It surpasses even Cameron's liquid-metal man of *Terminator 2: Judgment Day*, or Spielberg's Brachiosaurus in *Jurassic Park*. When the spectator has long since lost her fascination with the image in movement (Lumière's train can no longer fascinate as it did in 1895), the Wachowskis provide an image in stasis – not a still, but an image without the internal volition of narrative. This was for Bazin the essence of photography: the image in perfect reproduction, but without movement.[30] The body of Trinity holds in midair (the image stilled), and as the perspective shifts, we contemplate an image severed from its narrative housing, exhibiting itself from multiple perspectives. The movement inherent in the scene (the 180-degree spin of the point of view) is not the movement of the image in progression, but the affective movement of the image in space and time, crossing boundaries, opening up portals to new modes of creative imaging.

This chapter continues with an examination of a series of images of mainstream cinema that actively dissociate from narrative progression and present as affecting objects in themselves. These are objects that 'signify' outwardly and yet also reflect on an internal aesthetic composition. Such images stretch beyond the clarity of meaning, beyond storytelling and its required authorial intent, and encompass 'an entire world'.[31] The world of the image is of course still part of that world outside, that searches for 'truth' through the relationship between reality and the subjective consciousness.[32] But the world of this cinema is also contained *within* the image. I conclude the chapter with an analysis of the cinematic image reduced to a single frame, which I read not for an imprint of the fullness of feature narrative, but for the aesthetic potential of the image in 1/24th of a second.

---

[29] For a recent discussion of effect as event in bullet-time, see Eivind Røssaak, 'figures of Sensation: Between Still and Moving Images', in *The Cinema of Attractions Reloaded*, ed. Wanda Strauven (Amsterdam: Amsterdam University Press, 2006), 322–5.
[30] Bazin, 'The Ontology of the Photographic Image', 13–15. Cinema's evolution beyond photography is precisely its 'objectivity in time ... The image of things [in cinema] is likewise the image of their duration, change mummified as it were' (14–15).
[31] Tarkovsky, 110.
[32] Tarkovsky, 109.

Action cinema; the image of attraction; *The Road Warrior*

Taking Adrian Martin's lead in his exemplary formal analysis of the *Mad Max* films, I wish to examine a single cut in *The Road Warrior* (*Mad Max 2*, 1981), or more correctly, the relationship between two shots that inscribes a uniquely affective cinema image. It is this moment in the franchise that characterizes what Martin calls pure cinematicality: 'a cinema primarily of sensation'.[33] Indeed, Martin regards *Mad Max* (1979) as a cinema composed of the 'nitty-gritty fine grain of *images* (my emphasis), sounds, cuts and formal structures'.[34] I emphasize here Martin's use of image over some other formal component of the text such as story, character, or theme. The cinema of action is, in Martin's analysis, a cinema built of images in a series of complex relationships.

If Bordwell, Staiger and Thompson's 'obvious cinema' is in some sense a cinema of *narrative* action (which might also be read as a mode of realist cinema that dominated various traditions within Hollywood studio cinema),[35] in my reading of *The Road Warrior*, 'action cinema' is not a genre, and certainly not a narrative form *per se*. Rather, action represents a particular approach to rendering images through composition and cutting. Action might be inscribed through frenetic or chaotic cutting; Greengrass's *The Bourne Ultimatum* (2007) employs such a strategy; Friedkin's justly celebrated car chase in *The French Connection* (1971) employs several movements of discontinuous edits, almost jump cutting. Action might also be inscribed through compressing shot lengths such that the cut, rather than the shot, anchors the movement. This is a cinematic aesthetic in which the cut actively disorients the spectator and the image is at times, quite literally, an abstract aesthetic form, viewed by the spectator impressionistically. The image lingers as afterimage as the action shifts from one shot to the next. Bordwell's examination of *The Bourne Supremacy* (2004) reveals the average shot length to be approximately 1.9 seconds,[36] hardly enough time for the cogitating spectator to insert the abstractly rendered image into the complexity of progressive narrative movement.

---

[33] Adrian Martin, *The Mad Max Movies* (Strawberry Hills: Currency Press, 2003), 5.

[34] Martin, *The Mad Max Movies*, 6.

[35] For unparalleled precision in a formal examination of Hollywood's classical aesthetic, see Bordwell, Staiger and Thompson, *The Classical Hollywood Cinema*, 3–80.

[36] David Bordwell, 'Unsteadicam Chronicles', *David Bordwell's Website on Cinema* (blog), August 17, 2007, http://www.davidbordwell.net/blog/2007/08/17/unsteadicam-chronicles/ [accessed 13 December 2009].

Beyond cutting, action manifests also within the frame through movement of the camera. Fincher's hand-held chase sequence in *Se7en* (1995) [1:05:47–1:10:08][37] is exemplary of the moving camera to manifest the action aesthetic. This sequence recalls Bertolucci's death scene in the snow in *il Conformista* (*The Conformist*, 1971), radical at the time for its use of hand-held cinematography.[38] Greengrass's rapid cutting in the *Bourne* films is layered over a constantly moving, hand-held camera, foregoing the cleanliness of movement captured through Steadicam. Cutting on action takes on a new meaning, in which action is deliberately severed from narrative continuity and displays the potential of action in itself. The action image is subject to delimitation, departing from several conventions of narrative cinema, such as symmetrical composition, forced framing, match cutting, cutting on narrative action (generalized continuity), etc.

The image of action can also manifest through an object moving within, or through, the frame – the most obvious contemporary example is the bus in Jan de Bont's *Speed* (1994). *Speed*'s bus is literally beyond the control of conventional spatial and temporal constraints. Intriguingly, Richard Dyer characterizes *Speed's* mode of action cinema alongside Lumière's early cinema: '*Train Arriving at a Station* and *Speed* belong to a distinguished lineage. It includes all those celebrations of movement so prized by earlier commentators on film ... The celebration of sensational movement ... for many people *is* the movies.'[39] Here the train and the bus are forms of new locomotive experience. Lumière's train was no doubt as shocking to an audience in 1895 as de Bont's bus was to action fans in 1994. Dyer locates *Speed* alongside Lumière's early cinema because its action provides the thrill of the image in exhibition, providing the spectator with the intensity of movement. Even when the image of a moving object is in stasis – for example, an interior shot of the bus – the perceptually unmoving object is placed against a world in motion. *Speed* thus provides a sensation of speed through a world in perpetual motion: roads moving in a blur beneath the tires of the bus, backgrounds in a blur of abstractly rendered images (figures 3.3–3.9).

Action cinema is an experience of the image composed of the energy of movement. This is surely what accounts for the transformation from an action cinema that affirms continuity through progression (epitomized

---

[37] Time-code references are to *Se7en* (Deluxe Special Edition, DVD), Roadshow Home Entertainment, 1996.

[38] See Stuart Jeffries, '"Films Are a Way to Kill My Father"', *The Guardian*, 22 February 2008.

[39] Richard Dyer, 'Action!', in *Action/Spectacle Cinema: A Sight and Sound Reader*, ed. José Arroyo (London: BFI, 2000), 17–18.

FIGURES 3.3–5 *The image of action through abstraction:* Speed *(1994).*

FIGURES 3.6–9 *The object in perpetual motion:* Speed *(1994).*

in the classical era by the Western)[40] – and an action cinema of attraction, which renders movement as affective image-in-itself. Classical cinema is

---

[40] For an influential analysis of the Western film as movement, see André Bazin, 'The Western: Or the American Film *Par Excellence'*, in *What is Cinema? Volume 2*, trans. Hugh Gray (Berkeley and Los Angeles: University of California Press, 1967), 141: 'it is easy to say that because the cinema is movement the western is cinema *par excellence*. It is true that galloping horses and fights are its usual ingredients.'

not a cinema of action in the model proposed by Gunning's attraction of Lumière's locomotive. Yet action cinema, a modern phenomenon, partakes of this attraction of the image and its capacity to exhibit itself. *The Bourne Ultimatum*'s fight sequence in a Tunisian hotel room [1:04:56–1:06:47][41] is a 'pure' action sequence (connoting the action image of attraction), built of images of movement through frenetic framing, cutting and cinematography. Lighting and sound are appropriate for the diegetic space, but the rest is a conflation of energetic movements that disorient, and indeed assault, the senses of the spectator. I would further suggest that Greengrass's cutting is not only discontinuous, but that his approach to montage reveals a funda-mental spatial and temporal indeterminacy. *The cuts simply do not match.* And more radical than discontinuity is an editing ethos that deliberately fractures harmonious space and time (figures 3.10–3.12).[42] This is to suggest that Greengrass's action image is intrinsically indeterminate. The sequence refuses the conventional cut from the discontinuous action image to a wide shot, a cut that would neatly situate the moving objects spatially and tempo-rally. Rather, the fight is captured almost entirely in medium close-up and close-up, cut on frenetic camera movement, each image held for less than a second. The wide establishing shot of classical cinema makes no sense in the context of this fight sequence. What would a wide shot establish? Simply that the elemental spatial relationship between wide shot and close-up in classical cinema is fractured into so many arbitrary perspectives, so many flashes of images that display movement rather than deterministic spatial relationships.

Consider the obverse capture/editing strategy in Michael Mann's *Heat* (1995), in which a critical narrative turning point is inscribed through a bravura seven-minute shoot out [1:43:53–1:50:49].[43] Mann's sequence presents the most startling classical action sequence in modern American film simply because it is anchored through medium and long wide-angle shots. Mann's situating of the action within an actual space (rather than *Bourne*'s virtual space of the Tunisian room) through predetermined cuts to master shots

---

[41] Time-code references are to *The Bourne Ultimatum* (DVD), Universal, 2007.

[42] For an analysis of recent movements toward 'Chaos Cinema', see Matthias Stork, 'Chaos Cinema: The Decline and Fall of Action Filmmaking', *Indiewire*, 22 August 2011, http://blogs. indiewire.com/pressplay/video_essay_matthias_stork_calls_out_the_chaos_cinema [accessed 15 June 2012]. Stork's analysis of the action genre is thoroughly engaging, yet I would argue that he overplays the distinction between an action cinema post–2000 and an action cinema of the post-classic era (1960–2000). And clearly, the cinema of post–2000, whether that of Michael Bay or Paul Greengrass, partakes of various registers of continuity within an otherwise chaotic montage.

[43] Time-code references are to *Heat* (DVD), Warner Home Video, 1995. In this sequence, Mann intersperses tight angles/composition with consistent and measured reversions to wide compo-sitional shots (wide angles, overhead shots, over-the-shoulder point of view in extreme depth of field), anchoring the co-ordinates of space and time within the complex action movement.

FIGURES 3.10–12 *The image of action cut for radical discontinuity:* The Bourne Ultimatum *(2007).*

of the action renders it a classical narrative sequence (figures 3.13–3.16). The action is thus 'realistic', and thus progressively built. One might speak of the same monumental action of Kurosawa in *The Seven Samurai* (1954), *Kagemusha* (1980) or *Ran* (1985). This is not to suggest that Mann's or Kurosawa's films do not present cinemas of attraction – obviously they do. But these are attractions built on a classical register of action through the progressive and deterministic cinematic image.

The image of action – the image of action *in itself* – has increasingly become part of the genre of action cinema. This is again to distinguish between the action image of attraction (which one might discover in a horror film, or a romantic comedy, or a Pixar animation) and the action genre, which one can locate in a designated space in a video store, or on an Apple TV Menu Screen. The action image is not narratively constituted; the action *genre* is. Mainstream cinema rarely dissociates action from narrative entirely. Thus, we might read the image of action – and more broadly, Gunning's image of attraction – as an *intrusion* into a dominant narrative cinema of action. I wish to offer a close analysis of one such intrusion in George Miller's *The Road Warrior*.

The Road Warrior is a sequel to the enormously successful Australian film *Mad Max*, which Martin reads as a 'B-exploitation genre corral [which] is invariably a challenge – if not an affront – to middlebrow aesthetic values'.[44] In the era in which Australian cinema reinvigorated itself through *Picnic at*

---

[44] Martin, *The Mad Max Movies*, 14.

FIGURES 3.13–16 *Classical action: establishing shots, continuity cutting, action orchestrated in realistic space:* Heat *(1995).*

Hanging Rock (1975), *My Brilliant Career* (1979) and *Gallipoli* (1981), each a historical drama or period film, Miller adopted the aesthetics of American biker cinema, seeming to spill out of Corman's B-Grade AIP material that was lucrative on the fringes of Hollywood in the late 1970s. Fittingly, Corman's AIP distributed *Mad Max* when the film acquired a cult status in the US after early screenings.

The Road Warrior is less accurately a sequel to *Mad Max* than a reimagining of the Australian action cinema in an American context. If *Mad Max* is in some sense Australian, *The Road Warrior's* dystopian futurism is more obviously what Jim Collins calls 'genericity', or the performance of American genre.[45] Miller's purely sensational action cinema of *Mad Max* is recuperated in its sequel, yet the action makes space for several narrative and generic tropes recognizable in popular studio cinema of the late 1970s. *The Road Warrior's* construction of the figure of Max, an image in memory, partakes of Lucas's mytho-poetic narrative structure of *Star Wars Episode IV* and *Star Wars Episode V: The Empire Strikes Back* (1980).[46] The heroic quest figure (dystopian rather than utopian) stands on the road in a mist of smoke [1:08];[47] in the background, the sunset looks like a shot from *Star Wars Episode IV*

[45] Jim Collins, 'Genericity in the 90s: Eclectic Irony and the New Sincerity', in *Film Theory Goes to the Movies*, ed. Jim Collins, Hilary Radner and Ava Preacher Collins (New York: Routledge, 1993).
[46] See John Shelton Lawrence, 'Joseph Campbell, George Lucas, and the Monomyth', in *Finding the Force of the Star Wars Franchise: Fans, Merchandise and Critics*, ed. Matthew Wilhelm Kapell and John Shelton Lawrence (New York: Peter Lang, 2006), 21–33.
[47] Time-code references are to *Mad Max 2* (DVD), Warner Home Video, 2000.

(Luke gazing upon the dual suns of Tatooine, which in itself recalls an early sequence in Ford's *The Searchers*). The camera, placed at the level of the road and gazing upward at the distant figure of Max, slowly moves in, accompanied by the voiceover: 'I remember a time ...' This line strategically recalls for the early 1980s spectator Lucas's 'A long time ago, in a galaxy far, far away ...' The mytho-poeticism, and clear intertextual association with the studio High Concept film of the 1970s, is explicit in *The Road Warrior*. In its opening sequence, Miller's film demonstrates that hybridity of action common to the genre in the early 1980s: an action cinema composed of narrative, archetypal-mythological, cinematic and literary tropes.

The transition from narrative image to action image occurs in *The Road Warrior* at 3:28, in which exegesis accompanied by voiceover gives over to the shock effect of the pure image of action. This image is constituted on screen through each of the formal strategies discussed above: the object in motion, the world in motion, and the apparatus in motion, all joined through discontinuous, exhibitionist cutting. The image that remains a reflection on mythical history – on an undiscoverable past lost to war – opens on black as the sound of an engine assaults the spectator. Whereas in the previous narrative sequence the sound was non-diegetic, here the cut to diegetic sound, disproportionately loud over the soundtrack, literally pulls the spectator out of the meditative, trace-like exegesis. I use the word 'pull' deliberately because the image opens on the black of the aperture of an exhaust and *pulls outward* at speed through a fast zoom to reveal the front of Max's Interceptor. The zoom is traditionally an artificial visualization of the image. Here the zoom is not to depict frame and its contents; it is not to 'settle' the composition. Rather, Miller employs the zoom to render the affect of *movement*. In a similar fashion, Tarantino employs a 'Shaw Brothers Zoom' in *Kill Bill, Volume 1* to inaugurate the first action sequence of that film.[48]

The second shot occurs at 3:32: a low angle on the road moving beneath the vehicle. While Miller is clearly referencing this shot common to a great deal of road genre film (notably *Easy Rider*, 1969), here the cut provides the direct experience of speed. The road appears as an abstraction; the clear vanishing point and horizon line is a formal composition, stripping the image of its capacity to reveal more than what is contained in the energy of movement (figure 3.17). Shot 3 occurs at 3:34: the interior of the Inceptor, revealing the profile of Max (figure 3.18). Rather than cutting, the camera now fast pans to the left (figures 3.19–3.20) and displays the figures in pursuit of Max. The pan further unsettles the visual itinerary of this introductory sequence, in which

[48] Quentin Tarantino, 'Chapter 2', in *Kill Bill, Volumes 1 and 2* (Shooting Script). Internet Moviescript Database, http://www.imsdb.com/scripts/Kill-Bill-Volume–1-&2.html [accessed 6 April 2007].

both the environment (the Interceptor and the road) and the apparatus of the image (the camera) are energized through frenetic movement.

I focus on these three shots because they constitute an example of the uniquely affective qualities of the action image.[49] It is fitting that such an image provides an experience of speed, whether the speed of frenzied motion through camera movement and cutting in *The Bourne Ultimatum*, or the speed of a car on a road, an image that has become integral to the contemporary action genre. One could argue that a franchise such as *The Fast and the Furious* (currently in production on its sixth film) is built upon an action image ontology: the spectator detaches from the formulaic narrative structure (which functions as distraction) and engages in set pieces of action, in which the car, the road, its driver, and the experience of speed, are fetishized images.[50] Furthermore, such action images are not necessarily cinematic. Consider the commonplace image of the camera positioned on the front of the car, and at the level of the road, in the television coverage of NASCAR, or Australian V8 Supercars. Tony Scott's action film, *Days of Thunder* (1990), presents an intriguing visual itinerary of the image in its race scenes, effectively incorporating the aesthetics of action cinema and the aesthetics of television motor racing coverage. The vicarious thrill the spectator experiences through motor racing is surely not dissimilar to the thrill of the experience of Miller's action image in *The Road Warrior*, which is shot from the level of the road, from within the vehicle through the windscreen, and on each side of the vehicle. These are commonplace images in motor racing coverage, which is of course a non-narrative form. In *The Road Warrior*, the spectator also fetishizes the paraphernalia that gives meaning to speed. Thus speed is not merely a visual sensory mechanism, but is the product of the machinery of the car (the legendary Interceptor, supercharged for speed), as well as Max's clothing and accessories.

The transition from narrative to action in *The Road Warrior* is a jolt to the spectator. I have discussed the first three shots of Miller's action image, yet the film is infused with the intrusive presence of the image of action. Such images are necessarily perceived and experienced *as images* – attentive to their framing, composition and kinetic qualities. These are the cinematic attractions that continue to animate the contemporary action film.

---

[49] For a detailed discussion of speed in *Fast and Furious* (2009), see Lisa Purse, *Contemporary Action Cinema* (Edinburgh: Edinburgh University Press, 2011), 57–60.

[50] For a reading of the cinema of attractions as fetishized image, see Peter Cosgrove, 'The Cinema of Attractions and the novel in *Barry Lyndon* and *Tom Jones*', in *Eighteenth-Century Fiction on Screen*, ed. Robert Mayer (Cambridge: Cambridge University Press, 2002), 16–34.

FIGURES 3.17–20 *Visceral action through kinetic montage and intensified movement:* The Road Warrior *(1981).*

The close-up, and Sergio Leone

The close-up serves a dual purpose in the composition of cinema. First, it serves to unfold narrative, and to emphasize the importance of particular objects in space. The close-up directs the spectator's eyes, telling her where to look, what to think, but critically also what to *feel*. In a complex deep focus shot, populated with several objects at varying depths, where should the spectator's eyes rest? As so many theorists have suggested, Dreyer's close-ups in *La Passion de Jeanne d'Arc* (*The Passion of Joan of Arc*, 1927) are deeply affecting shots, leaving the spectator in 'extreme psychic proximity or intimacy'.[51] This is why Pina's death captured in medium long shot in *Open City* is so clearly the manifestation of a desire for aesthetic realism, distance and spectatorial detachment. Rossellini's camera foregoes the affective attraction of a close-up of the dying face, and instead reveals the banality, the ordinariness, of death during wartime.

This direction of the spectator's eyes through close-up clearly serves a narrative purpose. Consider the sequence in *Casablanca* in which Ilsa (Ingrid Bergman) waits for Rick (Humphrey Bogart) in his apartment [1:17:11].[52] Rick enters the room, turning on the light at the wall switch. The camera holds

[51] Jean Epstein, cited in Jacques Aumont, *The Image*, trans. Claire Pajackowska (London, BFI, 1997), 103.

[52] Time-code references are to *Casablanca* (DVD), Warner Home Video, 2000.

him in a medium shot. When he realizes Ilsa has entered the room from the balcony, his gaze directs the gaze of the camera toward the back of the room, holding Ilsa in a long shot. The length of shot provides the spatial contours of the setting, locating the principal objects, Rick and Ilsa, as well as the paraphernalia of the expressionist design of the set (*Casablanca* is, imagistically, a very expressionist film). From the medium long shot, the image cuts immediately to a close-up; Ilsa (from shoulders upward) composes the shot (figure 3.21). This close-up is held for two seconds, before the camera cuts again to Rick, who moves into the space of the room. The camera then captures the opening of the conversation in a wide two-shot of Rick and Ilsa.

What purpose does the intervening cut from long shot (establishing the space in its entirety) to close-up serve? Clearly, the transition forcefully brings the spectator into some contemplation of Ilsa's character and her predicament. The shot isolates Ilsa for a fleeting moment. This isolation accomplishes a psychological identification between spectator and character. At such closeness to Ilsa's face, we see her cut by the shadows cast by the blinds (a symbolic register); we see the fear in her eyes that are widened momentarily. But further, the intimacy serves the critical function of bringing the spectator into the psychological space of the character. The spectator transfers something of herself into this character. The close-up, at least in part, accomplishes the identificatory function of the classical apparatus. This psychological space is crucial to an acceptance of the reunion of Ilsa and Rick that concludes the sequence. The image in close-up is thus no less narratively imbued than the section of dialogue that immediately follows it.

In this reading of *Casablanca*, the close-up is a natural culmination of a spatial movement within the frame of classical cinema: from long shot to medium to medium close-up to close-up (the extreme close-up is rarely part of the natural composition of the object). In this itinerary, the close-up

FIGURE 3.21 *Ilsa (Ingrid Bergman) in a classical close-up:* Casablanca *(1942).*

brings emphasis to what is *already there*; the spatial contours of the shot are established (long shot) and will be revealed through increasingly closer shots. Such movements in shot lengths (from 'wide' to close-up) are characteristic of classical cinema, in which the director conventionally takes a master-shot (capturing the entirety of the set) and gradually shifts in for a series of additional shots. Each series brings a particular perspective, a particular angle and spectatorial view. In the master-shot approach to shooting (which continues to dominate film aesthetics), the close-up is merely a component of 'coverage', that which covers the space from various angles and will be set aside for assimilation or rejection in the editing room. For the classically trained film actor, the art of the performance is in close-up because the close-up reveals character to its extremity.[53]

This is one way of composing cinema through the close-up, in which the itinerary of the image moves from wide (master-shot) to tight (close-up). But the close-up can also present as compositional distortion – as *re-perspectivizing* – of the whole. This is the close-up that does not present the intimate psychological space of character within narrative, but displays the figure (or object) as a discrete aesthetic form. In this use of the close-up, the image is attentive to its compositional qualities; it detaches from the itinerary of a master-shot regime and becomes a fleeting (and potentially arbitrary) object in itself. The close-up in this regime is not the natural successor of the medium shot, or the medium close-up; such shot lengths are now merely possibilities that precede the revelation of a close-up. This is Balázs point in suggesting that a particular kind of close-up 'lifts some object or part of an object out of its surroundings'.[54]

Leone's opening to *Once Upon a Time in the West* employs the close-up and extreme close-up to reveal character as cinematic trope.[55] The extreme

---

[53] For an illuminating anecdote involving Al Pacino on the set of *Donnie Brasco* (1997), see Derek Malcolm, *In Conversation: Mike Newell* (Season 1, Episode 7), Sky Arts 1, UK, 2010. Newell describes the capture of a complex sequence shot on the set, at the conclusion of which, according to Newell, Pacino casually asked, 'Are we taking close-ups?' Newell, equally casual, replied: 'No.' According to Newell, Pacino then stormed off the set. Seeking to placate Pacino by inquiring what had upset him, Pacino apparently stated: 'You do not understand my art.'

[54] Béla Balázs, 'The Close-Up', in *Film Theory and Criticism: Introductory Readings*, ed. Leo Braudy and Marshall Cohen (Oxford: Oxford University Press, 2004), 316. Doane quite similarly argues that 'the close-up is always, at some level, an autonomous entity, a fragment, a "for-itself"'. See Mary Ann Doane, 'The Close-Up: Scale and Detail in the Cinema', in *differences: A Journal of Feminist Cultural Studies*, 14, no. 1 (2003), 90. Of course, while I ostensibly agree with Doane's position – that the close-up is an autonomous object – its placement within the classical narrative itinerary in *Casablanca*, while not precisely stripping the image of its capacity for autonomous life, relocates that life within (and subservient to) the flow of a progressive narrative logic. Doane's notion of an 'uncontainable excess' (105) is for me the determinant of the effect of a particular kind of close-up.

[55] For a detailed and comprehensive examination of *Once Upon a Time in the West* as narrative and image trope, see Christopher Frayling, 'Commentary', *Once Upon a Time in the West* (DVD, 2-Disc Special Edition), Warner Home Video, 2003.

close-up is not a 'natural' perspective – thus, Lynch's extreme close-ups on lips in *Wild at Heart* (1990), or Hitchcock's extreme close-ups on the body in *Psycho*, reveal fetishistic rather than narrative images (figures 3.22–3.26). In Leone, the villain *is* the close-up of a pair of boots (figure 3.27), or the lyrical motion of a dust jacket in a gust of wind. The threat of an impending confrontation in *Once Upon a Time in the West* is composed through hyperbolic sound (chalk screeching on a board; the squeak of the rusted metal of a windmill), ritual behaviours and actions (cleaning a gun, straightening a costume) and theatrical gesture. Leone's objects within the frame – a windmill, a dangling piece of string, a fly crawling on a wall, a telegraph – exist, in a sense, beyond the diegesis of the frame. Each image leaps out of the frame, performing in a register that is distinct from narrative, character and the formulation of story. Leone's camera maintains extreme close-ups and close-ups for excessive durations, gradually moving across objects and bodies. The opening sequence of *Once Upon a Time in the West* represents as formal an aesthetic composition – in which each shot is attentive to the aesthetic potential of the frame – as exists in genre cinema. The fact that Leone can hold the sequence – a harmonious aesthetic 'movement' – in excess of eleven minutes is astonishing.

At 9:23, the sound of Harmonica's (Charles Bronson) playing swells over the purely diegetic soundscape of the film; the harmonica is diegetic (present within the space of the film), yet its sound is produced non-diegetically, wildly inflated, ostentatious. As the harmonica continues to play, the image is held in long shot. The train moves off, revealing Harmonica in the background of what has become, through a subtle focal shift, a long shot. The camera moves backward (on a track) to compose the four bodies in what is clearly an artificial symmetry (figures 3.28–3.29). At 9:47, the image cuts to a close-up, revealing Harmonica's face, the brim of his hat, and critically, the harmonica in his mouth (figure 3.30). Unlike Curtiz's revelatory close-up of Ilsa in *Casablanca*, Leone's close-up is cut through by the brim of Harmonica's hat, subtly 'framing' the image. The extended sequence is a discrete movement within the film, a 'framed' duration subtly referenced through images of frames within frames in perpetual deferment (figure 3.31). The sequence then reverts to a series of shot reverse-shots in tight close-ups before the shoot out that presents a coda to the movement.

Here the close-up, and its relationship to varying shot compositions, is a plastic image; the spatial composition and temporal rhythms of Leone's close-ups share something with Eisenstein's montage of attractions. Leone's close-ups, more than merely autonomous images, are rhythmically composed, formed and cut to music and movement. The intrinsic rhythm of image movement and transition in Leone is nowhere more apparent than in the

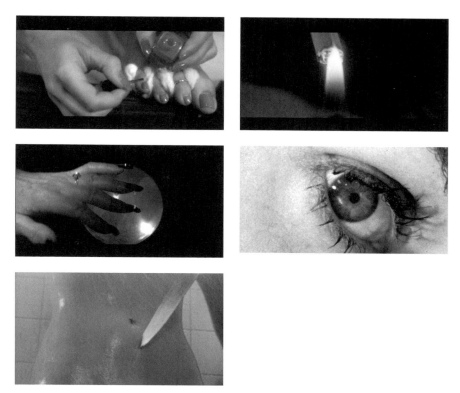

FIGURES 3.22–6 *Extreme close-up: the fetishistic image in* Wild at Heart *(1990) and* Psycho *(1960).*

climactic confrontations in *The Good, the Bad and the Ugly* (1966) and *Once Upon a Time in the West*. In fact, Leone's genre cinema might be appropriately engaged as a form of musical composition, in which the image attends to diegetic and non-diegetic sound. The filmmaker that attends to the internal rhythms of the film – seeking to make manifest a rhythmic composition of images – uses sound in unusual and deliberately ostentatious ways. Of course, this accompaniment of sound to image is part of all cinema traditions, and particularly present in the aesthetic of the classical Hollywood studio system. But whereas the score of the classical cinema accompanies and emotionally charges the visual image, Leone's sounds (including Morricone's score) have the power to organize the composition of images, to build rhythmic images and movements, to compose shots of varying length and compositional qualities that seem to pause, even momentarily, and exhibit their aesthetic objectivity: 'used this way, music does more than intensify the impression of the visual image by providing a parallel illustration of the same

FIGURES 3.27–32 *Leone's close-up: framing, performance and the autonomous image of cinema.*

idea; it opens up the possibility of a *new*, transfigured impression of the same material.'[56]

Leone's genre cinema reveals the essential artistic exhibitionism of the apparatus. For Baudrillard, Leone is the first postmodern filmmaker,[57] and postmodernity represents, if nothing else, the reification of form. There is continuity in the expression of the image between Leone and the later reflexive cinema of Tarantino, of which *Inglourious Basterds* (2009) is perhaps the most sophisticated rendition. The close-up in Leone is what Hitchcock called 'pure cinema', purely of the medium of moving images and their aesthetic and affective design. The close-up rendered in Leone, the image-in-itself, traverses narrative and non-narrative frames, such that Luhrmann's introduction of the Drover in *Australia* (2008) employs the free-floating signifier of a close-up in *A Fistful of Dollars* (1964) (figure 3.32). Leone's rhythmic montage informs the

---

[56] Tarkovsky, 158.
[57] See Frayling.

aesthetic expressivity of the recent trailer for *The Girl With the Dragon Tattoo* (2011).[58] Fincher's trailer is a seamless convergence of cinema, music video and image montage. Shots held for less than a second are animated in their composition and relation through music, colour, and rhythmic contrast. Such images inscribe a montage of attraction through which the spectator rightly contemplates the movement of cinema in a field incorporating vision and sound.

Leone displays this autonomous image most aggressively in his spaghetti Westerns. The rhythmic image is never as freely displayed in his later cinema, including the highly praised *Once Upon a Time in America* (1984). This is why Leone's Westerns, notably *The Good, the Bad and the Ugly* and *Once Upon a Time in the West*, transnational productions, accompanying the increasingly fragmented studio production ethos of the 1960s in the US, were not merely reflections on a classic American genre, but a reconfiguration of the aesthetic form of genre cinema itself.

The sound image in reproduction: *The Conversation*

Is the notion of cinema as the art of the image just an illusion? Of course: how ultimately, can it be anything else?[59]

Francis Ford Coppola's landmark exploration of sound (the sound of the world, and the sound of the cinematic diegesis) in *The Conversation* (1974) remains unsettling for the contemporary spectator. As was so much of the New American Cinema,[60] *The Conversation* is a film about the inability to perceive, the inability to record and capture, the elemental *lack* in the experience of the world. Keathley calls this a cinema of 'trauma',[61] and one might read *The*

---

[58] See *The Girl With the Dragon Tattoo*, Official Trailer, June 2, 2011, http://www.youtube.com/watch?v=WVLvMg62RPA [accessed 15 August 2011]. Fincher directed the trailer, which bears the visual and aural signatures of his feature cinema.

[59] Michel Chion, *Audio-Vision: Sound on Screen*, trans. Claudia Gorbman (New York: Columbia University Press, 1994), 5.

[60] The New American Cinema conventionally refers to a period of aesthetic and industrial transformation within the American film industry. See David Thomson, 'The Decade When Movies Mattered', in *The Last Great American Picture Show: New Hollywood in the 1970s*, ed. Thomas Elsaesser, Alexander Horwath and Noel King (Amsterdam: Amsterdam University Press, 2004), 73–82.

[61] Christian Keathley, 'Trapped in the Affection Image: Hollywood's Post-Traumatic Cycle (1970–1976)', in *The Last Great American Picture Show: New Hollywood in the 1970s*, ed. Thomas Elsaesser, Alexander Horwath and Noel King (Amsterdam: Amsterdam University Press, 2004), 293–308.

Conversation alongside other films of trauma – Altman's *Nashville* (1975) and Scorsese's *Taxi Driver* (1976) come to mind. Coppola's cinema turned this scepticism of the 1970s, which drew its inspiration from various modernist sources (the most obvious being Antonioni's *Blow Up*), back onto cinema's image and its attendant sound. If classical cinema's sound gave a fuller account of the visual image and was thus subordinated to the experience of the visual image,[62] cinema's modernity in *The Conversation* revealed the image as a pure sound bite, a spoken line or ambient noise that filtered over and above the itinerary of a narrative progression or visual cue.

In 1974, Coppola's film actualized what had been merely perceived, or felt, by the spectator. Altman had played with synchronicity and convergent tracks (*Mash* [1970]; *The Long Goodbye* [1973]); Scorsese had turned the pop song into an expressive aesthetic register unlike anything seen in the classical studio era.[63] However, Coppola's radical contribution to what was a developing modernist aesthetic was to turn the image into a *sound object* – to enable the visual image to engage with the equally autonomously functioning register of sound. I wish to illustrate two simultaneously functioning registers in which Coppola's sound image acquires autonomy from a visual itinerary: in the capacity of the image to function as reproduced utterance, or re-iteration; and in the capacity of non-diegetic sound (a piano score on the soundtrack) to converge with, and indeed, mediate, the diegetic sound of a saxophone in the film.

The lesson of Coppola's film is not that the protagonist's vision is affected by the condition of modernity; the visual image in modernist cinema had been suitably detached from the object, which we see clearly in Antonioni's vanishing body in *Blow Up*. In Coppola, modernity becomes an aural phenomenon, and modernist cinema, that infects the American cinema from the French New Wave, or Antonioni's expressive minimalism, is configured as a sound image that freely inhabits, and moves between, diegetic and non-diegetic cinematic space. Classical cinema manifests a soundscape that complements (and augments) the visual-scape. Sound and soundtrack are merely accompaniments in the majority of classical films.[64] Even Hitchcock's

---

[62] For an analysis of this prejudice, see William Johnson, 'Sound and Image: A Further Hearing', *Film Quarterly* 43, no. 1 (1989), 24–35.

[63] Consider the jump cut sequence early in *Mean Streets* (1973), clearly a quotation of Godard's precocious New Wave aesthetics, yet animated by an American pop song, The Ronettes's 'Be My Baby' (Phillies Records, 1963). For a useful discussion of the effect of popular music in Scorsese's early cinema, see Ben Nyce, *Scorsese Up Close: A Study of the Films* (Lanham: Scarecrow Press, 2004), 12–13.

[64] See David Bordwell and Kristin Thompson, 'Fundamental Aesthetics of Sound in the Cinema', in *Film Sound: Theory and Practice*, ed. Elizabeth Weis and John Belton (New York: Columbia University Press, 1985), 181–99.

collaboration with Bernard Hermann produces visual accompaniments; Hermann's score for *Vertigo* augments the escalation of Scottie's neurosis; Mother's jarring knife slashes in the shower scene of *Psycho* overwhelm any affective claim on the spectator made by Hermann's strings. Hermann's sounds throughout Hitchcock, and even in his last great score for *Taxi Driver*, give further expression to the virtuosity of the image.

But Coppola's modernism, and his contravention of the classical diegetic/ non-diegetic split, brings sound to the forefront of the mind – and sensory interfaces – of the spectator. The spectator must listen to the audio track of the conversation, picking up its words and sentences, the cadence of the speech between the speakers, the rhythm built through sound that actively integrates with, and configures, the visual image. Sound is played and replayed, heard and reheard, until it attains an ontological form quite separate from the narrative progression of the story. The remarkable mechanical zoom which opens the film functions only through the equally complex, and densely layered, soundtrack – in which sound is disoriented, asynchronous, and muddled, both organic and mechanical. When Harry Caul (Gene Hackman) is asked, 'how'd you get it [a recording]', he is deliberately evasive, wishing to protect his secret and possess the sound in its fixed form. Coppola requires the spectator to actively listen, 'to know that "the sound of x" allows us to proceed without further interference to explore what the sound is like in and of itself'.[65] The provocative question raised by Coppola's film is, simply, *what is this sound*? What is the ontological fabric of this conversation? Where is it heard? Through which mechanism is it produced? How does the conversation of Coppola's film manifest its strange and unsettling presence? This is again to ask more than what a sound *means*, but to ask what presents within the image beyond meaning, beyond narrative signification.

The Conversation opens on an oft-discussed mechanical zoom, a shot of some duration and complexity. The wide shot begins from a rooftop and gradually moves in to find form through an assortment of characters, the last of which is Harry Caul, the film's protagonist. Each image is destabilized through a confluence of sounds: dialogue, diegetic sounds emanating from Union Square at lunchtime, a jazz saxophone and vocal (presumably of a street performer), a barking dog that briefly enters the frame – and, almost imperceptibly, the interweaving of a conversation between a man and a woman on their lunch break. The initial vocal of the conversation, spoken by a woman, repeats the song lyric of the jazz vocal of the street performer. The conversation rises in volume and establishes coherent rhythm over the

---

[65] Chion, 33.

random sounds of the square. At 4:48,[66] the spoken 'what about me?' brings the conversation to the forefront of the image and reduces the background sound to random, indistinct and ambient noise.

Coppola's conversation occurs initially in the present-time of the film; one might say that in this elaborate zoom shot, the sound of the conversation, the dialogue between the man and woman that culminates in 'he'd kill us if he got the chance', is ontologically *present*. The spectator engages with the conversation as an event unfolding in time, a sequence comprising several minutes of fragmented dialogue. While the sequence begins as a disjointed asynchronous image (sound and vision in arbitrary relation), as the zoom shifts closer to the central action of the shot, Coppola brings the sound and visual image of the conversation into closer contact. The sound of the conversation begins somewhat muddled, emanating from an array of points in the town square. However, the conversation gradually becomes distinct, and is isolated from background noise as the spoken words of the two figures are brought up on the soundtrack. Word-sounds are cut over moving lips and matching facial cues. Coppola frames discrete shots of the man and the woman (or two-shots) through a shallow focus, emphasizing the centrality of the two figures to the spatial composition. The camera that begins in an impossibly long slow-zoom approximating the gaze of a telescopic site (an indeterminate panoptic gaze) increasingly cuts into the action below, visually and aurally situating the two figures, their sounds now cut to matching visual images. At the conclusion of the sequence, Caul believes he has acquired a 'nice fat recording', industry jargon for the capture of the event. For Caul, the conversation is crystallized as an occurrence in time, captured through the technology of sound-surveillance, reproduced on magnetic tape. At 8:57, the sound of a piano enters the frame, a conventional non-diegetic soundtrack in the form of a pleasant, if somewhat melancholy, waltz.

The conversation of the man and woman, recorded by Caul and his team, becomes an autonomous image *only in reproduction*. The conversation, performed for the spectator in the present, first captured in a disorienting zoom and then, incrementally, in the conventions of single and two-shots, is re-iterated as a sound-recording, and re-animated through the technology of sound production. At 16:26, now in his workshop, Caul begins to replay the conversation (his 'fat recording') on his sound equipment. This new sound emanates not from the spoken words of the conversation, but from the tape, from the reproduction in Caul's workshop. At 16:12, prior to the emanation of sound from the machine, Coppola cuts to a medium shot, framing Caul,

---

[66] Time-code references are to *The Conversation* (Widescreen DVD Collection), Paramount Home Video, 2000.

Stan (John Cazale), and the reels of tape that now contain the sound image (figure 3.33). The camera pans slowly, deliberately, to a set of large speakers on the wall. The image then cuts to an extreme close-up of Caul's fingers on the switches, knobs and dials – the transmission technology of the recorded conversation (figure 3.34). The conversation, an event captured in vision and sound, is past; the recorded version shifts into the present of the film, effacing the previous utterance. D'Escriván is thus correct to suggest that, at the conclusion of the first iteration of the conversation in actual time, the puzzle is solved: *he'd kill us if he got the chance.* 'Yet when [Caul] replays a segment ... the possibilities for meaning seem infinite.'[67] In reproduction, the sound of the conversation is now divested of its visual (present) itinerary in Union Square.

This sequence – a re-iteration of a conversation – recalls the mechanics of reproduction in Antonioni's present and past sound images in *The Passenger*. When, from inside Caul's workshop, Coppola cuts to the visual of the conversation, what does the spectator *perceive*? An image accompanied by sound, or the presence of sound accompanied by a projected (and imagined) image? In the re-iteration of the conversation, what are we watching? What are we listening to? Words lost in the surveillance are now enhanced through Caul's technology. Technology creates a new presence of sound in the workshop, distinct from the iteration of the conversation in Union Square. In a striking moment in this first re-iteration of the conversation, the visual of Union Square opens up. The words of the conversation are replayed, reheard by the spectator, yet each utterance is now disembodied, spoken through the technology of reproduction. Walter Murch, the sound designer on the film, brings up the mechanical registers of the voice, increasing echo and reverb. These mechanical affectations reconstruct the mellifluous, organic timbre of the voices (particularly the woman's) into a technologized (and reproducible) sound. When the spectator listens to the conversation in its second iteration, spun through the circuit of a recording system, the *visual* image is an accompaniment. Here the autonomous image of sound organizes a perceptual and affective engagement.

How can the spectator locate the subjectivity of a sound image (as the spectator conventionally searches for the subjectivity of a visual image)? When Coppola cuts to the visual in Union Square at 16:45, the image is asynchronous – the sound no longer matches the visual image, as it would in a classical cinematic soundscape. Shot and reverse-shot, the strongest indicator of point of view in cinema, is established between the object (the woman and man) and the sound engineer, Caul. Coppola cuts between

[67] Julio D'Escriván, 'Sound Art (?) on/in Film', *Organised Sound* 14, no. 1 (2009), 70.

FIGURES 3.33–4 *The first re-iteration of 'the conversation':* The Conversation *(1974).*

present and past, though the flashback is not a faithful rendition of the past, but its semblance, a simulation of that which took place and is lost in reproduction. This is Coppola's subtle rendition of the paranoid subjectivity of the modern self. At 16:43, the image cuts to a frame of the woman and man walking in the town square. The image deliberately approximates a point of view – the first component of a shot reverse-shot mechanism. Yet the cut that will present the reverse-shot, the perceiving subject, is not to Caul in the present of the conversation (its actual iteration initiated by the zoom) but to Caul *in his workshop*. Shot reverse-shot traverses present and past, its mechanical relation built on a recording. This is precisely the device employed by Antonioni in *The Passenger* (employing a tape-recorded conversation) to say something very similar about the existential (and ontological) spillage of past into present.

The itinerary of shot reverse-shot in the 'present' iteration of the conversation works through actual figures (Caul's team) situated in Union Square; the itinerary of shot reverse-shot in the re-iteration of the conversation in Caul's workshop works between the object (the man and woman projected in flashback) and the technologized subject of reproduction, the sound recording. At 17:32, the visual of the first iteration of the conversation holds the man and woman in a two-shot in shallow focus; their words are now clear over the background noise (Caul's mixing of the soundtrack and its visual representation are necessarily coterminous). Yet at precisely this moment, the characters in two-shot move out of the frame, and *Caul* is revealed in the background on a park bench (figure 3.35).

The image finds clarity in a sharp rack focus, and Caul is centralized. Who perceives Caul this way? In technologized reproduction, who authorizes these compositional inscriptions? While Caul sits before his state of the art recording system, for Coppola, the technologies of surveillance and recording give life to a new subjectivity of the image in sound, located within the panoptic mechanism of technological reproduction. The classical subjectivity of the shot (point of view) is effaced in *The Conversation*'s technologized sound reproduction. This is to suggest that if D'Escriván is correct in identifying

FIGURES 3.35 *The panoptic gaze: the autonomous image of reproduced sound:* The Conversation *(1974).*

narrative resolution in the first iteration of the conversation through the visual image, resolution at the point of the re-iteration of the conversation in Caul's workshop requires that subjectivity be located within the panoptic gaze of technology itself.

The Conversation: 'He'd kill us if he got the chance'

I conclude this meditation on Coppola's sound image with a re-examination of the famous utterance, 'he'd kill us if he got the chance'. I say re-examination because a great deal of work has been done on the unique auditory qualities of *The Conversation*,[68] and much of this work concludes with a reading of this utterance, initially obscured on Caul's soundtrack, revealed at the first act turning point on Caul's recording, and reheard (by Caul and the spectator) in the film's *dénouement*.

At 33:17, Caul initiates the second re-iteration of the conversation; a single spoken line remains obscured on the recording. On first playback, the line is an audible mix of speech fragment, mechanical interference and ambient noise. The voices are pronouncedly mechanical, further disembodied from the original source; the unique tonal and textural qualities of the mechanized voice are again contrasted with the initial (present) iteration of the conversation in Union Square that opens the film. At 39:24, after Caul boosts the sound through an external source, the purpose of the conversation, and the recording, becomes clear. The spectator hears: 'he'd kill us if he got

---

[68] See, for example, Kaja Silverman, *The Acoustic Mirror: The Female Voice in Psychoanalysis and Cinema* (Bloomington: Indiana University Press, 1988), 89–93; Dennis Turner, 'The Subject of *The Conversation*', *Cinema Journal* 24, no. 4 (1985), 4–22; Jay Beck, 'Citing the Sound: *The Conversation, Blow Out*, and the Mythological Ontology of the Soundtrack in the 70s Film', *Journal of Popular Film and Television* 29, no. 4 (2002), 156–63.

the chance'. The intonation is such that the emphasis falls on 'kill', with a lesser emphasis on 'us'; the audio track emanates from the tape with this emphasis. Coppola deliberately cuts images of the recording equipment – knobs and dials, as well as the exposed material of Caul's concocted booster – with the visual image from the conversation as it is played in the film's opening sequence. The attachment of image to the technology of recording is deliberate, suggesting that the spoken line emanates from its reproduced source. This utterance is thus absent from the initial iteration in the present-time of Union Square. As the sequence approaches the revelation of the line at 39:14, Coppola tightens the shots on the technology of the sound image, a movement culminating in a close-up of the booster, with its casing stripped away, revealing wires and boards (figure 3.36). The revelation of the spoken line at 39:24 is a critical plot point that catapults the narrative into its next movement (Act Two development). Then, at 1:45:50, in the film's *dénouement*, 'he'd *kill* us if he got the chance' becomes 'he'd kill *us* if he got the chance'. The story is revealed, Caul's mystery is solved, the narrative conflict resolved for the spectator. The man and woman have conspired to murder the director (Robert Duvall).

The orthodox reading (most explicit in Silverman)[69] of this strange re-iteration emphasizes the function of the utterance as narrative resolution. The shift in emphasis makes sense in the context of Caul's increasingly paranoid mind. This is how *Caul* hears the line. In its first revelation, Caul mishears the emphasis, the intonation, and thus the spectator receives a subjective rendition of the line. Caul is looking for a 'nice fat recording' rather than the meaning of the words, and thus misses the emphasis. The spectator listens through Caul's ears, not unlike the way in which the spectator sees through the subjective eyes of the protagonist in Polanski's *Repulsion* (1965) or Frankenheimer's *Seconds* (1966).

The revised utterance, with a revised emphasis, is a redubbing on the soundtrack (in industry jargon, Additional Dialogue Recording [ADR]): the sound plays over the visual image, but the lips of the man frame the initial utterance with its emphasis on 'kill' (figure 3.37). On the DVD commentary, Coppola suggests that the redubbing over the initial utterance was Murch's idea, and took place while cutting the film for picture and sound, well after Coppola had completed the shoot.[70] Thus it is Murch, the sound editor, that isolates sound from image, producing a sound image separate from the narrative itinerary of the film. On one level, of course, Murch's revised line

---

[69] Silverman, 90.
[70] Francis Ford Coppola, 'Commentary', in *The Conversation* (Widescreen DVD Collection), Paramount Home Video, 2000.

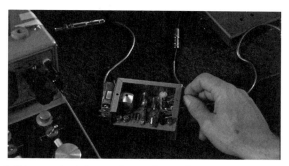

FIGURE 3.36 *A 'blow up' of the mechanical sound image:* The Conversation *(1974).*

permits the reading that Caul misheard the utterance on the tape. Yet Murch altered the line not to present an ontological truth, not to reveal the objectivity of the line as spoken, but to 'indicate to the filmgoer that the phrase now takes on a new emphasis for Harry. He hears the line *in his mind* [my emphasis] as it must have been all along]'.[71] What Caul hears in his mind effaces the initial utterance (spoken in the opening sequence of the film): 'he'd *kill* us if he got the chance'. That initial utterance is now lost to both Harry and the spectator; all that exists on the soundtrack are lines in re-iteration. The presence of both versions of the line within the film's diegesis, one created during production, the other during post-production, inscribes an autonomous image of sound, a line that signifies its intent, or more accurately, manifests its *presence*, in technological re-iteration. And what coheres in Caul's mind as 'the conversation' is the technological output of a recording. Murch's subtle hand in post-production represents merely one example of the under-theorized presence of the editor in the production of the autonomous cinematic image.

The Conversation: The autonomous image of sound

In the final scene of the film, two classically separate soundtracks, one diegetic (a jazz saxophone piece played by Caul), one non-diegetic (a piano piece), converge. The two soundtracks present separately in the film – Caul improvises to a jazz record in his apartment, while the piano score accompanies much of the dramatic movement of the film. Coppola employs the two soundtracks as discrete significatory (and symbolic) units.

[71] Cited in James M. Welsh, Gene D. Phillips and Rodney F. Hill, *The Francis Ford Coppola Encyclopedia* (Plymouth: Scarecrow Press, 2010), 46.

FIGURE 3.37 *A lost utterance in mechanical reproduction:* The Conversation *(1974).*

Caul finds an emotional outlet in the improvisational qualities of jazz; his accompaniment to a jazz record presents an opportunity to create, to break free of the metaphorical shackles of his life. Conversely, the melancholy piano track presents as a threat to Caul, its minor key unsettling, a sound metaphor for the ubiquity of the surveillance society. Caul's jazz saxophone and the non-diegetic piano piece are symbolically opposed, and musically inharmonious.[72]

At 1:47:54, Caul begins to search for a listening device in his apartment; this action (comprising several minutes of screen time) is accompanied by the non-diegetic piano track. Caul's desperation is matched by the increasing intensity of the piano, its phrases more pronounced, its tone and texture jarring. Unable to find the device, Caul retreats again to the sanctuary of jazz. The piano maintains on the soundtrack throughout the action. The visual image cuts to fleeting shots of the conversation in Union Square, now, in its fourth iteration, soundless, the ephemeral image from which all sound has been lost. At 1:51:40, the diegetic sound of the saxophone enters the frame as the piano continues to play its non-diegetic sound. The camera pans left to reveal Caul seated on a stool, oblivious to the ruination of his life (figure 3.38). He is immersed in improvisation, as he was in Act One of the film [13:20], yet now, astonishingly, the backing jazz record is absent. In the final sequence of the film, Caul effectively improvises to the non-diegetic (and thus 'absent') sound of the piano. At this point, the spectator must ask: what animates this improvisatory movement if the piano is a *non-diegetic score*? What is Caul listening to? The fullness of Coppola's metaphor materializes in sound: what begins as a somewhat jarring improvisational performance (inharmonious saxophone and piano) is gradually synthesized into a harmonious duet between the diegetic saxophone and the non-diegetic piano, concluding

---

[72] For an overview of compositional structure and harmony, see Nicholas Cook, *Analysis Through Composition: Principles of the Classical Style* (Oxford: Oxford University Press, 1996).

in a scale run on the piano that perfectly harmonizes with the expressive saxophone in Caul's hands. What presence within the diegesis of the film authorizes this synthesis, this artificial synchronicity?

Coppola thus concludes his landmark film with a simple, yet ingenious, metaphor. The duet between piano and saxophone reveals the sound image to be *more than* the signification of the cinematic diegesis. Sound explodes beyond the visually oriented frame. The image shifts outward from the hermetically sealed narrative, constructing and displacing boundaries. Coppola's soundscape demands a contemplation of cinema sound beyond the givenness of meaning, and Coppola demands that sound be engaged as an object, as the essential material of cinema, no less than a visual image that inscribes its presence through compositional form. Coppola's unique contribution to the ontology of the image is to cast the image *out of* sound.

In conclusion, I return to the line with which I began this analysis: in the several iterations of a line of spoken dialogue reconstructed through mechanical reproduction, or a soundtrack that moves cavalierly across diegetic and non-diegetic space, what does the spectator *see*? What does the spectator *hear*? From what source (the authentically original or mechanically reproduced) does cinema's image of sound emanate?[73]

Not a still, but a restless frame

I close a series of meditations on the autonomous image of cinema with a presentation of two cinematic frames, each drawn from Darren Aronofsky's *Requiem for a Dream* (2000). In September 2010, Professor Nicholas Rombes of the University of Detroit, Mercy assembled a group of scholars, practitioners, commentators and independent theorists of cinema to reflect on the cinema object. That object was *Requiem for a Dream*. The project, *Requiem 102* (accessible at http://requiem102.tumblr.com/) was not only a celebration of the 10th anniversary of the release of the film, but was also an attempt

---

[73] Richard King, an Oscar-winning sound designer and sound editor working freelance within the studio system, describes sound design as 'constantly innovating'. For King, the sound is frequently created separately from the image, and rarely recorded during production as a complete sound object. While attuned to the image, in some sense 'sticking to it', sound functions also autonomously from the diegesis of cinematic space. It is thus an experiential effect affiliated to yet not exclusively derived from the image of cinema. King provided the example of attempting to create the sound of the removal of a face mask for *The Dark Knight Rises* (2012), calibrated to an experience of the image rather than an inherent reality within the diegetic space. This is a soundscape that cannot 'sound like life' and for which a world has been 'completely created'. Interview with Richard King conducted 10 February, 2012 at Warner Bros. Studios, Los Angeles.

FIGURE 3.38 *Paranoia through panoptic surveillance:* The Conversation *(1974).*

to open a lively discourse about the nature of the cinematic image in an age in which cinema was reconfiguring itself – its shape, its boundaries, its claims on the twenty-first century individual. I was fortunate to be invited to contribute two entries – a reflection on each of two cinematic frames taken arbitrarily from the film. The arbitrary nature and spontaneous coming-into-being of a framed image were an integral part of the motivation of this project. My two frames (which I include as screenshots below) are merely two in an infinite array of discrete images that comprise a cinematic text. Rombes is a scholar at the forefront of thinking the ontological potentialities of the cinematic text in a past, present and future cinema. I thank him for the opportunity to contribute to this provocative project.

Requiem for a Dream: Random thoughts on the frame (10th minute)

10th minute. A random image, 1/24th of a second. A cinematic breath, in which narrative is held in stasis, waiting impatiently for the natural progression that attends the cinematic image.

A television set in a random space.

The deferment of the frame

Note here Aronofsky's display of the object: a television set, and 'television', its symbolic signified. The shot is a moment frozen in time. Perhaps this capture was preceded by a medium shot of the space, a nondescript room, the viewer reassured with an establishing shot – the connective tissue of screened space. But such suppositions are redundant. Now the frame – the

FIGURE 3.39

image in stasis – overwhelms the progression of story and character. The viewer anticipates a cut, a new image to eclipse the first, to animate the movement that is the essence of cinema. But that cut lies somewhere in a parallel frame that will not materialize here, at least not in this screening of Aronofsky's *Requiem for a Dream*.

In the 10th minute, cinema is again an image. Briefly, the frame comes alive, reporting on its capacity to reveal interior frames and frameworks, deferring sites of meaning as we peer into the frame within a frame that recedes into an imaginary life of the cinematic text. All this in a single 24th of a second.

Why a television set?

The dream-life of the cinematic image

> In societies dominated by modern conditions of production, life is presented as an immense accumulation of spectacles. Everything that was directly lived has receded into a representation.[74]

For Debord, the spectacle is deceptive, inculcating, pacifying, controlling. But in stasis, the image-spectacle is far from complete. It inhabits a literal space (a denotative meaning) and a dream-life. In a literal reading of the frame, the television is a signifier that speaks of inculcation to the dominant orthodoxy. We, as viewers, are the automatons bred in industrialized cultures. We are

---

[74] Guy Debord, *Society of the Spectacle*, (New York: Zone Books, 1994).

trans-fixed, glued to the set. But in a reading of the frame within a frame, the image is never final, never replete in its signification. This is image not as representation, but imbued with the rhythm of the dream-life of cinema. This is what Tarkovsky identified in his writing on cinema: the image manifest as unity of experience.

This is the accomplishment of *Requiem for a Dream* in so many image-frames, ever-expanding, ever-refreshing. The frame is not an artificial contrivance, but an expression of cinema in a very pure form. The fixation on the image-frame in Aronofsky, or Tarkovsky, or Lynch, is a fixation on cinema's imaginary life.

Affect and experience

'It's a reason to get up in the morning. It's a reason to lose weight, to fit in the red dress. It's a reason to smile. It makes tomorrow all right. What have I got Harry, hm? Why should I even make the bed, or wash the dishes? I do them, but why should I? I'm alone. Your father's gone, you're gone. I got no one to care for. What have I got, Harry? I'm lonely. I'm old.'
Sarah Goldfarb (Ellen Burstyn), *Requiem for a Dream*.

Embrace the televisual feast – the voracious appetite of the spectator on display.

FIGURES 3.40–1

It will set you free.

The television set

Postmodernity's cinematic explorations present two fascinations (among many) with the spectacle of the television set. Cronenberg's *Videodrome* (1983) presents the sensuality of the spectacle, in which addiction is experience – affective, hypnotic, sensual and co-sensual. *Requiem For a Dream*, a film also about addiction (Aronofsky's addiction is an evil incarnate), presents the television as the site of existential abandonment, the subject dispersed ever-further into intoxication, abandoning (and abandoned by) the world of the meaningful, cogent, industrious and regulated.

In the frame in which television is reified, and objectified, the interior and exterior of the frame bleed into each other. The object (television) swells to encompass the frame in its entirety, and then swells beyond, ballooning out like Cronenberg's television, so prescient in its reading of the co-sensual experience of cultural and aesthetic mediation.

The viewer, once outside, now reaches out into the expressive potential of the image-frame. The viewer is as vivid and intoxicated within the frame as without.

Convexity

As Cronenberg's screen swells ever further into a symbiotic relationship with the subject (immersion and detachment are not, in the end, mutually exclusive), so the frame is a spectacle screened on convex glass. The TV is not the denotative or connotative life of the frame. Rather, the essence is in the fullness of the screen, the convex desire to swell into the exterior, beyond the parameters of the object. If HD flat-screen technology (plasma, LCD, LED, 3D-TV) presents the image renewed as digital perfection, the retro-TV, shipped across Brooklyn, represents a nostalgia for the flawed image, the image bent, twisted and distorted through the expressiveness of old technologies.

FIGURE 3.42

Why are all of cinema's televisions retro-models, convex, with dials and knobs of the past, as if procured from the nearest pawnshop?

Why are drug-crazed projections convex images?

FIGURES 3.43–4

Requiem for a Dream: The memory of cinema (34th minute)

In search of …

'The most beautiful girl in the whole world' –
Harry Goldfarb

Nobody is as good with quotation as Umberto Eco. Eco's lexicon of textual images (to use his own terminology) is, it seems to me, infinite. I've always envied this. To be able to stretch an image infinitely, to suture it to any and all other images in a veritable history of experience. To create some new life out of the connections made renders the image always in communication, a functioning community of sorts that is as much about us – readers and spectators – as it is about text. What a great capacity Eco has to tell us not only what a text means, but – so much more important and dazzling in his work – how it stitches itself into the fabric of our lives.

Eco argues that cinema is a cult object, a thing that is made and remade, interpreted *ad infinitum*, a thing of beauty always in flux. So, a line of dialogue – 'Was that artillery fire or is it my heart pounding'[75] – becomes a wormhole through which we see the infinity of cinema past, present and future. A shot – Hitchcock's descending camera in Arbogast's death in *Psycho* comes back in full referential glory in Friedkin's *The Exorcist* (1973). Coming back in cinema is a reincarnation of sorts, but the ghost of the past subsists in the present. This is the continuous play of the text (and the image), as Eco would tell us. How else do we make sense of our love for this art form except that it encompasses the entirety of our experience?

Cinema is a search for the lost object in a labyrinth of images. 'In order to transform a work into a cult object one must be able to break, dislocate, unhinge it so that one can remember only parts of it'[76] – Eco, passionate about the interrelationships between cinema and life. This is the beauty of cinema – the part, the unhingeable text, is also the whole and the entirety of our experience of cinema. The part is wholesome and nourishing.

How richly playful – as an image is always playful – must a single film frame be? What would happen if our minds were to roam free of the boundaries of that temporal frame?

---

[75] For a discussion of cult cinema's and *Casablanca*'s textual fabric, see Umberto Eco, '*Casablanca*: Cult Movies and Intertextual Collage', in *Faith in Fakes: Essays*, trans. William Weaver (London: Secker and Warburg, 1986), 197–200.
[76] Eco, '*Casablanca*', 198.

Requiem for a dream – 34th minute:

FIGURE 3.45

A still woman, Marion Silver (Jennifer Connelly), black on white, the gray-white of the ocean. The ocean and the sky is a blank slate upon which to inscribe our cinematic fantasies.

A peephole into the past:

FIGURE 3.46

Surely we must first divest ourselves of Marion Silver. Character is so burdensome in opening up the frame. In doing so, we're divesting ourselves of the weight of the cinematic here and now. Cinema is much more than merely what we're looking at, or listening to. Marion is interesting: beautiful, delicate, damaged. But the image could be so much more.

We're not really looking at Marion here; we're looking at a simulacral ghost:

FIGURE 3.47

FIGURE 3.48

A fantasy, come to life:

FIGURE 3.49

A classical ideal:

FIGURE 3.50

And then we can dispense with Marion altogether:

The burden of identity in stasis, in still life. Now we glimpse the potential of the image-trope. But our search remains fragmented, confined. We're hung up on Marion imbued with the ghostly spirit of Jennifer Connelly. Might we not even divest ourselves of this signification, this identification trope, powerful as it is? Searching an image of a woman in a still, might we not only relinquish the hold of character ...

The image dissolves, a classical cinematographic trope. The woman is always in soft focus, always a fantasy, a memory.

Reading text is, for Eco, an act of creation; of breathing life into a dormant image.

The eyes:

FIGURES 3.51–3

Tighter on the lips:

FIGURES 3.54–5

The curve of the neck:

FIGURE 3.56

A cinematic memory-scape in still life

Which is why cinema and real life, our always-imagined real lives, are not distinct. And why a single frame of film is never quite a still.

FIGURE 3.57

I thank Rebecca Goldsworthy for the production of the composite image.

On the possibilities of a pure cinema

I love cinematic technique: montage, camerawork, and sound design used for its own pleasure, excitement, and emotional impact, not in subordination to literary and theatrical ends, but pure and free and strong as an autonomous art form, a sight and sound experience that is uniquely thrilling.[77]

Hitchcock's fascination with an autonomous cinema is evident in almost all of his films; surely no other filmmaker was as committed to affect – to the pure effect of the cinematic image on the spectator. The spectator, suggests Hitchcock, is 'aroused by pure cinema'.[78] But there is something more than the affective experience of the spectator at the heart of pure cinema. What prompts a uniquely cinematic affect– an affect, as Graves suggests, that is possible only in the cinema? Hitchcock's *North by Northwest* (1959) is a genre story, with a formulaic narrative structure. Yet Hitchcock plays with the form of cinema itself, its image as an aesthetic object. We see cinema's purity actualized in the abstract title sequence of *North by Northwest*; we see cinema's purity symbolized in the metacinematic raising of the curtain that opens *Rear Window* (1954), submerging the image of a studio lot apartment complex into the purity of a cinematic simulacrum. This is why Hitchcock's cinema – the pure cinema he discusses with Truffaut – could only have been produced within the classical studio system and its metacinematic frames. When the studio failed, Hitchcock seems ill at ease, and the return to the UK in a film like *Frenzy* (1972), while a high point in this later cinema, signifies a departure from a pure cinema.

In this chapter I have attempted to theorize through demonstration several unique properties of an autonomous cinematic image. I argue that this image is affective – it arouses the spectator into contemplation of an aesthetic exhibitionism. Malick's recent *Tree of Life* (2011) (and its natural precursor, *Days of Heaven* [1978]) resounds with the purity of image in sound and vision. We address Malick's origin of being in the hyper-aestheticized Big Bang sequence not as an image of the world in creation (a flashback), but as a cinematic *memory*, an image that bears some recourse to a past event in time, yet one that also brings that event into the present of a theatre and a screen. Malick's memory of the world can only make sense as a cinematic image, not unlike the way in which Vertov's city in *Man With a Movie Camera* only

---

[77] Douglas Graves, 'Pure Cinema Manifesto', *Pure Cinema Celluloid* (2009), http://www. purecinema-celluloid.webs.com/ [accessed 18 February 2011].
[78] Truffaut, *Hitchcock*, 349.

makes sense as a city constructed with the material of cinema: 'montage, camerawork, and sound design'.[79] Malick's autonomous image is a sound and vision object (planets and constellations, and hyperreal dinosaurs) animated through the material of cinema. This is why, it seems to me, Malick's film feels like a memory I've had, a conflation of my own past, and a past of the world captured in a cinematic image. This sensation is rendered through the most innovative image palette I've encountered in cinema for several years.

The potential of cinema has often been perceived as its capacity to show the world through narrative forms – encoded stories, archetypal figures, and mythologies across nations and cultures. The medium of cinema was globalized through narrative; it became an identificatory medium through narrativized fantasies. Yet the autonomous image, the image detached from the representation of the world as object or narrative, presents a uniquely affective register of cinema that works with, and yet also in some sense in isolation from, narrative progression. I argue that cinema's art is indelibly inscribed in this register of the autonomous image; it requires that we think about cinema as an aesthetic object that is both representative and self-attending, self-exhibiting. This is an image that has the capacity to function as pure composition; this image is always already abstract, even as it forms the shape of representation.

Part One of this book has attempted to trace a conceptual and aesthetic movement of the cinematic image from early cinema to the advent of digital capture and exhibition technologies. The autonomous image, in this study, is situated on the fringe of a mainstream aesthetic – Coppola's *The Conversation* exemplifies what Bordwell calls 'art cinema' in its structural movement toward ambiguity; Miller's *The Road Warrior* is reflexive postmodern genre, demonstrating a deliberate aesthetic departure from a classical genre itinerary; Leone's close-up is nearer to a tableau than it is to a narrative (master-shot) composition. The natural inclination is thus to read the autonomous image as a reaction to the classical narrative image of the studio cinema. In this model, the image of 'pure cinema' is read as an art cinema for its capacity to abstract from cinema's normative foundations: an art, industry and culture of narrative. In Part Two, I turn to the popular (narrative) cinema of Lucas, Spielberg, Cameron, Nolan, and other practitioners of what Wyatt calls 'High Concept', the most popular, pervasive and lucrative tradition in the history of the cinematic medium.[80] In

---

[79] Graves.

[80] Wyatt, *High Concept*. Emphasizing the properties of the movement-image, Deleuze suggests that the action-image has 'produced the universal triumph of American cinema' (*Cinema 1*, 141). Of course, while it isn't stated, the action-image in Deleuze's broader paradigm is bereft (except in special cases) of the cinematic image's capacity to effect new modes of thought, experience, and being.

reading an exemplary cinema of narrative *as a cinema of the image*, I conceive of the American High Concept film – what I will ultimately refer to as spectacle cinema – as a profound contribution to the evolution of cinematic art in the twentieth and twenty-first centuries.

PART TWO

The spectacle image

4

New American cinemas: 1967–79

Image, narrative and spectacle in mass entertainment

There are moments in cinematic history that galvanize the spectator with a virtuosity of spectacle. Spectacle, in my reading, connotes excess, to borrow a term usefully employed by Kristin Thompson. While excess is not, in Thompson's usage, associated with spectacle *per se*, the notion of a film as 'not contained by unifying forces' remains a critical formulation in studies of modern cinema.[1] In the moment in which Michael Bay's Transformers introduce themselves to the spectator (*Transformers*, 2007), there is an excess of material in the image that breaks beyond the parameters of narrative signification. The spectator does not need to know who speaks last. 'My name is Optimus Prime' is a sound object that traverses a lexicon of textual images, frames of reference, and performative pieces.[2] I anticipate this utterance, in the same way in which, as Eco writes, the spectator eagerly anticipates the performance of the cult cinema trope as textual object.[3] In *Transformers*, the

---

[1] Kristin Thompson, 'The Concept of Cinematic Excess', in *Film Theory and Criticism: Introductory Readings*, ed. Leo Braudy and Marshall Cohen (Oxford: Oxford University Press, 2004), 513. For an influential reading of style that stretches beyond the demands of narrative, see David Bordwell, *Narration in the Fiction Film* (Madison, WI: University of Wisconsin Press, 1985), 274–9. While Bordwell focuses on narrative style, I see no reason why the notion of an *excessive style* could not apply to image production through *mise en scène*, movement and editing.

[2] See, for example, a number of parody and referential pieces available online: ScreenTeamShow, 'I Am Optimus Prime' (2007), YouTube 2 February 2011, http://www.youtube.com/watch?v= rEwoY52Kw3I [accessed 16 November 2011].

[3] Umberto Eco, 'Innovation and Repetition: Between Modern and Postmodern Aesthetics', *Daedalus* 134, no. 4 (2005), 196: 'The series consoles us (the consumers) because it rewards our ability to foresee.'

spectacle image requires that I am distracted by the aesthetic form of the body, by its mechanical malleability, by the astonishment of scale and size, by the affective demarcation of the awe-struck Sam Witwicky (Shia LaBeouf), who stands below in shadow, secluded in a space not unlike the recess of a movie theatre (figure 4.1). Here the image of Optimus Prime functions as a material beyond narrative signification: the signifier that is always already displaced, asserting the play of spectacle over meaning. Ndalianis is correct to suggest that spectacle 'bombards the senses', but more provocative in her reading is the notion of the affective resonance of spectacle images. How does the spectacle image affect the spectator beyond its itinerary toward narrative closure? What is 'sensory bombardment' in the play of effects cinema, large-scale production, or the convergence of cinema, gaming and theme park attraction? Ndalianis calls such sensory experiences by an encompassing metaphor: the neo-baroque ride.[4]

The spectacle image is that material of cinema that springs forth from the screen to display more than the mechanics of narrative form. I have argued elsewhere that if spectacle is to be deployed as a coherent aesthetic in film analysis, it must signify more than the 'purely visual', or the 'purely aural'.[5] Bay's *Transformers* is a marvel of spectacle mass entertainment not least because of its commodity performance in the global marketplace. Yet the spectacularity of the *image* is, more specifically, a function of its relationship to a narrative encasement. Image excess is evident in the classical aesthetic of DeMille (the parting of the Red Sea in *The Ten Commandments* [1956] is the spectacle image *par excellence* in Paramount's classical studio cinema [figure 4.2]) as well as the contemporary studio cinema of Michael Bay, Roland Emmerich and Christopher Nolan. Spectacle resounds in the display of the image of excess. Spectacle and its distraction partakes of what Rodowick calls the 'figural', in the sense in which it encodes a 'logic of mass culture',[6] bereft of the aura of a once sacred aesthetic and cultural authenticity.

In July 2010, I was sitting in a cinema anticipating the next evolution of High Concept spectacle in Christopher Nolan's *Inception*; these are event films not least because they instantiate an event horizon in cinema history. As Dudley Andrew suggests, new cinema reminds us to ask not only what

---

[4] Ndalianis, 193–207. See also Geoff King, 'Ride-Films and Films as Rides', *Cineaction* 51 (2000), 2–9. King argues that the theme park ride draws on several of the experiential attractions of mainstream blockbuster cinema. I recently experienced the 'King Kong 360 3-D' ride at Universal Studios and was intrigued to discover Peter Jackson's voice-over introduction describing the ride as an extension of the filmic franchise. Presumably, Jackson (and Universal) read 'extension' as both an expansion of the narrative text, and an expansion of the modalities of experience of that narrative text.

[5] Isaacs, *Toward a New Film Aesthetic*, 85–8.

[6] Rodowick, *Reading the Figural*, 46.

FIGURE 4.1 *The distraction of the cinematic image:* Transformers *(2007).*

FIGURE 4.2 *Spectacle cinema in the classical era:* The Ten Commandments *(1956).*

cinema is, but also what cinema was.[7] There is perhaps a single moment in *Inception* that contributes to what I would consider an evolutionary movement of the spectacle image. Ariadne (Ellen Page), the Architect (more a symbolic designation in the film; how dreamscapes are built is left frustratingly vague) builds the interior physicality of the dream through a cognitive process. As she walks the streets of Paris, contemplating the composition of the physical space, the environment reconfigures, rebuilt by the architect of the dream. At this point in the film, there is a moment of the virtuosity of the image (what Bukatman calls sublimity),[8] in which the spectator is abruptly ejected from the narrative and borne into contemplation of the image-in-itself. The astonished contemplation of the spectacle image is, as Tom Gunning reminds us, a primal initiation.[9] Seated in a darkened theatre nearer in size to a stadium, a Parisian streetscape reconfigured itself before me on a gargantuan IMAX screen, and I let the narrative go, so to speak, brought into confrontation with

---

[7] See Andrew, *What Cinema Is!*, xxv–xxvi. For an illuminating discussion of cinema's many new technologies of the imagistic *real*, see 48–61.

[8] Bukatman, *Matters of Gravity*, 93.

[9] Gunning, 'An Aesthetic of Astonishment', 114–15.

the virtuosity of the spectacle as an object of my own astonishment. I turned to my partner and found myself murmuring, 'that's magical' (figures 4.3–4.5). The moment called to mind a similar experience of the impossibility of the image upon seeing *The Matrix* in 1999 and Trinity inaugurating bullet-time in the first action sequence of that film; seeing time and space so cavalierly dislocated on screen, I was astonished.

What must the spectator then make of *Inception's* convoluted, modular narrative that follows fast upon, and encompasses, the image of astonishment?[10] Nolan's narrative is not the kind of radical indeterminism one sees in an avant-garde experiment – Resnais's *Last Year at Marienbad* (1961) comes to mind, though Tykwer's more recent *Run Lola Run* (1998) instantiates just the same radical ontology of time and progression; neither Resnais's nor Tykwer's cinema is difficult to comprehend, or 'figure out'. Rather, such experimental narratives require what Barthes calls 'play', a performative engagement with the text.[11] But the spectator of *Inception* returns to the film time and again to *close it off*, to furnish it with a final significatory resting place. The thrill one experiences upon viewing *Inception* is derived from this act of fashioning narrative closure, bringing what was once formless and chaotic to resolution.

Indeed, *Inception* and *The Matrix* are, profoundly, cinemas of narrative. Both films are calculated genre productions; both films require complex processes of reading, interpretation and inference. But over and above narrative complexity, both films provide the mechanism of the individuated protagonist, the accessible pathway for identification between the protagonist (Neo/Cobb) and the spectator. Neo is the *tabula rasa*, the site at which all spectators are identified (or interpellated), and on which all fantasies are suitably transcribed. 'Neo' is precisely the pluralism of identity that High Concept cinema seeks to formulate, the simulacral everyman. In *The Matrix*, universality is an ontological given. While each film is a postmodern inflection of the quest narrative, the spectator attains fulfilment through narrative and character resolution. Cobb's spinning totem is a gesture not toward the indeterminacy of the present, but toward the affirmation of the values of family, home, and subjective, existential being. Is the spectator troubled by a final close-up of the spinning totem as Cobb loses focus in the background of the shot? Of course not. In the preceding sequence, Cobb attains subjective wholeness: 'I can't imagine you [Mal] with all your complexity, all

---

[10] I align *Inception's* narrative 'levels' with what Cameron identifies as 'modularization' in contemporary cinema narrative. See Cameron, 'Contingency, Order, and the Modular Narrative', 65–78.
[11] Roland Barthes, 'From Work to Text', in *Image-Music-Text*, trans. Stephen Heath (London: Fontana, 1993), 155–64.

FIGURES 4.3–5 *The astonishment of spectacle in contemporary studio production:* Inception *(2010).*

your perfection, all your imperfection. Look at you – you're just a shade.' Here the spectator receives the reassurance of the Cartesian affirmation of the subject. Like Neo's capacity to perceive the Platonic form within the virtual world of the Matrix, Cobb closes off the narrative trajectory of self-formation with the revelation of the artificial dream space, the perverse reproduction of Cobb's imagined world. In the context of such a declaration, Nolan's concluding shot of the token serves no purpose other than as a gimmick, akin to a Hitchcockian McGuffin. In *Inception*, rather than a genuine threat to existential harmony, the totem functions as pure narrative trope, or what Cubitt describes as a form of narration that 'becomes spectacular'.[12]

For Cobb's totem to unsettle the spectator, the spectator/protagonist dyad must be located within the disturbing presence of the unreal object. The totem must contaminate the mind of the protagonist, which would then, as it would in Kaufman or Lynch, contaminate the interiority of the text. Which is simply to say that, after several viewings of *Inception*, and having taught it twice to an undergraduate class, I remain less interested in whether Cobb is imprisoned in an infinitely deferred dream space than in the formal narrative elegance of precisely how Cobb and Saito get themselves back to the 'real'. Present and past, dream and reality, object and illusion are, in Nolan's *Memento*, *Insomnia* (2002), *The Prestige* (2006), and *Inception*, rigidly demarcated. The spectator momentarily intellectualizes the intriguing ontological

---

[12] Cubitt, *The Cinema Effect*, 239.

puzzle at the heart of Nolan's cinema, yet, affectively, the puzzle presents as intrinsically resolved, and the protagonist is reassured into submission.

When *Inception* concludes, and Cobb recedes into the imaginary of the deep background of the shot, when the narrative has attained its completion – what becomes of the image that was, momentarily, the very essence of the experience of cinema? What becomes of the autonomous image – its presence onscreen as an *object* – in what is ostensibly a narrative mode of cinema? At 28:14,[13] there is something startling in the exhibitionist capacity of a popular, narrative art. Art in this context, as in Gunning's image of early cinema, is a mode of creating and recreating the world of perception. In this moment, a cinema of mass entertainment reveals its aesthetic potential to formally compose a world of visual, aural, 'even kinesthetic conditions'.[14] Nolan cuts between the self-configuring Parisian street and the marvelling spectator (Ariadne). Yet while Ariadne is said to be architecturally rendering the dream space, simultaneously creating and inhabiting the environment, the space is subjected to its own formal compositional imperatives. The creator of the image is astonished not only by her creation (the neo-gothic cityscape recast through contemplation), but also by the capacity of the image to create form out of its own material. This is, for creator and image, a new physics of matter and movement. What animates this shape-shifting of buildings and streets? Is it not precisely the capacity of the image to create itself, in a sense to imagine itself into being? Is it not the display of 'optical, spectacular technologies that [create] immersive, overwhelming, and apparently immediate sensory experiences'?[15]

If *Inception* exemplifies contemporary cinema's predilection for narrative puzzles, the image-in-itself and its affective potential, even in a special effects film, must submit to the cognitive pathways and intellectual pleasures of convoluted stories. Such narrative constructions are conventionally severed from the aesthetic impulse toward formal image production and composition. *Memento*'s black and white is purely significatory, even if it is at times quite beautiful and expressive; *noir*'s aesthetic expressionism is absent in Nolan's lower contrasts. *The Dark Knight*'s neo-baroque comic aesthetic is astonishing in fleeting moments, but Burton's neo-gothicism and hyper-aestheticization in *Batman* (1989) is a distant memory. Yes, seated in that IMAX theatre, I was momentarily jolted by an image divorced from its natural progression toward a referent. And yet, even in the awareness of its autonomy, in what sense could I say that I *engaged* the image, as one might say that a spectator

---

[13] Time-code references are to *Inception* (Blu-Ray/DVD 4 Disc Set), Warner Home Video, 2010.
[14] Bukatman, *Matters of Gravity*, 90.
[15] Bukatman, *Matters of Gravity*, 91.

engages, and is engaged by, a story, or a character, or the imagined persona of a movie star – these building blocks of narrative fantasy?

Film Studies has, in the main, inflected its studies of spectacle through a Marxist discourse. In such readings, the spectacle image presents as an illusionistic object that distracts the spectator, or worse, affirms the enclosed and self-referential worlds of a spectacle cinema.[16] In Cubitt's reading, the effect is ideological: 'politics is here being conducted at a miniaturized level of micromarkets, lifestyle groups, and psychic intervention, wholly in keeping with shifts in marketing, advertising, consumption, and the intensifying individualism of North America.'[17] 'Mass entertainment' (to employ Cubitt's terminology, which is problematic in his reading of both a mass culture and a cinema of entertainment) presents an ideological fantasy, a hermetic world of spectacle no less constructed, or artificially inseminated, than the mythopoetic fantasies concocted by Lucas and Spielberg in the mid- to late 1970s. Beller reads this phenomenon most directly: 'Cinema and its succeeding (if still simultaneous) formations, particularly television, video, computers, and the internet, are deterritorialized factories in which spectators work, that is, in which we perform value-productive labor.'[18]

Of course, one would be foolish to reject the claim of the commoditization of the blockbuster film; Disney's recent re-release of *The Lion King 3-D* (September, 2011) in 3-D is precisely such a commercial imperative.[19] Yet, as I have argued, the cinematic image is necessarily more than a representative, or significatory, object, and I fail to be convinced that a cinematic effect that manifests astonishment in the spectator is best read in the crude Marxist discourse employed here. Could the autonomous image of cinema not provide some access to a mode of contemplation that constructs a new relationship between subject and image, in effect rendering the world anew, rather than merely the empty simulation of a lost (and pre-commoditized) past?

'The contemporary subject', for Cubitt, 'yearns for wholeness and integration',[20] which is promised by the technology of effects cinema (and

---

[16] Cubitt, *The Cinema Effect*, 246.

[17] Cubitt, *The Cinema Effect*, 246.

[18] Jonathan Beller, *The Cinematic Mode of Production: Attention, Economy and the Society of the Spectacle* (Lebanon, NH: University Press of New England, 2006), 1. Beller presents an interesting, though strangely reductive model of subjectivity through the machinery of postmodern capitalism. Such a position enables Beller to claim that the 'mediatic production of personality precisely reproduces that of other structures that create subjective agency by utilizing the leveraged pyramid of capital' (270). There is something fairly traditional here about the import of society's various psychopathologies in cinemas of excess.

[19] Aesthetic commoditization is exemplified in the development of 2-D to 3-D conversion and re-release; *The Lion King* re-release is a case in point.

[20] Cubitt, *The Cinema Effect*, 248.

digitization) but is never quite delivered. 'It is no longer the case that films in some way respond to, refract, express, or debate reality and society. Mass entertainment has abandoned the task of making sense of the world.'[21] Cubitt's readings of recent cinema are always detailed, inventive, and engaging. Yet his position on the age of late cinema seems determinedly inflected through a pessimistic dismissal of the aesthetic (or ideological) potential of mass entertainment. There is thus a distortion not of what a mass entertainment *is*, but of how it functions for the mass spectator. I have a very difficult time conceptualizing Tarantino's cinema as 'nihilistic'.[22] While Tarantino might be perceived as the postmodern textual flaneur, the purveyor of empty ideological positions, *Reservoir Dogs* (1992), *Pulp Fiction*, and certainly the recent *Inglourious Basterds*, present complex, historicized, and ideologically inflected images of the American subject. Cubitt's cinema of fantasy, read through Debord, draws all cinemas of effect (and explicitly, cinemas of digital technological production) into its nihilistic fold.[23] But surely even spectacle images, and the commodity of effects cinema, require subtle, nuanced, self-reflexive analysis. Not all cinemas of spectacle, of the neo-baroque, or of digital production (even if coordinated by a studio) are born of the same aesthetic, ideological, or ontological spirit.

Against such generalizations of contemporary cinema, I argue that mass entertainment must be examined as an affective image, inscribed by a highly sophisticated aesthetic register. This is the virtuosity Ndalianis argues underscores the new aesthetics of contemporary cinema, a neo-baroque impulse toward spectacle and ocular thrill.[24] Against Cubitt's reading of the neo-baroque aesthetic and its empty spectacle, Rombes presents a dialectical reading of the affective potential of the spectacle image of mainstream American cinema:

> Surely you have felt, even in the most terrible CGI movie, that there is something radical and beautiful lurking there in the images, beneath the surface, some image worth dwelling on, some moment of beauty undermined by the mundane dialogue, something flapping by, like silly pages and you want to say: wait, go back, show me that again. Yes, the movie comes up a little short on the 'please respect my intelligence' scale, but the sequence itself is beautiful, artistic, visually stunning. Despite the fact

---

[21] Cubitt, *The Cinema Effect*, 245.

[22] Cubitt, *The Cinema Effect*, 246–7.

[23] Thus, 'the digital corresponds so closely to the emergent loss of an ideological structure to social meaning because it no longer pretends to represent the world.' See Cubitt, *The Cinema Effect*, 250.

[24] Ndalianis, 23–7.

that the film is little more than visual highlights with no particular interest in coherence you find yourself wondering what would happen if you no longer judged the film by the usual, tired standards of the usual, tired critics, but rather by a new standard, one that took into account the crazy, incoherent tradition of innovation and experimentation that characterized early cinema.[25]

I quote Rombes at length because his articulation of a visionary aesthetics within the commercial imperative of High Concept narrative illuminates a path to a consideration of popular cinema as a meaningful engagement with an aesthetics and experience of spectacle. This is surely a position we must integrate into our analyses of cinema's 'being', and certainly if we are to ascribe some meaningful ontology of the 'new' or 'post' cinema milieu. Is it possible for an image ensconced in a formulaic, reductive, often insultingly haphazard, narrative structure to break free, to attain a status and stature as an autonomous image, and thus to engage the senses in astonishment? Might such an aesthetics evolve further toward a performance of pure spectacle, in which cinema attends to its status as a visual/aural production? In his most radical claim, Rombes argues that contemporary scholarship simply fails to recognize the 'avant-garde qualities of blockbuster films today because we get caught up in the stories they tell'.[26] If 'we' are the mass audience, we are also cinema's critics, commentators and theorists. We would do well to bear in mind Kristin Thompson's sound advice: 'The critic and his/her reader must resist the learned tendency to try and find a narrative significance in every detail, or at least they must realize that a narrative function does not exhaust the material presence of that detail.'[27]

My examination of the image of cinema now turns to the gargantuan images of scale, size, texture, colour – and even time – of American spectacle cinema. I locate the point of origin of this cinema in 1975, with the release of Spielberg's *Jaws*, the pure commodity of modern Hollywood studio production. I begin with a brief examination of the New American Cinema (beginning in 1967 and concluding with Coppola's *Apocalypse Now* in 1979) and the rise of the independent production company.[28] I argue, in effect, that the narrative cinema of the American independent provides the aesthetic and ideological platform for the emergence of spectacle cinema from the mid–1970s. Here the

---

[25] Rombes, *Cinema in the Digital Age*, 149–50.

[26] Rombes, *Cinema in the Digital Age*, 148.

[27] Thompson, 'The Concept of Cinematic Excess', 516.

[28] For a lively account of the rise of American independent film production, see Peter Biskind, *Easy Riders, Raging Bulls: How the Sex 'n Drugs 'n Rock 'n Roll Generation Saved Hollywood* (London: Bloomsbury, 1999).

benchmarks include the unprecedented return on studio investment of *Jaws* (1975), and the formation of Lucas's Industrial Light and Magic (ILM) in 1975, a special effects facility created for the production of *Star Wars Episode IV*. Upon release in 1977, *Star Wars Episode IV* eclipses *Jaws* as the highest grossing film of all time and instantiates an industrial and commercial commitment to spectacle production that maintains within the current studio system. The brief art cinema of Hollywood that introduced the American auteur to a popular art form – Coppola, Scorsese, Altman, Bogdanovich, Friedkin, among others – set the aesthetic and industrial foundation for the formation of an American spectacle cinema. This position is not, obviously, to value one textual modality over another, but to historicize and conceptualize an evolutionary trajectory in American cinema that has been all but neglected in film studies discourse. The spectacle image, I argue, materializes as the excess of the intellectual narrative image of the American independent cinema, which is exhausted in the middle of the 1970s.[29] In Part Two of this book, I extend the notion of cinema's autonomous image to conceptualize spectacle as a technological, aesthetic and affective formation integral to contemporary American cinema.

The new American cinema: An aesthetic of ambiguity

I had a dream about 1970s movies. There was that image from the end of *Deliverance* (1972), of the hand coming up out of the water – the corpse that refuses to go away. One hand. Where's the other hand? I wondered. Zinger! It erupted from beneath the cinders on the grave of *Carrie* (1976), a hand to drag us down into the darkness.[30]

'My film is not about Vietnam. It *is* Vietnam.'[31]

The exceptional quality of the films of the post-traumatic cycle becomes even clearer when they are contrasted with the two major film cycles which

[29] For an analysis of the formation of the New American Cinema, see David A. Cook, 'Auteur Cinema and the "Film Generation" in 1970s Hollywood', in *The New American Cinema*, ed. Jon Lewis (Durham: Duke University Press, 1998), 11–35. Cook describes the New American Cinema aesthetic as 'visually arresting, thematically challenging, and stylistically individualized' (12). For a reading of the exhaustion of the New American Cinema concurrent with the release of *Jaws*, see Biskind, 278–9.

[30] Thomson, 'The Decade When Movies Mattered,' 73.

[31] Francis Ford Coppola, Press Interview (Cannes, 1979), in *Hearts of Darkness: A Filmmaker's Apocalypse* (DVD), Paramount Home Video, 2007.

follow: the Vietnam and Blockbuster cycles. If the post-traumatic cycle replays the loss of confidence in American culture and values precipitated by our involvement in Vietnam, then the Vietnam and Blockbuster cycles represent a rebuilding, in very different ways, of this lost confidence.[32]

The edifice of the New American Cinema is, in Thomson's celebration of the decade, insurmountable. It remains an anomaly in the aesthetic, ideological and political evolution of the Hollywood studio cinema. In canonical cinema history, the New American Cinema is a cinema of 'travail and upheaval',[33] in which, for a brief but incandescent moment, the studios and fledgling production companies opened themselves to the artistic inclination of European art cinema: Antonioni, Fellini, Godard, Truffaut, Resnais, etc. These were European filmmakers recognizable for, among other things, their authorial (auteuristic) expressivity.[34] Biskind recounts the story of Paul Williams pitching a genre script to late–1960s Hollywood studio executives: '"No, no, no, no", they tell him. "We want to make movies that aren't about anything. Like that *Blow-Up* picture."'[35] American cinema, which had once conformed to the rigid aesthetic imperatives of a classical Hollywood, now exemplified a restless spirit. It was, in Thomson's assessment, a cinema that *observed*, that took note of the world and attempted, for a decade at least, 'to speak to us with unaccustomed candor'.[36] This was furthermore the decade in which Hollywood reflected the insurgence of alternative ideologies and cultures and, in its most radical incarnation, the image of a new American subjectivity. For Keathley, all of the New American Cinema, America's only genuine cinema of trauma, is about the experience of cultural and political upheaval.[37]

Schatz is correct to read the formulation of a distinctive aesthetic of Hollywood cinema through a transformation in the industrial and commercial structures of the system.[38] Corman's schlock horror or exploitation genre fare exists outside of the auspices of the studio system – it is, in name

---

[32] Keathley, 'Trapped in the Affection Image', 304.

[33] Thomson, 'The Decade When Movies Mattered', 73.

[34] Bordwell, 'The Art Cinema as a Mode of Film Practice', 58.

[35] Biskind, 22.

[36] Thomson, 'The Decade When Movies Mattered', 82.

[37] See Keathley, 304–6.

[38] Thomas Schatz, 'The Whole Equation of Pictures', in *The Film and Authorship*, ed. Virginia Wright-Wexman (New Brunswick: Rutgers University Press, 2003), 92–4. Schatz argues that 'the quality and artistry of all these films were the product not simply of individual human expression, but a melding of institutional forces' (92). While Schatz refers specifically to studio production of the classical era, I would argue that the institutional imperative is critical to the formation of the New American Cinema in the 1970s.

and spirit, an Independent American Cinema.[39] Rafelson's *Five Easy Pieces* (1970) came out of the evolution of an independent production company, BBS, which would also produce Bogdanovich's *The Last Picture Show* in 1971.[40] For Elsaesser, 'the old Hollywood studio-system worked according to a recognizably industrial model, which ... collapsed under its own weight and inflexibility. It was superseded by the more nimble, small-is-beautiful, artisanal mode of American independent film production.'[41] Production in the old system was rigidly formulated, regulated and systematized. Effectively, the shift from an old to the new, the studio to the auteur, and the classical to the post-classical, came out of the necessity for new industrial imperatives in the wake of the studio failure of the 1950s.[42] The notion of the 70s cinema as an allegory of post-Fordism makes sense in the context of the new, non-regulated industries of independent production companies, and studio corporations attempting to emulate the aesthetic and industrial context of independence.[43]

Independence in the late 1960s, or earlier if we include some of the studio work of Nicholas Ray or the New York productions of John Cassavetes,[44] connotes also a particular artistic sensibility. As Biskind argues, the independent filmmakers were philosophically opposed to the classical studio cinema's dictum of art as commerce.[45] A great deal of the New American Cinema was unbankable by the studios. How could a studio corporation predict what would make money in an age in which *The Graduate* (1967), *Easy Rider* and *Mash* turned enormous profits on modest budgets? Even more problematic,

---

[39] For a detailed account of the formation and development of American International Pictures (AIP), see Roger Corman, *How I Made A Hundred Movies in Hollywood and Never Lost a Dime* (New York: Da Capo Press, 1998).

[40] See Geoff King, *New Hollywood Cinema: An Introduction* (New York: Columbia University Press, 2002), 98–102.

[41] Thomas Elsaesser, 'American Auteur Cinema: The Last – or First – Picture Show', in *The Last Great American Picture Show*, ed. Thomas Elsaesser, Alexander Horwath and Noel King (Amsterdam: Amsterdam University Press, 2004), 53.

[42] For a comprehensive analysis of the formation, evolution and decline of the studio system, see Thomas Schatz, *The Genius of the System: Hollywood Filmmaking in the Studio Era* (Minneapolis: University of Minnesota Press, 2010). Schatz concludes his exhaustive analysis with an examination of the decline of the major studios and the entry into the era of New Hollywood production.

[43] See Elsaesser, 'American Auteur Cinema: The Last – or First – Picture Show'. See also in the same volume, Drehli Robnik, 'Allegories of Post-Fordism in the 1970s New Hollywood', in *The Last Great American Picture Show*, ed. Thomas Elsaesser, Alexander Horwath and Noel King (Amsterdam: Amsterdam University Press, 2004), 342–4. Robnik offers an analysis of the 1970s 'war movie' (notably *The Dirty Dozen* [1967] and *Kelly's Heroes* [1970]) as the representation of a post-Fordist subjectivity. In such films, Robnik perceives 'the emergence of a new conceptualization of purposeful, productive action' (335).

[44] See George Kouvaros, *Where Does It Happen?: John Cassavetes and Cinema at the Breaking Point* (Minneapolis: University of Minnesota Press, 2004).

[45] Biskind, 15–18.

such films clearly espoused the values of a counter-cultural (and thus fringe democratic) ideology. American cinema had turned from the masses to niche audiences, and studios were traditionally a mass production facility. The new independent filmmaker was an artist setting contractual terms.[46] Auteurism, a somewhat vague notion given substance in the US by Andrew Sarris,[47] became the widely accepted conceptual framework for the New American Cinema. Independence was a system itself, but for the filmmakers and the production company pioneers overseeing the transformation of American cinema (Corman, Rafelson, Coppola, etc.), it was an ethos.

While it is something of a generalization insofar as not all films exemplify a dominant trend aesthetically, culturally and politically, yet it remains the case that the majority of films of the New American Cinema tradition demonstrate two intersecting aesthetic tendencies: the tendency toward formal compositional ambiguity in narrative and image; and the tendency toward stories of personal and collective crises. I use the word tendency, rather than strategy, because composition, particularly composition of the image, is rarely a formal strategy in the literal sense of the word. A great deal of film composition takes place through accident and happenstance, and postproduction is always implicated in the creative process. Further, 'tendency' connotes a gesture toward a guiding principle rather than the rigid adoption of an aesthetic template. The New American Cinema, I argue, is infused with a 'spirit' of ambiguity, less a wave than a sensibility. Only Coppola genuinely entertained the notion of a movement, or artistic collective, in his development of American Zoetrope in 1969.[48]

The formal tendency toward ambiguity is exemplified in a film such as Altman's *The Long Goodbye*, a parodic and unsettling adaptation of Chandler's classic *noir* story. Altman's vision of LA *noir* is infused with the sensibility of disaffection and detachment exemplified in earlier New American films such as *Five Easy Pieces* and *The Last Picture Show*. In Altman's revisionist *noir*, the conventional detective is depicted as counter-cultural deviant, isolated from the social, cultural and political codes that authorize the LA lifestyle.

---

[46] One such case is Coppola's negotiation with Paramount for funding of *The Conversation* in exchange for directing *The Godfather, Part 2*. See Biskind, 183.

[47] See Andrew Sarris, 'Notes on the Auteur Theory in 1962', in *Film Theory and Criticism: Introductory Readings*, ed. Leo Braudy and Marshall Cohen (Oxford: Oxford University Press, 2004), 561–4. Sarris works hard to claim auteur theory as an incisive analytical (rather than purely critical) foundation, yet his model of a three-pronged auteur signature – technique, style, meaning – is very difficult to accept in a wide engagement with cinema and its inherently discursive meaning-making processes.

[48] For a fascinating account of Coppola and American Zoetrope in the New American Cinema era, see Gary Leva (director), *A Legacy of Filmmakers: The Early Years of American Zoetrope*, Leva FilmWorks, 2004.

Gould's Philip Marlowe wanders through the chaos of early 70s Los Angeles, resembling Antonioni's existentially bereft photographer of *Blow Up*. This figure is further reincarnated in any number of New American films: Michael Corleone (Al Pacino) reflecting on the possibility of losing his family in *The Godfather, Part II* (1974) or Harry Caul playing his saxophone in the final scene of *The Conversation*. Both Caul and Corleone allegorize a crisis in masculinity, family, society and state endemic in New American Cinema narratives of the late 1960s and early to mid–1970s. Both men present the obverse to the sustained certainty of self and society depicted in a great deal of studio genre cinema, notably the Western.[49] Travis Bickle (Robert De Niro) is exemplary of the flaneur of the new American modernity, whose paranoia reasserts its presence in a final series of jump cuts projected in the reflection of a mirror (figures 4.6–4.8). Friedkin's Popeye Doyle (Gene Hackman, *The French Connection*, 1971) pursues the criminal without bringing him to justice; the procedural narrative is existential rather than instrumental. For Altman's Marlowe, Michael Corleone, Harry Caul, Popeye Doyle, but equally Benjamin Braddock (Dustin Hoffman, *The Graduate*), Joe Buck (Jon Voight, *Midnight Cowboy*, 1969), Sonny (Al Pacino, *Dog Day Afternoon*, 1975), Jake Gittes (Jack Nicholson, *Chinatown*, 1974), George Roundy (Warren Beatty, *Shampoo*, 1975), Captain Willard (Martin Sheen, *Apocalypse Now*, 1979) – the goal, the *objective* of the guiding search of classical American film narrative vanishes in the context of the trauma of journeying. If the studio cinema was built on the optimism of a classical aesthetic in which the journeying protagonist acquired the lost object, Elsaesser is no doubt correct to charac-terize the New American Cinema as a cinema of failure, in which the classical journeyman is beset by a 'lack of motivation'.[50] Stasis, journeying without end, is an existential condition of America's cinematic modernity.

Bordwell's influential essay on the art cinema takes the notion of ambiguity further: 'the art cinema defines itself explicitly against the classical narrative mode, and particularly against the cause-effect linkage of events.'[51] Ambiguity is construed as the departure from classical narrative composition, which

---

[49] While of course genre cinema evolves throughout the classical era, I would argue that the narrative and character arc of the Western, particular from Ford's *Stagecoach* (1939) to Hawks's *Red River* (1948), traces the conflict formation and resolution of personal, collective and institu-tional crisis. For a recent useful analysis of identity formation in the classical era Western, see Robert B. Pippin, *Hollywood Westerns and American Myth: The Importance of Howard Hawks and John Ford For Political Philosophy* (New Haven: Yale University Press, 2010).

[50] Thomas Elsaesser, 'The Pathos of Failure: American Films in the 1970s', in *The Last Great American Picture Show*, ed. Thomas Elsaesser, Alexander Horwath and Noel King (Amsterdam: Amsterdam University Press, 2004), 284.

[51] Bordwell, 'The Art Cinema as a Mode of Film Practice', 57.

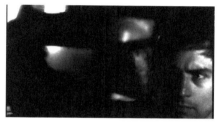

FIGURES 4.6–8 *The paranoid protagonist of the New American Cinema: Travis Bickle (Robert De Niro) in* Taxi Driver *(1976).*

accompanies the fragmentation of psychological causation.[52] Thus, Harry Caul's inability to perceive the world objectively provides the foundation for both his mental crisis and the film's ontological crisis of image and sound. For Deleuze, whose reading of a post-classical cinema traces a similar trajectory, 'the crisis of the action image [classical cinema exemplified in the studio era] was defined by a number of characteristics: the form of the trip/ballad, the multiplication of clichés, the events that hardly concern those they happen to, in short the slackening of the sensory-motor connections.'[53] Deleuze's trip/ballad is the 'beat journey',[54] mirroring the path of Sal Paradise across an America without a destination in Kerouac's *On the Road*.[55] Critically, for Deleuze, as for Elsaesser, the voyage 'has become detached from the active and affective structure which supported it, directed it, and gave it even vague directions'.[56]

Consider Rafelson's *Five Easy Pieces*, appearing in 1970 and a fermenting force in the evolution of the New American film aesthetic. What are we to make of the conclusion of the film, a wonderfully expressive sequence shot in depth, in which Bobby Dupea (Jack Nicholson) leaves Rayette (Karen Black) and hitches a ride north? If this is a character study, Bobby's

---

[52] Bordwell, 'The Art Cinema as a Mode of Film Practice', 58.
[53] Deleuze, *Cinema 2*, 3.
[54] Deleuze, *Cinema 1*, 208.
[55] Jack Kerouac, *On The Road* (New York: Viking, 1997).
[56] Deleuze, *Cinema 1*, 208.

character remains frustratingly beyond our grasp. Why can't Bobby progress in this story along conventional pathways? How can the spectator anticipate this monumental gesture, to turn one's back on a familial history and flee society? And this is not the flight toward social reintegration exemplified in the nineteenth-century American narrative.[57] Rather, this flight begins a movement that continues in perpetuity. We sense in *Five Easy Pieces* Dupea's crisis of self that is narcissistic and yet fraught with an existential insecurity. Dupea's movement is the same movement that animates Wyatt's (Peter Fonda) flight from society in *Easy Rider* and leads to a descent into the surrealist chaos of a post-countercultural America. The concluding shot of *Five Easy Pieces*, in which a truck grows smaller as it moves further from a gas station, is a metaphor for Dupea's inaccessibility – Bobby flees Rayette, but he also flees the exacting gaze of the spectator that seeks to resolve the conflict inherent in the character arc of a protagonist. The trauma of the protagonist results not merely from the failure to attain a goal, but the failure of narrative to render that journey in unproblematic terms. Is there any shot more radical in the New American Cinema than the projection of the death of Wyatt and Billy (*Easy Rider*) in a fleeting, almost subliminal image, tearing a classical temporality into so many freely associating parts (figures 4.9–4.10)?

While Rafelson's authorial expressivity is most clearly articulated in the departure from a narrative norm prescribing resolution and closure, it is precisely in the construction of narratives of ambiguity that the New American Cinema affirms the cinematic text as a narrative-based medium. Undermining classical narrative only serves to further emphasize the centrality and visibility of narrative form within the production of American cinema. The notion that narrative fragmentation, or destabilization, exemplifies a *non-narrative* cinema is for me misguided. Rafelson's, Scorsese's, Altman's or Coppola's narratives of ambiguity (which are indeed radical in the 1970s) assert the primacy of American cinema as a narrative text, and the fundamental experience of that cinema as an engagement with new narrative patterns and tropes. One could make the same argument of the 1990s American cinema and its puzzle narratives: modularization merely draws attention to new structural and functional components of story and character. Tarantino is an astonishing image stylist, yet almost all commentary on *Reservoir Dogs*, *Pulp Fiction* or the *Kill Bill* films read the Tarantino aesthetic in terms of narrative nonlinearity, hyper-genericity or unconventional dialogue. This is merely to say

---

[57] Consider, for example, the mythology inherent in flight and movement from civilization as restoration in the genres of the American Western, or indeed, nineteenth-century American literature. See Leslie Fiedler, *Love and Death in the American Novel* (New York: Stein and Day, 1966). See also Robert Jewett and John Shelton Lawrence, *The American Monomyth* (Garden City: Anchor Press, 1977).

FIGURES 4.9–10 *Fractured temporality in the New American Cinema:* Easy Rider *(1969).*

that the new narrative patterns of Bogdanovich, Coppola, Altman, Scorsese, or Paul Thomas Anderson, Tarantino and the Coen Brothers, affirm rather than implicitly subvert narrative form as the foundation of an American film aesthetic.

A historical departure (1)

If the person can tell me the story in 25 words or less, it's going to make a pretty good movie. I like ideas, especially movie ideas, that you can hold in your hand.[58]

Jaws changed the business forever.[59]

The Godfather (1972) and *The Exorcist* returned enormous profits on investment for their respective studios. Both films were released simultaneously in major cities on several hundred screens.[60] The success of each film set the platform for a production and distribution model that would be utilized by the major studios from the mid–1970s, and would in effect '[pave] the way for the ultimate destruction of the New Hollywood'.[61] The release of *Jaws* in 1975, and the phenomenon of *Star Wars Episode IV* (1977), profoundly transformed the environment of American cinema. The unprecedented market success of *Jaws* affirmed the commodity potential of the High Concept film. This production and distribution model originated within the New American Cinema's gravitation toward industrial independence; that is, the production and distribution model for what later came to be known as the 'blockbuster'

---

[58] Steven Spielberg, cited in J. Hoberman, '1975–1985: Ten Years That Shook the World', *American Film* 10, no. 8 (1985), 35.

[59] Biskind, 278.

[60] Biskind, 162. See also King, 'New Hollywood Cinema', 54–5.

[61] Biskind, 162.

effectively reoriented the movement of independence toward increasing integration into large-scale, generic, and special-effects-oriented production. By the early 1980s, in the wake of the financial successes of *Jaws*, *Star Wars Episode IV*, *Close Encounters of the Third Kind* (1977), *Superman* (1978), *Star Wars: Episode V: The Empire Strikes Back* (1980), *Raiders of the Lost Ark* (1981), *E.T.: The Extra-Terrestrial* (1982), *Ghostbusters* (1984), and *Back to the Future* (1985), the studio system was no longer the appropriate industrial context for an American art cinema. In the context of the blockbuster production and distribution model that now dominated the studio system, the American auteurs were fringe filmmakers.[62]

Of course, the transformation from art cinema to the studio blockbuster was not purely commercial, yet commerce provides a critical foundation to the evolution of the blockbuster film. As Schatz argues, the blockbuster represented a reversion to classicism inherent in studio production cinema.[63] If the New American Cinema was an art cinema, the blockbuster represented an aesthetic imperative toward mass consumption. Narratives of disaffection and alienation were recast as rites of maturation and self-discovery. Coppola's existentially adrift Harry Caul was offered the trajectory of recovery in Spielberg's Chief Brody in *Jaws*. The panoptic society of *The Parallax View* (1974) and *The Conversation* was thwarted (and politically challenged) by the ingenuity, innocence and secular faith of children in *E.T.: The Extra-Terrestrial*. Aesthetic realism was subordinated to the new image modalities of special effects, spectacle and action. The commercial failure of Altman's *Nashville* in 1975, perhaps the most radical and complex depiction of American trauma in 1970s cinema, presaged the unprecedented success of *Jaws* in the same year. If Altman's *Nashville* presented the spectator's experience as trauma, *Jaws* presented an American cinema of placation, wish-fulfilment and emotional well-being.[64]

---

[62] See Biskind, 408.

[63] Thomas Schatz, 'The New Hollywood', in *Film Theory Goes to the Movies*, ed. Jim Collins, Hilary Radner and Ava Preacher Collins (New York: Routledge, 1993), 34–6. See also Thomas Schatz, 'The Studio System and Conglomerate Hollywood', in *The Contemporary Hollywood Film Industry*, ed. Paul McDonald and Janet Wasko (Malden, MA: Blackwell Publishing, 2008), 19–25. Cavell argues that the genre cinema of the classical studio era is in fact a medium that could be recycled in later traditions. See Cavell, *The World Viewed*, 35–6.

[64] See Andrew Britton, 'Blissing Out: The Politics of Reaganite Entertainment', *Movie* 31/32 (1986), 1–42.

Transformations: *The Player*

Altman's *The Player* (1992) is a brilliant film for any number of reasons, but its opening eight-minute sequence shot is surely the apotheosis of what Cubitt calls the 'neo-baroque aesthetic' in the context of modern cinema's stylistic evolution.[65] Baroque aestheticism – Bordwell's authorial expressivity of the art film – is recast by Altman in 1992 as a reflexive commentary on the transition from the New American Cinema to High Concept Hollywood. In a very real sense, Altman's film is a product of the commoditization of cinema; while *The Player*'s genre structure coheres only in inverted commas, displaying its irony in the subtle and not so subtle references to a cinematic past, it remains, in my opinion, the film most radically removed from his auteurist works: *Mash*, *McCabe and Mrs. Miller* (1971), *The Long Goodbye* and *Nashville*. Against Altman's many baroque tendencies in the New American Cinema, *The Player*'s neo-baroque sensibility plays out in excess; the artistic (and auteuristic) virtuosity of the baroque is reframed as aesthetic excess. Altman's sequence shot of the New American Cinema is reconfigured as something bolder here, cavalier in its movement in space and time, rebellious in its audacity. *The Player*'s sequence shot is nearer in artistic restlessness to Welles's opening sequence shot in *Touch of Evil* (itself a departure from the sequence shot of *Citizen Kane* and *The Magnificent Ambersons* [1942]). Altman's quotation is thus not of his own baroque cinema, but of the Welles image of excess in 1958. It is fitting that Altman's sequence shot in *The Player* is captured entirely in a makeshift studio lot.

The critique of Hollywood High Concept in Altman's sequence shot functions through narrative diegesis (a pitch for *The Graduate, Part 2*; or a political thriller with a heart, couched as '*Ghost* meets *The Manchurian Candidate*') and the mechanism of the sequence shot: conventionally a shot of duration, often in depth. In *The Player*, the sequence shot, referenced in diegetic dialogue ('Welles's *Touch of Evil*'), is attentive to its own artistic distinction. On a studio lot in which executives green-light High Concept projects, Altman's sequence shot is not only anachronistic, but incongruous. Once exemplary of the auteur's virtuosity in the New American Cinema (for example, Altman's composition in the traffic jam sequence in *Nashville* [1975]), the shot becomes a quotation and a hyperbolic, flamboyant, self-conscious gesture. Altman's *The Player* is thus not a recuperation of the aesthetic agitation of the New American auteur, but a capitulation to the studio imperative that rendered the image of compositional ambiguity

---

[65] For a discussion of neo-baroque's expressive 'take', see Cubitt, *The Cinema Effect*, 219–23.

obsolete. *The Player* is not a dialectical move against the studio ethos, but a playful, ironic, self-aware, rebellious gesture, fleeting and anomalous.

In Altman's film, High Concept is presented as a dumbing-down of cinema's stories. What was once radical, confronting and irresolute takes on the reassurance and nourishment of formula.[66] 'Reassurance is keynote', suggests Robin Wood in an influential reading of 1980s American cinema. These reassurances 'diminish, defuse, and render safe all the major radical movements that gained so much impetus, became so threatening, in the 1970s'.[67] Wood here works through the orthodox reading of the transition from New American Cinema to High Concept's repetitive, and imminently repeatable, fantasies. Altman's camera in its continuous movement displays the radicalism of the sequence shot against the orthodoxy, or conservatism, of montage: 'My old man worked for Hitchcock … *Rope*, it's a masterpiece. Story wasn't any good, but he shot the whole thing without cuts. I hate all these cuts. Cut, cut, cut.' Yet the final joke is Altman's: the long take is invisible, and unremarkable, on a studio lot in the era of ubiquitous High Concept production. Once the distinction of the auteur, the long take is appropriated into the spatial and temporal coverage of the studio. Altman thus performs the effacement of his own authorial signature so visible in the 1970s.

By 1992 and Altman's release of *The Player*, Hollywood High Concept was a pejorative term. The New American Cinema was itself the object of nostalgia. While in the same year that Altman produced *The Player*, Eastwood produced *Unforgiven*, Neil Jordan produced *The Crying Game* through Miramax, and Tarantino produced *Reservoir Dogs*, Hillier is correct to conceptualize such films through the rubric of a Hollywood Independent Cinema of the 1990s rather than the New American Cinema of the 1970s. Altman's sequence shot in *The Player* demonstrates that the terrain of American film production had irrevocably changed. The allure of the New American Cinema, concluding perhaps with Coppola's tumultuous production of *Apocalypse Now* in 1979, maintains precisely because it has been overwhelmed. The allure of a past aesthetic represents the lost object of American cinema's history, and was, in 1980, or in Altman's simulacral studio lot of 1992, irrecoverable:

Says Bogdanovich, 'I felt that by the mid–70s, I'd blown it, Friedkin had blown it, Altman went into eclipse, one flop after another, Francis went crazy, even *Raging Bull* didn't do any business. Everybody kind of blew

---

[66] Schatz, 'The New Hollywood', 9.
[67] Robin Wood, 'Papering the Cracks: Fantasy and Ideology in the Reagan Era', in *Movies and Mass Culture*, ed. John Belton (New Brunswick: Rutgers University Press, 1996), 204–5.

it in varying shapes and sizes.' All but the most tenacious and disciplined directors of the 70s who had managed to walk the tightrope between art and commerce, fell to their deaths in the 80s.[68]

Beyond narrativity

I take narration to be, simply, *storytelling*. 'In any medium, narrative can be thought of as a chain of events occurring in time and space and linked by cause and effect … The clarity of comprehension [of narrative] is basic to all our other responses to films.'[69] This propensity to read cinema narratively is provocative, and in the main I agree with Thompson about the spectator's intuitive response to cinema's narrational fields. The contribution of Thompson to studies of classicism through narrative is not only invaluable, but critical to the discipline of film studies. In Bordwell and Carroll's designation of a 'post-theory' milieu, they are essentially asking for a commonsensical approach to cinema; cognition, in Bordwell and Carroll, is a way of making sense of the cinematic text through narrative. Such processes inevitably inscribe the spectator into a position of authority (against the spectator passivity postulated by 'grand theory' discourse) over the text, and thus reflect the dominant trajectories of contemporary film criticism, commentary and viewing practices.[70]

I've argued in this chapter that American cinema is fundamentally narratively based. While arguments about cinema's capacity for non-narrative forms are provocative, in my opinion, narrative is intrinsic to the industrial, aesthetic and commercial life of Hollywood. Perhaps this will change in time, and perhaps there are incremental shifts in the operation of new narrative forms.[71] But for now, narrative constitutes the arterial networks of story and character transmission in mainstream American cinema.[72]

I've also argued that the aesthetic of ambiguity that informs the New American Cinema, rather than exemplifying a non-narrative cinema, indeed

---

[68] Biskind, 408.

[69] Thompson, *Storytelling in the New Hollywood*, 10.

[70] See David Bordwell, 'Contemporary Film Studies and the Vicissitudes of Grand Theory', in *Post-Theory: Reconstructing Film Studies*, ed. David Bordwell and Noël Carroll (Madison, WI: University of Wisconsin Press, 1996), 6–18.

[71] Shaviro has coined the term 'post-cinematic affect' to attempt to describe what he perceives as departures from conventional narrative experience. See Shaviro, *Post-Cinematic Affect*.

[72] One need only take account of the proliferation of structural models of screenwriting pervasive in the contemporary studio system. See, for example, Robert McKee, *Story: Substance, Structure, Style, and the Principles of Screenwriting* (New York: Regan Books, 1997). For an astute analysis of the structural emphasis in the development of the modern screenplay, see Ken Dancyger, *Alternative Scriptwriting: Successfully Breaking the Rules* (Boston: Focal Press, 2007).

reaffirms the foundational presence of narrative within the studio and post-studio system. The spectator of *The Last Picture Show* or *The French Connection* or *The Conversation* is confronted by a new mode of narrative cinema in which conventional patterns of progression are interrupted, subject to contingency, and often stilled. The affection image of the New American Cinema presents an entrapment in stasis, in broken sensory-motor connections, and affect overcomes action as the dominant movement of cinema. Of course, there are moments in which the image functions as the excess of narrative, as the display of spectacle. Such images have manifested throughout cinema's history, and are present also in the New American Cinema (and European Art Cinema) of the 1970s, in which unsettled narratives 'freeze' (to use Wyatt's term)[73] and allow the play of exhibition images: Coppola's sound image in *The Conversation*, Bertolucci's frequent line crosses on movement in *The Conformist*,[74] Scorsese's jump cut to the beat of The Ronettes' 'Be My Baby' to open *Mean Streets*. But such moments are, in the aesthetic trajectory of modern American cinema, fleeting and episodic.

If the New American Cinema inscribes cinematic art, and cinematic experience, as *narrative* (the foundation of the aesthetic of ambiguity), High Concept cinema ('ideas that you can hold in your hand') – the cinema of the blockbuster aesthetic of the contemporary studio system – reconstitutes narrative progression as action rather than inaction, movement rather than stasis. The image that animates the 'blockbuster', the film produced as studio commodity,[75] is born of an impulse toward movement, and the display of that material Bukatman calls 'kinetic energy'. Thompson, and in another context Wood, are correct to suggest that the modern studio film is a vehicle for the unimpeded telling of stories;[76] it would be foolish to argue otherwise. But the High Concept film tells its stories precisely to deliver an experience of action through rhythm, movement, progression, and ultimately resolution. The historical/political/aesthetic crisis of action inherent in the New American Cinema is resolved in the emerging High Concept cinema, in which the affection image is reconceptualized as an image of sustained and aggressive action. The distinction between the aesthetic of ambiguity in the

---

[73] Wyatt, *High Concept*, 25.

[74] The 'line-cross', or 180-degree rule, the basic contravention of spatial continuity in *mise en scène*, intrudes in several sequences in Bertolucci's *The Conformist*, but perhaps most elegantly in the sequence in which Marcello Clerici (Jean-Louis Trintignant) visits his mother in her home. For a lucid explanation of the line-cross, see Tom Kingdon, 'The 180-Degree Rule,' in *Total Directing: Integrating Camera and Performance in Film and Television* (Los Angeles: Silman-James Press, 2004), 227–45.

[75] Alexandra Keller, *James Cameron* (London: Routledge, 2006), 21–3.

[76] See Thompson, *Storytelling in the New Hollywood*, 17–21; for Wood's account of the juvenilization of American cinema through narrativized ideology, see Wood, 'Papering the Cracks'.

New American Cinema and High Concept's 'disambiguated narratives' is thus one of *affect*, of the sensation of experiencing a mode of storytelling within a confluence of images and sounds.[77]

The aesthetic foundation of High Concept cinema has little to do with the simplification of story, or with the assimilation of character types into a recognizable framework, or indeed, with the projection of a conservative ideology through recognizable archetypal forms.[78] While simplistic storylines and universalized character types are one outcome of the High Concept aesthetic, the spectator should not construe High Concept cinema as the function of a narratively inscribed process. I could adequately demonstrate that *Midnight Cowboy* is composed of a very simple story; equally, I could argue that *Dirty Harry* (1971) is best read as a conservative response to an American countercultural ideology (I confess, this is not my inclination). Yet both *Midnight*

---

[77] While Wyatt's work on High Concept industry and aesthetics is invaluable, I wish to depart from the mode of instrumental analysis of High Concept cinema that locates its industrial, aesthetic and cultural life in the new formations of the studio system. See Wyatt, *High Concept cinema*. For a useful overview of the interrelationship of New American Cinema and High Concept cinema (the perceived transformation of an auteur-director into an auteur-producer), see Thomas Elsaesser, *The Persistence of Hollywood* (New York: Routledge, 2012), 283–9. Elsaesser draws on Jon Lewis's influential reading of High Concept cinema as a producer's medium. Yet clearly Lewis's conclusions about Spielberg's cinema are overly generalized: 'While the first wave auteurs focused primarily on *mise en scène* and took pride and care in directing actors during the production phase, Lucas and Spielberg are almost exclusively postproduction directors.' I hope that my analyses of several key sequences in Lucas, and particularly Spielberg, provide a more subtle analysis of *how* the aesthetic of High Concept functions in dialectical relation to the New American Cinema that preceded it. In any case, Buckland's *Directed by Steven Spielberg* is an exemplary close analysis of *mise en scène* in Spielberg. But Lewis's contention about a 'postproduction cinema', the notion of which is simply not feasible in the context of contemporary studio production (is Wong Kar-wai's *In the Mood For Love* (2000) a post-produced rather than produced film?), requires a more basic response: why is a cinema grounded in the immediacy of performance and *mise en scène* necessarily *more than* a cinema of composited images (the common practice of which in any case can be traced to cinema's origins)? See Jon Lewis, 'The Perfect Money Machine(s): George Lucas, Steven Spielberg, and Auteurism in the New Hollywood', in *Looking Past the Screen: Case Studies in American Film History and Method*, ed. Jon Lewis and Eric Smoodin (Durham: Duke University Press, 2007), 61–86. I could argue that the realism of performance and *mise en scène* in a film like *Rain Man* (1988) is equally a commercial and aesthetic imperative. *Rain Man* out-grossed the Zemeckis/Disney vehicle *Who Framed Roger Rabbit* (1988), McTiernan's action masterpiece *Die Hard* (1988) and Burton's *Beetlejuice* (1988). For an oft-cited piece on the integration of High Concept commercialism and the action genre, see Larry Gross, 'Big and Loud', *Sight and Sound* 5, no. 8 (1995), 6–10. Gross locates the turn to High Concept action in 1977, the release year of *Star Wars Episode IV* and *Close Encounters of the Third Kind*; of course, I argue that the High Concept film is industrialized through the production and distribution model exemplified by *Jaws*. Gross's piece is particularly interesting. I agree that Spielberg's cinema might be loosely affiliated with the action image promulgated by the James Bond franchise in the 1960s and early 1970s (especially *Goldfinger* [1964]), yet for me, *2001: A Space Odyssey* is anything but a High Concept action film (Gross, 8).

[78] See Jewett and Lawrence; Wood, 'Papering the Cracks'; Wyatt, *High Concept*.

Cowboy and *Dirty Harry* are texts that could emerge only within the industrial, aesthetic and cultural context of the New American Cinema; both films are animated through the image of inaction that accompanies the crisis of American subjectivity in the late 1960s and 1970s.

In the final sequence of *Dirty Harry*, the protagonist (Clint Eastwood) subdues the deviant Other, Scorpio. The confrontation between protagonist and antagonist takes place after a lengthy and elaborate chase sequence. Yet while Callahan recites the anticipated speech ('I know what you're thinking … Did he fire six shots or only five …'), in effect bringing narrative past and present together, the resolution to the action is subverted by the recuperation of the image of inaction: standing over the dead body of Scorpio, Callahan appears bereft of purpose, isolated in the empty space of the long shot (figures 4.11–4.13).

Why does he toss his badge into the lake at the end of the film? What can such a gesture signify? Is Callahan's emotional passage from the final sequence not to a *renewed* paranoia, to the schizophrenic subject position of a man at once part of the system and external to it? Could we not say that Callahan's final resting place (the journey without end) is precisely the subject position of Scorsese's Travis Bickle (*Taxi Driver*), who must resume his paranoid movement through the city?[79] The natural progression for Eastwood from *Dirty Harry* was thus not toward *Magnum Force* (1973), *The Enforcer* (1976) and *Sudden Impact* (1983), but toward *Tightrope* (1984), the film in which the normative figure of authority (Eastwood's cop, recast here as Wes Block) is revealed as the site of asocial, deviant, pathological desire. The elegant image of action that composes the most influential action sequence of the New American Cinema – a mid-Act Two car chase in *The French Connection*[80] – is unsettled by the transformation from action to inaction and stasis. While *The French Connection II* (1975) is obviously less successful than the original film, the relocation of Doyle some years later to Marseilles, increasingly immersed in a mid–1970s haze of disaffection, is entirely appropriate in the context of the irresolute narrative of the original film.

---

[79] For a very useful discussion of the disaffection of the New American Cinema protagonist, see King, *New Hollywood*, 19–21 and 33–4.

[80] Ramao identifies a discrete action genre of the 1970s as the 'car chase film'. Yet *Bullitt* (1968) and *The French Connection* sit uneasily for me as genre films formulated around an image of action. Granted, the sequences of both *Bullitt* and *The French Connection* play out astonishing action sequences, but the action is unsettled by the ambiguity of the narrative and image frame. Action thus remains unresolved. Rather, I would locate such action sequences in the wider display of ambiguity in the New American Cinema, in which, for example, a conventional genre piece such as *Point Blank* (1967) is reconfigured as a fragmented narrative whole. See Tico Ramao, 'Guns and Gas: Investigating the 1970s Car Chase Film', in *Action and Adventure Cinema*, ed. Yvonne Tasker (New York: Routledge, 2004), 130–52.

FIGURES 4.11–13 *The classical protagonist abandoned in the New American Cinema:* Dirty Harry *(1971).*

Contrast *Dirty Harry*'s concluding movement toward inaction and disenfranchisement with the image of social, psychological and existential recuperation in *Jaws*. In the film's first act, Chief Brody is presented as the damaged protagonist. Brody is cast, not unlike Callahan, Joe Buck *(Midnight Cowboy)* and Harry Caul (*The Conversation*), as the outsider: 'You're not born here, you're not an islander.' Brody's fear of the ocean has nothing to do with a predatory shark; it is, necessarily, irrational and paranoid: 'We know all about you, Chief. You don't go in the water.' Yet the narrative progression toward failure and abjection of the New American Cinema is interrupted – and re-animated – as *fulfilment through action*. Brody must not only leave land (on Quint's vessel) but must be, literally, submerged in the water. The destruction of the shark thus represents the conclusion of a narrative action that begins with inaction, stasis and paranoia on the land, and culminates in the active mastering of fear and trauma on the ocean. In *Jaws*, the destruction of the shark represents the guiding narrative action of the film; in *Dirty Harry*, the affective thrill of such fulfilment is subverted by the image of the isolated figure held in long shot, departing from the site of action. The image of action in High Concept cinema thus serves two elemental purposes: first, it creates narrative resolution through action; second, it materializes a profoundly affective image-in-itself.

Luke Skywalker's crisis of identity in the first act of *Star Wars Episode IV* finds its natural expression as action: trauma is resolved through psychological, existential (and, increasingly in the spectacle tradition, physical) rebirth. It is thus fitting that the endings to High Concept cinema display images of action: Brody's returning to shore and home in *Jaws*, Neary's (Richard Dreyfus) entrance into the Mothership in *Close Encounters of the Third Kind*, Luke's (Mark Hamill) destruction of the Death Star at the end of *Star Wars Episode IV*, Sarah Connor's crossing of the border into Mexico in *The Terminator* (this vehicular movement is reprised in the final scene of *Terminator 2: Judgment Day*), Neo's resurrection as the virtual One, constituting an actual/virtual rebirth in *The Matrix*, Jake Sully's (Sam Worthington) resurrection (and animation into action) in the final shot in *Avatar*, and so on. The animation of High Concept cinema through action effaces the image of inaction intrinsic to the preceding New American Cinema of conceptual ambiguity, political engagement and aesthetic realism. High Concept cinema is necessarily experienced as action – as movement and volition. European and American modernist cinema – or what Bordwell refers to as 'art cinema' – is necessarily experienced as inaction, stasis, contingency, unknowingness, and trauma.

The High Concept film, rather than conceptualized as a non-narrative cinema, or a cinema of simplistic, dumbed-down stories and characters (as has often been the case),[81] returns to studio cinema the image of action.[82] In *Jaws*, the image of action is bereft of the affective stasis of cinema's modernity evident in *Nashville*, released in the same year. Equally, in the contemporary studio system, Nolan's *Inception* is, in my estimation, a High Concept film not because of its majestic technological spectacle (though spectacle, in the wake of the exponential increase in effects production in the 1970s and 1980s, was the natural outcome of the High Concept aesthetic), but because Cobb's rejection of the outcome of the spinning totem is an *action*, a movement toward fulfilment and completion. The image of action of High Concept cinema thus serves a *conceptual* rather than purely narrative itinerary. The conceptual itinerary is necessarily archetypal and projected as universal; it remains the tacitly accepted studio position that films should be

---

[81] Wood, 'Papering the Cracks'; Andrew Britton, 'Blissing Out'; David Thomson, 'Who Killed the Movies', *Esquire* 126, no. 6 (1996), 56–63.

[82] Of course, a studio cinema comprised of an image of action exists throughout the New American Cinema. I am certainly not suggesting that the New American Cinema is bereft of narratives and images of action, or of a physical and existential progress toward resolution; such images are displayed in films as diverse as *Kelly's Heroes*, *Diamonds Are Forever* (1971) and *Enter the Dragon* (1973). Yet I agree with Biskind that *Jaws* 'changed the business forever', effectively illuminating a disambiguated narrative toward resolution and a spectacle image founded upon excess. Clearly, the High Concept cinema that evolves from 1975 is animated by new technologies, new aesthetic systems, and new affective modalities of the image, which I explore at length in the following three chapters.

accessible and universal in their facilitation.[83] This is simply to suggest that the affective register of the High Concept film has little at all to do with the radicalism of story and character so visible in the New American Cinema: narrative progression that stalls in Act Two, ontological determinism that materializes as indeterminism in a Third Act sleight of hand (*The Conversation*), the movement toward closure that is interrupted and recast as radical irresolution. Rather, the High Concept aesthetic is a conceptual framework that provides a foundation for the expression of the image of action. To build upon Wyatt's model, High Concept cinema is not purely a commodity aesthetic, nor a style integral to 'film's operation (and marketing)',[84] but a particular relationship of the moving image to a conceptual blueprint.[85]

High concept, effect, spectacle

For theorists of the blockbuster, or what I have addressed as High Concept cinema, the display of the image is a critical locus. Wood devotes a subsection of his article on 'Fantasy and Ideology in the Reagan Era' to 'Special Effects'. The special effect is the 'essence of Wonderland today … The unemployment lines in the world outside may get longer and longer, we may even have to go out and join them, but if capitalism can still throw out entertainments such as *Star Wars* … the system must be basically okay, right?'[86] The polemic aside, Wood is correct to identify the image of effects as central to the formation of a spectacle cinema. It is also integral to the aesthetic tradition in which American cinema manifests as concept and commodity

---

[83] This conclusion is based on a series of interviews conducted with practitioners currently active in the studio system, including Richard King (sound designer/editor, *The Dark Knight Rises*), John Lee (Assistant Editor, *The Dark Knight Rises*) and Rick Sayre (Senior Animator, Pixar Studios). See also Martin Flanagan, '"Get Ready For Rush Hour": The Chronotope in Action', in *Action and Adventure Cinema*, ed. Yvonne Tasker (New York: Routledge, 2004), 114.

[84] Wyatt, 23.

[85] I read High Concept more specifically in terms of the formation of genres of action, spectacle and adventure. While I agree with Wyatt that High Concept might be usefully applied to several genres, including the musical and romantic comedy of the late 1970s and 1980s (for example, *Grease* [1978] or *Flashdance* [1983]), the impact of High Concept on the industrial and aesthetic life of Hollywood is more obviously apparent in action and spectacle genres. For a reading of the distinction between action and adventure, see Yvonne Tasker, 'Introduction: Action and Adventure Cinema', in *Action and Adventure Cinema*, ed. Yvonne Tasker (New York: Routledge, 2004), 7–8. See also Bordwell, *The Way Hollywood Tells It*, for a similar formulation: 'Not all blockbusters are action movies, and not all action movies becomes blockbusters. Still, the action picture … remains the exemplar of the box-office triumphs of modern Hollywood' (113). I would trace this modernity through action to *Jaws* and its invigoration of an image of action.

[86] Wood, 'Papering the Cracks', 207.

object. Wood advances beyond Thomson's reductive reading of spectacle's artificial images[87] to critically center 'two levels of magic' in spectacle cinema: 'the diegetic wonders within the narrative and the extradiegetic magic of Hollywood ... The technology on screen, the technology off. Spectacle – the sense of reckless prodigal extravagance, no expense spared – is essential.'[88]

For Wood, a very astute Marxist critic of cinema, spectacle is an aberrant commodity of a hegemonic industry. Against the radical ambiguity of the New American Cinema, the commodity is conceptualized and historicized as regression. The spectacle of effects is either a nostalgia mode, or an amnesiac illusion.[89] Such accounts present a circumscribed history of what spectacle cinema *cannot* express: the radical irresolution of the modernist journey, the subject trapped in the 'affection image', the image and narrative of radical ambiguity, etc. But such readings, while serving noble purposes, miss what is, in very real terms, before the spectator's eyes: the image. It is precisely here that we encounter what Gunning perceived in his examination of early cinema: an image that exhibited itself *as spectacle*, that shocked its spectator, that drew a gasp from its audience. Is this not precisely what the spectator seeks upon confronting the contemporary 'event film', the effects spectacle that seeks to advance the technological, aesthetic and affective parameters of the image?

The influence of the Frankfurt School, particularly Adorno's 'consciousness as conformity', is evident throughout Wood's writing. Yet inadvertently, his acknowledgement of the spectacularity of effects, of the image of scale in production, presents an entry point into an analysis of the neglected image of spectacle in contemporary, studio-produced, cinema. For later theorists of spectacle cinema, or the neo-baroque aesthetic – Ndalianis, Bukatman, Cubitt – spectacle is merely a dimension of the image of cinema, whether of Gunning's early cinema that materializes in fits and starts, or Rombes's blockbuster film that attains the technological pinnacle of image production. Ironically here, a Marxist critic of the American cinema of the 1980s theorizes a mode of cinema in which the spectator is necessarily astonished by an image proffered in its purest commodity form. If High Concept cinema displays the image of action, the exponential increase in effects production industrializes a spectacle aesthetic intrinsic to High Concept's narratives, characters and image compositions.

---

[87] Thomson, 'Who Killed the Movies.'

[88] Wood, 'Papering the Cracks', 207.

[89] See, for example, Britton. For an influential analysis of High Concept's nostalgia aesthetic, see Fredric Jameson, 'Postmodernism and Consumer Society', in *The Cultural Turn: Selected Writings on the Postmodern 1983–1998* (London: Verso, 1998), 106.

The ontology of the spectacle image

Industrial Light and Magic: what is evoked by special effects sequences is often a hallucinatory excess as narrative yields to kinetic spectatorial experience … Cinematic images are indeed full and superbly weird.[90]

Inherent in the transformation of a Parisian street in *Inception* is the imprint of the technology of High Concept cinema – the medium and aesthetic framework that creates the spectacle image and exhibits it on a screen. Technology produces a trace imprint of itself, visible in the presence of the impossible image that springs up unexpectedly in so much spectacle cinema. The spectacle image is not a transmission, but a coming-into-being of a unique object infused with the presence of its technological brushstroke.[91] When the street moves in *Inception*, when the roads fold in upon each other and buildings seek new forms of visual expression, the image of cinema moves in its history, and in its relation to the past. This is no different from what Vertov captured in *Man With a Movie Camera* in 1929: filming the world not only shifted our perception of the world, but manifested it in ways we could not have imagined. And with each new cinematic articulation, the image of the world, and the image of cinema, *shifts*.

For Vertov, the medium was technologized – the camera *was* cinema, and cinematic perception, the Kino-eye, was mechanical.[92] *Man With a Movie Camera* remains one of the profound expressions of metacinema, the world imbued through the technology of film. For Vertov, a trace of technology in the image was not enough; the camera is a living object in the sense in which it is animated by the life of a machine technology. But even technology was merely one internal process of the creation of the cinematic image. For Vertov, as for Eisenstein, cinema was equally montage. Montage was as integral to cinema as the technology of the camera. Bazin later championed a freer mode of sequence composition, an image in depth and duration, yet for Bazin, Eisenstein and Vertov, film art was medium-specific; it made

---

[90] Bukatman, *Matters of Gravity*, 113.

[91] I am ironically appropriating Jameson's use of 'brush-stroke' to lament a realist modernism that no longer speaks to, and affects, the postmodern subject. As I am wholeheartedly immersed in the postmodern cultural imaginary, I can only but argue that the technology of effects cinema is no less an expressive aesthetic, no less artistic, no less individualized and communicative, no less affective in its import on the screen than the deeply affective modernist realism of a Joyce, or Mahler, or indeed, a work by Dziga Vertov. For Jameson's reading of postmodernity's 'waning of affect', see Fredric jameson, *Postmodernism, or the Cultural Logic of Late Capitalism* (Durham: Duke University Press, 1992), 15–19.

[92] See Manovich, *The Language of New Media*, xxix.

sense only in terms of the unique properties of the technology and aesthetic system of moving images. And beyond technology and image aesthetics, cinema provided an experience of modernity that gave life to new modes of experiencing the world, new modes of subjectivity, and a new affective relationship to the objective world. Early cinema was infected with the technology of modernity just as modernity was infected with a technology of a new visuality.[93] This, in spite of the awkwardness of identifying the originary impulse in cinema, was there at the beginning: technology, aesthetic language, sensation and affect.

I concur with Gunning that the early cinema shares a great deal in common with contemporary film practice. In the following three chapters, I trace three interrelated components of the spectacle image. In Chapter Five, I examine the increasing technologizing of the medium; I argue that the spectacle image and the cinema of effects manifest as a technological object through the formation of Industrial Light and Magic in 1975, and the turn to images of the 'technological sublime', to employ Bukatman's very useful terminology. In Chapter Six, I examine the neo-baroque aesthetic intrinsic to spectacle production; here I focus on stylistic expressivity in the cinema of Steven Spielberg. I argue that Spielberg pioneers a mode of High Concept image formation that functions explicitly as spectacle, or 'effect-oriented' cinema. In Chapter Seven, I theorize the affective properties of the spectacle image, examining the actual and virtual body as object in the cinema of James Cameron.

---

[93] See Murray Pomerance, 'Introduction', in *Cinema and Modernity*, ed. Murray Pomerance (New Brunswick: Rutgers University Press, 2006), 12: 'By invoking modernity, one has not said everything there is to say about cinema, any more than by invoking cinema, one has not said everything there is to be said about modernity. Yet without cinema, modernity is unthinkable; and without modernity, cinema would not exist.'

5

The technological image

Between reality, illusion and effect

Basically, special effects, whether optical or physical, are concerned with creating illusions on the screen.[1]

This chapter concerns a transformation, and exponential increase, in the production of mechanical, optical and digital effects in American High Concept cinema from 1975. In mapping this transformation, the chapter attempts to conceptualize the industrialization of a 'cinema of effect'. I turn from narrative to focus again on the image of cinema, and in particular, on the technology of production. I ask simply: what is the relationship of technology to the cinema of effect? 'Effect' here connotes more than merely reproduction, or the mirrored reflection of the real. The screened image and its apparatus, is, as Cubitt notes, a special effect.[2] The great Neorealist films, if we are to treat that aesthetic designation through Bazin, or Deleuze, or Bondanella, present images of a world effected by the apparatus of cinema. The apparatus of the moving image accompanies the evolution of perception and affect such that, as Vertov so elegantly displays in *Man With a Movie Camera*, perception no longer bears the trace of the subjective eye, but of the eye of cinema as a technological instrument.

For Brosnan, cinema's special effect is illusory. It is primarily concerned with obscuring the technological material that produces the image. The image, materialized on screen, seeks to render invisible the technology of effects production.[3] Thus, the accomplishment of a radically new special

---

[1] John Brosnan, *The Story of Special Effects in the Cinema* (London: Abacus, 1977), 7.

[2] Cubitt, *The Cinema Effect*, 1. Cubitt works through Metz's framework of the image as produced effect.

[3] See David Hutchison, *Film Magic: The Art and Science of Special Effects* (London: Simon & Schuster, 1987), xviii: 'The contradiction lies in the fact that everyone in the audience knows that

effect in Kubrick's *2001: A Space Odyssey* is astonishing: '*2001* created such a vivid and unforgettable impression of man in space that the actual moon landing, which took place in the following year after the picture's release, seemed an anti-climax.'[4] But while Brosnan is fascinated by Wally Veevers's use of models and miniatures and, like many other commentators on *2001*, is in awe of Douglas Trumbull's slit-scan device that 'opens' space and time,[5] for Brosnan the astonishment of the image does not derive from its technological creation, but from the illusion that the image manifests beyond technology, in a sense, of its own creation. When confronted with the image of a space station in rhythmic rotation, openly displayed against a complex matte background, the spectator stares in astonishment at the screen, wondering: how can such an image be *real*? How can it have materialized before me (figures 5.1–5.3)? Beyond the real, beyond the technology of production, the sublime effect astonishes the spectator through its unfathomable and uncontainable illusionistic properties.

In discussing Emmerich's *Independence Day* (1996), Cubitt searches for the affective material of the sublime image in its capacity to exceed the medium of cinema. Emmerich's image of effect 'throws before the audience the specificity of the medium as well as a terminal form of illusion that succeeds by exceeding the apparent limits of the medium.'[6] This is a highly provocative reading of the image of special effects. The image is at once greater than the medium (illusionistic) and circumscribed by it (subjected to the continued presence of the medium in the display of the image). But either way, the medium is subjugated to a functional role in the display of the image of effect; it facilitates the display of the sublime image. And thus, in affective terms, the image functions to efface the spectre of the medium that produces it. In Cubitt's model, Kubrick's revolving space station displays the sublimity of its form, the materialization of which is construed as a process of *mediation*: 'This is why effects must always be cutting edge', suggests Cubitt.[7] They must be of the here and now because they manifest the outcome of the latest image technologies that efface the imprint of technological creation – motion-controlled cinematography (*2001: A Space Odyssey*; *Star Wars Episode IV*), digital effects simulation (*The Abyss*; *Terminator 2: Judgment Day*; *Jurassic Park*), motion-capture (*Avatar*;

---

the destruction isn't real, that it is an illusion … but we delight in the completeness and believability of the illusion.' Here the contradiction in Hutchison's position remains unresolved: in what sense is the image of the destruction of the Earth in *2012* (2009) *unreal*? Of course, when I exit the theatre, the Earth remains intact; yet in what sense was the image of its destruction illusory?

[4] Brosnan, 153.

[5] Brosnan, 157.

[6] Sean Cubitt, 'Introduction. Le Réel, c'est le l'impossible: The Sublime Time of Special Effects', *Screen* 40, no. 2 (1999), 123–30.

[7] Cubitt, 'Introduction', 129.

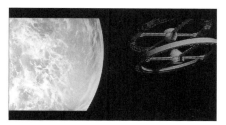

FIGURES 5.1–3 *Kubrick's groundbreaking mechanical visual effects:* 2001: A Space Odyssey *(1968).*

Rise of the Planet of the Apes, 2011; The Adventures of Tintin, 2011). The technical virtuosity of such effects merely displays to the spectator the image that exceeds the capacities of the medium to render a sublime effect.

Cubitt thus presents an intriguing notion of precisely how a cinema of effect functions affectively, and his theory of a temporality of effects cinema, or a temporality outside of progressive narrative, is provocative. Illusionistic effects 'lie athwart the narration, function[ing] as fetishistic interruptions'.[8] Clearly Cubitt's endeavour to account for the affect of the cinema *of effect* is a critical contribution to a theory of spectacle, acknowledging the incompatibility of effect and representation. Yet I remain uncomfortable with – and unconvinced by – the appropriation of the dominant discourse on effects theory, which is to regard the special effect of cinema – whether the Welles/Toland conflation of real and artificial in the image of Xanadu that opens *Citizen Kane*, or Kubrick's mechanical visual effects in *2001: A Space Odyssey* – as an *illusionistic* material. Illusion implies a deterioration of an *a priori* real, and re-inscribes a teleological itinerary of the image to attain the desired end point of representation – to make the image into the semblance of the real, or a mimetic object. As I have argued, the autonomous image *exceeds* representation, and in that display of excess we must seek the location of the 'ineffable' not in some projected sublimity, or representation thrown into crisis,[9] or in the inherent 'mystery' of the special effect that materializes as

---

[8] Cubitt, 'Introduction', 129.
[9] Cubitt, 'Introduction', 130.

magic, but in the technology that builds the impossible structures of contemporary effects images. For Cubitt, 'speaking the ineffable' is an appearance, a projection out of the ontological limitations of the medium. But in projecting the image beyond the medium, Cubitt recuperates effect as an illusion toward an encounter with an *a priori* real: a referent in flux, and in crisis. Contrary to Cubitt, or Brosnan, I locate the ineffable at the source of the technology of image production.

If the special effect presents as illusion, the screen is merely a site of manifestation of the real – to employ Baudrillard's useful schema in *Precession of the Simulacra*. Then, deferring the real, the screen potentially manifests a subjectively imagined, interior fantasy; and in final, absolute, destructive deferment, the screen manifests what Baudrillard calls the simulacrum, the pure effacement of the real.[10] But in such a conceptual model, surely the special effect can only ever be the paltry reproduction (if momentarily astonishing in sublime ineffability) of a once-authentic object (the real) that metamorphoses into pure simulation. Surely this is what Cameron means when he suggests that the purpose of special effects is to take 'these images in our minds … and get them onto the screen',[11] conforming to Baudrillard's second order of simulacra. 'The challenge is two-fold,' says Cameron. 'The wizards have to create the hardware and the software to realize the images; and the clients, the storytellers, have to come up with ideas worthy of these new techniques.'[12] For Cameron, effects are wizardry of a sort, and effects production is merely the imprint upon a screen of an image that was created in the mind of the artist/storyteller. The image in original form is pure and untainted; in technologized reproduction, the effects artist seeks to obscure, distract, distort and obfuscate the presence of effects technology – in effect, to efface the imprint of technology in the creation of the image. The image of effect, in Cameron, must display the inherent 'truth' of the real as illusion.[13]

I find Cameron's language revealing: the effects pioneer – for example, a Stan Winston or John Gaeta – is a wizard. The wizard is, for Cameron, a

---

[10] Baudrillard, *Simulacra and Simulation*, 6–7.

[11] Cameron, 'Effects Scene', 5.

[12] Cameron, 'Effects Scene', 5.

[13] Appropriately, a traditional filmmaker such as Christopher Nolan espouses the same antagonism toward the technological manifestation of special effects: 'The thing with computer-generated imagery is that it's an incredibly powerful tool for making better visual effects. But I believe in an absolute difference between animation and photography. However sophisticated your computer-generated imagery is, if it's been created from no physical elements and you haven't shot anything, it's going to feel like animation.' For Nolan, the overarching purpose of cinematic special effects is thus to 'fool the audience into seeing something seamless'. See Jeffrey Ressner, 'The Traditionalist: An Interview With Christopher Nolan', Director's Guild of America Interviews, Spring 2012, http://www.dga.org/Craft/DGAQ/All-Articles/1202-Spring–2012/DGA-Interview-Christopher-Nolan.aspx [accessed March 18, 2012].

magician, the possessor of a supernatural talent to create. Yet the wizard is also a conjuror or trickster, the illusionistic artist nearer in spirit to the nineteenth-century magician[14] than the practitioner of industrialized effects in contemporary studio production. How could one possibly describe the effect of *The Matrix*'s bullet-time as wizardry? For Gaeta, bullet-time is a radical intrusion into the ontology of cinema (and narrative) time-progression.[15] Gaeta's conceptual and methodological framework for the bullet-time image is created within a technological simulation.[16] The image thus materializes only as technologized reproduction, effacing the object real while displaying its technological material. Cameron's distinction between the effects practitioner (wizard) and the auteur-director (storyteller) makes little sense in an age in which the image bears the trace of a synthetic, technological material. The traditional auteur – Cameron's designation of 'storyteller' – is an ephemeral figure, abstracting from the hardware and software of technology to fashion images that are original, and maintain their virtuosity only in the mind. The fate of the storyteller-artist 'will depend on our mastery of technology'.[17] But consider Gaeta's rhetoric of a *creative* technologized production: 'The Wachowski brothers, myself and a spectrum of talented people tried pushing shot design through an emerging new paradigm dubbed Virtual Cinematography.'[18] The paradigm here is dislocated from Cameron's purity of the imagined image. The paradigm, in effect, emerges *out of technology*. The creative agent (surely artist is anachronistic) pushes the image through a virtual (technologized) itinerary. The filmmaker – or storyteller, if that is preferred – cannot experience, perceive or imagine the itinerary of the bullet-time image, or the image of the recreated ocean liner in *Titanic* (1997). Such images of effect are, in a very real sense, imagined through technology.

In this chapter and the two chapters that follow it, I attempt to overturn a number of orthodoxies surrounding the cinema of effect. First: that cinematic effect is a mode of illusionism. I have argued throughout this book that the film image is necessarily a synthetic production of the real; it must bear a trace of the real, as Bazin tells us, yet it is not, in image form, 'reality'. Perhaps this

---

[14] For a discussion of illusionistic practices and magic displays, see Andrew Darley, *Visual Digital Culture: Surface Play and Spectacle in New Media Genres* (London: Routledge, 2000), 40–2. See also Bukatman, *Matters of Gravity*, 81–8.

[15] Isaacs, *Toward a New Film Aesthetic*, 142–7.

[16] For an examination of Gaeta's method, and the wider implications of the use of digital simulation software, see Lev Manovich, 'Image Future', *Animation: An Interdisciplinary Journal* 1, no. 1 (2006), 26–31.

[17] Cameron, 'Effects Scene', 5.

[18] Quoted in Marco Trezzini and Danica Gianola, 'When Cinema Meets VR – John Gaeta Talks About *Speed Racer*', *VRMAG* 30 (2008), http://www.vrmag.org/speedracer/ [accessed March 31, 2012].

is to fall into a semantic muddle, distinguishing aesthetic realism from philo-sophical truth, yet the claims of realism on the spectator permit a complex register of unrealistic image itineraries: image effects. Welles's opening shot in *Touch of Evil*, bearing the signature of the complex sequence shot, is no more realistic in its movement itinerary than one of Busby Berkeley's orches-trated numbers in *The Gold Diggers of 1933* (1933). Welles's shot remains a pinnacle of the classical image of excess for its lengthy duration, functioning not as a barometer of realism, but as a gesture toward a baroque cinematic image so cavalierly exhibited in the Hollywood cinema of the late 1950s and 1960s. How then can a special effect – the stop-motion animated *King Kong* (1933) (figure 5.4), or the stop-motion animated ED–209 in Verhoeven's *Robocop* (1987) (figure 5.5) – be *merely* the illusion (and mediation, insofar as mediation functions to transmit material) of a prior, self-contained and self-animating image? There is an ontological space that opens up between the imagined image (a towering ape, or a military robot-machine) and the technological animation of the image on screen. Effects represent a form of technological life-giving, or life-animating, to the image. Cholodenko says it most explicitly in his examination of Spielberg's cinema of effect in *Jurassic Park*: 'the history of special effects … is the history of animation as the mechanism for the incorporation of the special effect in the cinema.'[19]

Second: I argue that the technologized image is necessarily an object in a process of production rather than reproduction. I argue that the image of cinema is the actualization of a technological process, whether the technology of digitization, stop-motion animation, or the elegance of mechanical effects in Kubrick's *2001: A Space Odyssey*.

Third: I argue that the effects artist (effects practitioner, designer, technician, or director-storyteller) is necessarily *in collaboration with* the material technology of image production. The medium functions as a technology of perception and affect; the technician produces out of the raw technology of the medium. This is a critical formulation because it recasts the ineffable image of cinema as the actual image-object of a cinema technology. Post-structuralist semiotics has emphasized the autonomy of the medium and its technology for some time, yet theories of cinema effect remain affiliated to a traditional and romantic notion of the image as snapshot of a pre-existing materiality.

Fourth: I argue that technology is a medium, but that technology transmits more than the screened image. Technology creates at the site

---

[19] Alan Cholodenko, 'Objects in Mirror Are Closer Than They Appear: The Virtual Reality of *Jurassic Park* and Jean Baudrillard', in *Jean Baudrillard: Art and Artefact*, ed. Nicholas Zurbrugg (London: Sage, 1998), 68.

FIGURES 5.4–5 *Technological animation in classical and new Hollywood:* King Kong *(1933) and* Robocop *(1987).*

of image development, digital simulation, production and post-production. Further, I argue that technology leaves behind an imprint of itself on the screen (akin to Bazin's trace of the real), which is best described as technology's synthetic material and processes. This is why technology presents as a fetishistic object in so much spectacle cinema; the sublime image draws its power from the display of new technologies, new technological uses, and new creative possibilities for imagining the world. The display of the image of technological effect is thus a revelation of the capacity of technology to create. Rather than a deterioration of the real, the image of effect represents a self-reflexive display of technology's creative material. The spectator experiences the thrill of the imprint (a displaced image) of technology in the revelation of the shark in *Jaws* (figure 5.6), Lucas's model of a space station in *Star Wars Episode IV* (5.07), the extreme wide-shot of the interior of an aircraft hangar in *Close Encounters of the Third Kind* (figure 5.8), or, more humbly, the fetishistic properties of surveillance instrumentation in television's *24* (figure 5.9).

The imprint of technology: On early cinema (Vertov) and late cinema (Spielberg)

The rise of the machine and its transformation of the human environment, as well as the rise of the masses, carried both apocalyptic and millennial possibilities – the possibilities of destruction often heralding the possibilities of renewal. As the harbinger of something new, something transformative, cinema, like other aspects of modern life, sparked an ambivalent reaction among not only artists but also intellectuals and politicians. Cinema, both

FIGURE 5.6–9 *The technological image in High Concept production:* Jaws *(1975),* Star Wars Episode IV *(1977),* Close Encounters of the Third Kind *(1977),* 24 *(2001–10).*

as a practice and as a force that was understood in a variety of ways, played a central role in the culture of modernity.[20]

Man With a Movie Camera proposes an untamed, and apparently endless, unwinding of techniques, or, to use contemporary language, 'effects', as cinema's new way of speaking.[21]

In the previous chapter, I discussed the unique spectacle properties of *Inception*; there is a radical cinematic beauty to that film's mindscapes. Ariadne's cathedrals of the mind require the elegant assemblage of techno-logical material: the physicality of a set, the interior of the frame, and in simulation, the ephemera of digital traces of shapes and forms, resembling reality and yet partaking of a substance quite apart from it. But it is in *The Prestige* that Nolan most effectively metaphorizes the image of technology. The film projects the spectator into the city of early modernity (London), which is at the time enraptured by the spectacle of new technology. Angier (Hugh Jackman) and Borden (Christian Bale) are magicians; each is also a trickster (Borden is an identical twin). As in *Inception*, Nolan is specifically attuned to the individual's capacity to create through technology. In *The*

---

[20] Tom Gunning, 'Modernity and Cinema: A Culture of Shocks and Flows', in *Cinema and Modernity*, ed. Murray Pomerance (New Brunswick: Rutgers University Press, 2006), 302.
[21] Lev Manovich, *The Language of New Media* (Cambridge: MIT Press, 2001), 11.

Prestige, creative illusionism materializes through the industrial technology of modernity;[22] in *Inception*, new technology allows the mind to synthetically formulate worlds.

The technologized images of modernity in *The Prestige* recall experiments with cinema and its image of the late nineteenth and early twentieth centuries. Angier's fascination with the new science is akin to the account of society's fascination with the moving image: 'The cinematograph reigns in the city, reigns over the earth … The cinematograph has crossed the borders of reality.'[23] Early cinema, and its protocinematic models, the Panoroma and Diorama, provides 'apparatical extensions of the spatial flânerie through the arcades.'[24] For Friedberg, modernity's technology, and its production through industrialized processes, provides new ways of seeing and engaging the architectural, social and public spaces of the city. But while early cinema, such as Méliès or Lumière, presents the 'spectacle of modernity' (including the image's capacity for novelty illusions), it remains for Gunning the experience of an illusion. Gunning's contention that early cinema has been 'theorized under the hegemony of narrative films' is no doubt valid. But I would add that the discourse of cinema's image of attraction (the exhibitionist image) equally marginalizes, or indeed renders invisible, the material of technology integral to early cinema's image production. For Gunning, the images of Lumière or Méliès are 'fascinating because of their illusory power'.[25] And while Lumière's image of the arrival of a train is a primal engagement beneath story, beneath narrative, the incredulity of the spectator is toward the strangeness of the *image* as illusion. Of course, Gunning's attention to the detail of exhibition is a landmark development in the analysis of the early film image, yet his focus is rarely explicitly attuned to the cinema apparatus and the imprint of the technology of image production on the screen. Could we not equally say that the experience of cinema in its early years was in some sense an experience *of technology*, and of a technological creation intrinsic to modernity's industrial processes? Could an early spectator experience a moving image through the *Cinématographe* in the same way that a citizen of modernity experienced *motion* in an automobile, or labour through the machinic processes of a production line (figure 5.10)?

---

[22] I would distinguish creative illusionism from Cubitt's reading of the neo-baroque tendency toward illusion as all-encompassing, and thus terminal. Of Angier's death, Cubitt writes: 'Without that reality, the reality of the self, what meaning can his death provide him with?' Yet I would argue that the spectator remains unaffected by this existential (and ontological) rabbit-hole of Nolan's cinema. See Sean Cubitt, 'The Supernatural in Neo-baroque Hollywood', in *Film Theory and Contemporary Hollywood Movies*, ed. Warren Buckland (London: Routledge, 2009), 59.
[23] Andrei Bely, cited in Gunning, 'Modernity and Cinema', 298.
[24] Anne Friedberg, *Window Shopping: Cinema and the Postmodern* (Berkeley: University of California Press, 1993), 90.
[25] Gunning, 'The Cinema of Attractions', 230.

FIGURE 5.10 *The experience of modernity: the production line in Chaplin's* Modern Times *(1936).*

Vertov's *Man With a Movie Camera*, read by Manovich as the 'guide to the language of new media', is exemplary for the production of the image as an imprint of a technological process. The film opens on a superimposed shot of a cameraman perched with a camera on top of a gigantic model of a camera; 'the camera, part of cinema's apparatus, becomes the main character'.[26] The image then moves into the space of a theatre, where Vertov's film will be exhibited to a mass audience. The first shot [2:45][27] displays the curtained screen and rows of seating; at 2:47, the image cuts to a reverse shot, displaying the point of projection of the finished film. Even in these early sequences, the image is exhibited as the technological creation of Vertov's camera. Vertov takes the technology of the apparatus – that captures, exposes, but also sequences (montage) and exhibits the image – to reconfigure the world of the organic eye through a cinematic perception. For Vertov, cinema's Kino-eye instantiates a mechanized perception.

At 3:00, Vertov superimposes an image of lights over a set of chimes, conflating two images in a uniquely cinematic synthesis (figure 5.11). A series of shots reveals the peripheral technologies of the apparatus, its exhibitionist tools, theatre seats, curtains, light coverings, and a barricade. At 3:08, the image cuts to a profile of the projector, openly displayed. It is, in Vertov's profile angle, a complex technological apparatus. The instrument is situated in an exhibitionist pose, its reels and knobs and intricate, once unfathomable technology now revealed to the spectator (figures 5.12–5.13). The sequence then moves to the performance (the exhibition of Vertov's film is no less than performance), revealing a theatre populated with spectators, and an orchestra that will accompany the image with sound.

The moment of revelation of the image of cinema – Vertov's Kino-eye capture of a cinematic space through a cinematic perception – is the

---

26 Manovich, *The Language of New Media*, 13.
27 Time-code references are to *Man With a Movie Camera* (DVD), Blackhawk Films Collection, 1998.

beginning of the film: the lavish raising of the curtain. Yet the moment is also, simultaneously, the coming to life of an inanimate technology. First, at 4:09, the trenchant beat of a cymbal simulates the sound of the mechanical ticking of a clock – the apparatus that is animated, as Manovich observes, by time. Then, at 4:41, the internal rods of the apparatus connect and illuminate the image (figure 5.14). The image (visual and aural) now springs to life, accompanied by the crescendo on the soundtrack. At 4:42, the image cuts to a profile of the projector and projectionist – the organic/technological synthesis/collaboration (figure 5.15). At 5:10, Vertov's cinematic perception of a Russian city and its people begins – exterior and interior of the cinematic frame are conflated, as are the instruments of the technological apparatus and human perception. The image in *Man With a Movie Camera*, birthed on the screen, is thus a triumph not only of a new mode of perception – a cinematic eye – but of the creative potential of the technology that brings cinema's image to life. This is a technological apparatus that indeed springs to life, grows legs, raises itself up from dormancy and walks across the screen (figures 5.16–5.18).

While Vertov's Kino-eye 'combined an aesthetic concept of documentary (unstaged film) with an ideological attitude toward art in general',[28] Petric is less than explicit when it comes to the impact of cinema technology on this ideologized perception. If the camera 'was a weapon in the ideological battle',[29] it was a technological instrument that divested the subject of the burden to perceive ideological 'truth' without mechanistic perception. The subject in Vertov thus perceives not only the world in a radically new and unimaginable way, but perceives through the technological apparatus of cinema, including the camera and its instruments, but also the technology of film language – for Vertov (as for Eisenstein), montage. This is why montage, in Vertov, is more appropriately thought of as a technology than a language.

Petric describes the famous editing sequence in *Man With a Movie Camera* in the following way:

She [Vertov's wife] does exactly what Vertov described – from miles of film strips, she culls the good pices [sic], those which will allow her 'to organize a good film.' After classifying 'the good film material' (arranged on the shelves above her editing table), she measures each shot and matches it with the others in various ways, building up the film's structure as a mason does by laying stones and bricks to make a house or oven. Throughout the film, Vertov continuously points to the thematic classification of shots into groups and sub-groups (which Svilova separates in many boxes, each

---

[28] Petric, 'Dziga Vertov as Theorist', 30.
[29] Petric, 'Dziga Vertov as Theorist', 30.

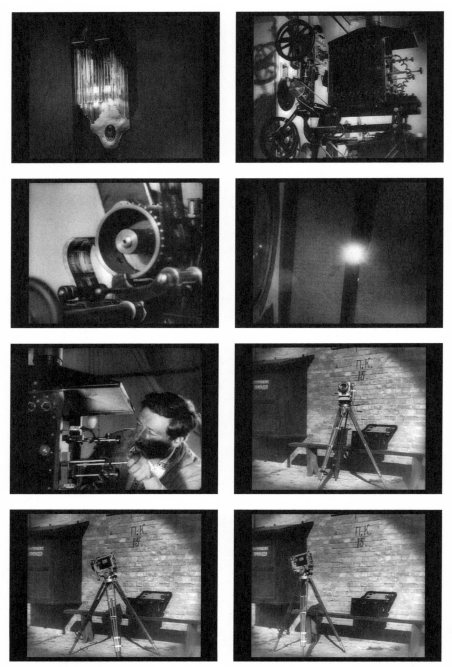

FIGURES 5.11–18 *The technological apparatus coming to life:* Man With a Movie Camera *(1929).*

related to a topic). By showing this repeatedly, he gives the viewer an insight into the very process of making a film.[30]

Petric is correct to emphasize the sequence as a self-reflexive commentary on the process of filmmaking. The transition from a still to moving image is Vertov's indication that the inanimate image is animated through a technologized movement; after all, 'there is no such thing as a moving image. No means has ever been devised of continually recording the sequence of changing light over an extended period of time'.[31] At 20:49, the radical mechanization of cinematic perception is displayed in two shots superimposed, both on a sharp tilt, veering away from an imaginary line that divides them. The film then moves into a series of frenetic sequences, capturing moving vehicles in profile, head-on, or from beneath. There is a gradual building of momentum, accompanied by the soundtrack. Then, suddenly, at 23:28, there is a pause in visual and sound. A galloping horse is stilled in mid-stride (figure 5.19); the music on the soundtrack abruptly cuts out. A series of stills follows, enveloping the screen with a single frame to present the illusion of a moving image stilled. At 23:51, the still of a child is revealed as a frame of film in series, each imperceptibly changed through infinitesimal movement (figure 5.20).

In the film's opening sequence, Vertov reveals the technological apparatus of cinema – projector, projectionist, theatre; it is, in production jargon, a cinematic reveal. Now, at 24:06, he reveals the editing suite. The film is spun onto a reel, examined, cut, glued, discarded, kept, etc. The processes do not 'reproduce' the image of Vertov's city, but produce (or create) an image through technology of a city radically divorced from its prior model. This is what Petric fails to emphasize in his reading of the editing process: that montage is a synthesis of the image captured through technology, and assembled through the technology of editing. It is thus not only Vertov's wife that 'organizes' the film, but the technology itself that reads the raw material of the city and establishes the binding mechanisms through the technology of montage. The image is the outcome of a technological process. Surely this is the point Vertov makes in bringing technology and the subject together in the final sequence of the film. While Manovich is correct to read Vertov's

---

[30] Petric, 'Dziga Vertov as Theorist', 34.

[31] Leo Enticknap, *Moving Image Technology* (London: Wallflower Press, 2004), 6. The early image was conventionally projected at 16 frames per second; current cinema practice (celluloid and digital) captures movement conventionally at 24 frames per second. Peter Jackson is currently in post-production on *The Hobbit*, captured at 48 frames per second, which is, even in early exhibition of its images, described as HD video rather than cinema's 24 frames per second texture. See Carolyn Giardina, 'Peter Jackson Responds to *Hobbit* Footage Critics, Explains 48-Frames Strategy', *The Hollywood Reporter*, 28 April 2012, http://www.hollywoodreporter.com/news/peter-jackson-the-hobbit-cinemacon–317755 [accessed May 18, 2012].

FIGURES 5.19–20 *The Technology of Montage:* Man With a Movie Camera *(1929).*

experiment as metatext, often neglected in analyses of *Man With the Movie Camera* is the indelible imprint of the technological apparatus on the image captured through Vertov's camera, cut by Vertov's wife, and exhibited in a theatre.

Could we not say that cinema's image is imprinted with its technological past, the itinerary that brought the image from its object-model into the cinematic form? That even as Vertov's eye presents the world of a city and its people, that such a world is never merely the image through human perception, but bears the trace of the technological apparatus that brought it to life? What might be at stake in suggesting that an image bears the trace of its technology, as Bazin once argued that an image bore a trace of the real?

I would argue that the spectacle image is no less imbued with the presence of its technological history. Rombes's avant-garde image of the blockbuster displays the imprint of its technological creation, and we might similarly read Cubitt's 'cinema effect' as the imprint of a technological apparatus ,that presents both the sublime and terminally threatening spectacle image.[32] The special effect is not merely an illusionistic image, but represents the outcome of a technologized itinerary, in which the subject is in some sense divested of the pursuit of the aura of the object-real. The subject gazes in awe at the spectacle of the impossible image and perceives with increasing acuity the imprint of the technology of its creation.

A mid-Act One point in Spielberg's *Jurassic Park*, a narrative turning point indicated by the revelation of the spectacle image, comes in the digitized shape of a Brachiosaurus. Indeed, Spielberg initially captures our astonishment (a combination of fascination, awe, and fear of the unknown) with a reaction shot of Dr Grant (Sam Neill) prior to the revelation of the object of fascination (figure 5.21). As Dr Grant must steer Dr Sattler (Laura Dern) toward a contemplation of the impossible image of the dinosaur (literally

---

[32] Cubitt, 'Introduction', 128.

a turning of Dern's head), so Spielberg alters the experiential mode of the spectator, previously immersed in the narrative exposition, to a contemplation of the dinosaur. It is a liminal moment in cinema's history, at which point an image materializes on screen in dialectical relation to a past cinema, evolving the potentiality of the technological (digital) apparatus.

The sequence cuts to a wide shot to visually composite the image – now Grant and Sattler comprise only peripheral figures and the image-in-itself is revealed against the open backdrop (figure 5.22). The camera pans with the dinosaur, panning not with the personification of the animal as character, but with the animation of the image as a spectacle of vision and movement. The shot compositing Grant and Sattler into the wide frame encapsulated by the dinosaur has less to do with establishing the astonishment of the characters (this is now redundant) than with establishing the technologized parameters of the image – size, clarity, rhythmic cadence, indexicality. In this cinematic reveal in 1993, astonishment is a function of the movement of digital effects beyond the celluloid effects of the optical printer. The material of digitality is *present* in the image. Grant and Sattler are never granted a close-up that functions separately from the reaction to the image. Much as Nolan shoots the reconfiguration of a Paris street from the ground, a veritable worshipping of the image by Cobb, Spielberg brings the spectator into contemplation of the image of the dinosaur from the ground, emphasizing the impossible size of the object. The cut to a wide shot to conclude Spielberg's spectacle performance holds momentarily as the dinosaur rises onto two legs, screaming at the moment of its cinematic birth: and the digital image *poses* for the gaze of the astonished spectator (figure 5.23). This is a birth of a cinema technology as surely as it is the revelation of a cloning technology within the diegesis of the film.

Williams's score, not unlike the soundtrack that accompanies the birth of Vertov's cinematic perception, emphasizes the grandeur of the image – not as representation, but as creation, as the digital materiality of cinema. The score draws on a lexicon of spectacle images that resonate quite apart from narrative, images cut to music rather than character action – the strings that incrementally build the 'image' of a shark in *Jaws*, the grandeur of the entry of a space cruiser in *Star Wars Episode IV*, a bicycle circumventing the stars in *E.T.: The Extra-Terrestrial*.

The performance of this spectacle – inaugurating an evolution in visuality through image technology – is rhythmic, and integrated into the spectator's experience (and memory) of spectacle cinema. Bukatman's reading of the science fiction genre is entirely appropriate here: 'the effect is designed to be seen, and frequently the narrative will pause to permit the audience to

FIGURES 5.21–23 *Revelation of the technological image of cinema:* Jurassic Park *(1993).*

appreciate the technologies on display.'[33] The final cut in the *Jurassic Park* sequence is to the capitalist Gennaro (Martin Ferrero). Equally astonished at the presence of a new technology of spectacle, he murmurs: 'We're going to make a fortune with this place.' The dialectic at the heart of spectacle aesthetics is revealed here in the dual impulses of the creator's vision. Spielberg materializes as the artist of a digital age, a pioneer of the evolving cinematic image, yet a plier of old stories and old mythologies, inscribed by familiar narrative structures. This is Spielberg as the capitalist-auteur, who will indeed make a fortune through a rendition of a revolutionary digitally composited image, affirming the interrelatedness of technology, image and commodity in American High Concept cinema.

Could we conceptualize such images, through Vertov and Spielberg – one the pioneer of a cinema apparatus created out of film stock, requiring light and chemicals to react with emulsive agents, various tools and instruments of capture, editing and exhibition; and the other the creator of a then relatively new and untested digital image of mainstream industrial production – as the creative output of a technological perception, in which the effects practitioner is a storyteller, and in which the storyteller's perception is spun through the mechanical processes of celluloid or digital technology? These are images, I would argue, that not only leave behind a trace of the organic world – the perception of the human subject of the real – but leave a trace also of the synthetic material of its technological apparatus. This is why no special effect

---

[33] Bukatman, *Matters of Gravity*, 95.

in cinema is purely an illusion. Can we contemplate the image of Kubrick's revolving space station in *2001: A Space Odyssey* and *not* perceive the technological virtuosity in its form and movement? In the wake of the success of *Avatar*, Cameron suggested that 'ideally, technology is advanced enough to make itself go away. That's how it should work. All of the technology should wave its own wand and make itself disappear.'[34] But how can the technology of spectacle make itself disappear? The spectacle image *requires* the material trace of its technological creation. Cameron's position, that again inscribes the effects artist as a magician (the illusionist), serves an ideological agenda that translates the image of technology with increasing swiftness and efficacy into studio cinema's commodity object. Spielberg's image of a Brachiosaurus, attentive to its own spectacular form, displays not only the image of astonishment, but also the commoditization of a radically new image technology.

The technological image and its properties

Whose vision is it? It is the vision of a computer, a cyborg, an automatic missile. It is a realistic representation of human vision in the future, when it will be augmented by computer graphics and cleansed from noise. It is the vision of a digital grid. Synthetic, computer-generated imagery is not an inferior representation of reality, but a realistic representation of a different reality.[35]

Baudrillard describes a simulacral space in which the map overtakes the physical space, and in which the abstraction, say a film image, 'is no longer that of the map, the double, the mirror, or the concept'.[36] In this simple but ambitious move, Baudrillard opens the way to thinking through the image as more than referent. In Baudrillard, though there is a deep and unsettling pessimism in his theory of simulation, there is also the possibility to see something more in the image, to account for it in terms greater than merely its purpose to mediate the common perception of the world. The simulacral 'America', catalogued as a series of networks, provides the thrill of the image as something in excess of the ordinariness of the real.[37]

---

34 Cited in Michael E. Harkins, 'The Spectacle in 3-D: Is *Avatar* Really Something New?', *Depth of Field*, February 19, 2010, http://myportfolio.usc.edu/meharkin/2010/02/is_avatar_really_something_new_the_spectacle_in_3-d.html [accessed July 8, 2011].
35 Manovich, *The Language of New Media*, 8.
36 Baudrillard, *Simulacra and Simulation*, 1.
37 Jean Baudrillard, *America*, trans. Chris Turner (London: Verso, 1988). For an evocative description of America as simulacral network, see 53: 'LOS ANGELES FREEWAYS –

Of course cinema is a medium, and it should be described initially in such terms; cinema carries an image of some prior substance. This is Salt's formulation in his argument for a positivist/scientific mode of film analysis: 'the most useful basic way of regarding the medium … is as a more faithful or less faithful reproduction of audio-visual reality.'[38] But mediation, as I have argued, is not a pure transmission of raw material; it is, in creative construction, the object aestheticized.

The notion of a trace material within the image is thus a critical formulation in coming to terms with how the image functions as mimetic form. Cinema, whether digital or celluloid, cannot divest itself of the trace of the real; I'm yet to encounter an image that manifests outside of the ontological space constructed by Bazin in his writing. But could we not argue that, in addition to the trace of the real, the image, whether of celluloid or digital creation, bears a trace of a synthetic material, a technology, and that such a material equally represents an encounter with cinema's essential form?[39]

Such trace images are clearly manifest in contemporary digital cinema. The simulated image of Gaeta's bullet-time displays the capacity of the image to form, and reform, outside of a realist itinerary, bearing a trace of the simulated real (a synthetic reality). I was more recently confronted with the digital image of *Rise of the Planet of the Apes*, the motion-captured facial expression of Caesar the Ape (figure 5.24). The Weta Digital effects in the film are pioneering.[40] The image of the young ape, particularly in close-up, is astonishing. While several shots of movement through space are less successful as an affective image, Caesar's facial expression seemed, at least on my initial

---

Gigantic, spontaneous spectacle of automotive traffic. A total collective act, staged by the entire population, twenty-four hours a day. By virtue of the sheer size of the layout and the kind of complicity that binds this network of thoroughfares together, traffic rises here to the level of a dramatic attraction, acquires the status of symbolic organization.'

[38] Salt, *Film Style and Technology*, 24.

[39] Here I reflect in part on the work of Aylish Wood in a superb reading of the interface of technology in the creation of screened experience. While Wood builds on a discourse increasingly interested in how subjects are engaged in technologized encounters, I conceive the trace of the technology of cinema in a much more elemental way. In the sense in which Bazin perceives a presence of the object in its ontological index (the photograph), I perceive the possibility for the presence of technology, its raw material and capacity to effect the real. See Aylish Wood, *Digital Encounters* (New York: Routledge, 2007), esp. 18–41. For an influential analysis of manifestations of the technological interface, see N. Katherine Hayles, *How We Became Posthuman: Virtual Bodies in Cybernetics, Literature, and Informatics* (Chicago: University of Chicago Press, 1999).

[40] For a discussion of the development of Weta Digital, see Scott Essman, 'Has Weta Digital Taken the Visual Effects Lead?', *Below the Line: Voice of the Crew*, August 15, 2011, http://www.btlnews.com/crafts/visual-fx/has-weta-digital-taken-the-visual-effects-lead/ [accessed November 8, 2011].

viewing, more than real, partaking of that uncanny register that has become associated with digital image technology.[41]

Seated in the theatre, I felt oddly confronted by the actualization on screen of a pure digital creation. The ape was not 'present' in the image in the same way in which Kubrick's apes are present in the Dawn of Man sequence of *2001: A Space Odyssey*, yet Caesar bore the essential trace of cinema, whether a trace image of the real or a trace image of a technological simulation through digital mapping and motion capture. I engaged affectively in this image not as one engaged an embodied being, but as one engages a synthetic material displaying its marvelous technological properties.

Such arguments about the affect of the digital image have been present in film studies discourse for more than a decade.[42] Yet I would argue that the continued fascination with film's 'end' through digitization has drawn an artificial line between the synthetic material of digital images and the authentic material of celluloid. Andrew frames the argument in the following way:

At the birth of motion pictures and again in the transition to sound, inventors, producers, and critics held ideas that did not quite overlap. The same is doubtless true in our transition to the digital. Still, throughout these transitions, and across the entire history of the medium's existence, cinema has raised (and sometimes pressed) a claim about realism that no other art before it could make.[43]

Andrew is clearly correct: we must acknowledge the aesthetic, affective and ontological continuities between the image of celluloid and the image of digital technology. Low-end digital capture has established a renewed

---

[41] For a discussion of the 'Uncanny Valley', see Catrin Misselhorn, 'Empathy with Inanimate Objects', *Minds and Machines* 19 (2009), 345–59. Catrin provides an overview of the original theory proposed by Masahiro Mori (1970) and theorizes an intriguing register of perception called 'imaginative perception', which is for Catrin specifically engaged with an imagistic (pictorial) rather than linguistic representation (352–3).

[42] For a fascinating attempt to recast the digital object as other-than-cinema, see Vivian Sobchack, 'Nostalgia for a Digital Object', *Millenium Film Journal* 34 (1999), 4–23. Tafler describes technology's intrinsic capacity to transform the image, and the experience of that image: 'We continue to invent the cinema. As film becomes video becomes digital, the cinema remains a fluid vehicle, perpetually in process, unstable in its projection and reception.' See David Tafler, 'When Analogue Cinema Becomes Digital Memory ...', *Wide Angle* 21, no. 1 (1999), 182. For Tafler, the turn to digital creates an experimental *newness* that anticipates 'the complete devolution of the screen' (184). For Rodowick's provocative reading of a digital break from the past, see *The Virtual Life of Film*, 98.

[43] Andrew, *What Cinema Is*, xxv.

FIGURE 5.24 *Life-animating through motion-capture technology:* Rise of the Planet of the Apes *(2011).*

interest in avant-garde realism, and in cinema's potential 'humanisms'.[44] Ndalianis traces what she calls the 'spiritual presence of the technological' in the neo-baroque science fiction blockbuster, yet her exemplary reading is of a celluloid film, Spielberg's *Close Encounters of the Third Kind*. Here the spirit of technology imbues the image with its trace presence. Digitization has no doubt altered the image of cinema. It presents the possibilities of a radically simulated image itinerary in a film like *300* (2006). Yet the experience of the presence, or trace, of technology in the image is evident in both celluloid and digital formats. At the heart of spectacle cinema is the presence of an effects technology, and, simply put, such technologies are equally part of celluloid and digital image systems that form the connective tissue of a century of cinema's image creation: *The Ten Commandments* (1956), *The Birds* (1963), *2001: A Space Odyssey* (1968), *Star Wars Episode IV* (1977), *Close Encounters of the Third Kind* (1977), *Superman* (1978), *Star Trek: The Motion Picture* (1979), *Raiders of the Lost Ark* (1981), *Blade Runner* (1982), *The Terminator* (1984), *The Fly* (1986), *Total Recall* (1990), *Jurassic Park* (1993), *The Matrix* (1999), *Transformers* (2005), *Cloverfield* (2008), and so on.

What does it mean to say that an image is technological, that it bears the trace of synthetic design, manufacture, production and commoditization? Not that it is produced through new technologies, or that it is the outcome of an assemblage of raw materials – but that the image and the techno-logical processes intrinsic to its creation are inseparable. In fact, the image

---

44 Rombes, *Cinema in the Digital Age*, 26–30.

of spectacle cinema is most appropriately conceptualized as a technology, which would enable the spectator to divest herself of the burden of the image as either pure mediation or the reproduction of the real. To regard the image as technology provides a form through which to theorize its aesthetic autonomy:

> In the special director's cut release [of *Close Encounters*], from the moment when the spaceship lands and up until the closing credits, over half an hour of screen time elapses. Half an hour of pure spectacle – with hardly a spoken word – accompanied by a highly emotive music track (composed by John Williams) invites the audience within the film to ponder the otherworldly experience of the arrival of alien technology within the diegesis, and the audience *beyond the diegesis* [my emphasis] to wonder over the special-effects technology that construct the film's spectacle.[45]

A historical departure (2): Industrialized effect

All art is technology.[46]

Peter Bogdanovich, one of the chief exponents of the New American Cinema, describes his methodology in working with actors during production on *The Last Picture Show* (1971):

> This movie had to be brilliantly acted ... I absolutely refused to have lunch or dinner or whatever it was with *anybody* but the actors. Nobody was allowed to sit at the actors' table except me and the actors. The crew was very annoyed ... The crew did not like me on that picture because I excluded them, paid them no attention and didn't even talk to them because I was so focused on the actors.[47]

Bogdanovich's comment is revealing about the perception of an American cinema grounded in an aesthetic of realism. Bogdanovich's performances are uniformly naturalistic, from Cybill Shepherd's Jacy Farrow to Ben Johnson's Sam the Lion; Johnson's performance in a lengthy monologue, shot in an

---

[45] Ndalianis, 212.
[46] George Lucas, cited in Michael Rubin, *Droidmaker: George Lucas and the Digital Revolution* (Gainesville: Triad Publishing Company, 2006), 6.
[47] Peter Bogdanovich, in 'The Last Picture Show: A Look Back', featurette, *The Last Picture Show* (DVD), Sony Pictures Home Entertainment, 2006.

extreme depth of field, is remarkable for its subtlety. Bogdanovich's black and white cinematography was inspired by Welles's classical realism in *Citizen Kane* and *The Magnificent Ambersons*. In Bogdanovich's method in working with actors (which shares something with Cassavetes's emphasis on the naturalistic aspects of performance),[48] the art of cinema is revealed through the realism of what happens in front of the camera; 'performance' is anathema to cinematic truth. Bogdanovich's enforced hierarchical relationship between actors and crew is a reflection of a mode of independent filmmaking attuned to the artistic authenticity of European experimental cinema (notably Truffaut)[49] and the American school of naturalism pioneered by Cassavetes in the late 1950s.

In 1975, four years after the release of *The Last Picture Show*, in the year of the release of *Jaws* and Altman's *Nashville*, George Lucas founded Industrial Light and Magic (ILM), an effects facility that would oversee the special effects production of *Star Wars Episode IV*. If *Jaws* had set the industrial framework for the emerging blockbuster, *Star Wars* ushered in the 'age of the effects movie'.[50] By 1975, Lucas had emerged as one of the film school generation, closely mentored by UCLA graduate Francis Ford Coppola. Coppola co-produced Lucas's first feature, *THX 1138* (1971), a dystopian science fiction film. After the failure of *THX*, Lucas directed *American Graffiti* (1973) for Universal, again co-produced through Coppola's American Zoetrope. On the strength of *American Graffiti*, Lucas acquired the funding to develop *Star Wars Episode IV*.[51]

As Cotta Vaz and Duignan argue, by the early 1970s the spectacle effects expansion of the 1950s and early 1960s (*The Ten Commandments*, 1956; *Jason and the Argonauts*, 1963; *2001: A Space Odyssey*, 1968) had gradually been overtaken by a tendency toward aesthetic realism in the American industry.[52] Prior to 1975 and the creation of ILM, American production championed

---

[48] For a useful overview of Cassavetes's improvisatory method, see Viera Maria, 'The Work of John Cassavetes: Script, Performance, Style, and Improvisation', *Journal of Film and Video* 43, no. 3 (1990), 34–40.

[49] For the influence of Truffaut on Bogdanovich, and Bogdanovich's thoughts more generally on Truffaut's influence on the New American Cinema, see Peter Bogdanovich, 'The 400 Blows', *Indiewire*, June 29, 2011, http://blogs.indiewire.com/peterbogdanovich/the_400_blows [accessed April 8, 2012].

[50] Mark Cotta Vaz and Patricia Rose Duigan, *Industrial Light and Magic: Into the Digital Realm* (New York: Ballantine Books, 1996), 2.

[51] For an account of Lucas's integration into studio production in the early 1970s, see Biskind, 235–8.

[52] Cotta Vaz and Duigan, 5–7. For a comprehensive account of the transition from early effects to industrialized effects through Industrial Light and Magic, see Julie Turnock, 'Before Industrial Light and Magic: The Independent Hollywood Special Effects Business, 1968–1975', *New Review of Film and Television Studies* 7, no. 2 (2009), 136–7.

in-camera and mechanical effects that were increasingly associated with a mode of cinematic realism.[53] Friedkin's landmark car chase in *The French Connection* is a case in point. Not only is the chase a marvel of editing for action, but the effects (the emphasis on location shooting, real-time capture eschewing slow-motion commonly used in the 1970s action film) complement what is ostensibly an art film aesthetic grounded in the actuality of the New York location.

Going against the grain of the American realism of the early 1970s, Lucas and a team of technicians, designers and engineers pioneered various technologies of image capture and composition that would not only evolve the industry of effects production in American cinema, but would in effect establish the cinema of effect as the dominant aesthetic in the studio system.[54] In Lucas's 'cinema effect', industrialized through an effects company, the image manifests through new technologies (and itineraries) of form and movement. Technologized motion control and regulated timing, rendered with precision in contemporary digital production, presents in primitive form in the effects development of ILM from 1975. Lucas's achievement with ILM is thus more than the production of new effects, or new effects technologies. Rather, ILM reorients the studio system to synthesize a High Concept narrative and character model with the technology and creative processes intrinsic to spectacle image production.

Simulated motion and complex compositing: The Dykstraflex system

I preface the following section with an acknowledgement of the exemplary analysis of *Star Wars Episode IV* as neo-baroque cinema in Angela

---

[53] Brosnan, 85–95.

[54] See Tomasovic, 'The Hollywood Cobweb', 311: 'If we look into the etymology of the French word *spectaculaire*, we find an ancestral neutral, coined around 1770 in the field of the theatre: *spectaculeux*. This term indicates a surplus of spectacle, an excess, an ostentatious sign of spectacle as machine, as apparatus. And, indeed, it is this exhibitionist and megalomaniacal determination that characterized, about two centuries later, the films of Steven Spielberg and George Lucas, unbeatable filmmakers of the spectacular.' Tomasovic's derisive reading of spectacle as anchored in Lucas and Spielberg betrays an affiliation to a legacy of theory that has dismissed spectacle cinema as the deterioration of the potential of cinema. Yet I agree with the more sober-minded claim that Lucas and Spielberg inaugurate a kind of filmmaking, which is for Tomasovic more nefariously a kind of cultural reality in the mid–1970s. It remains a truism nonetheless that Industrial Light and Magic inscribed an aesthetic that would determine the box office outcome for a number of benchmark-setting releases from 1975–85. See Thomas G. Smith, *Industrial Light and Magic* (London: Columbus Books, 1986), 217–51.

Ndalianis's *Neo-baroque Aesthetics and Contemporary Entertainment* (2005). I employ Ndalianis's work as a foundation to my own examination of Lucas's unique deployment of a technological image through motion-control cinematography.

Classical effects had always made use of complexly moving objects and cameras. Robert Wise's great science fiction film, *The Day the Earth Stood Still* (1951), used travelling mattes (common in production at the time) for foreground and background composition. Wheeler (the effects designer) oversaw the construction of an enormous spaceship, 350 feet in circumference and 25 feet high.[55] Classic science fiction, from Wise to Arnold Gillespie's optical effects in *Forbidden Planet* (1956), which Brosnan describes as 'almost equal to the astronomical simulations in … *2001: A Space Odyssey*',[56] display complex image compositions. Pinteau's vivid description of the image of the parting of the Red Sea in DeMille's *The Ten Commandments* illustrates the complexity of classical era effects production:

> One million dollars was allocated for the sequence of the parting of the Red Sea, out of a total budget of thirteen million dollars. It was John P. Fulton who had the responsibility for its conception. He built a thirty-five-foot-tall (ten meter) construction, a kind of barrier extended by a gently inclined ramp. Fifteen flood-gates linked to twenty-four reservoirs permitted control of the flow of water that flooded down the ramp to form a cascade. This wall of water was filmed twice, so as to create the right and left liquid walls as the Red Sea parted … In conjunction with this construction, he used a blue background, six hundred extras, dozens of optical effects, and a storm re-created with smoke machines.[57]

Critical to my argument is Pinteau's identification of 'dozens of optical effects' to distinguish optical from mechanical effects. Here optical effect is equivalent to what has come to be known as cinema's 'special effect' – a combination of mechanical and optical engineering. The optical effect is also commonly accorded the status of an 'impossible image' that manifests as illusion. Thus, while the opening of the doorway to Wise's spaceship in *The Day the Earth Stood Still* is a landmark mechanical effect, DeMille's composition employs the optics of cinema to *effect* the image. Clearly DeMille's image partakes of

---

[55] Brosnan, 138.
[56] Brosnan, 139.
[57] Pascal Pinteau, *Special Effects: An Oral History – Interviews With 37 Masters Spanning 100 Years*, trans. Laurel Hirsch (New York: Harry N. Abrams, 2005), 50.

a complex register of optical effects: background and foreground are compositional (here composition connotes the outcome of a compositing process rather than the compositional register intrinsic to *mise en scène* and framing). DeMille captures the process of water cascading onto the model twice to enable background and foreground to simulate a single image. Compositing of this kind is evident in cinema from the 1930s through the use of optical printing, which provides a relatively clear image after composition of separate captures.[58] Movements in background and foreground, in the late classical era in which DeMille was working, are commonly complex mattes that move and are coordinated with camera movements and the mechanical elements of the effect. In *The Ten Commandments*, in which the image is in actuality a complex composition of models, mattes and discrete images, the outcome is not an illusion as much as a harmonious celluloid simulation in movement and form.

If DeMille's effect is nearer to a classical effects itinerary, employing the optical devices that had been used for several decades in film production, Lucas's motion control cinematography regulates the production processes of effects through a radically new cinematographic technology. Even *2001: A Space Odyssey*'s astonishing optical effects were primarily in-camera: 'this amounted to shooting an element, rewinding the film, and then shooting the same film again with the next element in place.'[59] The in-camera optical effect was integral to the formation of effects production in the classical era. However, in-camera effects were inadequate for regulating complex motion and synthesizing the moving objects of background, foreground and camera. Simply put, 'Lucas' spaceships wouldn't be able to dogfight using the old methods'.[60] While the image of Tatooine's two suns attains a grandeur in the stillness of a shot (figure 5.25), Lucas would seek to combine the spectacular image in relatively slow motion (the revolutions of spaceship and space station in the trip to the moon in *2001: A Space Odyssey* are relatively slow and manageable through in-camera effects) with the spectacular image in aggressive motion (action) demanded of High Concept cinema's aesthetic design.

Critical to Lucas's innovation was control over the recording apparatus in a precise and repeatable way.[61] Whereas earlier mechanical and optical effects had been calibrated, such calibrations were often loose and unpredictable. A

---

[58] Salt, 235–6.

[59] Rubin, 64.

[60] Rubin, 64.

[61] For a discussion of innovation through technology in the mid–1970s, see David A. Cook, *Lost Illusions: American Cinema in the Shadow of Watergate and Vietnam 1970–1979* (Berkeley and Los Angeles: University of California Press, 2000), 383–4.

computer-controlled motion (before the advent of computer imaging in a film such as *Tron*, 1982) provided motion regulated through a computer system. 'ILM could synchronize many planes of action with precision; multiple space-ships could fly on the same screen, lights and engines on the ships could be added to the images, and so on. This "motion control" made the photography of miniatures suddenly a fairly realistic replacement for shooting live action.'[62] Motion control is thus an evolutionary leap forward in the production of cinema effects, not because it reveals the image with greater clarity or precision, but because it regulates the movement of the image (a composition of various depths of field, focus, and objects that proliferate with each series capture) with the precision of a computer technology. Such precision in movement was at the time unprecedented in the industry of effects production:

> Motion control is the ability to control the movement of the camera, the photo-graphic subject, and its lighting in synchronization to the movement of the film through the camera ... If we make a camera move that lasts two seconds on the screen, we can also say the camera moves forty-eight frames. Motion control records electronically the positions of the motors (which control the movement of everything – cameras and models) in the system on frame one through frame forty-eight. Now that we have a positional map for each frame, we can run the camera as often as we'd like, knowing that the camera and subject positions would track the map exactly based on frame count.[63]

The capacity to precisely track motion and match images to 1/24ths of a second through computer technology radically redefined the potential of classical compositing techniques in the production of optical effects. While *Star Wars Episode IV* is a marvel of miniature production and composition through models, the image attains a degree of perceptual realism through optical effects unprecedented in cinema.

In 1902, Méliès's *Le Voyage dans la Lune* (*A Trip to the Moon*, 1902) crafted the image as an in-camera effect. With the advent of optical printing in the 1930s, cinema became a simulation through image composition, evolving as a special effect in even its most realistic guise. Bazin's cinema of phenomenological realism in *Citizen Kane* is perhaps also the most effected by the apparatus, and Bazin's recognition of this paradoxical index is most illuminating in his work.[64] However, Dykstra's movement precision, originated

---

[62] Rubin, 64.

[63] John Dykstra, in Cotta Vaz and Duignan, 7.

[64] André Bazin, 'An Aesthetic of Reality: Cinematic Realism and the Italian School of Liberation', in *What is Cinema? Volume 2*, trans. Hugh Gray (Berkeley and Los Angeles: University of California Press, 1967), 16–40.

at ILM, enabled complex compositing that incorporated the movement of backgrounds, foregrounds and objects at significant speeds. Lucas's effects were indelibly marked with the lasting impact of Kubrick's spectacle cinema in *2001: A Space Odyssey*; Lucas acknowledged the influence of Kubrick's optical effects production in his work.[65] But while Kubrick's image displayed its spectacle qualities for the astonished gaze of the spectator (a great deal of *2001: A Space Odyssey* is nearer to an image still, or an image in gradual motion), Lucas incorporated spectacle into the itinerary of the image of action. Such speeds required a simulated environment mapped to relative precision (within 1/24th of a second – a single frame of film). Compositing in *Star Wars Episode IV* is thus an early form of image simulation that is conventionally theorized as part of the turn to digitization: 'In *Star Wars* films, it was not uncommon to have thirty to forty separate foreground pieces combined with a background onto one piece of duplicate negative film.'[66] Nicholson's language prefigures the kind of conceptual models and methodological terms that would be appropriated in describing the digital image of contemporary spectacle cinema.

ILM technologized movement and compositing through radical innovations from 1975, and this is nowhere more apparent than in the opening sequence of *Star Wars Episode IV*. At 1:55, the image tilts downward, moving evenly to reveal a black background etched with stars, a single small planet in deep background and a second planet in the foreground of screen left (figure 5.26). The astonishment of the reveal derives not only from the impressive size and clarity of the image,[67] but from the perfectly regulated, machinic movement that precedes the reveal. The cinematic image of outer space is a complex composition of models, mattes and compositing that draws attention to its technological construction. At 2:05, Leia's Corellian Corvette spaceship enters from the top of screen right, moving downward toward centre screen (figure 5.27). The ship moves across the frame at speed, accompanied by boosted diegetic sound and a lowering of Williams's score. The movement at speed of the ship is striking against the unmoving planets. At 2:07, the Empire's Star Destroyer enters the top right of screen, moving at the same speed, enveloping the frame and obscuring the small planet in the deep background of the shot (figure 5.28). The presence of the two spaceships, one in deep background, the other enveloping foreground and middle ground, moving at speed in a composited universe, is a staggering accomplishment in a single

---

[65] Biskind, 318. While for Lucas *2001: A Space Odyssey* was the exemplary cinematic effect, Biskind describes Lucas's assessment of the film as 'excessively opaque'.

[66] Bruce Nicholson, in Cotta Vaz and Duigan, 14.

[67] Ndalianis, 189.

shot in 1977. While Ndalianis's emphasis on neo-baroque perspectivism and virtuosic image manipulation is entirely appropriate, perhaps even more striking, though less visible, is the *movement* of the objects within the frame. This is a new kind of technologized movement that signals a transformation in the image in which spectacle is animated, and stimulated, through action *as well as* exhibition.

The reverse shot, at 2:21, is even more impressive. Here Dykstra's motion control enables the precise capture of the ships in relation to each other within the frame. So accurate is the movement and capture of the two objects in foreground and background that the perspective appears to elongate the foreground ship (Leia's Corellian Corvette) while maintaining the fixity of the Star Destroyer in the background (figures 5.29–5.30). It is an artificial contrivance, but Lucas's image is affiliated to a technological rather than indexical itinerary. The cut to the interior of Leia's ship at 2:28 concludes what is ostensibly a performance piece, animated through rhythmic, regulated movement. But it is also a demonstration of a new cinema technology that would redefine spectacle aesthetics in effects cinema.[68] This is not unlike the technologized image of bullet-time that inaugurates a new mode of cinematic perception and affect (digitized rather than celluloid compositing) in the first sequence of *The Matrix*. These are evolutionary movements in a history of the cinematic medium and its creation of images.

Conclusion: Image, effect, commodity

I perceive several points of continuity between what I have called the techno-logical image and the simulated images of digital cinema. Lucas's *Star Wars Episode II* represents the first film entirely composed of digitally captured and composited images. Lucas's commitment was again to a cinema future and a possible future of the image. During production on *Star Wars Episode II*, he claimed that he would never shoot film again; other filmmakers, including Robert Rodriguez (*El Mariachi*, 1992) have made similar claims.[69]

Yet it is equally significant that *Star Wars Episode IV* laid the groundwork for the embrace of a technology that would evolve effects production from an illusion to an image modality. Technology is, as Ndalianis argues, 'present'

---

[68] Cook, *Lost Illusions*, 384.
[69] For a revealing interview with Lucas discussing his commitment to cinema's digital future, see Ron Magrid, 'George Lucas Discusses his Ongoing Effort to Shape the Future of Digital Cinema', *American Cinematographer*, September 2002, http://www.theasc.com/magazine/sep02/exploring/ [accessed June 18, 2010].

FIGURES 5.25–30 *The sublime special effect animated through motion control technology:* Star Wars Episode IV *(1977).*

in the image. Such presences manifest evermore strongly as celluloid gives over to digital capture, post-production and, ultimately, exhibition. Theories of cinema have necessarily embraced affect as a guiding conceptual framework and methodology, as spectators attempt to situate themselves in relation to an image that is not 'real', and in which the object is, in a sense, absent. Such technologized bodies are clearly on display in Lucas's motion-controlled, composited images of a fantasy world in *Star Wars Episode IV*.

The rhetoric of effect as illusion maintains to the present, as is demonstrated in Cameron's description of *Avatar* as psychologically immersive experience. Gunning's reading of the early perception of the image as an alienated gaze seems equally appropriate to the 3-D image of attraction in contemporary cinema. Yet beyond mere illusionism, the image of spectacle cinema established a lasting commodity that radically differed from the images of the New American Cinema that preceded it. While of course I disagree with Thomson that Spielberg and Lucas 'killed the movies',[70] I acknowledge, as must all film commentators, the impact of a cinema of spectacle, effects and exponentially increasing technological innovation. Such images constituted a new cinema in which the technology of effects became its own industrialized process, and ultimately its own commodity form. By 1985, ILM had produced the effects on five of the ten highest-grossing films in the history of the studio era,[71] and it had been operational for only ten years. In the years since, the commodity of effects has seamlessly integrated vertically and horizontally into the industries of a global popular culture.[72]

As spectators, critics and theorists of cinema and its reception, we must avoid the well-trodden path: that the cinema of effects was purely commodity and that the blockbuster was merely a commercial product within an industrialized system. While there is some truth to this notion of the genius of a new studio system after 1975, neither Lucas nor Spielberg produced films as commodity fixtures. I have attempted to engage with a cinema of spectacle through an analysis of its spectacle properties – in this chapter, through the presence of technology in the image. This attempt to theorize what an effects cinema is, or what it might be, rather than what it lacks and can only continue to lack in a nostalgic reflection on cinema's various golden eras, seems to me a critical move in contemporary film studies discourse. To speak about blockbuster film, or High Concept cinema, or the cinema of spectacle, is to confront a cinematic tradition founded upon technological innovation, technological presences, and the grandeur of images. Spectacle cinema also happens to be the most lucrative and potentially influential cultural phenomenon of the last three decades. In the two chapters that follow, I continue my analysis of the spectacle image, shifting from technology to formal aesthetic strategies within the frame, and, in Chapter Seven, to affect and the sensory experience of the spectacle image.

---

[70] Thomson, 'Who Killed the Movies'.
[71] Smith, *Industrial Light and Magic*, x.
[72] See Marco Cucco, 'The Promise is Great: The Blockbuster and the Hollywood Economy', *Media, Culture and Society* 31, no. 2 (2009), 218–21. See also Keller, *James Cameron*, 21–34.

6

Neo-baroque form: Excess and disambiguation

The blockbuster auteur: On the cinema of Steven Spielberg

What role can a single director play in changing the course of Hollywood film history?[1]

In this chapter, I continue my examination of spectacle cinema through a sustained analysis of the filmic text. While I present numerous examples and several discrete image, shot, scene and sequence analyses, I focus on the work of Steven Spielberg. Spielberg is, in my estimation, the spectacle filmmaker *par excellence*, equally attuned to the technological, formal compositional and affective qualities of the cinema image. It is also Spielberg that is most explicitly associated with the rise of blockbuster cinema and spectacle aesthetics in the mid- to late 1970s. While *The Godfather* and *The Exorcist* are both 'blockbusters', if we are to adopt Biskind's model of saturation distribution and integrated marketing,[2] *Jaws* is a calculated spectacle production, integrating technological, aesthetic and commercial imperatives.[3] Coppola would follow *The Godfather* with *The Conversation* in 1974, a personal project funded by Paramount as payment for the production of *The Godfather, Part 2* (1974); the auteur filmmaker had gained the kind of power in the New

---

[1] Buckland, *Directed by Steven Spielberg*, 13.

[2] Biskind, 162. For a detailed examination of the development of saturation marketing as a studio practice, see Justin Wyatt, 'From Roadshowing to Saturation Release: Majors, Independents, and Marketing/Distribution Innovations', in *The New American Cinema*, ed. Jon Lewis (Durham: Duke University Press, 1998), 73–8.

[3] See King, *New Hollywood*, 55–6. See also Wyatt, 'From Roadshowing to Saturation Release', 78–83.

American Cinema that could hold a major studio to ransom.[4] Friedkin would follow *The Exorcist* with *Sorcerer* in 1977 and *Cruisin'* in 1980, films that attempted to recuperate a market share of Hollywood through the art-house distribution circuit. After the unprecedented success of *Jaws*, Spielberg would never again return to an alternative aesthetic, perhaps visible in various degrees in *Duel* (1971) and *Sugarland Express* (1974). In so doing, the success of Spielberg's American imaginary eclipses the commercial potential of the traumatic imaginary of Bogdanovich, Coppola, Altman, Scorsese, but also the fringe filmmakers, Cassavetes, Rafelson, Cimino, Friedkin, Ashby and Malick, among others.

In my reading of Spielberg's aesthetic, I refuse to distinguish between 'entertainment vehicles' – usually identified with the output of 1975–82: *Jaws, Close Encounters of the Third Kind, 1941* (1971), *Raiders of the Lost Ark*, and *E.T.: The Extra-Terrestrial* – and what are commonly referred to as the 'serious films': *The Color Purple* (1985), *Empire of the Sun* (1987), *Schindler's List, Amistad* (1997), *Saving Private Ryan* (1998) and *Munich* (2005). Perhaps Spielberg's subject matter engages with a historical realism in *Schindler's List* or *Saving Private Ryan,* and is for this reason nearer in spirit to the New American Cinema of Coppola, Altman or Cimino. Yet I would argue that Spielberg's so-called serious films are more appropriately modes of cinematic spectacle than cinematic realisms. *Schindler's List* and *Saving Private Ryan* are nearer technologically, aesthetically and affectively to the image itinerary of *Close Encounters of the Third Kind* and *Raiders of the Lost Ark* than the war narratives of Cimino's *The Deer Hunter* (1978) or Coppola's *Apocalypse Now.* Coppola's image of Vietnam is surely the profound modernist image of American art cinema. 'Horror' is an aesthetic, political and existential determiner; 'horror' seeds the destructive tendency of the colonizing individual ('My film is not about Vietnam. It *is* Vietnam'); 'horror' theorizes the destruction of the hermetic text, and specifically, war cinema's transformation from realist to surrealist aesthetics; 'horror' manifests the traumatic stasis of a political system exhausted with its incapacity to represent a citizenry.

But in 1993, in *Schindler's List*, Spielberg's image of war and destruction is *recuperative*. Representation's modernist horror is recoded as an American utopian progressivism. Perhaps it is enough to account for this recuperation as a fantasy narrative, what Farrell describes as the 'fantasy of heroic rescue from death and malice'.[5] But the recuperation of the utopian ideal is as much *imagistic* as narrative. Consider the introductory image of Willard (Martin

---

[4] Biskind, 183.
[5] Kirby Farrell, 'The Economies of *Schindler's List'*, in *The Films of Steven Spielberg: Critical Essays*, ed. Charles L. P. Silet (Lanham: Scarecrow Press, 2002), 191.

Sheen) in *Apocalypse Now*: the superimposed images of the burning jungle and spinning fan blades present a schizophrenic consciousness (figure 6.1). Coppola cuts the image to a rendition of 'The End' (The Doors), an incantation toward death and madness.

In contrast, *Schindler's List* opens on a communal gathering and proceeds to isolate the unique, contained subjectivity of an individual, a figure that will stand in as the perceptual itinerary of the war and the Holocaust. At 0:40,[6] the image opens on a gathering of six figures, adults and children. Spielberg shoots the assemblage from a low angle, accentuating brown and yellow hues in the colour grade (figure 6.2). It is only after a moment that we realize that the somewhat mannerist low angle shot[7] is naturalized through the compositional emphasis on the child in the right foreground of the shot: what is a low angle shot for the collective is in fact a natural eye-line shot for the child. The child's singular importance is established through the eye-line, foreground position, as well as the subsequent cut to a profile close-up. The spectator is effectively shifted into a detailed perception (and affective engagement) with the child. The child, as numerous commentators have observed, is a recurrent motif in Spielberg.[8] Yet in this sequence the child serves more than a narrative itinerary, establishing also a perceptual itinerary founded on wonder, astonishment and incredulity. At 0:50, the profile close-up on the child is captured in shallow focus, accentuating the formal distinction of the figure (figure 6.3). Spielberg cuts the frame with a single vertical line; at screen right, the child's shadowy profile (lit with a heavy backlight) is set in relief against the lit background. On screen left, the shallow focus shot composes the distinct image of a candle, the flame accentuated against the black background of a curtain that marks the vertical division of the frame. This image is a marvel of composition for a significatory, but more deliberately affective register. Here Spielberg infuses the image with the mechanism for perception and affect. The spectator is suitably transfixed by the child, and is transposed into a subject position common in Spielberg's cinema.[9] This itinerary toward perception, affect and interpretation, I would argue, is encapsulated in this procession of two very simply composed shots. Composition within the frame reveals the intrinsic harmony of perception in Spielberg's war film.

---

[6] Time-code references are to *Schindler's List* (DVD: Two-Disc Special Collection), Universal Home Video, 2006.

[7] Buckland, 38. Building on the framework of Adrian Martin, Buckland conceptualizes an 'expressive' element in Spielberg's compositional strategies.

[8] See, for example, Farrell, 192–3. See also Wood, 'Papering the Cracks', 206–7.

[9] The spectator encounters similar perceptual itineraries through the child in *Close Encounters of the Third Kind*, *E.T.: The Extra-Terrestrial*, *Indiana Jones and the Temple of Doom* (1984), *Empire of the Sun*, *Jurassic Park*, *A.I.: Artificial Intelligence* (2000), and *War of the Worlds* (2004).

FIGURE 6.1 *'The horror, the horror': Coppola's imagistic modernism in* Apocalypse Now *(1979).*

FIGURES 6.2–3 *Disambiguated lines of perception:* Schindler's List *(1993).*

In this comparative examination of two images, we see the performance of the image of High Concept cinema (founded upon concept, archetype and disambiguated lines of perception, action and affection) against Coppola's modernist surrealism. While perception is individuated through Willard (Martin Sheen) in the opening sequence of *Apocalypse Now*, Coppola depicts that perception as fractured, and the consciousness as dispersed spatially and temporally. 'Saigon … shit' – the spatial/temporal location is also a site of the traumatized consciousness of modernity. But in *Schindler's List*, it makes sense that we are to be located perceptually alongside one of Spielberg's children (and one who surely resembles Eliot [Henry Thomas] in *E.T.: The Extra-Terrestrial*). Epstein reads the child as motif for the film's ideological subtext: 'a beautiful boy is up to his shoulders in a reeking latrine. His expression is troubled and angelic, an expression that denies the experience of being in a real latrine, as the film evades the lesson of the Holocaust.'[10] The expression of this child, occurring at a mid-Act Two turning point in *Schindler's List*, is not dissimilar to the expression of stern bewilderment of the child that opens the film.

---

[10] Jason Epstein, cited in Farrell, 192.

In subjecting the work of Spielberg to a close, functional analysis of the image, I supplement my reading of the technological imprint of spectacle cinema evident in *Star Wars Episode IV*, *Jurassic Park* and *Inception*, to name three films discussed in Part Two of this book. I conclude this chapter with an attempt at what Bordwell calls an 'exceptionally exact perception' of the second shark attack sequence in *Jaws* and the arrival on Omaha Beach in *Saving Private Ryan*. I present an analysis of an exemplary film from both Spielberg's 'entertainment' and 'serious' works to argue that, as Buckland demonstrates, Spielberg's cinematic aesthetic is identifiable and eminently traceable in his cinema from 1975 to the present.[11] While I cannot claim to bring the level of precision or sheer invention of Bordwell to my own formal analyses, I seek to reveal the compositional aspects of spectacle cinema through close, sustained and contextualized observations of *mise en scène*, compositional movement and shot relations.

Film style, method and analysis

Stylistic history is one of the strongest justifications for film studies as a distinct academic discipline. If studying film is centrally concerned with 'reading movies' in the manner of literary texts, any humanities scholar armed with a battery of familiar interpretive strategies could probably do as well as anyone trained in film analysis. This is especially true as hermeneutic practices across the humanities have come to converge on the same interpretive schemas and heuristics. But if we take film studies to be more like art history or musicology, interpretive reading need not take precedence over a scrutiny of change and stability within stylistic practices.[12]

Film analysis has no single methodology; this is one of the perennial frustra-tions of attempting to account for the meaning, or effect, of cinema. How precisely does one read the film image? Should we attune our perception to the shot as a narrative cell, or the image as a formal compositional unit? Can the image subvert the itinerary of the narrative cell, as it seems to do, for example, in Carol Reed's Dutch tilts that capture a world askew in *The Third Man* (1949)? The spectator's engagement with cinema, at least in its

---

[11] While I would argue that Buckland privileges narrative over image, his analysis of Spielberg's work is comprehensive and persuasive in its perception of a thematic, aesthetic and structural unity. See Buckland, *Directed by Steven Spielberg*.

[12] Bordwell, *On the History of Film Style*, 8.

industrial and commercial context, is a 'confluence of artistry, industry and technology'.[13] The history of film production and reception displays an almost incalculable array of images, each composed, recorded and exhibited through a special configuration of artistry, industrial and technological production. The image might come about through necessity: the rawness of Pennebaker's early vérité images in *Don't Look Back* (1967) are the outcome, at least in part, of the necessity to map the movements of its subject, Bob Dylan.[14] The grandeur of Riefenstahl's crane cinematography in *Triumph des Willens* (*Triumph of the Will*, 1935) captures the larger-than-life monumentalism of its subject, Adolf Hitler. Are these two forms of cinema partaking of the same elemental material, such that we might say cinematic viewing requires image literacy, as reading requires a literacy to make sense of its words? Eisenstein argued for the essential language of cinema, but here it was a particular notion of language accorded a special status in the Soviet cinema. For Eisenstein, the language of cinema inscribed the shot and its relationship to other shots – this is a system in which cinema's substance was made of 'each particle of a film fragment', and in which montage is a 'purity of film form'.[15]

But Eisenstein's images require more than reading. Eisenstein's montage through conflict is built through tension and resistance, and such tensions and resistances stem from movement and temporal relations – in short, montage inscribes rhythm and sensation, as well as signification. The spectator is jolted by the jarring confluence of images in *Potemkin*'s Odessa Steps sequence. In the case of *Potemkin*, it is instructive to compare Eisenstein's Odessa Steps sequence and De Palma's Steps sequence in *The Untouchables* (1986) to appreciate the way in which a montage of conflict is reanimated through principles of classical composition (continuity editing) and neo-baroque aestheticism (mannerist slow-motion). Eisenstein's montage functions as inscription; De Palma's is more appropriately the excess of quotation.

Bazin treated cinema as a language, or at least alluded to such in 'The Evolution of the Language of Film'. It was precisely against montage that the language of film evolved for Bazin. Again, this language was predicated on more than signification. Bazin's conception of deep focus was less attuned to the technology of the camera, less obviously attuned to the external

---

[13] Maria Pramaggiore and Tom Wallis, *Film: A Critical Introduction* (London: Lawrence King Publishing, 2008), 4.

[14] See Jeanne Hall, '"Don't You Ever Just Watch?": American Cinéma Vérité and *Don't Look Back*', in *Documenting the Documentary: Close Readings of Documentary Film and Video*, ed. Barry Keith Grant and Jeannette Sloniowski (Detroit: Wayne State University Press, 1998), 223–37.

[15] Sergei Eisenstein, 'Film Language', in *Film Form: Essays in Film Theory*, trans. Jay Leyda (Orlando: Harcourt, 1977), 111.

properties of composition than it was to the experience of the spectator: 'independently of the contents of the image, its [the deep focus shot] structure is more realistic … It implies, consequently, both a more active mental attitude on the part of the spectator and a more positive contribution on his part to the action in progress.'[16] As Bazin acknowledges, even Renoir and Welles used montage, but in such cases '[the filmmaker] makes it an integral part of his plastic'.[17]

The question of cinema's composition and mode of analysis, the question of its *language*, is critical to the discourse of studies. In fact, the evolution of film theory, from early theory's medium specificity debates to *Screen's* psychoanalytic Marxism to Deleuze's mode of phenomenology, asks us to consider how the film text *functions*, how it manifests on the screen of the theatre, or the screen of the spectator's mind. It is often permissible in theoretical discourse to make sweeping generalizations about a cinematic text, or its creator. For example, consider Deleuze's suggestion that 'it was also Hitchcock's task to introduce the mental image into the cinema and to make it the completion of the cinema, the perfection of all the other images … In Hitchcock, actions, affections, perceptions, all is interpretation, from beginning to end.'[18] To substantiate the claim in part, Deleuze cites Narboni in *Cahiers du Cinema*. There is nothing especially radical in this comment, as it takes the subjective shot of Hitchcock (famously, in *Psycho*, but *Notorious*'s (1946) equally famous crane move to reveal a key) and turns it into a purely mental image that manifests through *relation* rather than action or perception. Deleuze's inscription of a mental image strategically locates Hitchcock's *oeuvre* within the broader schematic of the movement image and its crisis. But what is exceptional is the size of Deleuze's claim. To say that Hitchcock introduced an 'image' through cinema's apparatus (an image that had not manifested in the cinema up until this point) is intriguing. But then to also suggest that such an image accounts for Hitchcock's 'cinema' is surely excessive. Here I am sympathetic to the commonsensical view that Hitchcock's image metamorphosed from his early cinema (the British silent and sound period) to the studio years, and then again to the late American and British films.[19] Hitchcock's image rhythms change, as do narrative, character and thematic scaffolds. Perhaps the mental image is again explicit in *Frenzy*,

---

[16] Bazin, 'The Evolution of the Language of Cinema', 35–6.

[17] Bazin, 'The Evolution of the Language of Cinema', 35.

[18] Deleuze, *Cinema 1*, 200.

[19] *The Wrong Man* (1956) radically revises the trope of the innocent man suspected of a crime in *Saboteur* (1942), which equally departs from the suspense itinerary displayed in *The 39 Steps* (1935). I would argue that innocence and guilt, or freedom and entrapment, are dissimilar affective gestures in these three films.

but can it equally be applied to all of Hitchcock's films? Would we perceive the same image of relation in *Psycho* (in part, a deliberate departure from the Hitchcockian suspense film of the studio era in the 50s) that we might in *To Catch a Thief* (1955)? If, as Deleuze argues, the mental image constitutes the substance of Hitchcock's 'cinema', how does the spectator account for the differences in Hitchcock's work across several decades of production? For Deleuze, the crop-duster of *North by Northwest* is a 'demark', which takes the 'term' outside of a series to presumably manifest the image (of thought). Deleuze reads the crop-duster as demark because it dusts crops where there are no crops to spray, hence bringing forth the image divorced from subjective/objective relation, the pure mental image of relation.[20] Yet a close examination of the sequence not only reveals the refuse of dying crops on the surface of the ground, but the sequence in fact concludes with Thornhill (Cary Grant) escaping the crop-duster by secluding himself in a field of crops. The reason Hitchcock exposes Thornhill to a crop-duster in a barren field is to provide the narrative conditions for what is a thrilling, though entirely conventional, action sequence. If Thornhill were to seclude himself in a crop field in the beginning of the chase, the action sequence would have nowhere to go.

Such broad generalizations have established complex and discursive film theory traditions.[21] Thompson describes such approaches and methodologies as unconcerned with the 'specificity of the aesthetic realm'.[22] I am sympathetic to arguments made by Bordwell, Thompson and others that a great deal of analysis of cinema engages with the image, or narrative, only superficially to establish broad theoretical paradigms across aesthetic and industrial contexts. My engagement with cinema in this book attempts to celebrate the capacity of the image to signify and affect through a complex and prolifer-

---

[20] Deleuze, *Cinema 1*, 203.

[21] Here of course I refer to a Deleuzian semiotic system influential in contemporary film studies that, while provocative, seems to engage whole bodies of work, and whole filmmaking traditions, paradigmatically. See Mullarky, 78: 'It is nonetheless striking how closely Deleuze watches the films of his choice with an eye to recreating his own philosophy in their image.' Surely Hitchcock is the one great filmmaker for whom nothing was a given, and in which the image was at least as much the creation of an apparatus as a philosophical modality. For a broad examination of the paradigmatic generalizations of 'Grand Theory' discourse, see Bordwell, 'Contemporary Film Studies and the Vicissitudes of Grand Theory'. For a lucid and strongly waged challenge to the psychoanalytic use of the concept of pleasure in feminist criticism, see Malcolm Turvey, 'Philosophical Problems Concerning the Concept of Pleasure in Psychoanalytic Theories of (the Horror) Film', in *Horror Film and Psychoanalysis: Freud's Worst Nightmare*, ed. Steven Jay Schneider (Cambridge: Cambridge University Press, 2004), 68–83. For a challenge to Fredric jameson's Marxist-utopian film analysis, see Michael Walsh, 'Jameson and "Global Aesthetics"', in *Post-Theory: Reconstructing Film Studies*, ed. David Bordwell and Noël Carroll (Madison: University of Wisconsin Press, 1996), 481–500.

[22] Kristin Thompson, *Breaking the Glass Armor: Neoformalist Film Analysis* (Princeton: Princeton University Press, 1988), 9.

ating system of aesthetic tools and strategies. I am unsure whether theorists (myself included) fully appreciate the aesthetic distinction of a single shot (or image) in a standard large budget effects vehicle; and if we are aware of the complexity of such aesthetic systems (and production practices), this awareness has yet to properly filter down into the various discourses of film studies research.

To this end, Bordwell and Thompson provide the framework for a mode of formalist textual analysis, examining the film text as a systematic operation of narrative and image composition. Formalist analysis is sensitive to cinema's stylistic apparatus: its *mise en scène* formations, its technological mannerisms, its essential language of connecting one shot to the next. Since the early 1980s, Thompson and Bordwell have been associated with a method of analysis termed 'neoformalism', which Thompson describes as: 'a two-way exchange between theory and criticism … Neoformalism as an approach does offer a series of broad assumptions about how artworks are constructed and how they operate in cueing audience response. But neoformalism does not prescribe how these assumptions are embodied in individual films.'[23] This approach is built upon the foundations of Bordwell and Thompson's theory of the cognitive engagement with cinema founded on perceptual cues and active spectatorship. Essentially, I would argue that Bordwell and Thompson employ a 'direct' method, following the most clearly established line between the spectator's perceptual mechanisms and the formation of image and narrative.[24]

The common criticism levelled at neoformalism, or at formalist analysis *per se*, is that such methods prevent a more imaginative or explorative mode of film analysis, or in even more basic terms, that such analytical methods limit perception to an instrumental and crude apparatus. I can appreciate such concerns in contemporary film studies discourse, in which theories of being, consciousness and embodiment have given rise to imaginative ways of thinking about the film object. Yet one can still argue that film analysis, regardless of 'approach', must employ a methodology appropriate to the medium, and Thompson and Bordwell appear not only cognizant of, but expressly articulate, the necessity of engaging with an aesthetic object in a variety of industrial, artistic and commercial contexts. The celebration of the primacy of the aesthetic object is precisely to render a *non-instrumental* formalist analysis, and such analyses, I argue, not only incorporate a

---

[23] Thompson, *Breaking the Glass Armor*, 6.

[24] See David Bordwell, 'Common Sense + Film Theory = Common-Sense Film Theory?', *David Bordwell's Website on Cinema*, May 2011, http://www.davidbordwell.net/essays/commonsense. php#_ednref13 [accessed June 15, 2012]. Bordwell is very direct in his confrontation with what he considers 'far-fetched' theories of cinematic perception, cognition and affect.

contextualized reading of the image and narrative, but a wider, more subtly informed view of production, post-production, distribution and reception practices.[25] Bordwell's declaration of the importance of film style is directed not only toward the spectator of cinema, but also toward the theorist, who must attend to cinema's stylistic idiosyncrasies as he or she must to its industrialized and commercialized styles, strategies and internal processes.

Framing spectacle: *Jaws* and neo-baroque excess

Bordwell presents an astonishingly precise analysis of the evolution of depth cinematography in *On the History of Film Style*. This analysis enables him to contribute to, and expand upon, several of the formulations of key theorists on depth cinematography, notably Bazin and Comolli. Against Comolli's reading of the evolution of depth in the film image as ideologically motivated, Bordwell provides an examination of the technological and compositional complexities inherent in early cinema, including the attempt to provide the impression of depth in the image. The value of Bordwell's analysis of depth is in its concordant analyses of authorial signature (for example, Toland, working with Welles or Ford) and industrial development. Depth is not merely a function of ideological purpose and directorial intent, but is also determined by new lenses, stocks, modes of lighting, and compositional strategies.[26] Thus, while Welles is conventionally the pioneer of depth within the studio system, Bordwell presents a striking shot of three depth planes in Huston's *The Maltese Falcon* (1941), released only a few months after *Citizen Kane*.[27] Bordwell is thus able to critique the foundational position of Bazin on depth with recourse to cinema's technological evolution:

> Bazin believed that Welles's shots displayed a respect for recording an integral time and place within the continuum of phenomenal reality. In many of these shots, though, there was no coherent phenomenal reality to be recorded: the space we see is closer to the artificiality of an animated cartoon.[28]

---

[25] For a lucid account of the evolution of Bordwell's neo-formalist method, see Colin Burnett, 'A New Look at the Concept of Style in Film: The Origins and Development of the Problem-Solution Model', *New Review of Film and Television Studies* 6, no. 2 (2008), 127–49.

[26] Bordwell, *On the History of Film Style*, 159–63.

[27] Bordwell, *On the History of Film Style*, 221–6.

[28] Bordwell, *On the History of Film Style*, 225.

I have argued elsewhere that, against an inherent realism, deep focus constituted an evolution of style in Welles, and later in Hitchcock.[29] Deep focus might be more appropriately termed a 'reality effect'. Bordwell's close image analysis is most valuable as a way of historicizing cinema's evolution as a technology, industrial system, aesthetic template, and critically, mode of effect. I have read this evolutionary movement toward the advent of a High Concept cinema in the mid–1970s studio system, and the industrialization of a cinema of special effects. I argue that the spectacle image demonstrates two formal aesthetic imperatives: toward excess in the compositional elements of the image (neo-baroque aestheticism); and toward conceptual, narrative and image disambiguation.

The discourse surrounding spectacle remains problematic in contemporary film analysis, and I agree with Lavik that the conventional pathway through Debord's *Society of the Spectacle* (taken by a great number of theorists of spectacle) offers little value to the film theorist.[30] The society of the spectacle, so closely affiliated with culture industries and passive aesthetic, cultural and political engagement, presents few avenues for careful exploration of how spectacle functions in contemporary society, let alone cinema. In my usage throughout this book, spectacle connotes more than what is seen or heard on the screen; it is more than simply a heightened visuality, 'a heightened degree of spectacle or spectacular action: the "big" explosion or the "big" outburst of special effects'.[31] Spectacle is also more than a capitalist ideology. In image terms, spectacle describes a cinematic aesthetic in which the image manifests beyond the itinerary of narrative – which I conceptualize as the autonomous image, or the image-in-itself. This image manifests through the imprint of technologies of production (the technological image) and the compositional strategies increasingly visible, and regulated, in the production of American High Concept cinema.

While I engage in part with the narrative framework of *Jaws*, my reading is more deliberately formalist in its address of Spielberg's image composition. This reading attempts to build upon, and yet also depart from, Buckland's notion of 'organic unity' in his analysis of Spielberg's poetics. Buckland works through Thompson's neoformalist method in accounting for the organic unity in a successful work of art:

'Organic unity' names a very particular organization of form. An organic unity is a whole that is more than the sum of its parts, for the whole

---

[29] Isaacs, *Toward a New Film Aesthetic*, 26–36.
[30] Erlend Lavik, 'The Battle for the Blockbuster: Discourses of Spectacle and Excess', *New Review of Film and Television Studies* 6, no. 2 (2008), 169–70.
[31] Geoff King, cited in Lavik, 171.

possesses an added value not contained in any of its parts. All the parts of an organic unity are necessary and sufficient to its status as a unity … In an organic unity, the parts reach their highest degree or best possible level of integration.[32]

This is an intriguing position, and Buckland's willingness to elevate Spielberg's poetics to the status of art (achieved through organic unity) is a much-needed contribution to current discourses of cinema that invariably privilege the realist aesthetic over spectacle. In Buckland's work, Spielberg's images of scale, subtlety and complexity are harmonious and organically interconnected. To this end, I agree. If terms such as 'masterpiece' and 'classic' (as an evaluative determiner) have meaning any more, they should be applied to a great deal of Spielberg's cinema – *Jaws, Close Encounters of the Third Kind, Raiders of the Lost Ark*. I'm less confident with Spielberg's later work, but this is expressly where I would depart from Buckland's revelation of an authorial organic unity. Buckland is committed to the revelation of the whole – the artwork in its organic unity that exceeds its compositional elements.[33] But the question of organic unity returns to the more problematic question of how the film image manifests on the screen. Is it through the hand of a creator (director), through a technological and aesthetic apparatus, or through the perceptual mechanism of the spectator? The attribution of an organic unity to Spielberg's *oeuvre* relies in too great a measure on artistic intent. The industrial and commercial imperatives of the studio system require the intervention of external agents at every stage of production. Perhaps the collaborative nature of mainstream studio production has been overstated in reaction to classical auteur theory, yet it is true that stars are more valuable commodities than directors, and actively write, perform and direct production. And while Spielberg had 'final cut' throughout the 1980s and 1990s, and continues to enjoy that privilege within production practice,[34] final cut is always a conditional entitlement in the studio system.

Against the whole, I would argue that spectacle reveals the unity of the *part, sequence, or movement*. Against classical unity, I perceive in spectacle cinema what Calabrese terms neo-baroque form, in which text is 'born from mechanical repetition'.[35] Calabrese appears to work through Eco's

[32] Buckland, *Directed by Steven Spielberg*, 31.
[33] Buckland, *Directed by Steven Spielberg*, 33.
[34] See Tatiana Siegel, 'Fade-Out on Final-Cut Privileges?', *Variety*, January 22, 2010, http://www.variety.com/article/VR1118014187?refCatId=13 [accessed January 8, 2011].
[35] Omar Calabrese, *Neo-Baroque: A Sign of the Times* (Princeton: Princeton University, 1992), 27. See also Calabrese, 55: 'Pulsation toward the limit of the system, as we have already seen, might be motivated by the noncentrality of a system's organizing center.'

notion of repetition in the postmodern textual condition. Repetition implies a circuit, a relation of one part to another that forms discrete units attended to the autonomy of each object rather than an organic whole.[36] The texts of spectacle are subject to cutting up, dispersal and renewed integration. At the level of image form, a neo-baroque aesthetics implies expressiveness or excess, and a performance of the unit as an autonomous object. Thus, while I would argue that *Saving Private Ryan*'s synthesis of the realist and fantasy registers is uneven, even strategically ideological, it seems entirely appropriate to perceptually, intellectually, and affectively engage with the arrival on Omaha Beach as a discrete unit within the whole. This is not a segment of a film (the organic whole), but a contained neo-baroque *performance*. Could one not say the same of *Jurassic Park*'s technological wonders in a film that is narratively and dramatically uneven (comprising a strangely distended first act)? But further still, can the theorist in all confidence perceive the whole, when cinema extends ever more deliberately into cross-mediated platforms, industries and cultures? Can one locate an organic unity on the screen, when cinema increasingly manifests *off-screen*, in the domestic spaces of homes, or the virtual environments of contemporary gaming and avatar experiences? In this book, I privilege the image as an autonomous object, that might be stitched together with other images to form a series, that might then comprise a sequence (a narrative movement), that might then comprise larger segments of narrative. But while I entertain the notion of narrative coherence (which I take to be some move toward organic unity), I am unconvinced that the spectacle cinema manifests unity in image form beyond a discrete series that requires detaching from the whole in a modulated performance. Therefore, against the notion of organic textual unity (and authorial signature), I wish to read Spielberg's second shark attack in *Jaws* as a discrete signifying and affecting unit – a neo-baroque set piece.

Second shark attack: Spielberg's neo-baroque aestheticism

First movement: From invisibility to excess

The image opens on a pan left as a woman walks toward the ocean. A dog plays in the background. The image registers the dog of secondary importance within the frame, situated in the background; appropriately, the dog

---

[36] Umberto Eco, '*Casablanca*', 446–55.

will die off-screen in this sequence. As Buckland suggests, the shot's primary significance is to pick up the figure of Alex Kintner as he returns from the ocean (figure 6.4).[37] Alex's movement now organizes the movement of the camera, which pans right. The framing of the primary figure – Alex – is a crucial indication of the classicism of the shot (figure 6.5). The pan – left to right – manifests inconspicuously if not invisibly. The camera attains a static position in a dialogue between Alex and his mother, a relatively shallow shot that again places the narrative emphasis on the boy, maintaining the classical certainty of composition (figure 6.6).[38] At 13:13,[39] the camera begins its first conspicuous itinerary – the transition from the left-right pan to stasis is inconspicuous, but the transition from stationary to mobile camera, *without cutting*, is a highly visible gesture. The camera elevates and pans right in a fluid movement, framing the background in the widescreen composition. Sound materializes as the camera pans across a family – again, a conspicuous, visible departure from a classical itinerary. The sound materializes as if on cue, a deliberate sound-tracking of the camera move. The reveal of Brody, still in the single shot, accompanied by a rack focus, establishes the virtuosity of the continuous shot (figure 6.7).

Second movement: Disambiguation

The width and depth of the previous movement in single shot now transitions to a series of shots identifying the principal figures of the action: Alex Kintner re-entering the ocean (figure 6.8), the dog paddling with stick in mouth (figure 6.9), the woman in the ocean depicted in long shot (figure 6.10), culminating in a shot of the dog fighting over the stick (figure 6.11) – appropriately, the stick will identify the absence of the dog in a subsequent shot. Narrative is inscribed through objects within the frame, discrete figures as yet unrelated. Spielberg deliberately charts a movement from ambiguity to coherence in depicting in series the key protagonists of the action to follow. We might contrast this gesture toward narrative coherence with the earlier discussion of the ambiguity of the sound image of *The Conversation* in which the essential discord between image and sound remains unresolved.

---

[37] Buckland, *Directed by Steven Spielberg*, 95.
[38] Calabrese, 192–3.
[39] Time-code references are to *Jaws* (DVD, 25th Anniversary Collector's Edition), Columbia Tristar Home Video, 2000.

FIGURES 6.4–7 *From invisibility to virtuosity:* Jaws *(1975).*

FIGURES 6.8–11 *Disambiguation:* Jaws *(1975).*

Third movement: Brody and the neo-baroque gesture

The cut to Brody [14:07] is to a conventional medium-long shot – his position in the top right of frame is naturalized through his eye-line toward screen left (figure 6.12). However, the convention of an invisible style – a presumed shot reverse-shot relation with the woman floating on the ocean – is broken through a self-conscious, mechanistic contrivance. The image jump cuts twice to move from medium to close-up on Brody; the jump cut as an image-break recalls the self-conscious stylistics of Godard's *Breathless* (1960), which had been recently incorporated into the cinema of the New American filmmakers, from Boorman (*Point Blank*, 1967) to *Penn* (*Bonnie and Clyde*, 1968) to Scorsese (*Mean Streets*, 1973). In Spielberg's rendition, the aberrant effect of the neo-baroque jump cut is softened by a 'wipe' – as a figure walks across the shot, Spielberg cuts, simulating a wipe between frames (figures 6.13–6.15).[40] The wipe also emphasizes the width of shot, now common in widescreen aesthetics, but especially significant in spectacle cinema. For Belton, 'something basic had changed in the motion picture experience that redefined the spectator's relationship with the screen, which now entered further into the spectator's space, and with the soundtrack, which reinforced this extension of the image and exceeded even the image's border.'[41]

Here jump cut and wipe demonstrate the excess of cinematic style, even as that style is rendered partially invisible through Spielberg's clever manipulation of shot and shot relation. Spielberg repeats the jump cut on wipe several times in a series to conclude the itinerary of the (now neo-baroque) classical shot reverse-shot.

Fourth movement: Excess and artistic virtuosity

At 14:39, the image returns to a close profile on Brody in conversation. Spielberg composes the close two-shot in depth to prepare for the conventional reverse-shot movement from Brody's perspective – Brody's continued search for signs of the shark (figure 6.16). Yet the point of view shot at 14:44 is the most explicit contrivance yet: an extreme shot in depth, superimposed with an extreme close-up of the figure in conversation (figure 6.17). Naturalized perception is foregone in this shot and lays the groundwork for the artificial contrivance of the 'Vertigo shot' that will conclude the sequence. A series of expositional shots follows, leading into the culminating movement.

---

[40] See Buckland, *Directed by Steven Spielberg*, 97. Buckland notes Bordwell's examination of the 'wipe-cut' in David Bordwell, 'Intensified Continuity: Visual Style in Contemporary American Film', *Film Quarterly* 55, no. 3 (2002), 16–28. While I acknowledge the importance of a method (Buckland) and a technological innovation in lensing (Bordwell, 18–19), more visible, in my opinion, is a register of stylistic expression, a neo-baroque tendency toward virtuosity that reflects upon a classical model, and yet seeks to revise it. While perhaps hypothetical, I would argue that more important than the visibility of method and technology is a dialectical relationship between classical and neo-baroque style exemplified in the sequence; the wipe 'cuts' continuity into discrete sections.

[41] John Belton, *Widescreen Cinema* (Cambridge: Harvard University Press, 1992), 187.

FIGURES 6.12–15 *Expressive montage:* Jaws *(1975).*

FIGURES 6.16–17 *Contrived perspective through dual focus cinematography:* Jaws *(1975).*

Fifth movement: The spectacle image

The final movement follows the shot itinerary of the film's opening – beginning beneath the water, cutting to the surface, followed by the frenzy of the attack. However, in this second shark attack, in this turning of the screw, Spielberg incorporates Brody's perspective. Williams's score departs from the diegesis; the image is momentarily soundless. The cut to Brody at 16:40 is accompanied by an eerie non-diegetic sound. The stylistic mannerism of the sequence shot, rack focus, and jump cut in the preceding movements of the sequence now materialize as a quotation of Hitchcock's 'Vertigo shot', a contrivance of perspective through a simultaneous zoom and dolly movement in opposite directions (figures 6.18–6.22).

This sequence partakes of the register of the neo-baroque cinematic image identified by Ndalianis and Cubitt. Cubitt suggests that the neo-baroque

FIGURES 6.18–22 *The synthetic image of spectacle:* Jaws *(1975).*

cinema 'gathers the forces of film about its moments of spectacle'.[42] The technological and aesthetic apparatus of film is on display throughout the sequence. The spectacle presents as a mode of excess, an image that increasingly seeks to move beyond the parameters of the classical frame. Classicism's invisibility of style gives over to the artist's playful and self-reflexive virtuosity. Establishing shots enter into a rhythm of movement; classical composition and shot relation metamorphose into an expressive stylistics.

I have attempted to trace the way in which the medium of cinema, as well as a neo-baroque stylization, is inscribed in what for most spectators is a conventional sequence founded upon coherent exposition and action. Contrary to a great deal of commentary on Spielberg's poetics, in *Jaws* he shares the affinity for the stylistic excesses of the medium that characterized the American cinema of the 1970s. In this sense, Spielberg demonstrates here, and throughout his *oeuvre*, a mode of stylistic expressiveness that

---

[42] Cubitt, *The Cinema Effect*, 217.

displays the signature of the filmmaker as self-consciously as Scorsese's tracking shot in the early sequence of *Mean Streets* or Altman's asynchronous soundscapes in *McCabe and Mrs. Miller*. Spielberg is no less of the neo-baroque school of filmmakers that came out of UCLA, USC and the New York film schools, who had spent a decade studying the European filmmakers they admired.

There is clearly a cinematicality, a reflexive awareness of cinema's perception, in the development of the second shark attack sequence. Spielberg's procession of images is not to formulate an organic unity, but to contrive a series of movements that express the aesthetic autonomy of the image within the progression of the sequence; each shot builds incrementally on the last. The itinerary of the image is toward excess, toward revelation and a hyperbolic image of perception – the 'Vertigo shot' that reveals the destructive potential of the shark. Buckland argues that the shot 'is motivated and expressive in this scene, for it has a psychological meaning, just as it did when Hitchcock invented it in *Vertigo*'.[43] But clearly the motivation for the shot has less to with Brody's perspective than with a hyperbolic mode of perception Spielberg mechanically simulates. Hitchcock's 'Vertigo shot' simulated the protagonist's perceptual condition – that is, Scottie's (James Stewart) physical perception, which Hitchcock attempted to transpose to the spectator. Hitchcock had in fact attempted the shot in *Rebecca* (1940) to simulate the sensation of fainting.[44] But in *Jaws*, Spielberg does not imply that Brody sees the world in a way captured by the 'Vertigo shot'; nor is the shot purely the expression of a contained psychological state. Rather, the perspective is what I would call a cinematic contrivance, an image itinerary in excess of the common visual perception of the spectator. I would argue that Spielberg's camera move partakes of the register of the cartoon and its graphic excesses: Bugs Bunny, or Daffy Duck, or Roger Rabbit, their eyes popping out of their heads (figure 6.23). Perhaps, as Ndalianis suggests, neo-baroque style inscribes a mode of participatory spectatorship,[45] yet in this shot the effect is more appropriately to magnify the image, and to exceed the dimensions of the image in its naturalized (or classical) form. There is thus a psychological participation in the image that requires the distantiating effect of the cinematic apparatus.

Of course, the image the camera seeks is that of the shark. Spielberg's cinema formulates narratives founded upon the revelation of an imagined object, a shark, or a spaceship, or the Ark of the Covenant, or a newly realized

---

[43] Buckland, *Directed by Steven Spielberg*, 99.
[44] Truffaut, 372–4.
[45] Ndalianis, 152.

FIGURE 6.23 *Perceptual excess:* Who Framed Roger Rabbit *(1988).*

digital T-Rex. Such objects, paltry images in the mind, swell through cinema's apparatus of excess. Cinema's spectacle images do not simply materialize our mental images. The fascination – or obsession – with the spectacle image is exemplified in Roy Neary's (Richard Dreyfus) attempt to unearth the mystery of an alien encounter in a pile of mash potato (figure 6.24). Neary's crude construction is superseded by a domestic model (figure 6.25), and then by the astonishment of Spielberg's technological image in the final sequence of the film. The spectator desires the profound image reveal, the excess of an image of technology, rendered through a neo-baroque style in which classicism (or spatial and temporal unity) metamorphoses into grand aesthetic gesture. Neo-baroque excesses of style and technology in *Jaws*, *Close Encounters of the Third Kind* and *Star Wars Episode IV* establish an industrial and commercial production model. In the second shark attack sequence in *Jaws*, the shark remains unseen, incrementally swelling in the mind of the spectator. When we first see the shark, the mechanical apparatus dubbed 'Bruce', Brody's reaction – 'you're going to need a bigger boat' – is inevitably a let-down. It is both the image of a technological sublime and the deterioration of the mental projection. How could it not be? The shark had been storyboarded into all of the attack sequences, and would have been used extensively in production had it not broken down prior to shooting; the absent image is, ironically, a function of technological failure.[46] Yet by the late 1970s, as *Jaws* was superseded by *Star Wars Episode IV* as the highest grossing film in history, to be superseded by *E.T.: The Extra-Terrestrial* in 1982, Spielberg and Lucas (and the new studio system) had recognized the primal desire of the spectator to encounter images of excess, technologies of exhibition, and mass cinema's orientation toward spectacle.

---

[46] For a vivid and entertaining account of the several production catastrophes that beset *Jaws,* see Carl Gottlieb, *The Jaws Log, 30th Anniversary Edition* (New York: Newmarket, 2005).

FIGURES 6.24–5 *The obsessive desire for revelation:* Close Encounters of the Third Kind *(1977).*

Incitement to action, realist spectacle and the neo-baroque aesthetic: Omaha Beach, *Saving Private Ryan*

By the late 1990s, Spielberg's *oeuvre*, once exemplified by cinematic fantasies, included the Oscar-winning *Schindler's List* and the historical account of the uprising of African slaves in 1839, *Amistad* (1997). LaPorte's *The Men Who Would Be King* recounts in titillating detail the desire of Spielberg to cast himself as a serious filmmaker in the mould of the great studio directors of the past.[47] The Oscar for *Schindler's List* provided superficial evidence of the seriousness of Spielberg's cinema. While *Jaws* and *Close Encounters of the Third Kind* are also regarded in some sense as classic American films, the stigma of a uniquely spectacle (and thus 'adolescent') sensibility continues to define Spielberg's output for many commentators and theorists.

Saving Private Ryan, released in 1998, is perhaps Spielberg's most deliberate engagement with a serious cinema in the contemporary American tradition. Its subject matter recalls the chaotic realism of Cimino's *The Deer Hunter* and Coppola's *Apocalypse Now*. The narrative of a platoon of soldiers engaging in war is couched as both a gritty human story and a historical recreation of the actual experience of war veterans: 'They [veterans] all said there were two wars fought, there was our war and there was Hollywood's war.'[48] The film's gesture toward a cinematic realism that at times manifests a documentary aesthetic is radical in the context of Spielberg's studio production in the 1990s. A film about veterans, for veterans, recalls Oliver Stone's claims to authenticity of *Platoon* (1986) and *Born on the Fourth of July*

---

[47] Nicole LaPorte, *The Men Who Would Be King: An Almost Epic Tale of Moguls, Movies, and a Company Called Dreamworks* (Boston: Houghton Mifflin Harcourt, 2010).

[48] Steven Spielberg, cited in Toby Haggith, 'D-Day Filming – For Real. A Comparison and "Truth" and "Reality" in *Saving Private Ryan* and combat film by the British Army's Film and Photographic Unit', *Film History* 14, no. 3/4 (2002), 333.

(1989).⁴⁹ In *Saving Private Ryan*, the sequence in which the American soldiers disembark onto Omaha Beach is appropriately described as 'a landmark in the history of war films, because of the visceral power and brutal realism of its treatment of combat'.⁵⁰

Yet conceptualizing an aesthetic distinction between Spielberg's cinema of fantasy and a cinema of reality is problematic. As Plantinga has recently argued, cinema bears a necessary similarity to the spectator's individual and shared reality: 'the spectator has emotions and affects in response to narrative events in a film that suggests that she perceives and responds to a fictional world in some of the same ways she would perceive and respond to the actual world.'⁵¹ Spielberg's fantasy narratives engage directly, and profoundly, with the image of reality accorded to the spectator through her senses. The cinematic figure of E.T. bears no pleasant relation to an actual physical being – its bodily form is initially shocking, even repulsive. Yet the narrative scenario involving E.T.'s encounter with a family in suburban California is experientially familiar to the early 1980s mass culture spectator.⁵² Spielberg normalizes the alien form by displaying a reaction shot of a child (Drew Barrymore) upon discovery of E.T. (figure 6.26); incredulity, fear and repulsion ultimately mature into acceptance, sympathy and love (figure 6.27). These are narrative scenarios that reflect upon, and indeed converse with, the narrative scenarios intrinsic to several rites of maturation in spectacle cinema.

More significantly, Spielberg's concertedly realist cinema partakes of an aesthetic register (*mise en scène*, composition through movement, montage) identifiable in his fantasy films. In the previous section of this chapter, I provided an example of the neo-baroque aestheticism of a sequence in *Jaws*, in which the image is affiliated to a discrete movement within the broader compositional structure of narrative. I wish to provide an analysis of two similar movements, one extracted from *Jaws* and exemplary of High Concept spectacle cinema, the other extracted from *Saving Private Ryan*, and projected as cinematic 'realism'. Each movement, I argue, is underscored by the incitement to action, imagistic excess and narrative disambiguation.

---

⁴⁹ See Chris Salewicz, *Oliver Stone: The Making of his Movies* (London: Orion Media, 1997).

⁵⁰ Haggith, 332.

⁵¹ Carl Plantinga, 'Trauma, Pleasure and Emotion in the Viewing of *Titanic*: A Cognitive Approach', in *Film Theory and Contemporary Hollywood Movies*, ed. Warren Buckland (London: Routledge, 2009), 240.

⁵² This suburban setting bears a striking similarity to the idyllic community of Amity (*Jaws*). Spielberg captures small-town Americana with familiar cinematic, but more explicitly popular cultural, tropes: a community of kids moving through a space, the boundaries of which must be transgressed; figures of authority who remain oblivious to the significance of supernatural elements in their midst; rituals of gatherings that move outward from family to civic institutions to repressive state apparatuses, and so on.

FIGURES 6.26–27 *A narrative of encounter and maturation:* E.T.: The Extra-Terrestrial *(1982).*

In the first encounter with Jaws on the ocean [1:11:40], Spielberg begins an orchestrated action sequence with an elaborate ejection from the preceding action – a dissolve. The image materializes in close-up on Brody's continued attempts to tie a seaman's knot (figure 6.28); his failure to accomplish the task provides a stultifying rhythm to the movement. The setting displays the banality of inaction: Quint (Robert Shaw) sits in his position over the rod, Brody situates the centrality of the frame (figure 6.29), Hooper (Richard Dreyfus) steers the boat. A series of cuts display the characters in relation – images bereft of action, or indeed, the potential for action (figure 6.30). Williams's distinctive non-diegetic soundscape is conspicuously absent. Yet in High Concept cinema, inaction serves merely as counterpoint to aggressive action and character volition. The commencement of the movement from inaction to action occurs through a single image: a close-up on Quint, low-angled, displaying the exaggerated proportions of the rod and reel. The shot strategically locates the central focus of the ensuing action (figure 6.31). When the reel begins to turn, indicating the presence of the imagined Other, the transition from stasis, passivity and inaction to movement and action is initiated. Brody, oblivious to the inciting incident (the turning of the reel, the sound of which is amplified on the audio track), continues the repetitive (but unfulfilled) turning of the rope. It is critical that Hooper and Brody are displayed in poses of inaction, and indeed, distraction, within the frame that composes Quint and the turning reel (figures 6.32–6.33). The movement toward action can be completed only through the simultaneous incitement to action of the central figures within the sequence: Brody (the film's protagonist) and the imagined Other (the film's antagonist). A series of discrete images builds the spectator's anticipation of the image of action, intensifying an inherent continuity in the movement:[53] Quint straps himself into the harness; Williams's unsettling score swells gradually in intensity. It is imperative that Brody and Hooper are oblivious to these diegetic and non-diegetic gestures.

---

[53] Bordwell, 'Intensified Continuity'.

FIGURES 6.28–33 *The image of inaction prefiguring the incitement to action:* Jaws *(1975).*

At this point, the image of action is initiated. Brody yells, 'Ay! I got it!', successfully tying the knot and completing one of several rites of maturation he will undergo at sea. But more important than tying the knot is the aggressive action of snapping the rope taut and displaying the knot to the audience – Spielberg shoots Brody's action in a medium close-up (figure 6.34). Attentive to Brody's accomplishment (from ineptitude to maturation, inaction to action), the imagined Other flees from the boat, bringing the reel to full and aggressive life within the frame (figure 6.35). The synchronicity of action between Brody and the imagined Other is integral to the formation of the image of action.

We see such movements from inaction to action throughout Spielberg's *oeuvre*, and indeed, throughout the American High Concept cinema. An almost identical set piece occurs in the revelation of the T-Rex in Act Two of *Jurassic Park*. Dr Malcolm (Jeff Goldblum) sits in the back of a jeep as Dr Sattler and Peck (Robert Muldoon) search for signs of Dr Grant and the children. This brief sequence functions as a pause in the narrative, awaiting the incitement to the next action sequence. A single shot mediates the transition

FIGURES 6.34–5 *The incitement to action:* Jaws *(1975).*

from inaction (Sattler and Peck moving arbitrarily within the space, Malcolm isolated in the jeep) and action: the ripple in a rainwater puddle signaling the arrival of the T-Rex. Spielberg deliberately shifts from the metonymic image of the imagined Other (the puddle of water) to a series of cuts displaying the characters assembling and moving with renewed purpose, animated through increased intensity. The sequence concludes appropriately on the reveal: a T-Rex of impossible scale, constituted out of a digital material new to cinema. The revelation of the impossible image requires the formal transition from stasis to movement, inaction to action, passive engagement to intensified volition. Such movements not only characterize, but fundamentally materi-alize, the image of action in High Concept cinema.

Could we not argue something very similar about the explicit and brutal image of action displayed on Omaha Beach in *Saving Private Ryan*? Could we not say that 'realism' in the sequence on Omaha Beach is inscribed through precisely the same neo-baroque aestheticism demonstrated in *Jaws*, and that Spielberg's images of war partake of the same register of excess as the image of a shark, or a digital dinosaur? Essentially, I would argue that the spectator's desire to encounter the impossible image of combat in *Saving Private Ryan* is founded upon the same desire to encounter the image of excess materialized through action in Spielberg's so-called fantasy cinema. Neo-baroque aestheticism in *Saving Private Ryan* merely masquerades as an aesthetic of reality; images of war are less a historical record (and certainly not an indexical impression of the real) than a performance of spectacle cinema's image and narrative poetics.

The set piece in which Captain Miller (Tom Hanks) arrives at Omaha Beach is not precisely an image *of history*, but a subjectivized reflection; indeed, the subjectivized memory of war is a strategic device deployed throughout *Saving Private Ryan*.[54] The perceived realism of image, shot, and cut during

---

[54] For an excellent analysis of affective mechanisms in the Omaha Beach sequence in *Saving Private Ryan*, see Michael Hammond, '*Saving Private Ryan's* Special Affect', in *Action and Adventure Cinema*, ed. Yvonne Tasker (New York: Routledge, 2004), 153–66. I ostensibly agree with Hammond's position on the film, though Hammond is more acutely focused on aesthetic style as a mechanism of affect. Hammond appropriately dubs the sequence 'melodramatic dramaturgy' (159).

the Omaha Beach sequence (a series of three movements comprising 18 minutes) effaces the spectator's memory of an elegiac low-angle, sun-dappled medium shot of the American flag that opens the film (figure 6.36). Private Ryan, an old man at Arlington cemetery, reflects on the heroism of the men who gave their lives so that his could be spared. In the narrative frame closure in the final sequence of the film (the past is flashback), Ryan asks of his wife: 'Tell me I've led a good life. Tell me I'm a good man', to which she replies, 'You are'. The film closes on the image of the American flag with which it opened (figure 6.36). The frame functions not only as a point of entry and exit into a conventional flashback, but isolates the perceptual mechanism through which the war will be imagined and visualized. As in the opening to *Schindler's List*, Spielberg focuses on the eyes of the perceptual mechanism with a slow dolly from medium shot to extreme close-up (figures 6.37–6.39).

The hard cut to the beach, displacing the image of Ryan's gaze, materializes as memory, a strategically deployed reflection. The spectator now encounters an image with a reduced colour saturation of 60 per cent,[55] shot from a low angle (figure 6.40). After a brief overhead establishing shot of the boats coming in to the beach, Spielberg cuts to the frenetic hand-held camera cinematography he will employ for much of the action that follows.

The set piece is a performance of various registers of cinematic realism, modulated to present the impression of reality while overlaying that impression with a subjectivized (and ideologized) reflection on the past. I perceive three modalities of cinematic realism operating as discrete movements within the sequence. First: documentary realism; second: what I describe as 'orchestrated realism', in which a documentary aesthetic (resembling cinéma vérité, though without that aesthetic's tendency toward voyeurism) is supplemented by story and character elements fashioning a narrative movement; third: narrative realism (inscribing progressive action), in which the itinerary of the war image is framed in its entirety against the narrative of volition that will return the past to the present (enclosing the framed memory) in the final sequence of the film.

Movement 1, documentary realism, is evident in Spielberg's recreation of the chaos of the arrival on the beach, which commences with the approach of the boats on the water. This introductory sequence is shot primarily with hand-held camera, eschews forced framing (a compositional aesthetic), and covers the image only through diegetic sound. In much the same way as Greengrass shoots hand-held to capture the spontaneity of action in *United 93* (2006), Spielberg shoots interiors (of the boat) and exteriors,

---

[55] See Blain Brown, *Cinematography: Theory and Practice* (Waltham, MA: Focal Press, 2002), 223–4.

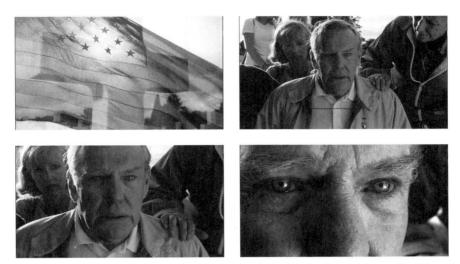

FIGURES 6.36–39 *A subjective recollection of war:* Saving Private Ryan *(1998).*

medium-to-long shot, in hand-held. The aesthetic mannerism contrives an aesthetic of spontaneity, of unanticipated encounter. Hand-held cinematography also captures the effect of the natural undulation of the setting, on the water, and on the land. The sequence accentuates the documentary realism of diegetic sound in the underwater shots, in which sound is muffled for the spectator. The presence of blood and other matter on the camera in the early sequences [6:08],[56] while clearly orchestrated, is a striking indication of the desire for aesthetic realism (figure 6.41). The inference is that the spectator encounters an aesthetic reproducing historical actuality; the affective import is that we are watching history in the unfolding. Spielberg thus presents himself as a documentarian, and the cinematic image as historical document.

The documentary aesthetic continues in the initial outpouring of soldiers, the arbitrary nature of death and violence, and the unpremeditated response of soldiers to the trauma of the assault. The sequence from 8:01–8:19, in which the hand-held camera captures the action in depth with various levels of diegetic sound, is convincingly realistic. Reverse shots from the 'murder-holes' display the action in depth (figures 6.42–6.43), and in lengthy takes [8:23–8:36]. The entirety is shot in real-time, at natural speed, with only diegetic sound to accompany the image. The first movement concludes at 9:20, with a shot of Captain Miller alighting on the beach. The image shifts to a subtle slow-motion, diegetic sound is muffled, and a non-diegetic sound enters the frame. At this point, Spielberg relocates the perceptual presence

---

[56] Time-code references are to *Saving Private Ryan* (DVD – Widescreen Special Limited Edition), Dreamworks Home Entertainment, 1999.

of the film; Miller (Hanks) is substituted for the older Ryan of the film's prologue – critically, the clearly differentiated protagonist as subject-position is maintained.

The slow-motion sequence inaugurates a shift in register from documentary realism to orchestrated realism (Movement 2). The image is strategically subjectivized through Miller's perception; the movement is a discrete narrative section calculated to guide the spectator to an interpretation of the chaos. The maelstrom of the arrival on the beach, the arbitrary nature of the action in Movement 1, is organized (and narrativized) for the spectator through Miller's point of view. At 10:24, the camera shifts into a close-up on Miller (figures 6.44–6.46), which commences the movement up the beach.

In the second movement of the sequence, unforced framing is interspersed with an increasing number of forced frames [for example, 11:46–11:50; 12:18–12:20; 14:25–14:31], providing a measured compositional quality to the previously 'non-compositional' (spontaneously unfolding) action. Scattered diegetic sound is lowered to provide access to instrumental dialogue that will progress the narrative and character development: a medium close-up on a dying soldier crying 'Mama!' (figure 6.47); the forced frame on a soldier's tirade: 'Just give us a fucking chance, you sonofabitch!' (figure 6.48); the exchange between Miller and Horvath (Tom Sizemore): 'Captain, if your mother saw you do that, she'd be very upset'/'I thought you were my mother.' At 16:14, the image cuts to a forced frame in depth, a group of soldiers gathered in foreground over a dying man (figure 6.49). As in the landing on the beach, blood and other matter is displayed on the lens (or added in post-production), conflating diegesis with non-diegetic material. Yet now there is clearly an orchestration to the 'realism' of the presence of the camera. Whereas the first image of the spotted lens fluctuated through the hand-held movement of the camera, now Spielberg brings the image to rest, and the camera's 'presence' in the diegetic space presents as a compositional element of the movement. The arbitrary location of people and objects transforms into the strategic isolation of Miller and his platoon. Violence is now calculated for dramatic effect: a soldier, feeling a bullet strike his helmet, removes the helmet, only to be shot in the head [18:44–18:52]. Movement 2 concludes at the first resting point on the beach, providing the setting for the narrative action that will lead into the subsequent, and concluding, movement.

Orchestrated realism is fully integrated into a conceptual scenario through a ritualized performance of a genre trope: the sniping of the enemy. This single action provides the first visualization of the protagonist and antagonist in relation to each other. While the film begins with an arbitrary set of character relations on a beach, it now recasts random violence and arbitrary character

FIGURES 6.40–43 *Arrival at Omaha Beach:* Saving Private Ryan *(1998)*.

relations in a Manichean morality exemplary of American High Concept cinema.[57] The cut to an extreme close-up on the sniper with a movement outward (figures 6.50–6.52) functions as a conventional cinematic movement – a shot reverse-shot execution common in contemporary action cinema.[58] The taking of the hill (a series of 'murder-holes') accomplishes the movement from orchestrated realism to what Menand calls 'possibly the most tried-and-true dramatic plot known to man: a life is saved'.[59] The sequence concludes with Miller's subjective perception of the destruction and carnage on the beach (again, the movement into extreme close-up), accompanied by the return of Williams's overarching theme (figures 6.53–6.56).

In the Omaha Beach sequence, Spielberg demonstrates his virtuosity in the use of the cinematic medium to produce not a recreated reality, but a 'reality effect'; the cinematic image materialized in excess of a naturalized perception of the world. The image in *Saving Private Ryan* demonstrates a uniquely cinematic itinerary, in which *mise en scène*, movement and rhythm through montage provides an experience of the image of cinema: of its purity through the technology and aesthetic of the medium. As in Spielberg's virtuoso rendition of the image of excess in *Jaws*, in *Saving Private Ryan* the

[57] For an analysis of a monomythic foundation to the American superhero film, see John Shelton Lawrence and Robert Jewett, *The Myth of the American Superhero* (Grand Rapids: Wm B. Erdmans, 2002). For an examination of the 'evil other' in the genre, see especially 36–42.

[58] A similar action interchange take place in *The Hurt Locker* (Bigelow, 2008).

[59] Louis Menand, '*Saving Private Ryan*: Jerry Don't Surf', in *The Films of Steven Spielberg: Critical Essays*, ed. Charles L. P. Silet (Lanham: Scarecrow Press, 2002), 251.

FIGURES 6.44–49 *Orchestrated Realism:* Saving Private Ryan *(1998).*

excess is that which lies beyond the real, that which is more than reality and must be imagined through a cinematic itinerary. This image in *Saving Private Ryan* is no less a product of the apparatus of cinema than the overwhelming image of the Mothership and hangar in *Close Encounters of the Third Kind*, or the impossible image of a realist dystopian cityscape in *Minority Report (2002)*. *Saving Private Ryan* is thus no more 'realistic' a mode of cinema than Spielberg's fantasy narratives, which give back equally, and in equal portion, the unattainable image. This is not a criticism of Spielberg, who is in my estimation the consummate film stylist operating in the aftermath of the New American Cinema. Instead, I offer this reading of Spielberg's aesthetic design in an attempt to account for the affect of such images in contemporary global film culture. Such self-exhibiting images are nearer to *revelation* than depiction, nearer to the experience of a thrill, the viscerality of movement and action, than instrumental signification.

The neo-baroque excess of the image is radical precisely because it is conventionally framed within a recognizable, and hermetically sealed, scenario. Spectacle requires accessible narrative structure, archetypal characterization,

FIGURES 6.50–56 *Narrative disambiguation:* Saving Private Ryan *(1998).*

and an aesthetic of excess. Spielberg's aesthetic functions to disambiguate the image – much as the aesthetic of Antonioni, or Coppola, or more recently a filmmaker like Haneke, functions to present images of radical ambiguity.[60] What begins as the randomness and spontaneity of documentary realism metamorphoses into a spectacle in which the image is disambiguated and

---

[60] Consider, for example, the open endings inscribing the aesthetic of ambiguity supplemented by the image of contemplation and inaction in *Caché* (*Hidden*, 2005) and *Das Weisse Band* (*The White Ribbon*, 2009).

concretely conceptualized. Once disambiguated (Movement 2 and 3 within the Omaha Beach set piece), the image functions as an exhibit, a veritable artwork built of the technology and aesthetic material of cinema. While I cannot hope to account for every shot, scene, or sequence in *Saving Private Ryan*, or indeed, Spielberg's cinema, I argue that a spectacle aesthetic is not only present in the poetics of Spielberg, but that, increasingly, and with increasing image-literacy, the contemporary mass spectator discovers herself attuned to the unique shapes, rhythms and compositional networks that inscribe a cinema of spectacle, and therein, the image modalities of the contemporary blockbuster film.

7

Spectacle affect

Image, narrative and affect: Theoretical paradigms

I have suggested that spectacle is a function of a particular narrative stylistics, and a particular image modality founded on an orientation toward excess. Narrative orientation tends toward structural simplification; toward concrete conceptual design (a High Concept framework) and formal patterning. Formal patterning is accessed, and indeed anticipated, through several mechanisms analyzed in assiduous detail in Thompson's *Storytelling in the New Hollywood*: 'Hollywood favors unified narratives, which means most fundamentally that a cause should lead to an effect and that effect in turn should become a cause for another effect, in an unbroken chain across the film.'[1] These are narrative mechanics in Thompson's study, though we might equally say that such mechanics of causality – implying open access to character motivation, and a spatial and temporal realism – inhere in conceptual design. It is a reality of the contemporary studio system that a large proportion of speculation film scripts are optioned for a conceptual framework and rewritten for production.[2] High Concept story requires the mechanics of narrative progression outlined in Thompson's study of ten films, each a studio vehicle, each differing in some fundamental way, yet each essentially classical in its narrative and conceptual orientation. There are of course anomalies (Payne's *The Descendants* [2011]

---

[1] Thompson, *Storytelling in the New Hollywood*, 12.
[2] See Stephen F. Breimer, *The Screenwriter's Legal Guide* (New York: Allworth Press, 2004), 88–9. Breimer suggests that the predicament is changing under new Writers Guild of America rules, yet ownership of the original optioned script remains a matter for negotiation (86). For a colourful account of the misadventures of the Hollywood screenwriter, see William Goldman, *Adventures in the Screen Trade: A Personal View of Hollywood and Screenwriting* (New York: Warner Books, 1984). While Goldman's account is somewhat dated, the material context of the production from screenplay to film remains relevant in the era of contemporary Hollywood.

seems oddly assimilated into a classical system,[3] as does Anderson's *There Will Be Blood* [2007]), yet I would concur with Thompson that the system maintains in significant measure for producers and mass culture consumers across the classical and new studio eras.

Thompson, and for that matter the majority of formalist theorists, have less to say about modalities of the image, and less to say about cinema's affective register, in which the spectator is carried away not only by narrative mechanics (and cognitive cues), but also by what several recent theorists refer to as 'intensities': movements, rhythms, sound motifs, image motifs, energies, the substance of cinema that functions in concert with narrative. Movement seems to be key here, or at least, movement as transformation from one form into another. Working through Deleuze's all-encompassing notion of the movement-image (which is of the same 'set' as the time-image, though separate in its properties),[4] Colman suggests that affect 'is what will cause the movement from one state to another … A movement (or action) occurs, giving rise to an affect, in turn generating a reaction and perception of both the affect and the action.'[5] In Deleuze, affect presages action; an affective transformation materializes as an action-image. And of course, such action-images then create new affective potentialities, that again build to create further actions, and so on.[6] This notion of affect, whether in Deleuze or elsewhere, again asks what cinema is beyond a transparent mediation of signs. How is sensation triggered by a flow of images and sounds, or even a colour that prompts something beyond the spectator's cognitive reach but remains affecting all the same? Is there some faculty that opens itself to, or is

---

[3] The final shot of *The Descendants* displays the elegant (and subtle) negotiation of a cinematic classicism and the tendency toward what Sconce and others have called 'Smart Cinema'. In the shot, the scattering of bodies within the lounge room resolves into an image of a family brought together by tragedy. Yet over and above what is a familiar trope of classical narrative, Payne maintains the shot in depth and significant duration, imposing upon it the façade of an alternative, avant-garde ethos. For recent readings of the 'Smart Cinema' aesthetic, see Jeffrey Sconce, 'Irony, Nihilism and the New American "Smart" Film', *Screen* 43, no. 4 (2002), 349–69; see also Claire Perkins, *American Smart Cinema* (Edinburgh: Edinburgh University Press, 2012).

[4] See Colman, *Deleuze and Cinema*, 14–15.

[5] Colman, *Deleuze and Cinema*, 82.

[6] For an enchanting anecdote of movement inherent in stillness, see Raùl Ruiz, *Poetics of Cinema*, trans. Brian Holmes (Paris: Dis Voir, 2005), 65: 'Another memory: in Canton province not far from Guilin, I was out on a boat with some friends. We had just had lunch, and we were lazy and intermittently napping, when somebody woke us up saying: "Look, look, there is a Taoist monk over there." I looked, and I saw an immobile monk on the banks of the river, in the position of somebody getting ready to take a big leap. He was so immobile that I had the impression that everything so apparently immobile, like the stones, the hills, the clouds in the sky, was teeming with movement – everything but the monk. Immobility called for movement, movement engendered immobility. Behind every immobile thing movement lurked. I said to myself: "These things were falsely immobile. Immobility conceals movement."'

opened by, the image, and thus experiences it as something more than what it means, or what it carries?

In recent studies of cinema, affect is commonly conceptualized as more than an emotional response. Plantinga describes emotion as merely 'one sort of psychological entity among a broader class of affects'.[7] In Carroll's oft-cited study, affect refers to 'felt bodily states',[8] or the 'life of feeling',[9] a complex set of emotional, visceral, cognitive and perceptual transformations. While Carroll very usefully distinguishes between emotion and affect, the body remains critical to the affective experience. More recently, Sobchack has described cinematic affect as embodiment, 'not merely with the body as an abstracted object belonging always to someone else but also with what it means to be "embodied" and to live our animated and metamorphic existences as the concrete, extroverted, and spirited subjects we all objectively are'.[10] I could apply the notion of embodied experience to the affect created by Lars von Trier's *Melancholia*, a film that deliberately works through a complex affective register. Von Trier's images materialize in some sense beneath an instrumental perception, moving fluidly between past and present, subjectivity and objectivity, substance and insubstantiality. The final shot of *Melancholia* confronts the spectator with stunning intensity: this is an encounter between image and self that engages with a narrative outcome (the end of the world is surely the most dramatic of all narrative outcomes), and yet, even momentarily, the image of an ending seems to exceed such spatially and temporally constrained boundaries (figures 7.1–7.3). This totality of the experience of the image seems to be what Sobchack aims at: 'We need to alter the binary and bifurcated structures of the film experience suggested by previous formulations and, instead, posit the film viewer's lived body as a carnal "third term" that grounds and mediates experience and language, subjective vision and objective image.'[11]

But what then is the relationship between an experience of an image – the final image of *Melancholia* would not recede from my mind for days afterward – and an experience of an encapsulating narrative form? What is the relationship between my body, my embodied being, and more than merely 'the image', but *this image* in a narrative progression, which displays

---

[7] Carl Plantinga, *Moving Viewers: American Film and the Spectator Experience* (Berkeley: University of California Press, 2009), 9.

[8] Noël Carroll, *The Philosophy of Motion Pictures* (Malden, MA: Blackwell, 2008), 149.

[9] Carroll, *The Philosophy of Motion Pictures*, 147.

[10] Vivian Sobchack, *Carnal Thoughts: Embodiment and Moving Image Culture* (Berkeley: University of California Press, 2004), 1.

[11] Sobchack, *Carnal Thoughts*, 60.

FIGURES 7.1–3 *The intensity of cinematic experience:* Melancholia *(2011).*

its material unique to a spatial and temporal moment?[12] Or do all of cinema's images necessarily provide the same 'experience of seeing, hearing, touching, moving, tasting, smelling in which our sense of the literal and the figural may sometimes vacillate, may sometimes be perceived in uncanny discontinuity, but most usually configures to make undifferentiated sense and meaning together'?[13]

Drawing on Miriam Hansen's influential work, Anne Rutherford has recently theorized a cinema that 'reveals the potential to shake the disparate elements of the film free from the conventional narrative sequences'; this is an aesthetic that 'reveals how the format of narrative can be adapted to open onto a cinematic experience that is rich, layered and exhilarating'.[14] In Rutherford's evocative description, these material elements constitute the rhythms that underlie storytelling. Of course, cinematic narrative might be rich and layered, and the spectator might be exhilarated by the complexity

---

[12] In fact, Plantinga argues that 'emotions (and other affective experiences) unfold in time; they are not like snapshots, but rather more like narratives' (*Moving Viewers*, 9; see also 80–2). This is an intriguing position and illuminates the essential interconnectedness of experiencing a film as an image-form while simultaneously experiencing those images within a temporal system, narrative. I would therefore agree that 'the spectator's emotional experience is largely directed to the film's narrative' (*Moving Viewers*, 10; see also 83–4). Affective engagement is part of the wider operation of the cinema commodity within the contemporary Hollywood studio cinema, and such affective processes are in the main founded upon narrative form and function, or what Plantinga calls 'a chronological pattern of emotional response' (91).

[13] Sobchack, *Carnal Thoughts*, 76.

[14] Anne Rutherford, *What Makes a Film Tick?: Cinematic Affect, Materiality and Mimetic Innervation* (New York: Peter Lang, 2011), 28.

of a narrative system. We see such narratives in classical *noir*, in which the experience of cinema is derived, at least in part, from resolution. Turning points, plot points within acts, reversals, and so forth, provide various measures of intensity. The exhilaration occasioned by the *dénouement* of *The Usual Suspects* (1995) is surely founded upon the revelation of narrative 'truth', which is distilled into the neatness of the identity of Keyser Söze. The conflict internal to irresolution gives over to the reassurance, and exhilaration, of resolution – Singer's zoom into extreme close-up of the Kobayashi mug is less for a calculated affective response than to provide the requisite pause in narrative, the necessary duration that enables the spectator to make sense of the revelation. The perception of narrative truth is thus *distended*, and all the more astonishing for its distension (figures 7.4–7.6).

But Rutherford's exhilaration at Malick's images in *Days of Heaven* speaks of something else that animates narrative progression, and overlays narrative with its own affective register. Precisely what constitutes the material of affect is more difficult to conceptualize, and frequently requires the substitution of metaphor and generalization for detailed, and functionally oriented, film analysis. Thus, for Rutherford,

> At the climax of the film [*Days of Heaven*], this energetic charge is focused on the locusts. This intensity is not about emotion … An anthropomorphic moment it may be, on one level – but this is more about the way the motion, texture and sound are experienced across the sensorium of the viewer, the way they stir up the viewer, hook them into the moment on a level of heightened awareness, out of the habitual, into the senses, into the materiality of the image.[15]

Here the prose is evocative, and indeed, stirring. The prose of course further stirs up an emotional experience in the reader, animating a memory or future experience of the concluding sequence of the film. Rutherford projects a radically subjective experience of a cinematic movement as a confluence of images, a stream of affect and sensation, particular to the spectator yet in some sense quite generalized. Even more subjectivized is Sobchack's account of the experience of a sequence in *The Piano* (1993), cited in Rutherford: 'Watching *The Piano*, my skin's potentiality streams toward the screen to rebound back on itself. It becomes literally and intensely sensitized to texture and tactility.'[16] This is again a radically personal experience; sensation 'streams'

---

[15] Rutherford, 29.

[16] Cited in Rutherford, 50. For a more expansive revelation of the sensation of encountering *The Piano's* opening shots, see Sobchack, *Carnal Thoughts*, 62–6. For Plantinga, the issue

 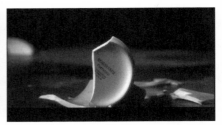

FIGURES 7.4–6 *The intensity of narrative revelation:* The Usual Suspects *(1995).*

and 'rebounds', vaulted gestures that attempt to 'account for' a modality of image experience. But how can affect be sufficiently described, or explained, through such metaphors of experience? I acknowledge that, for Sobchack, such verbs are not employed metaphorically.[17] But would such active experiences apply to all modes of cinematic encounters, to all films, or only films with the unique affective propensity of *The Piano*? What does it mean for the 'skin's potentiality' to '[stream] toward the screen'? While Rutherford herself takes issue with Sobchack's non-specific account of cinema's affect, in her description of the affect of Malick's images, words such as 'energetic charge' or 'intensity', or even the more banal 'hook', create an impression of, rather than functionally describe, the experience of cinema. Malick's images resonate through the 'orchestration of a material pulse'.[18] The image is thus some kind of material, some kind of objective matter, beyond merely the shell of progressive storied elements. Yet such images remain in Rutherford, or in Sobchack's account, generalized across all modes of spectatorship, springing

---

with Sobchack's phenomenological mode of affect is in the notion of film experience as dual embodiment: the embodiment of the spectator, and the embodiment of the *film*, that displays its own affective capacities and experiences. Thus, Sobchack's language in this account of a film experience seems to imply a knowing (or at least affectively operating) communication between cinema and the spectator. See Plantinga, *Moving Viewers*, 115–16.

[17] Sobchack, *Carnal Thoughts*, 79. See also Vivian Sobchack, *The Address of the Eye: A Phenomenology of Film Experience* (Princeton: Princeton University Press, 1992), xviii. Sobchack's project indeed is to '[destabilize] language' and its reliance on metaphors of phenomenological experience.

[18] Rutherford, 29.

forth and moving outward from a more conventional cognitive enjoyment of cinematic story. 'The close-up', suggests Rutherford 'is like an exclamation mark – like the deflection onto a gestural moment of intensity.'[19] Perhaps this is the case, and the potential of the close-up is provocative in a great deal of cinema. And yet as I attempted to show in a discussion of Leone's *Once Upon a Time in the West*, even the close-up is rarely a discrete cinematic perspective; an image, or a shot, has the capacity to function differently in the hands of different filmmakers. In Leone, the close-up is not exclusively a barometer of intensity, but expresses also the potential of the image to exceed the compositional and textual (image as cinematic trope) frame.

Rutherford's (and Sobchack's) position seems too aggressive a turn away from an engagement with narrative form and narrative experience. Cinematic images are affecting. Yet such images are also redolent with semiotic content. In Rutherford's methodology, narrative presents merely a convenient assemblage of images, or image intensities. The spectator experiences the image first (and primarily) as non-narrative intensity; narrative then sorts a series of intensities into a functional and reproducible framework. If narrative remains an incidental shell, intensity is privileged as *more than* instrumental stimulus. This is why Rutherford's study of affect leans toward Malick and not, say, John Carpenter, Brian De Palma, or indeed, Steven Spielberg, all filmmakers working through the medium's capacity for affect, yet attuned to the affective disposition of causal narrative progression. This is why Sobchack's most primal encounter with the cinematic sensorium in *Carnal Thoughts* is through *The Piano*. One might therefore argue that Malick's cinema (or Campion's cinema, for that matter) demonstrates less a 'radical conception of what narrative is – what its place is and how it progresses'[20] than a series of narrative episodes loosely integrated into a somewhat dispersed whole. The spectator encounters in Malick – particularly *Days of Heaven*, *The New World* (2005) and *Tree of Life* (2011) – a filmmaker at best casually affiliated to the affective potential of narrative form.[21]

Rather, in shaping rhythmic affect, as Pearlman notes, the image in flow is necessarily a confluence of narrative and movement:

> In film editing, an editor is rarely simply making an experience of time, energy, and movement; she is also shaping story, character relationships,

---

[19] Rutherford, 20.

[20] Rutherford, 27.

[21] See, for example, Carl Plantinga, 'Defending *Tree of Life*', *The Society for Cognitive Studies of the Moving Image*, July 9 2011, http://scsmi-online.org/forum/defending-the-tree-of-life [accessed June 2, 2012]. Plantinga reads the story elements of *Tree of Life* 'less like cogs in a narrative wheel than poetic interludes or ruminations in a cosmic pastiche'. I would argue that one could say the same of *Days Of Heaven*, several sequences in *The Thin Red Line* (1998) and *The New World*.

and other kinds of information … In shaping the rhythm of the film, time, energy, and movement are the salient factors; they shape the qualitative experience of the story and information.[22]

This is particularly the case in a cinematic aesthetic that privileges narrative form, which is not to say complexity, but the affective experience of story, character and theme in logical relation. In a similar vein, I have argued for a consideration of the image as a material that infuses, and indeed substantiates, narrative and yet which might be experienced, even momentarily, as an autonomous object. This is not to reject Thompson's classical paradigm of the contemporary Hollywood cinema, in which narrative structure is accorded a special status. Indeed, it is to attempt to build on this foundation by establishing a conceptual and methodological bridge between narrative mechanics and image modality. Such a bridge would illuminate the essential relationship between the autonomous image and narrative progression in which intensities, the embodied effect of sounds and images in flow, and the rhythmic performance of this flow, enrich and substantiate, rather than enervate, narrative form. Rather than disabling the progression of narrative, I argue that the spectacle image imbues narrative with a special intensity experienced by the spectator. Could we not be equally evocative about Cameron's image intensities in *The Terminator*, or *Titanic*, or *Avatar* – films that match, in movement, rhythm, and momentum, the classical narrative itinerary expounded in Thompson's study? Could we not describe our engagement with the spectacle film as an experience of image intensity, of an image affect *in concert with* an experience of High Concept design and narrative? Further, could one argue that the spectacle image is attuned to a unique mode of cinematic affect built of an intensity expressed *within* the parameters of classical narrative form?

This is to ask, simply, why narrative and image intensities continue to be viewed in film studies as oppositional and antagonistic, rather than the integrated parts of an aesthetic system. Why must the contemplation of image intensities in cinema occasion a 'paradigm shift'?[23] Surely all theorists of cinema, and all spectators, must acknowledge that narrative presents a progression of images, and that the particular progressive form of these

---

[22] Karen Pearlman, *Cutting Rhythms: Shaping the Film Edit* (Burlington, MA: Focal Press, 2009), 39. Pearlman's edited film thus functions as an experiential whole, in which movement, time and energy works with narrative progression, story information and character development. While I am not particularly committed to the notion of an experiential whole in cinema (or the fullness of the revelation of story), this formal synthesis of narrative and energy seems a critical development in ways of thinking through cinema's experiential capacities.

[23] Rutherford, 37–9.

images imbues cinema with an affective life. While Plantinga's contention that 'it is a film's narration, consisting of its narrative structure, style, and point of view, that shapes the overall experience it offers'[24] might be seen to marginalize the kind of image intensities perceived by Rutherford in *Days of Heaven*,[25] there is surely something commonsensical in locating the image and its narrative flow in an organic, and mutually affecting, relationship.

In this chapter, I attempt to account for the unique experience of the spectacle image, spectacle cinema's capacity for affect. I confess this attempt to explain experience channels through a stream of memories of my own first, and subsequent, experiences of cinematic spectacles. I recall an experience of *Superman II* (1982) at a cinema in Cape Town, South Africa, overwhelmed by the battle between Superman (Christopher Reeve) and General Zod (Terence Stamp). I recall the impression of the speed of flight of the body through the streets of Metropolis. The spectacle was less impressive viewed as an adolescent in the late 1980s. As an adult, I recall the experience of a stunningly beautiful underwater sequence in Kostner's *Waterworld* (1995) in an otherwise thinly veiled reworking of *The Road Warrior*; the sequence maintains as the entirety of that cinematic experience. In Bay's *Transformers*, I was awed by the mechanical figure of the body set to rhythmic slow motion (figures 7.7–7.9); *Transformers* reflects a fascination with both the machine and the body, two of contemporary culture's abiding fetishes. Here of course my model of affect is somewhat cognitively tuned; the profound site of my cinematic experience is a personal and collective memory: private, public, cultural, in perhaps varying orders of affective import. But memory is for me the provocative site at which affect gains traction – memory is something more than cognition, more than sense-making. I sense that my fascination with cinema began through its experiential, affective mechanisms, and such mechanisms seem to potentially predate conscious, or cognitive, engagement. I encountered cinema's critical discourses only after I had been ineradicably altered by an affective experience of moving images.

I again reflect upon the elements of spectacle thus far considered: the imprint of technology in the image, the orientation toward neo-baroque excess in image form, and the orientation toward disambiguation in concept and narrative design. Affect, while a significant part of contemporary film studies, remains problematic. The language of affect is built of metaphors and descriptive terms and phrases that attempt to substitute for cinematic experience. While I maintain the position I articulated at the beginning of

---

[24] Carl Plantinga, *Moving Viewers*, 33.
[25] This is clearly not the case in Plantinga's work, which is sensitive to affect across narrative and non-narrative systems. See Plantinga, 'Defending *Tree of Life*'.

FIGURES 7.7–9 *The affect of the machinic body:* Transformers *(2007).*

this book – that a description of cinematic experience cannot provide the framework through which to comprehensively account for that experience – I argue that a theory of spectacle requires engaging with affect, experience, and the primal encounters between cinema's image and its spectator. In this chapter, as in the previous two, I focus my attention on a filmmaker: James Cameron. If Lucas and Spielberg are the formative filmmakers of the High Concept era, Cameron's output builds upon the image of technology, incorporates the aesthetic orientation toward excess, and explores with increasing sophistication cinema's affect through the genre narratives of *The Terminator*, *Aliens* (1986), *Terminator 2: Judgment Day*, *Titanic* and *Avatar*. If classical auteurism is incompatible with a contemporary studio system, Cameron's cinema maintains a tendency toward an aesthetic and ideological vision. In the assessment of McVeigh and Kapell, his films 'contain recurring patterns, themes, visual and narrative signatures and motifs'.[26] Cameron's recent turn to 3-D inaugurates a new era of spectacle production, and a new affective capacity in the cinematic image. For Cameron, cinematic 3-D is primarily an affective phenomenon. While I touch on 3-D briefly in this chapter, I return to the phenomenology of 3-D experience in a more complex analysis in Part Three of this book.

---

[26] Steven McVeigh and Matthew Kapell, 'Introduction: Persistence of Visions – Approaching the Films of James Cameron', in *The Films of James Cameron: Critical Essays*, ed. Matthew Wilhelm Kapell and Stephen McVeigh (Jefferson: McFarland Press, 2011), 4.

Image functionality and affect: Sensation and *mise en scène*

If our analysis focuses on the body – on sensory experience – to the exclusion of the film and its materiality, we end up with the erasure of *mise en scène*, the loss of the film itself and the short circuit of any real engagement with the film as film.[27]

How does affect function if film – its material presence and its significatory content – is put into the frame? Thompson's neoformalist methodology in *Breaking the Glass Armor* (1988) emphasizes the importance of cinema's functional imperative.[28] Thompson invokes cinema's *aesthetic*, its special characteristic of being of the art of cinema.[29] We see this measure consistently explored in the work of Thompson and Bordwell, but also, in a simpler means-end hypothesis, in the functional analysis of screenwriting in the work of Robert McKee or Syd Field.[30] McKee's book, simply titled *Story*, subjects the cinematic aesthetic to the operation of a narrative frame that gives life to story elements, character 'arcs' and thematic texts and subtexts. This functionalist methodology continues to inform the majority of screenwriting, production and post-production rhetoric, in which cinema's experiential capacities are rationalized within the deterministic parameters of a narrative form. In this model, affect is the outcome of a particular structural disposition: three-act, four-act narrative, incorporating structural movements within acts and scenes that build the organic narrative whole. To Thompson's reading of narrative functionality (motivation), I would add 'narrative rhythm' in my reading of affect to acknowledge movements, ebbs and flows, subtle or aggressive turns, and variations in narrative film form.

The great contribution of Rutherford's work on affect is to return cinematic experience to a contemplation of *mise en scène*. On a more fundamental level, this is to return affect to a contemplation of cinematic form. While Bordwell is unparalleled in the specificity of description of *mise en scène*, there the concept has something of a traditional import to describe the internal elements of the scene (frame), and thereby account for the aesthetic style of the cinematic unit. For example, in a discussion of contemporary

---

[27] Rutherford, 50.

[28] See Thompson, *Breaking the Glass Armor*, 14–21.

[29] See Thompson, *Breaking the Glass Armor*, 36: 'Art's main concern is to *be* aesthetic.'

[30] See McKee, *Story*; see also Syd Field, *Screenplay: The Foundations of Screenwriting* (New York: MJF Books, 1994). Field's book is often credited with inaugurating a functionalist narrative approach to screenwriting in the post-classical Hollywood tradition.

Hollywood's style, Bordwell suggests that, 'at the level of stylistic texture, we can trace out a spectrum of more or less aggressive uses of intensified continuity – stylistic registers, we might say'.[31] While a number of theorists have taken issue with Bordwell's reading of intensified continuity to explain the changes in Hollywood's new aesthetic,[32] I am suitably persuaded that the films of Michael Bay, Roland Emmerich, Christopher Nolan and Steven Spielberg are not only founded upon a classical continuity aesthetic, but render experiences affiliated to an image of the inherent continuity of perception. But when Bordwell turns this meditation on style to affect, the description of experience is less clearly articulated, even somewhat generalized. Working through Geoff King's theory of action-spectacle, affect is manifest in 'violent motion punching out of the screen or engulfing the viewer'.[33] Affect, or an experience of a complex, carefully articulated stylistics, is generalized motion, and the viewer's contact with such motion is merely a vague sense of immersion, or absorption. Spielberg's concluding action sequence in *Indiana Jones and the Last Crusade* (1989) is astutely described in terms of style through technology and technique: the sequence 'displays his [Spielberg's] characteristic mix of long and short focal-length shots, it gives crammed depth compositions a rhythmic pulse, thanks not only to cutting but also to pans, tilts, and rack focusing. Movements jump from plane to plane, and some gags seem designed specifically for wide-angle and telephoto framings.'[34] But affect is again merely 'rhythmic pulse' occasioned by a series of movements. The spectator as affected subject is absent in the analysis of style, and image intensity, which I take in Rutherford to be the material that derives from a confrontation between image and subject, is subordinated to a sustained itinerary of stylistic devices.

If the image is on some level affecting, and if the shot is not conclusively, or purposively, a discrete narrative cell, we might begin to speak about an autonomous image in which narrative boundaries are transgressed. But further, and more valuably, we might begin to speak about a cinematic image that is expressed as a function of affect, and not purely, or essentially, as a function of cinematic style. This is to contemplate the image and its narrative form as an organic material, subject to fluctuations in experience, subject to varying modes of affect, and subject to highly individual ways of experiencing cinematic images. In the most banal way, this is to suggest that cinema is resolutely experiential, and that experience is subject to change, in varying

[31] David Bordwell, *The Way Hollywood Tells It*, 158.
[32] See, for example, Steven Shaviro, 'Post-Continuity', SCMS Paper Presentation (Boston, 2012), *The Pinocchio Theory* (Blog), http://www.shaviro.com/Blog/?p=1034 [accessed May 21, 2012].
[33] Bordwell, *The Way Hollywood Tells It*, 158.
[34] Bordwell, *The Way Hollywood Tells It*, 158.

degrees, from one spectator to the next. It follows that *mise en scène* must be more than a stylistic and functional index, but a manifestation also of cinematic affect. This is one way to think through the fraught terrain of affect in cinema studies – to describe the sensations we feel, overtly or subtly, directly or through mechanisms that mediate the effect of the image (editing, for example), and conceptualize their contours through a carefully observed and sustained analysis of *mise en scène*. In so doing, we might perceive the spectator's engagement with cinema's image as a necessary confrontation between image and spectator. But against Sobchack's indifference to content within the frame, affect might usefully explain cinema's *meaning* while simultaneously explaining its various registers of experience.

Unlike a great deal of affect theorists, I find it difficult to reject entirely the close analytical studies of narrative form in the exhaustive analyses of Bordwell and Thompson. I find such accounts, while at times generalized and broadly encompassing, persuasive. But more pressing is an affective burden I cannot divest, which returns again and again to the profound experience of narrative systems.[35] I disagree that narrative affect is not in some sense manifest in the image, and that narrative's several intensities within cinema's classicism cannot in some way be fathomed as affective material. Indeed, I would argue that synthetic narrative structures inform the greater part of industrial production strategies from the classical studio era to contemporary studio practices. Consider Gittes's (Jack Nicholson) 'pathos of failure' (to use Thomas Elsaesser's evocative phrase)[36] in the final sequence in *Chinatown* (1974). On one hand, the sequence functions as a narrative, rather than imagistic, movement – here I deliberately use a language of affect to describe the function of narrative form. *Chinatown*'s ending constitutes what Eco calls a genre innovation, in which narrative form stretches its boundaries while reflexively engaging on a prior iteration of that form.[37] The shot, scene, sequence, and movement are, in effect, textual tropes. Fittingly,

---

[35] Geoff King, to some degree following the approach of Bordwell and Thompson, has challenged the notion that spectacle renders narrative obsolete. For example, King makes the commonsensical point: 'The demands of the blockbuster may have led to an emphasis on certain genres and on episodic forms of narrative, but this is not the same as narrative being displaced.' See King, 'Ride-Films and Films as Rides', 8. Like King, I am constantly surprised at the claim that contemporary blockbuster cinema functions *non-narratively*, embracing spectacle as an overarching aesthetic sensibility. The enterprises of *The Matrix*, *The Lord of the Rings*, *Harry Potter*, *Transformers*, *Spiderman*, Marvel's conglomerate franchises (Disney Corporation), *Avatar*, function through accessible and recognizable concept structures mapped through the coordinates of a tested (and strategically implemented) narrative patterning. Further, the convergence of cinema and extra-cinematic text (gaming, theme park rides, merchandizing, etc.) functions significantly through narrative points of contact.

[36] Elsaesser, 'The Pathos of Failure'.

[37] Eco, 'Repetition and Innovation', 194–9.

Towne's script concludes, as all obedient *noirs* should, with the restoration of order, justice, and the progress of urban modernity.[38] Polanski's 'pessimistic ending', a dramatic revision of the ending of the screenplay, is not merely an ideological departure from the norm, but an explicit revision of a narrative outcome anticipated by the spectator. We see in Gittes the narrative revision of Bogart's Sam Spade in *The Maltese Falcon*. It is thus not coincidental that Huston appears as antagonist in *Chinatown*. These are narrative materials that render intensities of cinematic experience. In the final sequence of *Chinatown*, affect manifests as a confrontation between the spectator and the raw material of story:

> A long shot of the street as Evelyn Mulwray's car comes to rest in darkness – the intrusion of the horn in the relative quiet – the palpable duration of the shot – Gittes's movement onscreen from behind the camera while the shot is held – the increase in intensity of the movement, accompanied by a woman's scream, held longer than anticipated – the fast pan from right to left as Gittes enters the frame of the car – the reveal of the repulsive wound –

This material (image and rhythm inscribed through movement) animates the screen through carefully modulated intensities negotiated by spectator and image. For Rutherford, such intensities materialize beyond the play of narrative, beyond structural and functional indices, beyond story and character movements. And yet, clearly, Towne works within the narrative framework of *noir*; clearly, Polanski captures an image in movement animated through *noir*'s distinctive stylistics. Why then should the narrative itinerary inherent in this sequence be subordinated to image-intensity as cinema's overarching affective material, as its essential 'glue'?

Rutherford describes *mise en scène* as a 'dynamic concept'. Working through the *Cahiers du Cinema* critics of the 1950s, she suggests that *mise en scène* 'must be understood as not just what has been put into the frame but what has been put into the moment of experience, that it cannot meaningfully be understood as inert elements in the frame – these elements must be explored for how they draw the spectator into the scene, materially, experientially, as the scene unfolds in time'.[39] What a radical notion – to perceive the internal components of the frame as elements of experience, alongside elements of style, structure, functionality, and the conventions of aesthetic form. In this model, *mise en scène* extends from conventional frame and

---

[38] See Biskind, 166.
[39] Rutherford, 61.

shot assemblage to incorporate movement and rhythm in montage.[40] *Mise en scène* is the 'basic layer that comes in under the level of narrative ... [that] is more like the glue that holds narrative together'.[41]

But here there is again something that attests to Rutherford's reification of image affect as a pure experience of cinema, onto which narrative is mapped for functional (and usually commercial) purposes. What purpose does narrative serve in this mode of affect theory but to conceptualize cinemas bereft of the image's more subtle and mature intensities? To suggest that cinema is made of that which 'comes under the level of narrative' can only but marginalize an aesthetic founded upon concrete narrative form, clear conceptual frameworks, and the manifest stylistic mechanisms that carry story from first frame to last. Granted, Rutherford's model is provocative when applied to Malick, Angelopoulos or the montage kinetics of Lee Myung-Se's *Nowhere to Hide* (1999).[42] One could speak of the elemental image intensities in the cinema of Jean-Luc Godard, Abbas Kiarostami, Michael Haneke, Wong Kar-Wai and Spike Lee. But how is such a model of affect – that deliberately seeks out the intensities *beneath* narrative, that conceptualizes *mise en scène* as more than an assemblage of objects and yet quite apart from narrative form – applied to a spectacle aesthetic that seeks to inscribe the clearest line of access to story (narrative) and character (archetypal) development?

In what remains of this chapter, I attempt to trace the function of affect in the cinema of James Cameron. My analysis is certainly not exhaustive, and clearly some of my claims apply to work outside of Cameron's directorial *oeuvre*. A broader analysis might encompass the Kathryn Bigelow-directed *Strange Days* (1995), one of the more sophisticated meditations on virtual experience and affect in recent cinema.[43] In my analysis, I treat the image as the essential material of cinematic experience, yet I acknowledge the allure of narrative form, substance and engagement – in short, the varying intensities unique to a mode of storytelling. Cameron's cinema is sensitive to the exhibitionist (and affective) qualities of the image, and yet I would argue his films function explicitly through the paradigm of a classical narrative form. While Cameron's cinema partakes of the technological and neo-baroque image, and is clearly a continuation of the spectacle aesthetic Bukatman describes as 'sublime experience',[44] in Cameron the register of affect is deliberately

[40] Rutherford, 62–3.
[41] Rutherford, 72.
[42] See Rutherford, 145–216.
[43] See Steven Shaviro, 'Straight From the Cerebral Cortex: Vision and Affect in *Strange Days*', in *The Cinema of Kathryn Bigelow: Hollywood Transgressor*, ed. Deborah Jermyn and Sean Redmond (London and New York: Wallflower Press, 2003), 159–77.
[44] Bukatman, *Matters of Gravity*, 93.

deployed within the interconnected image and narrative system. The image of the body is a visceral experience in *The Terminator*; that image, built of a synthetic polycarbonate material, is again affectively wielded in the exhibition of a digital effect in the T–1000 (*Terminator 2: Judgment Day*). Perhaps Cameron's most sophisticated meditation on the cinema of affect is his sequel to Ridley Scott's *Alien* (1979), itself one of the great vehicles for spectacle affect in the High Concept tradition. In *Aliens*, the body is an instrument of affect, first as human form, then as female alien (and alienated body), and then as hybrid, or cyborg being (*Alien: Resurrection*, 1997).[45] In *Avatar*, the synthetic (vision and body) becomes virtual, negotiating movements and states between embodiment, disembodiment and re-embodiment. In short, Cameron's cinema, from *The Terminator* to *Avatar*, is about perception and affect, vision and bodily sensation.

Affect and the spectacle image

Affect takes place at the site of the screen, in confrontation with the image that might appear suddenly (the shock and absurdity of a man impaled through a milk carton in *Terminator 2: Judgment Day* [figure 7.10]); or slowly, gradually, and in subtle, almost imperceptible intensities (the slow zoom that opens Coppola's *The Conversation*); or more mysteriously, the virtuosic movement of a camera that breaches the classical frame in a complex sequence shot in Spike Lee's *Do the Right Thing* (1989) (figures 7.11–7.15).

But affect is also grounded in the self, the mental faculties, and the body and its sensory faculties. Affect might materialize through reflection – accounting for the popularity of what Jameson terms the nostalgia mode of cinema in the 1980s.[46] The image and spectator are always interacting in a circuit, as image is perceived and affectively experienced, and then layered onto the experience of subsequent images, and such circuits proliferate as the experience of cinema becomes ever more discursive and complex.

---

[45] For an excellent reading of the capacity of the cyborg to represent cultural, and especially, gendered identity, see Sue Short, *Cyborg Cinema and Contemporary Subjectivity* (New York: Palgrave, 2005), 81–105. Working through Donna Haraway's notion of gendered progressivism in the cyborg-being, Short suggests that 'The cyborg's ability to transcend gender has thus proved to be largely ineffectual within SF cinema, yet in its exaggerated depiction of male and female roles it has nevertheless provided the opportunity by which to question whether they are truly as "natural" as has traditionally been perceived' (104). For a classic reading of the cyborg body and vision apparatus, see Donna Haraway, *Simians, Cyborgs, and Women: The Reinvention of Nature* (New York: Routledge, 1991).
[46] Fredric Jameson, *Postmodernism*, 19–21.

FIGURE 7.10 *The shock of the spectacle image:* Terminator 2: Judgment Day *(1991).*

FIGURES 7.11–15 *The affect of a virtuosic camera move:* Do the Right Thing *(1989).*

Accounting for the affective qualities of cinematic experience is also more difficult in the age of ubiquitous digital image medias (that are cinematic, yet simultaneously 'more than cinema') than in the contained celluloid past.

I have explored the notion of the spectacle image as a synthetic material built out of new cinema technologies and evolving aesthetic styles. But spectacle is as much a cultural as aesthetic formation. We might equally apply the notion of spectacle to the function of cinema as commodity. I have argued elsewhere that commodity consumption (of a film product, or its strata of commodity experiences) might provide a unique affective charge.[47] The attraction of *The Avengers* (2012) is not precisely its genre conformity, or indeed, an aesthetic tradition (High Concept studio cinema), but the felt perception of the movement of the commodity across a personalized, and yet collectively acculturated, space. This is how cinema is experienced in the variously convergent interfaces of contemporary culture, in which, as Elsaesser argues, the text in production, dissemination and consumption is 'opened up'.[48] Could we not transpose this model of the spectacle image onto a model of spectacle affect? Could we not speak of the uniquely affective material of spectacle, as affect theorists are wont to do with the 'unseen' but intensely felt sensations of avant-garde cinema?

Such a model attempts to conceive of spectacle as a distinctive mode of affect in much the same way that I have conceived of spectacle production as a distinctive mode of technological and aesthetic creation. Surely a studio-produced spectacle cinema inscribes its own itineraries of engagement, its own mechanics of narrative and image intensities, its own visual and aural signifiers that function to charge the circuit between image and spectator. Of course, not all images are the same, and not all films described as spectacle partake of the same technological, aesthetic and affective register. Yet commonalities are clearly apparent. The visceral experience of speed is, as Arroyo suggests, intrinsic to spectacle.[49] The sustained contemplation of the image of astonishment maintains in most major productions; for example, the astonished gaze directed at the digital Brachiosaurus in *Jurassic Park*. Sensations of speed are now commonly incorporated into the experience of spectacle through shot duration (exponentially decreasing), disorientation through intensified (and occasionally fractured) montage, and increased motion-control of the technological apparatus. In *Jurassic Park*, we see the convergence of the technological image and the image of action in the T-Rex

---

[47] Isaacs, *Toward a New Film Aesthetic*, 64–8.

[48] Elsaesser, *The Persistence of Hollywood*, 291.

[49] José Arroyo, 'Mission: Sublime', in *Action/Spectacle Cinema: A Sight and Sound Reader*, ed. José Arroyo (London: British Film Institute, 2000), 21–4.

set piece, in which astonished and terrified contemplation incorporates the viscerally charged action of the pursuit. Spielberg's T-Rex reflected in a mirror thus manifests the image of excess innervated through the intensity of speed (figure 7.16).

Why then should we apply the same model of affect as one we might apply to the experience of the cinema of Malick or Angelopoulos, for whom conventional narrative mechanics are 'clunky and archaic'?[50] Even if one rejects the distinction between a classical and an art film genre, surely the expressive silences and explicitly orchestrated 'empty spaces' in Malick and Angelopolous, or Truffaut, or Antonioni, or Kiarostami, or early Scorsese and Altman, or Paul Thomas Anderson with *Punch Drunk Love* (2002), or Godoy's recent *Ulysses* (2011), provoke a mode of affect quite distinct from an experience of the image of astonishment, or its movement at speed and intersecting intensities cut within the shell of an overarching narrative. Why should we privilege an intensity that charges beneath narrative – drawing on the canon of affect cinema, conventionally selected from the archive of modernist, experimental, avant-garde European, or New American cinemas – when cinematic spectacle clearly moves toward disambiguation and excess, and the intensities such modalities inscribe? In the majority of affect theory models seeking intensities beneath narrative, narrative is not merely of a register oblivious to 'pure' affective material, but functions explicitly to conceal what lies beneath cinema's commoditized narrative shell – a privileged mode of image experience deemed by Rutherford and others to be all but effaced in contemporary mainstream studio production.

Spectacle cinema, such as the image of action in Lucas's motion-controlled cinematography in *Star Wars Episode IV*, facilitates not only new ways of creating the image, but new modes of experiencing cinema. The experience of motion-controlled cinematography and capture is unprecedented in the history of the moving image. The experience of a digital body – a morphing T–1000 in *Terminator 2: Judgment Day*, a digitally simulated recreation of the Titanic, the avatar of a paraplegic soldier deployed in a digitally simulated cinematic world – is unprecedented in the history of the moving image. Such images call for a new discourse on cinematic affect that confronts the material of cinema across a variety of spectra, from Malick's vast and empty spaces of the universe in *Tree of Life* (2011) to the experience of a moving image such as Lumière's *Arrival of a Train at a Station* in 3-D, created anew and re-experienced as a spectacle image in Scorsese's *Hugo* (2011).

Cameron's spectacle manifests as the image of excess – increasingly sophisticated in the exponentially swelling production budgets of major studio

---

[50] Rutherford, 27.

FIGURE 7.16 *The astonishing digital effect animated through aggressive action:* Jurassic Park *(1993).*

projects. The image evolves as the industry seeks evolution through technology; it further evolves as a classical stylistics metamorphoses into a neo-baroque aesthetic. Beyond image mechanics, Cameron's narratives perform the cinema of spectacle, effectively enabling the image evolution to function within the frame of a High Concept story. Thus, films such as *The Terminator* or *True Lies* or *Titanic* not only manifest new forms of vision, but also dramatize the experience of new visual modalities, new textures, new bodily forms and sensations. The narrative of *The Terminator* is perhaps most perfectly realized through the franchise aesthetic: what begins as evolution from organic body (Sarah Connor, Kyle Reese) to metal indo-skeleton (the Terminator) evolves again from metal indo-skeleton to digitized liquid-metal in *Terminator 2: Judgment Day.* Ndalianis offers a provocative reading of the evolution of a mode of vision and affect as *Terminator 2: Judgment Day* evolves further into the Universal Studios exhibit, *T2 3-D: Battle Across Time,* in which the 'illusionistic outcome is not only technologically groundbreaking but also phenomenologically new'.[51]

All of Cameron's films are in some sense about the newness of vision and its affective properties. Cameron's spectator is an experiential vessel, partaking of an evolved mode of perception and affect. A close analysis of Cameron's work (in subsequent sections, I focus on *The Terminator,* *Terminator 2: Judgment Day, Aliens* and *Avatar*) reveals the extent to which Cameron's cinema attempts to create a spectacle affect, attentive to the requirements of cinematic narrative, and yet also increasingly cavalier in the manifestation of a new technological, aesthetic and affective image.[52]

---

[51] Ndalianis, 201.

[52] While in a very different context, the work of Laura Marks on the intersection of information and affect is provocative in the context of spectacle cinema. The difficulty in conceptualizing the ontology of the spectacle image (or any cinematic image, for that matter) stems from a complex

The technology of vision and visuality: The technological image reprised

The cosmic displays of science fiction cinema, produced by technologically advanced optical effects, surely derive from a similar drive for scopic mastery. The overwhelming perceptual power granted by these panoramic displays addressed the perceived loss of cognitive power experienced by the subject in an increasingly technologized world.[53]

Rather than inevitably promoting an awareness of what it might mean at any given place and time to be a spectator of a big budget spectacle ... these moments intensify the spectator's experience of the film at the level of seeing itself.[54]

While High Concept cinema conventionally displays a world affectively familiar to the spectator (frequently an idealized imaginary, a utopia, such as Spielberg's Amity in *Jaws* or Lucas's site of the rebellion in *Star Wars Episode IV*), always beneath the register of the image is the exhibition of the technology of its creation; this is what I have referred to as the technological image intrinsic to spectacle cinema. Cameron's cinema seeks to further push the boundaries of image technology; in Cameron, the trace of technology is more pronounced, and thus, more deliberately affecting. Each new Cameron production is an orchestrated technological spectacle advancement, re-imagining a prior cinematic materiality. The industrial structure of Hollywood is increasingly technology-oriented, perhaps most openly displayed in the production and reception of *Avatar*,[55] and such experiences are couched in the rhetoric of newness.[56] In April 2012, *Titanic* was re-released in cinemas

---

and problematic relationship between the image and what it signifies; this is the elemental lack experienced in the image as material, and the signified as representation. Marks describes a cinematic image that 'struggles to emerge from information' in its relation to the plane of immanence; working through Bergson, Marks identifies the origin of the image in the 'infinite set of all images'. There is thus the implication of a process of partaking of the realm of the image in communicating information. 'Screen theory', suggests Marks, 'can ask images where they came from: did they unfold from information or from the universe itself? ... Screen theory can evaluate the ways in which films struggle to bring information into the perceptible.' See Laura Marks, 'Information, Secrets, and Enigmas: An Enfolding-unfolding Aesthetics for Cinema', *Screen* 50, no. 1 (2009), 86–98.

[53] Bukatman, *Matters of Gravity*, 81–2.

[54] Keller, 105.

[55] See Elsaesser, *The Persistence of Hollywood*, 297–8.

[56] Appropriately, a marginalized, auteurist-styled filmmaker such as Terry Gilliam laments the contemporary studio obsession to render the technological image anew: 'I've seen great chunks

for the experience of cinematic 3-D.[57] The image in composition remains the same. The narrative structure remains the same. But the technology of image exhibition changes, and new affective relationships between spectator and screen are commoditized as new experience.

While technology infuses all cinema traditions, in spectacle, as I have argued, technology is materially infused in the image; technology manifests an affecting *presence*. Whether we seek to call this presence the 'trace' of technology, or technology's imprint, essentially, the image as it filters through the effects production apparatus of High Concept cinema is a technological exhibition. Spectacle cinema thus necessarily provides the experience of the technological image, as well as the experience of a technologized vision and sensorium. Each new Cameron film is an entry point to a new mode of technologized experience. The newest, most resplendent incarnation of Cameron's vision-machine is a remodelled stereoscopic apparatus. For Cameron, stereoscopic perception is an evolution of seeing; in phenomenological terms, an evolution of being. The spectator is thus affected by the technological lens through which spectacle cinema is perceived, and felt.

This is the critical formation in the cinema of spectacle production: narrative moves toward the artifice of concept storytelling (is this not the fermenting ground for quotation, referentiality and nostalgia as affect charted in the work of Eco, Jameson, Hutcheon, and others?) as, concurrently, the image expands the technological parameters of the apparatus. Cameron's most sophisticated concept narrative, *Aliens*, functions suitably as pastiche, or what Collins calls 'genericity', the genre form that is attentive to its artificial structure.[58] Yet the image swells to excess in the increasingly complex and sophisticated technologies of image production. Optical and mechanical effects exhibit in casual gestures – the holographic screen in an early sequence of the director's cut of *Aliens*[59] (figures 7.17–7.18); the loader, a utilitarian object in Act One of the film, reconfigured as a technological body in the confrontation between Ripley and the Alien Queen[60] (figure 7.19). While

---

of *Avatar* in 3-D, but I don't know if the experience is any better. And perhaps what they have to do with *Avatar* is make the same experience, the same film we've seen before only that it is 3-D and more glorious. I mean, it is very beautiful looking … But is it a new experience?' An interview conducted by César Alberto Albarran with Terry Gilliam, November 4, 2009 (*Cine-Premiere Magazine*). I gratefully acknowledge Mr César Albarran in providing this source.

[57] The re-release grossed 200 million in its opening fortnight. See Pamela McClintock, 'Box Office Report', *The Hollywood Reporter*, 16 April, 2012, http://www.hollywoodreporter.com/news/titanic-box-office-james-cameron–312497 [accessed 28 May 2012].

[58] Collins, 'Genericity in the Nineties'.

[59] This image is quoted in Verhoeven's *Total Recall* more than a decade later.

[60] This image is quoted in the performance of an army of robotic shells in *Matrix Revolutions*.

Lucas and Spielberg reprise the aesthetic spectacle of an early serial show,[61] *Aliens* works at the edges of hybrid genre, reflecting on the construction of character types, narrative movements, and prior iterations of generic form.

Affect is inscribed in the majority of Cameron's narratives through the activity of perception, which is an active rather than passive engagement with the physical world. Thus the body and the visual apparatus evolve through the technology of new cinema as, narratively, stories and characters trace the evolution of an increasingly technologized world. Vision in Cameron is the 'definitive articulation of [machine nature]'.[62] Keller refers specifically to the machinic perception of the Terminator in *The Terminator*, Cameron's first major spectacle production, but the affective potential of a machinic vision applies equally to his later spectacles, *Terminator 2: Judgment Day*, *Titanic*, and particularly, *Avatar*. For Keller, 'the machine eye computes the world in terms of very particular information that is mathematical, weapons-related, and task and goal oriented.'[63] What appears as mathematical readout is, affectively, the experience of a technological vision; the spectator experiences, vicariously *and* directly, a machinic perception. Here technology is not merely a distantiated point of view, but inscribes the experience of a new way of seeing. For the spectator, there is an affective charge in the perception of a cyborg-being in *The Terminator* and *Terminator 2: Judgment Day*. We are not merely positioned to observe the Terminator in secret, but subjectively inhabit a machinic body, perceptual faculty, and increasingly in *Terminator 2: Judgment Day*, a machinic consciousness. These are now 'our eyes', 'our body'.

The cyborg machinic vision is the natural precursor of virtual perception in *Avatar*, in which the spectator awakes anew in the body of a virtual construct, and simultaneously experiences the new image of spectacle cinema through the machinic vision of the 3-D apparatus. Here again, and perhaps most sophisticatedly, spectacle cinema is more than a medium for the conveyance of an *a priori* reality. Here the special effect, the technology of cinematic effect, is not mimetic, but profoundly transformative. Spectacle seeks to render the subjective self perceptually and affectively (through machinic eyes and machinic bodies) anew. And the affect of the image in spectacle, experienced through its several intensities, is felt also as excess, as the beyond of the normative standards of wonderment, awe, repulsion, desire, and so on.

---

[61] A great deal has been made of the self-conscious recycling of the matinee serial in *Star Wars Episode IV* and the *Indiana Jones* films. But while such films clearly reflect on a past cinema, the affect of the spectacle image is not purely nostalgic, which is essentially where Jameson misunderstands the affective import of High Concept cinema. See Jameson, *Postmodernism*, 19.

[62] Keller, 105.

[63] Keller, 105.

FIGURES 7.17–19 *The exhibition of optical and mechanical effects:* Aliens *(1986).*

The machinic perception perhaps approaches Rombes's insight into the spectator of contemporary media, in which perception, experience and consumption inter-relate as mediated processes:

> Instead of a relationship between a spectator and a screen, we now have one between the spectator, the screen and the spectator's avatar, who watches the screen on an intermediary screen on behalf of the spectator. The avatar becomes a character, too, an illusion, but one projected from the flesh-and-blood spectator, and endowed with a certain degree of agency.[64]

When we don the oversized glasses required for 3-D perception, do we remain our perceptual and experiencing 'selves'? Or are we projected into a technologically created space, reflecting on a new simulacral (avatar) identity, as we recall the ordinariness, and potential obsolescence, of 2-D perception and affect? But this is precisely why 3-D isn't cinema at all, at least not in the orthodox treatment of cinema as a narrative media.[65] I prefer Rombes's model of an avatar vision, which permits a wholesome synthesis between organic subject and image/vision machine (nearer in essence to Hayles's

[64] Rombes, *Cinema in the Digital Age*, 58.
[65] For a more expansive treatment of this position, see Bruce Isaacs, 'Technologies of New Experience: On Cinema, 3-D and the Imaginary', *Stereoscopic Media*, November 30, 2011, http://www.stereoscopicmedia.org/?p=110 [accessed December 21, 2011].

conception of a 'post-human' as liberated form), to Virilio's vision-machine, which effaces the organic and factual, and submits to the empty location of a virtual subject.[66]

The technology of material and non-material bodies (including ocean-liners): Endo-skeletons, morphing shapes and machines

Zooropa, vorsprung durch technik.
U2, 'Zooropa' (1989)

Long live the new flesh.
Max Renn (James Woods), *Videodrome* (1983)

Cronenberg's *Videodrome* presents the subject as a synthesis of human consciousness and technology. The New Flesh reaches outward to an evolved consciousness, yet it also presents the mechanism for the destruction of self and a descent into madness. Max Renn kills himself to be reborn in a televisual fantasy, only to kill himself again, then to be reborn, *ad infinitum*. The credits roll, but Cronenberg's film remains unsettling because of the projection of a synthetic self. What is the outcome of a technologized consciousness? How does the subject experience selfhood if self and a technological Other are somehow synthetically joined? This is Virilio's concern with postmodernity's machine consciousness:

> Aren't they talking about producing a 'vision machine' in the near future, a machine that would be capable not only of recognising the contours of shapes, but also of completely interpreting the visual field, of staging a complex environment close-up or at a distance? Aren't they also talking about the new technology of 'visionics': the possibility of achieving sightless vision whereby the videocamera would be controlled by the computer?[67]

Virilio's machine consciousness is present in a great deal of Cronenberg, notably *Videodrome*, *The Fly* and *Existenz* (1999). If several of Cronenberg's

---

[66] Paul Virilio, *The Vision Machine*, trans. Julie Rose (Bloomington: Indiana University Press, 1994), 59.
[67] Virilio, 59.

films partake of the spectacle of the science fiction genre, his relationship to the technology of the synthetic body is decidedly ambivalent. Cronenberg's bodies are fetishistic objects; the body is a site of abjection in films like *Videodrome*, *The Fly* and *Crash* (1996). The narrative tracing a symbiosis of body and machine reaches for the ideal, the perfection of body and consciousness, yet the attempt to invent a new consciousness is Promethean, and Cronenberg's protagonists, male and female, organic/synthetic/virtual, for the most part end up alienated and disfigured. The spectator experiences the body in Cronenberg as an object of revulsion, and body parts are frequently in the process of decay, disfigurement and horrific transformation (figure 7.20). Cronenberg's images of the body also sit uneasily with more conventional horror genre images of the body (for example, those of the alien/human symbiosis in Carpenter's *The Thing* [1982]). Whereas Carpenter displays monstrosity within the body of the Other, Cronenberg fetishizes the anatomical object. Carpenter's body is narrativized as repulsive or erotic object; Cronenberg's bodies exhibit themselves as taboo offerings, neither purely the site of erotic pleasure nor generic repulsion.

This disfigurement of the body in Cronenberg – this abjection – is clearly *not* the image of the body the spectator experiences in Cameron's spectacle cinema. This is one way we might differentiate the body within spectacle cinema from the body of what has come to be called the 'body horror' genre.[68] The body horror genre repulses the spectator through the inescapable presence of the monstrous body. The spectator thus identifies (though that term remains problematic) with bodily abjection – Max Renn in *Videodrome*, Seth Brundle (Jeff Goldblum) in *The Fly*. Cronenberg's films affirm the threat of the body against the veneer of a normative (and illusionistic) ideal. In spectacle cinema, however, the abject body is necessarily absent. If materially present within the story, the monstrous body is projected as antagonist, and is eradicated in the final act of the narrative. Thus, Schwarzenegger's body must be subdued by the normative male/female subject-position: Sarah Connor/Reese in *The Terminator*. The Alien Queen must be subdued by Ripley, a human who has slept through the last 50 years of post-human technological evolution; Ripley's living quarters, 50 years in her future, are decidedly unfuturistic. In *Terminator 2: Judgment Day*, Sarah Connor must again subdue the monstrous body (the liquid-metal

---

[68] See Linda Badley, *Film, Horror, and the Body Fantastic* (Westport, Conn.: Greenwood Press, 1995). Badley argues that 'In the 1980s the horror film became an agonistic "body language" for a culture that perceived itself as grotesquely embodied and in transformation' (8). The definition of the horror of the body *genre* implicates Browning's *Freaks* (1932) as something of a point of origin. This fetishization of the body (and the repulsive affect of the body in transformation) is clearly demonstrated in Cronenberg's *Videodrome* and *The Fly*.

FIGURE 7.20 *The abject body in Cronenberg:* The Fly *(1986)*.

T–1000), this time even less human than Schwarzenegger's Terminator of the first film. Subduing the body of the monster is thus integral to the formation of spectacle narrative, and affirms the categorical distinction between the ideal body of spectacle and the monstrous body of the body horror genre.

Spectacle cinema reveals the potential of technology to improve the embodied substance of the self, including its perceptual and affective faculties. While Cameron's spectacle cinema begins with the primacy of organic being over technology (the idealization of the human body in *The Terminator*), it evolves through a period of 25 years into a synthesis of human consciousness and technological apparatus – the embodiment of a virtual new flesh in the final shot of *Avatar*. At the conclusion of *Avatar*, Jake Sully is re-embodied in a virtual shell. The opening of the eyes in *Avatar* signals the realization of an ideal embodiment – the human consciousness resurrected into a virtual form. We see such awakenings throughout spectacle cinema: Luke Skywalker's awakening to the presence of the force in the final run at the Death Star in *Star Wars Episode IV*; Neary's awakening to the immensity of the universe in his entry into the Mothership in *Close Encounters of the Third Kind*; Neo's awakening (and resurrection) into the actual/virtual consciousness of the One in the final sequence of *The Matrix*.[69]

In spectacle cinema, the image of the future, and the image of a technologized perception and affect, is necessarily utopian. Against Cronenberg's horror that commonly results in existential and bodily disfigurement, the spectacle image presents the *idealization* of the body in technological form. As technology evolves to produce ever more astonishing spectacle images, so the affect of the screened body provides the thrill of enhancement of the embodied self. In *Avatar*, the disabled organic body of the protagonist-spectator evolves into the technological body (synthetic/virtual) of an avatar.

---

[69] For a discussion of 'narratives of becoming' in recent action cinema, see Purse, *Contemporary Action Cinema*, 32–5.

For Cameron, we experience ourselves through the image of technology; and the technological image is at its most vivid, and at its most intense, in depictions of the ideal machinic/organic body. Indeed, I would argue that the body is the primary site through which spectacle cinema manifests affectively.[70]

The subject and body seek technologies of renewal and radically enhanced perceptual and affective experiences that improve upon the quotidian self. In my use of the term body, I include the body of all animate objects, whether a cyborg-being (*The Terminator*) or a recreated ocean liner (*Titanic*). The line between animate and inanimate threshold, in the image of spectacle cinema, is increasingly subject to effacement. Indeed, I would argue that one of the foundational aesthetic gestures (narrative and image) in spectacle is to animate the inanimate object (a body): a fossilized dinosaur is animated into a living animal (*Jurassic Park*); a machine is animated into a cyborg-being in *The Terminator* and *Terminator 2: Judgment Day* (the Terminator's ability to re-energize, and reform, demonstrates the capacity of the digital image to re-animate dormant material); a relic of the past is animated into the digitized simulation of the present (*Titanic*).

Why should we distinguish between living bodies (a problematic term in any case in the age of digital simulation) and inanimate objects? Surely bodies are in a perpetual state of animation through cinema's moving image technology. As an image, and thus as the material of a cinematic object, is Caesar the Ape in *Rise of the Planet of the Apes* any more 'real' than Cameron's mechanically and digitally simulated Titanic? In what sense is the digitally effected creation of Titanic less affecting than the image of a simulated face, or a body animated through motion-capture technology? One of Cameron's most profoundly affective moments reanimates the image of the Titanic for a contemporary mass cultural audience. The parallelism of present and past in the film does not inscribe a narrative movement into the past, but an animating *of the past* through digital simulation technology. Cameron shoots the relic of Titanic in murky, documentary-style, which he then brings back in the glory of a digitized present. In this sequence, affect is not merely felt through the experience of a technological image, but more complexly inheres in the capacity of cinema to create a simulation (in the present) of an object lost to a historical past.

In this sense, *Titanic* displays a technologically created and narratively inscribed awakening of the body. The critical movement from present to past

---

[70] For a detailed discussion of the body as central to contemporary action cinema affect (though of course I would extend this genre reading to incorporate spectacle cinema *per se*), see Purse, *Contemporary Action Cinema*, 42–8.

occurs at 19:06.[71] A computer monitor displays the image of the relic of Titanic beneath the ocean. The camera moves slowly from left to right, not in a conventional wide pan, but in a circular movement that emulates a computer image simulation. Critically, there is no cut between present and past. This is not a point of view itinerary, as occurs at 18:10; this is not the elderly Rose's flashback. Rather, it is the revelation (through simulation) of the spectacle of a cinematic technology. The cinematic reveal is not that of the original ship, or of the ship recreated in recollection (flashback), but of its digital simulation in the present (figures 7.21–7.25). The simulation, and not the original artifact, is the affecting object. The digital simulation takes the image of the past (now scattered in its cultural resonance in personal and collective memory) and makes of it an object anchored within the present. In the same way, the spectator is not overwhelmed by the image of a dinosaur in Jurassic Park; rather, she is overwhelmed by its digital materiality on a screen, precisely as the spectator was overwhelmed not by a train pulling into a station in 1895, but by the image of a train Lumière had concocted through a new technology. As in all spectacle images, in the moment of revelation of the new Titanic, narrative guides the affective itinerary, notably through the first notes of a conventional music cue that builds to crescendo within the movement.

While Avatar is an obvious end point for the exploration of a post-human life form (though Hayles's notion of the post-human is almost diametrically opposed to Cameron's more conventional, and ideologically normative, post-human), Cameron's oeuvre displays an exponentially increasing fascination with the human/machinic synthesis. The display of the machinic body in The Terminator, while a narrative image, functions also fetishistically. In the sequence in which the Terminator repairs his body, the spectator is repulsed by the disfigurement of the organic outer layer of flesh. Yet Cameron's revelation of machine material beneath organic material is a sequence of some duration, in which the visceral experience of the disfigurement of flesh (through cutting and the exposure of a bodily wound) is sutured to the astonishment of the material, and movement, of the machinic body. The image displays the organic fingers that move in symbiotic relation to the machinic endo-skeleton (figures 7.26–27). In Terminator 2: Judgment Day, the T–1000 liquid metal Terminator presents the image of an early digital simulation (figures 7.28–7.29); morphing technology would be more gratuitously employed in Michael Jackson's 'Black or White' music video, released six months later. The spectacle body as affective vessel undergoes its own morphological transformation as Cameron presents a gender subversion of

---

[71] Time-code references are to Titanic (DVD), Twentieth Century Fox Home Video Entertainment, 2002.

FIGURES 7.21–5 *The affect of the digitally simulated object:* Titanic *(1997).*

the mainstream norm through Sarah Connor's hyper-masculine physicality (figure 7.30), Schwarzenegger's effeminate paternalism (the Terminator's affective evolution is toward a cyborg-being that has learned how to feel emotion, and can thus shed tears!), and the T–1000's asexuality. The image of greatest astonishment displays the confrontation between the real and simulated body in a hospital foyer. The inanimate floor swells as the image morphs into the shape of a human (figure 7.31). The spectator experiences the astonishment of the effect, and the uncanny sensation of being confronted by the perfection of the technological simulation. Confronting the real, the simulation (the T–1000) appears momentarily astonished at its own image-reflection (figure 7.32).

Cameron's most complex body is exhibited in *Aliens*. In Ridley Scott's *Alien*, which is perhaps nearer to a dystopian body-horror text than a utopian spectacle, the female body is the organic ideal. Clearly Ripley (Sigourney Weaver) is not an erotic object in conventional patriarchal display, yet bodily she manifests the image of the female in opposition to a male alien predator. In the final sequence of the film, Ripley subdues the alien through a passive evasion, hiding in a space suit while setting the instruments to open the hatch.

FIGURES 7.26–32 *Affect and bodily transformation in the cinema of James Cameron.*

In the final sequence of *Aliens* (Cameron's sequel), Ripley is again confronted by an alien, this time the greater threat of a Queen, which provides an intriguing gender subtext to the film. However, rather than enacting a passive evasion, Cameron activates the body of the protagonist by placing Ripley in the loader, a mechanical vehicle for heavy lifting. The loader works as a narrative cue, returning the spectator to Act One of the film, in which Ripley attempts to 'make herself useful'. Now, in the final act confrontation, her activation within the loader implies a conventional High Concept maturation, or developmental process. Ripley is again empowered and purposive in the final sequence of the film.

Cameron's protagonist-female metamorphoses into an organic/machinic hybrid through a symbiosis of organic and technological body. It is thus critical that the narrative displays Ripley's prowess with the loader in Act One. While her function in Act One is utilitarian ('I don't know, what can you do?'), in the final sequence, the loader is more intensely, more elementally, part of Ripley's body. Cameron foreshadows the metamorphosis from organic to organic/machinic being in Ripley's gradual 'hardwearing' – first, through the demonstration of Ripley's prowess with the loader in Act One; second, through Ripley's assumption of control of the vehicle during the escape sequence, in effect emasculating Gorman (William Hope); third, through Hicks's instruction on working military hardware prior to the attack of the Alien army; fourth, through Ripley's embodiment within a suit of military technology – guns, grenade launcher, flame thrower, surveillance device, and so on; fifth, through the revelation of Ripley's organic/machinic body in the confrontation with the Alien Queen.

The final confrontation inaugurates a conceptual movement toward narrative resolution [2:18:54]: triumph over the monstrous Other, recuperation of the maternal female role (Ripley), the journey toward home and civilization. Cameron shoots the spectacle revelation in a conventional low angle, accentuating size, scale and proportion. Heavy backlighting renders a silhouette of the machine, such that the illusion of synthesis between organic and machinic material is uncanny (figure 7.33). Sound is brought up within the diegetic space – movements, gestures, the internal workings of the organic/machinic body are amplified. Ripley advances through the low angle image, pausing in a close-up (figure 7.34).

How does the spectator experience such an image? How are its various intensities manifested? The trope of the loader functions to disambiguate the image: there is the anticipated natural movement toward story and character resolution. If the reappearance of the loader is unanticipated, the spectator is nevertheless reassured by the hybrid body's familiarity. Narrative prompt manifests a mode of intensity in the sequence. Narrative coordinates

FIGURES 7.33–4 *The machinic/organic body in spectacle cinema:* Aliens *(1986).*

are further inscribed through the Queen's reverse-shot perspective, which constructs the spatial environment of the confrontation. The point of view itinerary is clearly not a form of spectator identification; instead, the coordinates further disambiguate the image and steer it toward resolution.

Yet the body that moves through the space is an image of excess. It is experienced as a technological object, pausing in fits and starts, moving in frenzy in defense or attack. The body displays its organic/machinic material, its several component parts in synthetic movement. The mechanical body is something of a trope in postmodern science fiction – visible in Verhoeven's *Robocop*, *Matrix Revolutions* (2003), and most recently in *Avatar*. Yet the affect of this image in *Aliens* is experienced as the utopian ideal of a technological embodiment. Here Cameron displays the profound contribution of a spectacle aesthetic to the medium of moving images: the industrialization of a mode of production and reception engaged in a perceptual and affective evolution of self through technology. Ripley is profoundly human (bearing the archetypal patterning of the High Concept narrative) and yet *more than human.*

In this series of analyses, I argue that Cameron represents the epochal transformation of the classical auteur. For Cameron the image of cinema is reified as a pure technological production.[72] This is a production and consumption ethos founded upon the exponential research and development of technologies of production, increased scales of effects and technological creation, increasingly complex and discursively mediated strategies for disseminating and marketing the image of spectacle in global cultures. In Cameron's unflagging enthusiasm for new spectacle forms, a cynic might conclude that his cinema represents merely a commercial enterprise, a consistently expanding capital base, which in turn provides the justification for the zealous commitment to 3-D, increased frame-rate capture, motion-

---

[72] For a discussion of various evolutions of the modernist auteur into the contemporary filmmaker, see Lewis, 'The Perfect Money Machine(s)', and Elsaesser, *The Persistence of Hollywood*, 289–304.

capture imaging technology, digital simulation software, and so on. I am not so cynical. Spectacle is necessarily a convergence aesthetic. It is necessarily a synthesis of a mode of creation that is profoundly technology-oriented. It is energized through a commodity-ethos, in which the performance of the image as commodity is intrinsic to its status as representation, art and cultural object.

PART THREE

On the characteristics of future cinema

8

New cinematic imaginaries

Teleological and transcendental narratives in image media: *The Dark Knight Rises*, IMAX film, and HFR cinema

Every new development added to the cinema must, paradoxically, take it nearer and nearer to its origins. In short, cinema has not yet been invented![1]

One of the peculiarities of cinema is that it tends, despite the best efforts of Bazin and Kracauer, to separate itself from … the natural environment.[2]

Christopher Nolan is a contemporary master of American High Concept cinema. *The Dark Knight Rises* (2012) will surely deliver the next chapter in the evolution of a career that no longer seeks to demonstrate an alternative sensibility (*Following*, 1998; *Memento*), but is increasingly concocted of the grandest machines the studio system can proffer. Nolan's image objects are indeed cathedrals of a simulacral imagination. These images are also, of course, the purest form of commodity, engaging a market itinerary that shifts freely between screened media, merchandizing, and cultural capital.[3] The

[1] Bazin, 'The Myth of Total Cinema', 21.
[2] Cubitt, *The Cinema Effect*, 359.
[3] For an analysis of the creation of the cinema commodity, see Janet Wasko, 'Financing and Production: Creating the Hollywood Film Commodity', in *The Contemporary Hollywood Film Industry*, ed. Paul McDonald and Janet Wasko (Malden, MA: Blackwell Publishing, 2008), 43–62. Acland describes contemporary cinema production in terms of a 'narrative path for the film commodity as it moves from conception to consumption' (Acland, *Screen Traffic*, 229). I wish to read this 'movement' in two ways: one, as the indifferent itinerary of the commodity within the global marketplace; and two, as *volition*, as the potential energy of the cinema commodity to enter and affect global culture.

image expresses what Tuck refers to as the 'capitalist sublime', affiliated to discourses of truth, beauty, the commodity and contemporary acculturated experience.[4]

I am therefore excited about the prospect of *The Dark Knight Rises*, due for release in Sydney, Australia July 19, 2012. This, it must be confessed, after having been somewhat disappointed by *Inception*, *The Dark Knight*, *The Prestige*, *Batman Begins* or indeed, any of Nolan's previous films, including the audacious *Memento.* Why then do I anticipate the coming of the tent-pole release of the Warner Bros. summer catalogue?[5] Simply put: *The Dark Knight Rises* represents the cultural object that most explicitly engages the ontological tensions within the medium of contemporary cinema; it is part of the material of cinema's current becoming. *The Dark Knight Rises* is forcefully composed of cinema's present and future material, yet it engages with equal force the century-long history of the medium. Each shot in Nolan's cinema projects an encounter with cinema's historicity. Nolan speaks in the rhetoric of the classical auteurs, seeking 'improvements' of the image, or essential experiences that only cinematic subjectivity can offer.[6] IMAX film (upon which Nolan shot an hour's worth of material for *The Dark Knight Rises*) exhibits the amped-up purity of celluloid: 'IMAX is the best film format that was ever invented' (figure 8.1).[7] Each shot in IMAX form establishes a movement away from, and yet also toward, cinema's origin. In purifying film, Nolan seeks to take it nearer to the essence of the medium. For Doane, 'today, the gigantic screens of IMAX theatres work to reassert, to reconfirm, that possibility of absorption … In other words, it seems necessary today to exaggerate, to hyperbolize the cinema in order to be assured it works.'[8] The filmic material of the IMAX image is celluloid hyperbolized in dialectical relation to the conventionally scaled celluloid image (35mm), or the miniaturization of the

---

[4] Greg Tuck, 'When More is Less: CGI, Spectacle and the Capitalist Sublime', *Science Fiction Film and Television* 1, no. 2 (2008), 249–73. I find Tuck's conclusion particularly appropriate to the experience of contemporary High Concept cinema: 'We are not simply duped by commodities, because we are complicit with them. We "know" they value capital above all else, but they remain in excess of it because they can, in the last instance, generate it only through us, through our labour, our needs, our wants. That is, the structure in dominance here is not simply a desire to have but a profound desire to *belong*' (272).

[5] For a discussion of 'tent-pole' distribution, marketing and industrial organization, see Acland, *Screen Traffic*, 159–62.

[6] Nolan, quoted in Ressner, 'The Traditionalist'. Nolan describes his method (or 'style') as an 'absolute concern with point of view. Whether in the pure camera blocking or even the writing, it's all about point of view.' What interests me is the essentialism of Nolan's doctrine, expressed as an aesthetic absolute, or even a moral aesthetic.

[7] Nolan, quoted in Ressner, 'The Traditionalist'.

[8] Mary Ann Doane, 'The Close-Up', 110.

'large-scale' digital image.[9] In an age in which auteurs are reanimating images through digital technology, *The Dark Knight Rises* represents the 'incomparable ecstasy' of an early, uncontaminated cinema. Nolan is thus appropriately a 'traditionalist' in a studio environment in which the rhetoric of the survival of cinema is couched within the rhetoric of technological innovation.

If Nolan had been relatively quiet up until this point on the use (and abuse) of digital technology within the studio system, *The Dark Knight Rises* constitutes a more deliberate confrontation with current production practice. It is a timely intervention: Spielberg's *War Horse* (2011) established the temporary viability of film within studio production even as *Hugo* demanded the digital apparatus of 3-D capture and projection. *The Artist* (2011) is not only radical for its appropriation of a silent film genericity, but openly displays the textural presence of celluloid: originally shot in colour, the film was transposed to black and white to capture the aesthetic tonality of celluloid in the late silent era. Tarantino's *Django Unchained* (2012) was shot on 35mm anamorphic film stock, demonstrating Tarantino's continued commitment to the preservation of a celluloid aesthetic.[10]

Other self-professed pioneers of contemporary cinema have recuperated similar teleological narratives of moving image evolution. Cameron projects a cinematic futurism in his advocacy of 3-D stereoscopic imaging and high frame-rate cinema (HFR). Peter Jackson recently exhibited a section of *The Hobbit*, the first mainstream production to utilize high frame rates through digital technology. Experimentation with frame rate is not altogether new,[11]

---

[9] While significantly larger in scale than the largest conventional movie theatre, the digital IMAX image initially represented a significant diminution of the filmic IMAX image. See James Hyder, 'IMAX Reacts to Controversy Over Digital Theatres', *LF Examiner*, 26 May 2009, http://www.lfexaminer.com/20090525a.htm [accessed 13 October 2011].

[10] Nick James, 'Tarantino Bites Back' (Interview), *Sight and Sound*, Feb 2008, http://www.bfi.org.uk/sightandsound/feature/49432 [accessed 12 June 2010]. Tarantino recuperates the overly simplistic dichotomy between celluloid cinematography as artistic creation (sculpting with the material properties of cinema: film, light, etc.) and digital cinematography as simulation: 'No cinematographer should be promoting digital. It makes them as obsolete as a dodo bird.' Tarantino then qualifies his own brand of hyperbole: 'But in the case of *Sin City*, and probably *300*, you know you could never have made those movies on film.'

[11] Douglas Trumbull developed the 'Showscan System' in the early 1980s, capturing on 70mm film stock, projecting at 60 frames per second. Trumbull has indeed been one of the most vocal advocates of high frame-rate cinema. See Jeff Labrecque, '*2001: A Space Odyssey's* Tech Pioneer on "Hobbit" Footage: A fabulous and brave step in the right direction', *Entertainment Weekly*, May 2 2012, http://insidemovies.ew.com/2012/05/02/douglas-trumbull-hobbit-frame-speed/ [accessed 28 July 2012]. Trumbull describes the effects aesthetic of *2001: A Space Odyssey* as the 'ultimate trip because it abandoned conventional cinematic wisdom in favor of a pure experience'. After several tests with increased frame rates, Trumbull concluded: 'We proved to ourselves and the United States Patent Office that it was absolutely true. There's a perfect curve of increased stimulation with increased frame rate.' For a more expansive analysis of the potential of new technologies (primarily stereoscopic imaging and increased frame rates, see 'Statement by Douglas Trumbull', *DouglasTrumbull.com*, 11 January 2012, http://douglastrumbull.com/ [accessed 24 March 2012].

FIGURE 8.1 *The amped-up celluloid image on IMAX film.*

but Jackson, Cameron and other key industrial figures operating within the studio system have strategically reoriented the debate: much as 3-D for Cameron projects an immersive experience of the moving image, so an increased frame rate provides 'more' of the object in its natural movement on screen. Duration is now mapped with double the framed 'images' of the traditional moving image of cinema projected at 24 frames per second. There is, simply put, more of the object within the same duration. A two-second shot (for example, a series of three cuts in an action sequence of *The Bourne Ultimatum*) displays 48 discrete images in constant motion through the projecting apparatus. Spaces between images (the image of black that sutures one frame to the next) are evenly condensed, fixed to smaller and smaller durations as the frame rate increases. Cameron has already speculated about the mainstream adoption of HFR cinema as high as 60 frames per second.[12]

Against Nolan's revitalization of the indexical filmic ideal, hyperbolically displayed in IMAX, Cameron's teleological narrative of the materialization of cinema works through digitality: the image's capacity for malleability through compositing and simulation. Stereoscopy is not exclusively a digital platform, nor is HFR cinema. Yet digital technology resituates stereoscopy and HFR production from an experimental (and financially risky) industrial process toward an industrial (and perceptual) norm. Recently speaking to Richard Hollander, a leading effects pioneer within the studio system, I asked: 'Precisely what has digital technology brought to cinema?' Hollander replied: 'With digital effects, we can do anything.'[13] This is not hyperbole, but a valid statement about the elemental relationship between reality and its manifestation in a digital image. The technology of digitality returns cinema – and cinema theory – to foundational questions about the origin of the medium of

---

[12] See Carolyn Giardina, 'James Cameron Urges Industry to Use Faster Frame Rates', *Hollywood Reporter*, 31 March 2011, http://www.hollywoodreporter.com/news/james-cameron-urges-industry-use–173577 [accessed 8 July 2012]. Cameron has projected the possibility of shooting *Avatar 2* and *Avatar 3* in stereoscopic 60 frames per second.

[13] Phone interview conducted with Richard Hollander, 14 February 2012, San Francisco.

moving images. What is the purpose of image production? In what sense are we – our material and non-material selves – engaged and invested in image production? For Hollander, digitization recasts the moving image medium from a necessarily constrained photographic reproduction (a shell) to the openly accessed possibilities of digital simulation. Hollander described such images of pure simulation as 'full-cloth images'. And yet this simulated image is only one part of the radical material of digitality. The image is not only built through simulation, but the simulation – the digital medium itself – is in a constant state of evolution, of *being built*. Code is in a natural state of filiation. The process of simulation – its tools, its technological processes – rather than medium-fixed, or indeed even medium-specific, are subject to change through enhancement. The simulation is thus perhaps best thought of as a trial and error laboratizing of the transcendental purpose of cinema. Ironically, Cameron perceives an end-point to the process: the image that attains a technological maturity to efface the imprint of its technological production. This is a technology 'advanced enough to make itself go away'.[14] I'm not quite sure how such a claim works within the rhetoric (and industrial mandate) of perpetual technological expansion.

I sense that for Nolan, as for Bazin, the medium of the moving image takes the spectator back to the world: 'I feel very lucky to be a member of probably the last generation who cut film on a Steenbeck flatbed, physically taping it together and dropping out shots.'[15] Of the essential characteristics of the cinematic image, Nolan adopts a classical position: 'When I look at a digitally acquired and projected image, it looks inferior against an original negative anamorphic print or an IMAX one.'[16] And further: 'I believe in an absolute difference between animation and photography. However sophisticated your computer-generated imagery is, if it's been created from no physical elements and you haven't shot anything, it's going to feel like animation.'[17] For Nolan, film *looks* better. But it is also imbued with the indexical presence of the object in photographic reproduction. 'Better' connotes two teleological positions: toward more reality in the image; and toward the greater capacity for aesthetic virtuosity in celluloid production. Each position maintains the status of the auteur-filmmaker, the creative genius that affirms the authenticity of the celluloid image. In the age of digitality, how a film looks is increasingly a question of immateriality rather than materiality.

For Cameron, as for the advocates of digitality, the medium, always in some sense affiliated to reality (studio cinema could not function otherwise),

---

14 Cited in Harkins.
15 Nolan, quoted in Ressner, 'The Traditionalist'.
16 Nolan, quoted in Ressner, 'The Traditionalist'.
17 Nolan, quoted in Ressner, 'The Traditionalist'.

takes the spectator to a world of immersion, interactivity, and transcendental body and mind experience – the avatar. Both Nolan and Cameron seek the essence of the medium in a technological material. Yet a perceived break has occurred, to use Rodowick's words. A projected cinematic future (at least within the studio system) seems to take one of two forms: toward the purity of filmic (photographic) form, which will require a significant investment in film technology, maintenance and cultural discourse;[18] and toward the reification of a digital image, stripped of its aura of indexicality. In my opinion, the lack of enchantment of the image has nothing to do with digitality *per se*; celluloid accomplished such a stripping away of the aura in its capacity for reproduction.[19] But, as Rodowick astutely observes, digitality constitutes a stripping away of the existential life of film. HFR thus seems to me the most interesting (and potentially conflicted) image material. On the one hand, HFR moves toward reality in providing more of the object; more of the object will be present to our sensory engagement. Yet, even at its point of inception (which is not exclusively photographic), that object will be a digital doppelganger, with its capacity to unnerve the spectator through its increasingly emphatic presence.[20] What will be our response to digitality that is ever more present, ever more acutely perceived, ever more cavalier in its simulated potentiality, composed of exponentially multiplying pixels that mould bodies to form at increased speeds?

Is it even cinema? 3-D, *Avatar*, and immersive cinema experience

Wouldn't 3-D have heightened the expressiveness of, say, the opening of the door onto Monument Valley in *The Searchers*, the wide-angle distortions and camera movements in *Touch of Evil*, the interplay between reality and the photographic image in *Blowup*, the climactic psychedelia in *2001*, and the foreground/background complexities in *Nashville*?[21]

---

18 Granted, such an investment is increasingly unlikely. For a comprehensive examination of the global take-up of digital production and exhibition, see David Bordwell, 'Pandora's Digital Box: In the Multiplex', *David Bordwell's Website on Cinema* (blog), 1 December 2011, http://www.david-bordwell.net/blog/2011/12/01/pandoras-digital-box-in-the-multiplex/ [accessed 2 April 2012].

19 Here I refer to Benjamin's seminal work, 'The Work of Art in the Age of Mechanical Reproduction'.

20 Early reactions to *The Hobbit* describe the film as looking like a 'made-for-TV movie. It was too accurate, too clear'. See Ben Child, 'The Hobbit: First Glimpse Gets Mixed Response', *The Guardian*, 25 April 2012, http://www.guardian.co.uk/film/2012/apr/25/the-hobbit-first-screening-cinemacon [accessed 8 June 2012].

21 Michael Kerbel, '3-D or Not 3-D', *Film Comment* 16, no. 6 (1980), 20.

What are we to make of the new 3-D cinematic imaginary? I refer to contemporary 3-D as 'new' because mainstream 3-D production had previously attempted to imagine the world anew in the early 1950s through the B-Grade Hollywood film.[22] *Bwana Devil* (1952) represents 3-D's first encounter with a mass culture and a mass cinema industry. Hitchcock attempted to bring 3-D into the mainstream through the Warner Bros. production of *Dial M For Murder* (1954); Warner Bros. had had some success with *House of Wax* (1953) in 3-D the previous year. But whereas *House of Wax*'s camp horror translated to 3-D's capacity for image excess, the transposition to *Dial M For Murder*'s conventional, dialogue-heavy situational-drama was less successful.[23] The cinematic flamboyance of *The Birds* (1963) or *Marnie* (1964), or perhaps even *Rope*, that curious experiment with depth and duration in 1948, might have been more suited to stereoscopic image production. There have since been several revitalizations of 3-D production, but in the long history of Hollywood studio cinema, 3-D is little more than an affectation, a pleasurable distraction from the evolution of the moving image in 2-D, privileging generic narrative and recognizable character types. My first encounter with 3-D was *Jaws 3-D* in 1984, a film nearer in aesthetic spirit to *House of Wax* than *Dial M For Murder*. The 3-D image of the unrelenting predator was, in the most literal sense, in excess of its 1975 2-D image.

The legacy of 3-D stereoscopic cinema is its hyperbolic aesthetic. We enjoy the thrill of an image dislocated from the itinerary of our perception. 3-D is *more than* real. It engages our perception in a way that is at once immersive and participatory. *Hugo* is said to draw us into the innermost depths of the simulacrum of Paris (which is equally the site of a simulacral history of cinema's origins) while isolating the point of view of the spectator within the theatre. We *feel* our presence as perceptive beings, dislocated from objects that suddenly reach out toward us, or occasionally recede in startling depth of field. 3-D exhibits the materiality of spectatorial affect, presenting the novelty of an image that takes the spectator back to the medium of astonishment. For Kerbel, who is by his own acknowledgement fanatical about stereoscopic cinema, '[3-D] reminds us that gaudy, circus-like spectacle was one of cinema's roots'.[24]

In 2009, Cameron's *Avatar 3-D* was projected as one such new experience, a mediated image so completely and perfectly immersive that its cinematic shell is effaced, and the spectator confronts the thrill of cinema produced,

---

[22] See Dave Kehr, '3-D or Not 3-D', *Film Comment* 46, no. 1 (2010), 60. For a very useful examination of the formation of stereoscopic cinema, see Ray Zone, *Stereoscopic Cinema and the Origins of 3-D Film* (Lexington: University of Kentucky Press, 2007).

[23] Kerbel, 12.

[24] Kerbel, 15.

post-produced, exhibited and experienced in three dimensions. Spectators are traumatized by the abrupt ejection from the spatially replete eco-world of Pandora. How does the spectator confront the world of the real, the paltry originary image of the technicolored simulacrum? How does the spectator re-encounter the banality of a shark in 2-D after being subjected to the terror of a shark that leaps beyond the screen in negative parallax, threatening the spectator's body with its own newly embodied form?[25] This is why *Avatar's* final shot – the virtual eyes opening – is both a cliché in High Concept cinema and an unsettling truth: cinema ends, credits roll and hyper-real technological worlds cut to black. How does the spectator return to the immersive fantasy when movies end, when 3-D reformulates into 2-D perception, when the fluidity of motion capture in simulated space becomes the jerky, unpremeditated, unmapped movements of actuality? My experience of ejection from a stereoscopic viewing experience – *The Adventures of Tintin*, *Hugo*, or more humbly, *Jaws 3-D* – is of returning to the phenomenological *real*. The ejection is thus from a phenomenological fantasy, or at least a novel phenomenological contrivance of vision, cognition and affect.

It is difficult to project precisely what the new 3-D is, or indeed what it might be. The thrill of a projectile intruding into the virtual space before the screen is subdued now, or at least, subtly rendered. The new 3-D, inscribed in the conceptual paradigm of James Cameron, is said to render the technological brush-stroke of cinema invisible:

> The irony with *Avatar* is that people think of it as a 3-D film and that's what the discussion is. But I think that, when they see it, the whole 3-D discussion is going to go away … That's because, ideally, the technology is advanced enough to make itself go away. That's how it should work. All of the technology should wave its own wand and make itself disappear.[26]

For Cameron, immersive 3-D experience should be a hermetic, interior phenomenon. It should naturalize rather than hyberbolize perception, cognition and affect; it should realize the mythic potential of cinema to manifest new worlds, and new perceptual and psychological experiences.

Reading much of what came out in the months after *Avatar's* release, I could not help but reflect on the project of André Bazin, who privileged

---

[25] Zemeckis nicely parodies this thrill of excess of stereoscopic vision in *Back to the Future Part II* (1989). Strolling through Hill Valley of 2015, Marty McFly is set upon by Jaws in stereoscopic 3-D. The shark leaps out in negative parallax from a theatre billboard, attacking Marty (who screams in terror!). When the shark recedes, and Marty recognizes the illusion of the shark in 3-D, he declares, 'Shark still looks fake'.

[26] Cited in Harkins.

the capacity of the image in depth and duration to reveal the real, to bring the spectator into a phenomenological encounter with the world.[27] Bazin is quite explicit on the subject of depth: 'That is why depth of field is not just a stock in trade of the cameraman like the use of a series of filters or of such-and-such a style of lighting, it is a capital gain in the field of direction – a dialectical step forward in the history of film language.'[28] Bazin champions the experiential potential of the image in depth against flatness, usually contrived through invisible editing, or classical continuity. Depth maintains the image in spatial unity; flatness accentuates an object on a plane, strategically directing the passive gaze of the spectator. Intriguingly, Bazin's description of the evolution of the cinema image through depth is not dissimilar from Cameron's celebration of stereoscopic depth. For Bazin, as for Cameron, the image in depth is revelatory.

And yet, with each new 3-D film I watch, and re-watch, it occurs to me that my experience of stereoscopic depth is *not* the same as that of traditional depth cinematography in 2-D cinema. In fact, after re-examining the depth cinematography used by Welles in *Citizen Kane*, *The Magnificent Ambersons*, *The Stranger* (1946), *The Lady From Shanghai* (1948) and *Touch of Evil* – films that display astonishingly virtuosic images of depth and duration – I would argue that the two spatial registers of the moving image are in some sense diametrically opposed; stereoscopic depth takes me further from the experience of depth cinematography I admire in Renoir, or Welles, or Altman, or Cuarón. I necessarily engage these separate images of depth as *different* objects, manifesting very different images of the world. I am thus increasingly perplexed by analogies drawn between classical cinema's depth cinematography, so explicitly rendered in a filmmaker such as Welles,[29] and stereoscopic 3-D that claims to render a newly immersive experience of depth: 'What is different about *Avatar* in 3-D as compared to more recent 3-D movies is its immersive effect. Rather than using the technology as a visual gimmick, Cameron worked to create a cinematic experience. The aesthetics of three-dimensional depth perception utilized and the visuals required by the storyline work in concert, lending particularly well to a *real-world* [my emphasis] experience.'[30] Can classical depth cinematography in 2-D and stereoscopic depth cinematography in 3-D equally claim to manifest the

---

[27] Bazin, 'The Myth of Total Cinema'.

[28] Bazin, 'The Evolution of the Language of Cinema', 35.

[29] Bordwell has usefully demonstrated that depth cinematography manifests quite a bit earlier as a concerted 'style'. See Bordwell, *On the History of Film Style*, 158–68.

[30] Harkins.

'world', to 'bring the spectator into a relation with the image closer to that which he enjoys with reality'?[31]

The paradox of immersive 3-D

You can always ask, pointing to an object in a photograph – a building, say – what lies behind it, totally obscured by it … A photograph is *of* the world.[32]

3-D is a misnomer. Films are 3-D. The whole point of photography is that it's three-dimensional. The thing with stereoscopic imaging is it gives each audience member an individual perspective. It's well suited to video games and other immersive technologies, but if you're looking for an audience experience, stereoscopic is hard to embrace.[33]

In the opening sequence of *Avatar*, Sully awakes from hibernation in a cryogenic chamber, one of William Gibson's coffins of the cyberpunk tradition. Cameron employs a familiar setting, recalling Ripley's awakening from hibernation in *Aliens*. The sequence in *Avatar* is thus quotation. Rendered now in 3-D in *Avatar*, the cryogenic chamber is Cameron's self-reflexive demonstration of a technological advancement in cinema. This is a display of the depth capacity of stereoscopic imaging.[34]

In 3-D, we see the spectacle of the Bazinian real, materialized in the striking depth of a shot (figures 8.2–8.3). Cameron holds on the cryogenic chamber, the camera moving almost imperceptibly, permitting the uninterrupted contemplation of the space. Bodies float in zero gravity at various depths of field, collapsing the classical composition of foreground, middle ground and background (figure 8.4). The chamber is cut through by bodies in motion that display a spatialized 'relationship between audience and filmed body'.[35] *Mise en scène* is orchestrated for stereoscopic depth perception. Objects seem unnaturally aware of their presence in relation to the depth of the shot, strikingly interposed against the openness of the chamber. We might say that these bodies are animated by a form of 'depth perception'.

---

[31] Bazin, 'The Evolution of the Language of Cinema', 35.
[32] Cavell, *The World Viewed*, 23–4.
[33] Nolan, quoted in Ressner, 'The Traditionalist'.
[34] On stereoscopy and new media self-reflexivity, see Barbara Klinger, '*Cave of Forgotten Dreams*: Meditations on 3D', *Film Quarterly* 65, no. 3 (2012), 42–3.
[35] Miriam Ross, 'Spectacular Dimensions: 3D Dance Films', *Senses of Cinema* 61 (2011), http://sensesofcinema.com/2011/feature-articles/spectacular-dimensions–3d-dance-films/#b7 [accessed 10 March 2012].

There seems a self-reflexive mannerism in *mise en scène* that opens stereo-scopic cinema to its performative potential: the crystalline features of the shot held for 45 seconds (a sequence shot of some duration in High Concept cinema), the materiality of the space in depth. Much as Renoir uses vertical lines to accentuate depth in complex sequence shots in *Le Règle du Jeu* (*The Rules of the Game*, 1939) (figures 8.5–8.8), Cameron provides a grid structure through which to display depth as a material form. Cameron's cryogenic chamber displays the aesthetic imprint of Renoir's corridor.

This sequence in *Avatar* reflects the aesthetic expressivity of stereoscopic effect, or a mode of cinema in which 'spectacle [is] primary experience'.[36] Clearly Cameron has orchestrated a spectacle to open his landmark film. The shot exhibits an innovative new stereoscopic technology (the image of technologized perception and affect). It displays framed space orchestrated for stereoscopic visualization, extending from the interior of the theatre in negative parallax to the interior of the screen in positive parallax. It seeks to immerse the spectator in a fantasy world wholly contained by the stereoscopic apparatus. This is a space in which depth has been 'opened up' to the presence of the spectator.

But what is *contained* in this stereoscopic image? In what sense is stereoscopic spatiality revealed? In what sense can we say that depth had materialized anew in stereoscopic 3-D, in dialectical advancement of classical depth cinematography? I agree with Klinger that stereoscopic cinema opens up old questions about depth and phenomenological reality.[37] 3-D cinema projects immersive space, encapsulating the spectator in a potentially infinitely expanding depth field. Ross emphasizes stereoscopy's 'infinite depth planes and pop-out effects', moving freely between negative and positive parallax. Indeed, she persuasively argues that the stereoscopic image '[problematises] the distinction between diegetic and non-diegetic space'.[38] But whereas I think Ross and Klinger quite correctly identify stereoscopic depth cinema-tography as the spectacle of *depth* – this is stereoscopic cinema's '3Dness'[39] – I would identify classical depth cinematography (the display of continuous space in Renoir or Welles) as the spectacle of *movement*. While stereoscopic imaging materializes depth in potentially infinite planes, classical depth cinematography materializes spatialized movement within a continuous field, or what Cavell calls the image '*of* the world'.

Let me attempt to work through this distinction. In 2-D depth cinema-tography, the image reveals a spatial 'whole'. This is a space that is at once

---

[36] Ross, 'Spectacular Dimensions: 3D Dance Films'.
[37] Klinger, '*Cave of Forgotten Dreams*', 40.
[38] Ross, 'Spectacular Dimensions'.
[39] Klinger, '*Cave of Forgotten Dreams*', 40.

FIGURES 8.2–8 *Composition in depth in 3-D stereoscopic and 2-D cinematography:* Avatar *(2009) and* The Rules of the Game *(1939).*

framed through *mise en scène*, and yet exceeds the frame. I agree with Cavell (and Deleuze, who picks up the point from Cavell)[40] that the moving image is necessarily 'beyond the frame'; why should this movement stop at an arbitrary boundary, for example, at the edge of the framed image? There is an astonishing moment in *Taxi Driver* in which the camera sets about its own itinerary, oblivious to the drama affecting its protagonist. The image holds Travis (Robert De Niro) in a medium shot as he speaks into a payphone (figure 8.9). After what seems an inordinate length of time, the camera begins a track right, no longer attending to the subject of the frame. The track ends on an empty corridor, isolating the open space in depth as the 'principal object' within the frame (figures 8.10–8.11). In what sense can we say that Travis is no longer present within this spatial whole? Surely Travis forcefully inhabits the *expanded* frame, which builds upon the spatial whole. The camera track infuses the space with movement, encompassing Travis, the corridor, and the space between the two. Similarly, Antonioni's movement of the camera in the classic final shot of *The Passenger* breaks beyond the frame, not only holding the shot in depth, but breaking beyond the bars of the room, intruding into the framed space that is now opened up into the whole. This is precisely the radicalism of the camera in autonomous movement: the subjectless camera leaves the body, expanding the spatial whole beyond the perceptual mechanism of the protagonist (who suitably dies off-screen) (figures 8.12–8.14).

This image in Antonioni – striking for depth of field and focus – is not the display of depth, but the coming into being of a cinematic space *through depth*. The sequence displays the performance of spatial movement: the orchestration of the camera through a slow dolly, the artifice of the hotel façade that must give way to permit the autonomous movement of the camera, bodies that move in and out of shot, radically dissociated from a narrative itinerary. The movement of the camera animates the space, inscribing a spatial continuity that coheres from foreground to deep background, and then infinitely beyond the frame of the screened image. This is the kind of image Bazin accords the special status of aestheticized reality, referring specifically to Welles in his essay, 'The Evolution of the Language of Cinema'. In *Citizen Kane*, Welles tracks from a close-up on Kane's mother, then moves into the interior of the house to capture Thatcher and Kane's parents in the foreground, all the while maintaining focus on the image of the young Charlie in deep background (figures 8.15–8.17). In what sense can we say that this legendary camera move reveals depth, that it is an image *of* depth?

Clearly, the special status of Welles's image has something to do with the technology of depth cinematography and duration (the sequence shot);

---

[40] Deleuze, *Cinema 1*, 29–32.

FIGURES 8.9–14 *The expanded frame in depth in 2-D cinematography.*

Bordwell is thus correct to emphasize depth cinematography as the outcome of an industrial process.[41] But the image in depth is no less *of depth* than it is of some other form of spatial representation. Rather, in Welles, depth serves the purpose of 'opening up' the space within, and outside of, the frame, in effect opening the image to the potential for increasingly expressive movement. And this is precisely how Bazin describes the sequence shot: not as the revelation of depth, but as the revelation of an image that brings the spectator into contact with a particular phenomenological experience. Whether we agree that this is an experience of the real, or of some other synthetic image form, depth is *infused into* a phenomenological space. In classical depth cinematography, depth is merely background; it sustains the image of space. Of course there are sequences in Welles, or Antonioni, or Scorsese, in which images in depth are bereft of perceptible movement. But movement, as Deleuze suggests, is internal to the image, whether that image

---

[41] Bordwell, *On the History of Film Style*, 160–64.

FIGURES 8.15–17 *The signature expanded frame in Welles:* Citizen Kane *(1941).*

is of an object in stasis, or an object animated by aggressive motion within the frame.[42]

There is something in this image of spatialized movement that is absent in stereoscopic depth. While I agree with Klinger that '*Citizen Kane's* deep-focus moments or *Touch of Evil's* legendary opening crane shot and long take convey the majesty and exhilaration of highly self-conscious presentations of space',[43] in stereoscopic 3-D, space is materialized as the display *of depth*. Depth is less the evocation of a spatial unity that extends infinitely beyond the frame, than the display of an object isolated in depth for the gaze of the spectator. I would thus argue that stereoscopic depth is a form of what Manovich calls spatial montage: 'a number of images, potentially of different sizes and proportions, appearing on the screen at the same time.'[44] Stereoscopic depth displays a hierarchy of planes, each plane materializing an object, each plane materializing a localized space divorced from the whole. In stereoscopic depth, the plane is again *foregrounded* in much the same way that classical montage foregrounds perception of the separate planes

---

[42] See Ruiz, *Poetics of Cinema*, 65.
[43] Klinger, '*Cave of Forgotten Dreams*', 40.
[44] Manovich, *The Language of New Media*, 322.

of a spatial whole. Granted, Manovich's spatial montage refers to the kind of assemblage we rarely see in mainstream narrative cinema, in which separate images appear on screen at the same time. Figgis's *Time Code* (2000) is an effective example; De Palma uses split-screen to occasionally astonishing effect in films such as *Dressed to Kill* (1980) and *Body Double* (1984). Manovich is explicitly talking about separate images that inhabit the same screen-time, the same frame. And yet, isn't stereoscopic cinema an *assemblage* in depth, a montage in depth? My experience of 3-D is of the exhibition of an image that isolates *this* object, or *that* one, pulling the spectator's gaze this way or that way.

Immersive stereoscopic depth, at least in my experience of contemporary 3-D, is thus a paradoxical notion. Christie cites Eisenstein in making a claim for the experiential potential of 3-D.[45] But surely Eisenstein (whose original piece I've not been able to access) equates stereoscopy with conflict through montage, the montage of attractions that innervates the spectator's intellectual faculties. I thus concur with Eisenstein, and my experience of contemporary 3-D plays out the same conclusion: in 3-D, the image revelation is not of a spatial whole, but of an object materialized in a depth relationship (spatial montage), reflexively aware of its status in depth, and no less explicit in its plasticity. Confronted with the 3-D image, the spectator cannot contain the whole in stereoscopic perspective, but cuts the image into discretized segments, which is essentially why 3-D cinema requires constant focalizations on discrete depth planes. Klinger is perfectly correct to suggest that stereoscopic depth 'explicitly limns dimensionality'.[46] This is stereoscopy's revelatory effect: the illumination of 'multiple planes of action', dimensionality rather than spatial continuity. The limn effect converges a single point of view, a single depth perceptual capacity of the image.

I saw *Avatar* in 3-D on a Saturday afternoon soon after it was globally released in 2009. Some time later, but no more than a few hours after the screening, I encountered great difficulty recalling the experience *in 3-D*, as stereoscopic perception. The depth image of the film had diminished. I could not recollect an experience of the image in depth, and even less the experience of the image in duration. It seemed my initial point of experiential contact with the film had crystallized in 2-D, displacing the affective experience of spatiality while simultaneously bringing to the foreground the flatness of narrative form. And so the film, as an experiential whole, was significantly diminished. Bazin's depth/flatness dialectic seemed part of some

[45] Ian Christie, 'Clash of the Wonderlands', *Sight and Sound* 21, no. 11 (2011), 36–8.
[46] Klinger, 39.

other spatial ontology, some other way of experiencing space as continuous form.

What had become of *Avatar*'s 3-D? What becomes of the next projection of stereoscopic spectacle? Perhaps it fixes in the spectator's experience as a memory of the materiality of depth on screen, fused awkwardly into the immersive shell of High Concept narrative. The affective import of contemporary 3-D in the wake of *Avatar* is the supplementation and augmentation of vision, not as a function of visuality, but as a function of the technology of the glasses we gleefully wear in the multiplex and collect for future 3-D events.[47] It seems to me the current fascination with 3-D is not to see the world anew, but to see the world through new eyes.[48]

The mobility of the image

Against the grain of a great deal of theory of the digital image, Rombes suggests that 'digital cinema has opened up striking alternatives to Hollywood's multimillion dollar productions'.[49] For Rombes, 'haunted by the spectre of perfection, there is a tendency in digital media – and cinema especially – to reassert *imperfection*, flaws, an aura of human mistakes to counterbalance the logic of perfection that pervades the digital'.[50] If digitality at the high end of industry production constitutes a technological evolution toward ever more perfect cinemas (images perfect in their immersive capacities), digitality at the low end of production promises precisely the opposite: a humanistic engagement with flaws, degradation and decomposition. This is not far from Dudley Andrew's assertion of cinema's capacity to engage lived experience: 'the films some of us care most about ... have a mission quite other than lying or agitating: they aim to discover, to encounter, to confront, to reveal.'[51] Andrew makes no distinction between celluloid and digital images in discerning films that aim to reveal; rather, such aims, as I suggested in Chapter One, seem founded upon an ethical imperative to

---

[47] 'Ownership is the most intimate relationship that one can have to objects. Not that they come alive in him; it is he who lives in them.' See Walter Benjamin, 'Unpacking my Library: A Talk About Book Collecting', in *Illuminations: Walter Benjamin: Essays and Reflections*, ed. Hannah Arendt (New York: Shocken Books, 1988), 67.

[48] For an analysis of Cameron's auteur aesthetic founded upon 'prosthetic vision', see Keller, 15–16. While the prosthetic vision is not overtly incorporated into the narrative of *Avatar*, Cameron's fascination with sight here transposes to the prosthetic sight of cinematic spectatorship in 3-D.

[49] Nicholas Rombes, 'Introduction', in *New Punk Cinema*, ed. Nicholas Rombes (Edinburgh: Edinburgh University Press, 2005), 2.

[50] Rombes, *Cinema in the Digital Age*, 2.

[51] Andrew, *What Cinema Is!*, xviii.

communicate. But Rombes seems to take this generalization about cinema's overarching purpose further. If both Andrew and Rombes seem committed to the notion of the image's humanistic potential, Rombes explicitly suggests that a humanistic desire for mistakes is intrinsic to the *digital* image, and to its radically different production and reception itineraries. Rombes is thus interested in the capacity of digital technology to render 'fragile images ... in a shaky, pixilated way'. If the digital image is in a state of permanent decomposition, if it is always threatened by the spectre of its own degradation, the moving image that arises from the digital apparatus carries within it the sensation of loss, of existential uncertainty.

At the high end of digital production, cinema narratives conventionally trace the utopian evolution of self toward a state of technological transcendence. Such transformations are exemplified in two High Concept allegories of digitality: the resurrection of the One in *The Matrix* and Sully's resurrection within the virtual body of the Na'vi warrior in *Avatar*. Both *The Matrix* and *Avatar* are suitably described as landmark achievements in the evolution of the moving image; both films embrace the digital imperative beneath a classical High Concept narrative system. Both films provide the spectator with a 'digital awakening' within worlds that function through computer-generated simulations. Elsaesser suggests that 'after spending time on Pandora, young viewers contracted the inevitable Avatar Blues, feeling so distraught that they were in need of serious professional counseling.'[52] But while Elsaesser reads such pathological responses as merely one possible response to the film, I would argue that this incapacity to withdraw from the simulation is the foundational aesthetic and ideological imperative of the High Concept film. For Mike (a viewer who contemplated suicide after seeing the film), Pandora is a 'wonderful world',[53] redolent with digitally simulated colours, movements, textures, emotional arcs, and narrative trajectories of becoming.

At the low end of digital technology, the apparatus employs the bodily shape (and digital image capacity) of a mobile device – an iPhone 4. In 2011, Park Chan-Wook directed *Night Fishing*, a 33min film (though of course the outcome is in no way filmic) budgeted at $133,000 US. The narrative is simple: a man fishing at a lake encounters a supernatural being, and is able to communicate with his daughter 'on the other side'. We discover at the film's conclusion that the man is recently deceased and struggles to accept his own death. This story is quite conventional, even clichéd. Yet what elevates the material is precisely what Rombes refers to as the decomposition of the

---

[52] Elsaesser, *The Persistence of Hollywood*, 293. I've heard that many adults had much the same experience!

[53] Quoted in Elsaesser, *The Persistence of Hollywood*, 293.

image in digital form. In *Night Fishing*, Park employs the iPhone camera as a mobile image-capture device. In its strangely unsettling departures from conventional cinematography, the iPhone does not express a neo-baroque virtuosity as much as an unstable mode of perception. This is a mode of perception not only specific to digitality, but to cinema's inherent mobility in an iPhone 4 body. The phone has access to small spaces, to odd angles, to ways of capturing the world that have little to do with common cinematic perception. The image moves haphazardly, as if it cannot be fixed or held steady – which of course it cannot. This instability in image composition is directly affiliated to the mobility of the image. And the mobility of the gaze is a radical transformation in the image of cinema, a vital expansion of the capacity of digitality to reflect contemporary experience.

But there is more at stake than a radically altered gaze. Such images are inherently *transient*; such images are exchangeable. We hold such images in our possession, as part of our person or community. In perceiving a world captured on a device that is increasingly a global communication medium, cinema is less a projection than a communication, less a gaze *upon* the world than a mode of perceptual exchange engaged *in* the world. Even projected digitally in a theatre, *Night Fishing* presages the increasingly open-access territories built of digital technologies. Such objects are of course not films. But neither are they 'movies' in the cultural connotation of that word.

Jafah Panahi's *This Is Not a Film* (2011) is a documentary depicting the filmmaker's house imprisonment. It was shot primarily on an iPhone, with additional material captured on a consumer digital video camera. Panahi's film is the profound expression of the capacity of a personal digital apparatus to reveal life: to offer contemporary cinema as a mode of confrontation. Here Panahi's plight is deeply affecting. Yet there is a spontaneity to this assemblage that we recognize in the technological images of our own everyday lives. Panahi's life captured on an iPhone feels tragically connected to my own. The medium of digital mobility is thus deeply affecting; it is a very strange kind of image affect radically different from the affective experience of industrialized cinema production.

Panahi's film was smuggled out of the country on a flash drive, that most portable of experiential containers. For those transporting the drive hidden in a cake, I wonder if the digital image had not reacquired the aura Benjamin had deemed lost in the age of mechanical reproduction? Could the medium of mobile digitality recapture that enchantment of life in a moving image that is all the more affecting for its grainy, pixilated imagery, for its mobility and exchangeability? Ironically, Panahi's film is *not a film*. Thus, while a symbol of powerful resistance through moving images, it is not a transgression of the restrictions imposed on him by Iranian authorities. In attempting to explain what the film is (how does the reviewer classify a film that explicitly disavows that medium?), A. O. Scott concludes his *New York Times* review with a provocative reflection on the medium of cinema: 'How did Mr. Panahi do this? I'm at a bit of a loss to explain, to tell you the truth, since my job is to review movies, and this, obviously, is something different: a masterpiece in a form that does not yet exist.'[54]

A vivid philosophy of the image espoused by Pixar's Rick Sayre[55]

I was recently privileged to spend a few hours talking to Rick Sayre, a senior animation scientist working at Pixar Studios. Sayre was a key figure on some of Pixar's most significant productions, notably *The Incredibles* (2004); *The Incredibles* remains for me Pixar's outstanding aesthetic achievement. Sayre shifts between animation scientist and occasional theorist of the moving image. On this evening in particular, he was forthcoming about his relationship to image technologies, moving and still (including painting), past, present and future.

We had spent some time discussing a philosophy of the moving image, and the relationship between a moving image in photographic reproduction and a moving image animated through a variety of processes. Sayre had spent some time prior to his career at Pixar as a visual artist, training and exhibiting. Pixar was thus a continuation of a long and discursive engagement in visual arts production and culture. I was especially interested in Sayre's position on the impact of computer animation, and more broadly, the impact of digitality on the experience of the moving image. I was astonished by the extent of Sayre's knowledge of various theories of the ontology of the moving image.

The foundation of the philosophy of animation Sayre espoused was what he referred to as a 'discretized image', a phrase commonly used in the industry. Discretization refers to a movement animated through a procession of frames, 24 frames per second in traditional film, 48 frames per second in *The*

---

54 A. O. Scott, 'A Video From Tehran: It's Not What It Isn't, but What It Is', *The New York Times*, February 28, 2012, http://movies.nytimes.com/2012/02/29/movies/hes-jafar-panahi-but-this-is-not-a-film.html [accessed 1 June 2012].

55 Interview conducted 15 February 2012, Emeryville, San Francisco. I should emphasize that our meeting was less formal interview than a discussion about various philosophies of the moving image. I therefore attempt to maintain the open, exploratory nature of this engagement in my account of it.

Hobbit, and so on. For Sayre, animation represents the purity of discretization. This discretization is traditionally accomplished through the progression of animation cels; more recently, discretization is performed through computer animating systems. Sayre further suggested that directors of animation (and no doubt animators as well) viewed the physical environment as 'discretized space', as discrete sections of a whole. Yet the whole was less significant than the movement encapsulated by a series of frames. The spatialized and temporalized image is thus subjected to the itinerary of animated frames, individual space and time segments stitching an environment into an arbitrarily formed unity. I mentioned a theoretical trajectory within cinema studies – an ontological theory of the medium of cinema – that entertained the notion of movement as discretized progression, and indeed, that traced the origins of the medium of the moving image to *animation*, an 'animating' of an object, or a sort of spontaneous life-giving to an object within an environment.[56] Sayre suggested that he would have no problem with such a notion, that it seemed only natural to entertain a historical and ontological affiliation between live action image capture and animation. For Sayre, an animated environment – any environment enlivened through discretized movement – was a profoundly synthetic object.

We concluded a long conversation that shifted from ontologies of the image to the capacity for industrialized production to produce art through digital animation, an interest we shared. Prior to parting ways, Sayre mentioned his peripheral involvement in a sub-cultural practice called, simply, 'Demoscene'. He suggested I might investigate Demoscene further, particularly as I'd expressed an interest in the function of artistic imperatives (virtuosity) within the increasingly technologized medium of cinema. If the conventional wisdom was that digitality had removed the material brush-stroke from the process of moving image production, rendering the artist subservient to the technology, I asked Sayre how he would conceptualize the art of digital animation? It was thus to Demoscene that he turned in 'animating' a philosophical position on computer-generated animation, on the implication of physical and virtual discretized environments, and on the potential for a phenomenological experience of digitality.

A demo is a presentation (demonstration) on computer, formulated through code and run in real-time through the computer platform. Sayre thus

---

[56] For a passionate statement of this position, maintained through a long and sustained challenge to conventional thinking on film ontology, see Alan Cholodenko, 'Introduction to SCMS Panel: Animation – Film Studies and Media Studies' "Blind Spot"', *Society for Animation Studies Newsletter* 20, no, 1 (2007), 15. Cholodenko argues that 'For me not only is animation a form of film, film – all film, film "as such" – is a form of animation, calling for the thinking of all film through animation!'

forbid me to 'watch' a demo through an easily accessed medium such as YouTube; rather, a demo required *running*, it required *animation* through the computer platform. The demo was simultaneously an image in production, the code through which the image had been inscribed, and the technological medium through which the object moved; the code provided the life-source for the moving image production from conception to demonstration. Sayre described Demoscene as a subversive (and little-known) movement within the contemporary environment of mainstream digital culture. I asked Sayre if Demoscene was equivalent to Machinima, which I knew something (though admittedly little) about at the time. No, it was precisely Demoscene's deviation from Machinima's conventions that fascinated Sayre, particularly in Machinima's evolution toward filmic and game aesthetics. Machinima, according to Harwood, 'is an art form in evolution. A Machinima manifesto would recognize its distinctive attributes, creative endeavor, its techno-logical, social and cultural context, and political position in relation to digital commerce.'[57] But this art form is flexible in its production, operating platform and mode of exhibition. Contemporary Machinima increasingly integrates post-production editing technology, refining the production, steering the production nearer toward the itinerary of the cinema image. For this reason, Nitsche locates the material and ontological essence of Machinima in a time 'before audiences got used to rendered single versions of game movies [now broadly described as Machinima], before these recordings were combined with traditional CGI, visual postproduction effects, and any other animation technique available'.[58] In short, in a time when Machinima was in its nascent state as a demo, 'before it entered the media mashup'.[59] This is a Machinima that 'switch[es] to the machine as performing entity'.[60]

Yet it is not precisely the machine that performs in Demoscene, but the *code* that is animated through the technology of digital production. And it is code that provides the creative, constructive material for Demoscene. Here Sayre's philosophy of digital virtuosity sounds very much like Rombes's humanist digital cinema. Rombes reads digital cinema through its engagement with the fragility of the image, the threat of its own design toward an impos-sible-to-attain perfection in visual, aural and kinetic clarity. Digitization is thus enhanced through the awareness of its capacity for decomposition. For Sayre, Demoscene strips the image of the world to its elemental code, the essence

---

[57] Tracy Harwood, 'Towards a Manifesto for Machinima', *Journal of Visual Culture* 10, no. 1 (2011), 6.
[58] Michael Nitsche, 'A Look Back at Machinima's Potential', *Journal of Visual Culture* 10, no. 1 (2011), 14.
[59] Nitsche, 14.
[60] Nitsche, 15.

of digitality. But unlike the lavish production of a great deal of contemporary Machinima, Demoscene limits its capacity within a computer environment. Sobol vividly describes his first encounter with Demoscene:

> So I looked.
> What I saw was one of the most imaginative and beautifully rendered computer animations that I had ever encountered. The screen was alive with intricate shadows and reflections, all effortless morphing from one complex 3-D form into another … I was awed. But I still hadn't fully understood what made it so special.
> 'It's real-time 3-D', I was told in an almost reverential tone by a teenage computer animator. 'It's a 64k file. The whole thing is 64k', added a wet-behind-the-ears programmer in wonderment. I looked at them in confusion … I did not immediately grasp the significance of this statement.[61]

What is this digital code? What is it that materializes in relation to a technological constraint, 64k of data, or more appropriately, 64k of *memory*? Code is an impression. Code manifests as a presence within the production, beneath the image. The image manifests the pictorial form and, simultaneously, the trace impression of its code. Demoscene is thus a technological object, and yet it remains perpetually confronted by its own fragility, its inherent limitations. 'What is it?' asks Sobol, staring at a computer screen. What is this medium that is neither cinema, nor game, but is affiliated to the historical itineraries of both mediums?

For Sayre, digital virtuosity is expressed through imaginative renderings of code within the constraints of a computer system. The code is at once virtuosic expression – a digital brush-stroke – and an affirmation of the constraints on that mode of expression. The experience of this object is radically removed from an experience of cinema, or gaming, or indeed, multi-media Machinima.

When we had all but exhausted this discussion about Demoscene, Sayre concluded with one further provocation: 'Simply, that code can be beautiful.' I paused for a moment to contemplate the gravity of this statement. I had a vague notion of what Sayre meant, though I'm not a programmer. *Not* that the pictorial representation of digitality could be beautiful – as it is in the image of digital code in *The Matrix*, or in an elaborate image simulation in Machinima. But that 'beauty' inheres in the space between the technological medium

---

[61] John Sobol, 'Demoscene and Digital Culture', in *The Sharpest Point: Animation at the End of Cinema*, ed. Chris Gehman and Steve Reinke (Toronto: YYZ Books, 2005), 207.

and the image, spilling out as a trace presence of digital material. Beauty manifests in the image of what digital code *could do*, and what it *had done*, less than in the image of what it was. Demoscene is of course not digital cinema, and certainly not digital cinema as it is produced within the studio system. Cinema can only metaphorize the phenomenon of digitality through films like *The Matrix*. Yet Demoscene expresses something vital about the capacity of images of spatial and temporal environments to manifest through code, and perhaps to project a mode of perception attuned to material objects and the codes that create them.

Nostalgia for a lost object: A visit to the museum

In March of 2012, I attended an exhibition of Christian Marclay's *The Clock* at the Museum of Contemporary Art in Sydney. Marclay's work of art is a video installation that tells time, mirroring the flow of time for the duration of the spectator's visit. But instead of clock hands or digital readout displays that analogize the flow of time in our daily lives, *The Clock* measures time by the assemblage of narrative sections of film, each clip displaying 'the time' within a point in time within a film. At noon, for example, Zinnermann's *High Noon* (1952) indicates that outside the MCA in Darling Harbour, it is twelve o'clock (figures 8.18–8.19).

The object is a magnificent accomplishment; imagine the hours spent trawling through cinema's history of images to put this time-piece together. In some basic sense, it was thrilling simply to see time told *through cinema*, to be there at the moment of *High Noon*, in preparation for the showdown. I was forcefully brought into the same time as *The Clock*, which was a kind of cinematic time, the flow of which I marked by my own watch. Perhaps

FIGURES 8.18–19 *High noon in Marclay's* The Clock.

Bergson would say that our separate durations had found a point of contact. I shared a brief temporal connection with Will (Matt Damon) in *Good Will Hunting* (1997) and Audrey Hepburn in *Wait Until Dark* (1967).

I think Marclay is right to describe the effect of *The Clock* as anxiety-inducing. Time is more commonly an abstraction from life, subordinate to what we do, or to what we experience – the content of each second, minute, hour, and so on. But *The Clock* makes time material, it makes time into a *felt* thing. I left the MCA at 5 p.m., having the distinct sense of time lost. This was the anxiety Marclay talked about. And yet I also had the sense that cinema had been invigorated through this digital assemblage. *The Clock* displayed film cut to a new temporality. This was the simulated material digitality offered: not objects, not the content of a frame, but spatialities and temporalities unique to a digital medium. I wondered if this would be the outcome of digitality, the display of the image of the spatial and temporal world in ways new cinema had only begun to explore.

Bibliography

Abel, Richard. *The Ciné Goes to Town: French Cinema 1896–1914*. Berkeley and Los Angeles: University of California Press, 1994.

Acland, Charles R. *Screen Traffic: Movies, Multiplexes, and Global Culture*. Durham: Duke University Press, 2003.

Adorno, Theodor. 'Culture Industry Reconsidered'. In *The Culture Industry: Selected Essays on Mass Culture*, J. M. Bernstein ed., 85–91. London: Routledge, 1991.

Albarran, César Alberto. 'Interview With Terry Gilliam'. Conducted on behalf of *Cine-Premiere Magazine*, 4 November 2009.

Andrew, Dudley. *Concepts in Film Theory*. Oxford: Oxford University Press, 1984.

—'Introduction'. In *The Image in Dispute: Art and Cinema in the Age of Photography*, Dudley Andrew ed., 3–7. Austin: University of Texas Press, 1997.

—*What Cinema Is!*. Malden, MA: Wiley-Blackwell, 2010.

Arroyo, José. 'Mission: Sublime'. In *Action/Spectacle Cinema: A Sight and Sound Reader*, José Arroyo ed., 21–4. London: BFI, 2000.

Aumont, Jacques. *The Image*. Claire Pajackowska (trans.). London, BFI, 1997.

Badley, Linda. *Film, Horror, and the Body Fantastic*. Westport, Co.: Greenwood Press, 1995.

Balázs, Béla. 'The Close-Up'. In *Film Theory and Criticism: Introductory Readings*, Leo Braudy and Marshall Cohen (eds), 314–20. Oxford: Oxford University Press, 2004.

Barnouw, Eric. *Documentary: A History of the Non-Fiction Film*. New York: Oxford University Press, 1993.

Barthes, Roland. 'From Work to Text'. In *Image-Music-Text*, Stephen Heath (trans.), 155–64. London: Fontana, 1993.

Baudrillard, Jean. *America*. Chris Turner (trans.). London: Verso, 1988.

—*Simulacra and Simulation*. Sheila Faria Glaser (trans.). Detroit: University of Michigan Press, 1994.

Bazin, André. 'The Evolution of the Language of Cinema'. In *What Is Cinema? Volume 1*, Hugh Gray (trans.), 23–40. Berkeley and Los Angeles: University of California Press, 1967.

—'The Myth of Total Cinema'. In *What Is Cinema? Volume 1*, Hugh Gray (trans.), 17–22. Berkeley and Los Angeles: University of California Press, 1967.

—'The Ontology of the Photographic Image'. In *What Is Cinema? Volume 1*, Hugh Gray (trans.), 9–16. Berkeley and Los Angeles: University of California Press, 1967.

—'An Aesthetic of Reality: Cinematic Realism and the Italian School of Liberation'. In *What is Cinema? Volume 2*, Hugh Gray (trans.), 16–40. Berkeley and Los Angeles: University of California Press, 1967.

—'Bicycle Thief'. In *What is Cinema? Volume 2*, Hugh Gray (trans.), 47–60. Berkeley and Los Angeles: University of California Press, 1967.

—'In Defense of Rossellini, a Letter to Guido Aristarco, Editor-in-Chief of Cinema Nuovo'. In *What Is Cinema? Volume 2*, 93–101. Berkeley and Los Angeles: University of California Press, 1967.

—'The Western: Or the American Film *Par Excellence*'. In *What is Cinema? Volume 2*, Hugh Gray (trans.), 140–8. Berkeley and Los Angeles: University of California Press, 1967.

—'The Myth of Stalin in the Soviet Cinema'. In *Bazin at Work: Major Essays and Reviews from the Forties and Fifties*, Bert Cardullo ed., Alain Piette and Bert Cardullo (trans.), 23–40. London: Routledge, 1997.

—'De Sica: Metteur En Scène'. In *Vittorio De Sica: Contemporary Perspectives*, Howard Curle and Stephen Snyder (eds), 62–76. Toronto: University of Toronto Press, 2000.

Beck, Jay. 'Citing the Sound: *The Conversation*, *Blow Out*, and the Mythological Ontology of the Soundtrack in the 70s Film'. *Journal of Popular Film and Television* 29, no. 4 (2002), 156–63.

Beller, Jonathan. *The Cinematic Mode of Production: Attention, Economy and the Society of the Spectacle*. Lebanon, NH: University Press of New England, 2006.

Belton, John. *Widescreen Cinema*. Cambridge: Harvard University Press, 1992.

—'Digital Cinema: A False Revolution'. *October* 100 (Spring, 2002), 98–114.

Benjamin, Walter. 'Unpacking my Library: A Talk About Book Collecting'. In *Illuminations: Walter Benjamin: Essays and Reflections*, Hannah Arendt ed., 59–68. New York: Shocken Books, 1988.

—'The Work of Art in the Age of Mechanical Reproduction'. In *Film Theory and Criticism: Introductory Readings*, Leo Braudy and Marshall Cohen (eds), 791–811. Oxford: Oxford University Press, 2004.

Biskind, Peter. *Easy Riders, Raging Bulls: How the Sex 'n Drugs 'n Rock 'n Roll Generation Saved Hollywood*. London: Bloomsbury, 1999.

Bogdanovich, Peter. 'The Last Picture Show: A Look Back' (featurette). *The Last Picture Show* (DVD), Sony Pictures Home Entertainment, 2006.

—'The 400 Blows'. *Indiewire*, 29 June 2011, http://blogs.indiewire.com/ peterbogdanovich/the_400_blows.

Bondanella, Peter E. *Italian Cinema: From Neorealism to the Present*. 3rd edn. New York: Continuum Press, 2001.

Bordwell, David. 'The Art Cinema as a Mode of Film Practice'. *Film Criticism* 4, no. 1 (1979), 56–64.

—*Narration in the Fiction Film*. Madison, WI: University of Wisconsin Press, 1985.

—'Contemporary Film Studies and the Vicissitudes of Grand Theory'. In *Post-Theory: Reconstructing Film Studies*, David Bordwell and Noël Carroll (eds), 3–36. Madison, WI: University of Wisconsin Press, 1996.

—*On the History of Film Style*. Cambridge: Harvard University Press, 1997.

—'Intensified Continuity: Visual Style in Contemporary American Film'. *Film Quarterly* 55, no. 3 (2002), 16–28.

—*The Way Hollywood Tells It: Story and Style in Modern Movies*. Berkeley and Los Angeles: University of California Press, 2006.

—'Unsteadicam Chronicles'. *David Bordwell's Website on Cinema* (blog), 17 August 2007, http://www.davidbordwell.net/blog/2007/08/17/unsteadicam-chronicles/.

—'Common Sense + Film Theory = Common-Sense Film Theory?'. *David Bordwell's Website on Cinema* (blog), May 2011, http://www.davidbordwell.net/essays/commonsense.php#_ednref13.

—'Pandora's Digital Box: In the Multiplex'. *David Bordwell's Website on Cinema* (blog), 1 December 2011, http://www.davidbordwell.net/blog/2011/12/01/pandoras-digital-box-in-the-multiplex/.

Bordwell, David and Noël Carroll (eds). *Post-Theory: Reconstructing Film Studies*. Madison, WI: University of Wisconsin Press, 1996.

Bordwell, David, Janet Staiger and Kristin Thompson. *The Classical Hollywood Cinema: Film Style and Mode of Production to 1960*. New York: Columbia University Press, 1985.

Bordwell, David and Kristin Thompson. 'Fundamental Aesthetics of Sound in the Cinema'. In *Film Sound: Theory and Practice*, Elizabeth Weis and John Belton (eds), 181–99. New York: Columbia University Press, 1985.

Bouzereau, Laurent (director). 'A Conversation With Steven Spielberg' (featurette). *Lawrence of Arabia* (DVD), Collector's Edition (2-Disc Set), Sony Pictures, 2001.

Breimer, Stephen F. *The Screenwriter's Legal Guide*. New York: Allworth Press, 2004.

Britton, Andrew. 'Blissing Out: The Politics of Reaganite Entertainment'. *Movie* 31/32 (1986), 1–42.

Brosnan, John. *The Story of Special Effects in the Cinema*. London: Abacus, 1977.

Brown, Blain. *Cinematography: Theory and Practice*. Waltham, MA: Focal Press, 2002.

Buckland, Warren. *Directed by Steven Spielberg: Poetics of the Contemporary Hollywood Blockbuster*. New York: Continuum Press, 2006.

Buckland, Warren ed. *Puzzle Films: Complex Storytelling in Contemporary Cinema*. Chichester: Wiley-Blackwell, 2009.

Bukatman, Scott. *Matters of Gravity: Special Effects and Supermen in the Twentieth Century*. Durham: Duke University Press, 2003.

Burnett, Colin. 'A New Look at the Concept of Style in Film: The Origins and Development of the Problem-Solution Model'. *New Review of Film and Television Studies* 6, no. 2 (2008), 127–49.

Butte, George. 'Suture and the Narration of Subjectivity in Film'. *Poetics Today* 29, no. 2 (2008), 277–308.

Calabrese, Omar. *Neo-Baroque: A Sign of the Times*. Princeton: Princeton University, 1992.

Cameron, Allan. 'Contingency, Order, and the Modular Narrative: *21 Grams and Irreversible*'. *The Velvet Light Trap* 58 (2006), 65–78.

Cameron, James. 'Effects Scene: Technology and Magic'. *Cinefex* 51 (1992), 5–7.

Campbell, Joseph. *The Hero With a Thousand Faces*. Princeton: Princeton University Press, 1968.

Capps, Emma. *Time, Consciousness, and the Potential of Cinema*. Masters Dissertation, University, 2011.

Carroll, Noël. *The Philosophy of Motion Pictures*. Malden, MA: Blackwell, 2008.

Caton, Steven Charles. *Lawrence of Arabia: A Film's Anthropology*. Berkeley and Los Angeles: University of California Press, 1999.

Cavell, Stanley. *The World Viewed: Reflections on the Ontology of Film*. Cambridge: Harvard University Press, 1979.

Child, Ben. 'The Hobbit: First Glimpse Gets Mixed Response'. *The Guardian*, 25 April 2012, http://www.guardian.co.uk/film/2012/apr/25/the-hobbit-first-screening-cinemacon.

Chion, Michel. *Audio-Vision: Sound on Screen*. Claudia Gorbman (trans.). New York: Columbia University Press, 1994.

Cholodenko, Alan. 'Objects in Mirror Are Closer Than They Appear: The Virtual Reality of *Jurassic Park* and Jean Baudrillard'. In *Jean Baudrillard: Art and Artefact*, Nicholas Zurbrugg ed., 64–90. London: Sage, 1998.

—'Introduction to SCMS Panel: Animation – Film Studies and Media Studies' "Blind Spot"'. *Society for Animation Studies Newsletter* 20, no. 1 (2007).

Christie, Ian. 'Clash of the Wonderlands'. *Sight and Sound* 21, no. 11 (2011), 36–8.

Collins, Jim. 'Genericity in the 90s: Eclectic Irony and the New Sincerity'. In *Film Theory Goes to the Movies*, Jim Collins, Hilary Radner and Ava Preacher Collins (eds), 242–63. New York: Routledge, 1993.

Colman, Felicity. *Deleuze and Cinema: The Film Concepts*. Oxford: Berg, 2011.

Conrad, Joseph. *Heart of Darkness*. New York: Penguin, 1999.

Cook, David A. 'Auteur Cinema and the "Film Generation" in 1970s Hollywood'. In *The New American Cinema*, Jon Lewis ed., 11–35. Durham: Duke University Press, 1998.

—*Lost Illusions: American Cinema in the Shadow of Watergate and Vietnam 1970–1979*. Berkeley and Los Angeles: University of California Press, 2000.

Cook, Nicholas. *Analysis Through Composition: Principles of the Classical Style*. Oxford: Oxford University Press, 1996.

Coppola, Francis Ford. 'Press Interview' (Cannes, 1979). *Hearts of Darkness: A Filmmaker's Apocalypse* (DVD), Paramount Home Video, 2007.

—'Director's Commentary'. *The Conversation* (Widescreen DVD Collection), Paramount Home Video, 2000.

Corman, Roger. *How I Made A Hundred Movies in Hollywood and Never Lost a Dime*. New York: Da Capo Press, 1998.

Cosgrove, Peter. 'The Cinema of Attractions and the Novel in *Barry Lyndon* and *Tom Jones*'. In *Eighteenth-Century Fiction on Screen*, Robert Mayer ed., 16–34. Cambridge: Cambridge University Press, 2002.

Cotta Vaz, Mark and Patricia Rose Duigan. *Industrial Light and Magic: Into the Digital Realm*. New York: Ballantine Books, 1996.

Cubitt, Sean. 'Introduction. Le Réel, c'est le l'impossible: The Sublime Time of Special Effects'. *Screen* 40, no. 2 (1999), 123–30.

—*The Cinema Effect*. Cambridge, MA: MIT Press, 2004.

—'The Supernatural in Neo-baroque Hollywood'. In *Film Theory and Contemporary Hollywood Movies*, Warren Buckland, ed., 47–65. London: Routledge, 2009.

Cucco, Marco. 'The Promise is Great: The Blockbuster and the Hollywood Economy'. *Media, Culture and Society* 31, no. 2 (2009): 215–30.

Dancyger, Ken. *Alternative Scriptwriting: Successfully Breaking the Rules.* Boston: Focal Press, 2007.

Darley, Andrew. *Visual Digital Culture: Surface Play and Spectacle in New Media Genres.* London: Routledge, 2000.

Debord, Guy. *Society of the Spectacle.* New York: Zone Books, 1994.

DeBruge, Peter. 'Editors Cut Us in on Tricky Sequences'. *Variety,* February 16, 2007, http://www.variety.com/article/VR1117959745?refcatid=13.

Deleuze, Gilles. *Cinema 1: The Movement Image.* Hugh Tomlinson and Barbara Habberjam (trans.). Minneapolis: University of Minnesota Press, 2009.

—*Cinema 2: The Time Image.* Hugh Tomlinson and Robert Galeta (trans.). Minneapolis: University of Minnesota Press, 2009.

DeLillo, Don. *White Noise.* New York: Viking, 1985.

—*Underworld.* London: Picador, 1998.

Deutelbaum, Marshall. 'Structural Patterning in the Lumière Films'. *Wide Angle* 3, no. 1 (1979). 28–37.

Diawara, Manthia. 'Black Spectatorship: Problems of Identification and Resistance'. *Screen* 29, no. 4 (1988). 66–79.

Dixon, Wheeler Winston. *The Transparency of Spectacle: Meditations on the Moving Image.* Albany: State University of New York Press, 1998.

Doane, Mary Ann. 'The Close-Up: Scale and Detail in the Cinema'. In *differences: A Journal of Feminist Cultural Studies* 14, no. 1 (2003): 89–111.

—'The Indexical and the Concept of Medium Specificity'. *differences: A Journal of Feminist Cultural Studies* 18, no. 1 (2007): 128–52.

—'Indexicality: Trace and Sign: Introduction'. *differences: A Journal of Feminist Cultural Studies* 18, no. 1 (2007), 1–6.

Robnik, Drehli. 'Allegories of Post-Fordism in the 1970s New Hollywood'. In *The Last Great American Picture Show*, Thomas Elsaesser, Alexander Horwath and Noel King (eds), 333–58. Amsterdam: Amsterdam University Press, 2004.

Dyer, Richard. 'Action!'. In *Action/Spectacle Cinema: A Sight and Sound Reader*, José Arroyo ed., 17–20. London: BFI, 2000.

Eco, Umberto. '*Casablanca*: Cult Movies and Intertextual Collage'. In *Faith in Fakes: Essays.* William Weaver (trans.), 197–211. London: Secker and Warburg, 1986.

—'Innovation and Repetition: Between Modern and Postmodern Aesthetics'. *Daedalus* 134, no. 4 (2005), 161–84.

Eisenstein, Sergei. 'The Cinematographic Principle and the Ideogram'. In *Film Form: Essays in Film Theory*, Jay Leyda (ed. and trans.), 28–44. Orlando: Harcourt, 1977.

—'Film Language'. In *Film Form: Essays in Film Theory*, Jay Leyda (ed. and trans.), 108–21. Orlando: Harcourt, 1977.

Elsaesser, Thomas. 'American Auteur Cinema: The Last – or First – Picture Show'. In *The Last Great American Picture Show*, Thomas Elsaesser, Alexander Horwath and Noel King (eds), 37–69. Amsterdam: Amsterdam University Press, 2004.

—'The Pathos of Failure: American Films in the 1970s'. In *The Last Great American Picture Show*, Thomas Elsaesser, Alexander Horwath and Noel King (eds), 279–92. Amsterdam: Amsterdam University Press, 2004.

—*The Persistence of Hollywood*. New York: Routledge, 2012.

Elsaesser, Thomas, Alexander Horwath and Noel King (eds). *The Last Great American Picture Show: New Hollywood Cinema in the 1970s*. Amsterdam: Amsterdam University Press, 2004.

Elsaesser, Thomas and Malte Hagener. *Film Theory: An Introduction Through the Senses*. New York: Routledge, 2010.

Enticknap, Leo. *Moving Image Technology*. London: Wallflower Press, 2004.

D'Escriván, Julio. 'Sound Art (?) on/in Film'. *Organised Sound* 14, no. 1 (2009), 65–73.

Essman, Scott. 'Has Weta Digital Taken the Visual Effects Lead?'. *Below the Line: Voice of the Crew*, 15 August 2011, http://www.btlnews.com/crafts/visual-fx/has-weta-digital-taken-the-visual-effects-lead/.

Farrell, Kirby. 'The Economies of *Schindler's List*'. In *The Films of Steven Spielberg: Critical Essays*, Charles L. P. Silet ed., 191–214. Lanham: Scarecrow Press, 2002.

Fiedler, Leslie. *Love and Death in the American Novel*. New York: Stein and Day, 1966.

Field, Syd. *Screenplay: The Foundations of Screenwriting*. New York: MJF Books, 1994.

Filser, Barbara. 'Gilles Deleuze and a Future Cinema: Cinema 1, Cinema 2, and Cinema 3?'. In *Future Cinema: The Cinematic Imaginary After Film*, Jeffrey Shaw and Peter Weibel (eds), 214–17. Cambridge, MA: MIT Press, 2003.

Fincher, David (trailer director). *The Girl With the Dragon Tattoo*. Official Trailer, June 2, 2011, http://www.youtube.com/watch?v=WVLvMg62RPA.

Flanagan, Martin. '"Get Ready For Rush Hour": The Chronotope in Action'. In *Action and Adventure Cinema*, Yvonne Tasker ed., 103–18. New York: Routledge, 2004.

Flaxman, Gregory. 'Introduction'. In *The Brain is the Screen: Deleuze and the Philosophy of Cinema*, Gregory Flaxman ed., Minneapolis: University of Minnesota Press, 2000.

Frampton, Daniel. *Filmosophy*. London: Wallflower, 2006.

Frayling, Christopher. 'Commentary'. *Once Upon a Time in the West* (DVD, 2-Disc Special Edition), Warner Home Video, 2003.

Friedberg, Anne. *Window Shopping: Cinema and the Postmodern*. Berkeley and Los Angeles: University of California Press, 1993.

Giardina, Carolyn. 'James Cameron Urges Industry to Use Faster Frame Rates'. *Hollywood Reporter*, 31 March 2011, http://www.hollywoodreporter.com/news/james-cameron-urges-industry-use–173577.

—'Peter Jackson Responds to *Hobbit* Footage Critics, Explains 48-Frames Strategy'. *The Hollywood Reporter*, 28 April 2012, http://www.hollywoodreporter.com/news/peter-jackson-the-hobbit-cinemacon–317755.

Goldman, William. *Adventures in the Screen Trade: A Personal View of Hollywood and Screenwriting*. New York: Warner Books, 1984.

Gordon, Andrew. '*Star Wars*: A Myth for our Time'. *Literature/Film Quarterly* 6, no. 4 (1978), 314–26.

Gottlieb, Carl. *The Jaws Log, 30th Anniversary Edition*. New York: Newmarket, 2005.

Graves, Douglas. 'Pure Cinema Manifesto'. *Pure Cinema Celluloid* (2009), http://www.purecinema-celluloid.webs.com/.

Gross, Larry. 'Big and Loud'. *Sight and Sound* 5, no. 8 (1995), 6–10.

Gunning, Tom. 'The Cinema of Attractions: Early Film, Its Spectator and the Avant-Garde'. In *Early Cinema: Space, Frame, Narrative*, Thomas Elsaesser ed., 56–62. London: BFI, 1990.

—'An Aesthetic of Astonishment: Early Film and the (in)Credulous Spectator'. In *Viewing Positions: Ways of Seeing Film*, Linda Williams ed., 114–31. New Brunswick, NJ: Rutgers University Press, 1995.

—'Modernity and Cinema: A Culture of Shocks and Flows'. In *Cinema and Modernity*, Murray Pomerance ed., 297–315. New Brunswick: Rutgers University Press, 2006.

—'Moving Away from the Index: Cinema and the Impression of Reality'. *differences: A Journal of Feminist Cultural Studies* 18, no. 1 (2007), 29–52.

Haggith, Toby. 'D-Day Filming – For Real. A Comparison and "Truth" and "Reality" in *Saving Private Ryan* and combat film by the British Army's Film and Photographic Unit.' *Film History* 14, no. 3/4 (2002), 332–53.

Hall, Jeanne. '"Don't You Ever Just Watch?": American Cinema Verité and *Don't Look Back*'. In *Documenting the Documentary: Close Readings of Documentary Film and Video*, Barry Keith Grant and Jeannette Sloniowski (eds), 223–37. Detroit: Wayne State University Press, 1998.

Hammond, Michael. '*Saving Private Ryan's* Special Affect'. In *Action and Adventure Cinema*, Yvonne Tasker ed., 153–66. New York: Routledge, 2004.

Hansen, Miriam. 'Early Cinema, Late Cinema: Permutations of the Public Sphere'. *Screen* 34, no. 3 (1993), 197–210.

Harkins, Michael E. 'The Spectacle in 3-D: Is *Avatar* Really Something New?'. *Depth of Field*, 19 February 2010, http://myportfolio.usc.edu/meharkin/2010/02/is_avatar_really_something_new_the_spectacle_in_3-d.html.

Haraway, Donna. *Simians, Cyborgs, and Women: The Reinvention of Nature*. New York: Routledge, 1991.

Harwood, Tracy. 'Towards a Manifesto for Machinima'. *Journal of Visual Culture* 10, no. 1 (2011), 6–12.

Hayles, N. Katherine. *How We Became Posthuman: Virtual Bodies in Cybernetics, Literature, and Informatics*. Chicago: University of Chicago Press, 1999.

Hillier, Jim. 'Introduction'. In *The New American Cinema*, Jim Hillier ed., ix–xvii. London: BFI, 2001.

Hoberman, J. '1975–1985: Ten Years That Shook the World'. *American Film* 10, no. 8 (1985), 34–59.

Hutchison, David. *Film Magic: The Art and Science of Special Effects*. London: Simon & Schuster, 1987.

Hyder, James. 'IMAX Reacts to Controversy Over Digital Theatres'. *LF Examiner*, 26 May 2009, http://www.lfexaminer.com/20090525a.htm.

Isaacs, Bruce. 'Do Not Screen – Frames 1321–1332 (19 June 2011)', http://donotscreen.net/.

—'Nonlinear Narrative'. In *New Punk Cinema*, Nicholas Rombes ed., 126–39. Edinburgh: Edinburgh University Press, 2005.

—*Toward a New Film Aesthetic*. New York: Continuum Press, 2008.

—'Technologies of New Experience: On Cinema, 3-D and the Imaginary'. *Stereoscopic Media*, 30 November 2011, http://www.stereoscopicmedia.org/?p=110.

James, Nick. 'Tarantino Bites Back: An Interview With Quentin Tarantino'. *Sight and Sound*, February 2008, http://www.bfi.org.uk/sightandsound/feature/49432.

Jameson, Frederic. 'Postmodernism and Consumer Society'. In *The Cultural Turn: Selected Writings on the Postmodern 1983–1998*, 1–21. London: Verso, 1998.

—*Postmodernism, or the Cultural Logic of Late Capitalism*. Durham: Duke University Press, 1992.

Jeffries, Stuart. '"Films Are a Way to Kill My Father"'. *The Guardian*, 22 February 2008.

Jewett, Robert and John Shelton Lawrence. *The American Monomyth*. Garden City: Anchor Press, 1977.

Johnson, William. 'Sound and Image: A Further Hearing'. *Film Quarterly* 43, no. 1 (1989), 24–35.

Keathley, Christian. 'Trapped in the Affection Image: Hollywood's Post-Traumatic Cycle (1970–1976)'' In *The Last Great American Picture Show: New Hollywood in the 1970s*, Thomas Elsaesser, Alexander Horwath and Noel King (eds), 293–308. Amsterdam: Amsterdam University Press, 2004.

Keating, Patrick. 'The Fictional Worlds of Neorealism'. *Criticism* 45, no. 1 (2003), 11–30.

Kehr, Dave. '3-D or Not 3-D'. *Film Comment* 46, no. 1 (2010), 60–7.

Keller, Alexandra. *James Cameron*. London: Routledge, 2006.

Kerbel, Michael. '3-D or Not 3-D'. *Film Comment* 16, no. 6 (1980), 11–20.

Kerouac, Jack. *On The Road*. New York: Viking, 1997.

King, Geoff. *New Hollywood Cinema: An Introduction*. New York: Columbia University Press, 2002.

—'Ride-Films and Films as Rides'. *Cineaction* 51 (2000), 2–9.

Kingdon, Tom. 'The 180-Degree Rule'. In *Total Directing: Integrating Camera and Performance in Film and Television*, 227–45. Los Angeles: Silman-James Press, 2004.

Klinger, Barbara. '*Cave of Forgotten Dreams*: Mediations on 3D', *Film Quarterly* 65, no. 3 (2012), 38–43.

Kouvaros, George. *Where Does It Happen?: John Cassavetes and Cinema at the Breaking Point*. Minneapolis: University of Minnesota Press, 2004.

Kundera, Milan. *The Unbearable Lightness of Being*. Michael Henry Heim (trans.). London: Faber and Faber, 1984.

Labrecque, Jeff. '*2001: A Space Odyssey's* Tech Pioneer on "Hobbit" Footage: A fabulous and brave step in the right direction'. *Entertainment Weekly*, 2 May 2012, http://insidemovies.ew.com/2012/05/02/douglas-trumbull-hobbit-frame-speed/.

LaPorte, Nicole. *The Men Who Would Be King: An Almost Epic Tale of Moguls, Movies, and a Company Called Dreamworks*. Boston: Houghton Mifflin Harcourt, 2010.

Lavik, Erlend. 'The Battle for the Blockbuster: Discourses of Spectacle and Excess'. *New Review of Film and Television Studies* 6, no. 2 (2008), 169–87.

Lawrence, John Shelton and Robert Jewett. *The Myth of the American Superhero*. Grand Rapids: Wm B. Erdmans, 2002.

Lawrence, John Shelton. 'Joseph Campbell, George Lucas, and the Monomyth'. In *Finding the Force of the Star Wars Franchise: Fans, Merchandise and*

Critics, Matthew Wilhelm Kapell and John Shelton Lawrence (eds), 21–33. New York: Peter Lang, 2006.

Leva, Gary (director). *A Legacy of Filmmakers: The Early Years of American Zoetrope*. Leva FilmWorks, 2004.

Lewis, Jon. 'The Perfect Money Machine(s): George Lucas, Steven Spielberg, and Auteurism in the New Hollywood'. In *Looking Past the Screen: Case Studies in American Film History and Method*, Jon Lewis and Eric Smoodin (eds), 61–86. Durham: Duke University Press, 2007.

Lewis, Jon ed. *The New American Cinema*. Durham: Duke University Press, 1998.

Lim, Bliss Cua. *Translating Time: Cinema, the Fantastic, and Temporal Critique*. Durham: Duke University Press, 2009.

Lumière, Auguste, and Louis Lumière. ' L'arrivée D'un Train À La Ciotat (Arrival of a Train at a Station)'. YouTube Video (0.50sec.), http://www.youtube.com/watch?v=BO0EkMKfgJI.

—'La Sortie Des Usines Lumière À Lyon (Workers Leaving the Lumière Factory)'. YouTube Video (1.50sec.), http://www.youtube.com/watch?v=1dgLEDdFddk.

McClintock, Pamela. 'Box Office Report'. *The Hollywood Reporter*, 16 April 2012, http://www.hollywoodreporter.com/news/titanic-box-office-james-cameron–312497.

McKee, Robert. *Story: Substance, Structure, Style, and the Principles of Screenwriting*. New York: Regan Books, 1997.

McVeigh, Steven and Matthew Kapell. 'Introduction: Persistence of Visions – Approaching the Films of James Cameron'. In *The Films of James Cameron: Critical Essays*, Matthew Wilhelm Kapell and Stephen McVeigh (eds), 1–13. Jefferson: McFarland Press, 2011.

Magrid, Ron. 'George Lucas Discusses his Ongoing Effort to Shape the Future of Digital Cinema'. *American Cinematographer*, September 2002, http://www.theasc.com/magazine/sep02/exploring/.

Malcolm, Derek. *In Conversation: Mike Newell* (Television). Season 1, Episode 7, Sky Arts 1, UK, 2010.

Mangolte, Babette. 'Afterward: A Matter of Time'. In *Camera Obscura, Camera Lucida: Essays in Honor of Annette Michelson*, Richard Allen and Malcolm Turvey (eds), 261–74. Amsterdam: Amsterdam University Press, 2003.

Manovich, Lev. *The Language of New Media*. Cambridge, MA: MIT Press, 2001.

—'Image Future'. *Animation: An Interdisciplinary Journal* 1, no. 1 (2006): 25–44.

Marks, Laura. 'Information, Secrets, and Enigmas: An Enfolding-unfolding Aesthetics for Cinema'. *Screen* 50, no. 1 (2009), 86–98.

Martin, Adrian. *The Mad Max Movies*. Strawberry Hills: Currency Press, 2003.

Martin-Jones, David. 'Demystifying Deleuze: French Philosophy Meets Contemporary U.S. Cinema'. In *Film Theory and Contemporary Hollywood Movies*, Warren Buckland ed., 214–33. New York: Routledge, 2009.

Menand, Louis. '*Saving Private Ryan*: Jerry Don't Surf'. In *The Films of Steven Spielberg: Critical Essays*, Charles L. P. Silet ed., 251–6. Lanham: Scarecrow Press, 2002.

Michelson, Annette. 'Bodies in Space: Film as Carnal Knowledge'. *Artforum* 7, no. 6 (1969).

Misselhorn, Catrin. 'Empathy with Inanimate Objects'. *Minds and Machines* 19 (2009), 345–59.

Mullarky, John. *Philosophy and the Moving Image: Refractions of Reality*. London: Palgrave, 2009.

Mulvey, Laura. 'Visual Pleasure and Narrative Cinema'. In *Feminism and Film Theory*, Constance Penley ed., 57–68. London and New York: Routledge, 1988.

Musser, Charles. 'The Travel Genre in 1903–1904: Moving Towards Fictional Narrative'. In *Early Cinema: Space, Frame, Narrative*, Thomas Elsaesser ed., 123–32. London: BFI, 2010.

Nagib, Lúcia. *World Cinema and the Ethics of Realism*. New York: Continuum Press, 2011.

Natoli, Joseph P. *Memory's Orbit: Film and Culture, 1999–2000*. Albany: State University of New York Press, 2003.

Ndalianis, Angela. *Neo-Baroque Aesthetics and Contemporary Entertainment*. Cambridge, MA: MIT Press, 2005.

Nitsche, Michael. 'A Look Back at Machinima's Potential'. *Journal of Visual Culture* 10, no. 1 (2011), 13–18.

Nyce, Ben. *Scorsese Up Close: A Study of the Films*. Lanham: Scarecrow Press, 2004.

Pearlman, Karen. *Cutting Rhythms: Shaping the Film Edit*. Burlington, MA: Focal Press, 2009.

Perkins, Claire. *American Smart Cinema*. Edinburgh: Edinburgh University Press, 2012.

Petric, Vlada. 'Dziga Vertov as Theorist'. *Cinema Journal* 18, no. 1 (1978), 29–44.

Pfeil, Fred. 'From Pillar to Postmodern: Race, Class, and Gender in the Male Rampage Film'. In *The New American Cinema*, Jon Lewis ed., 146–86. Durham: Duke University Press, 1998.

Pinteau, Pascal. *Special Effects: An Oral History – Interviews With 37 Masters Spanning 100 Years*. Laurel Hirsch (trans.). New York: Harry N. Abrams, 2005.

Pippin, Robert B. *Hollywood Westerns and American Myth: The Importance of Howard Hawks and John Ford For Political Philosophy*. New Haven: Yale University Press, 2010.

Plantinga, Carl. *Moving Viewers: American Film and the Spectator Experience*. Berkeley and Los Angeles: University of California Press, 2009.

—'Trauma, Pleasure and Emotion in the Viewing of *Titanic*: A Cognitive Approach'. In *Film Theory and Contemporary Hollywood Movies*, Warren Buckland ed., 237–56. London: Routledge, 2009.

—'Defending *Tree of Life*'. *The Society for Cognitive Studies of the Moving Image*, 9 July 2011, http://scsmi-online.org/forum/defending-the-tree-of-life.

Pomerance, Murray. 'Introduction'. In *Cinema and Modernity*, Murray Pomerance ed., 3–15. New Brunswick: Rutgers University Press, 2006.

Pramaggiore, Maria and Tom Wallis. *Film: A Critical Introduction*. London: Lawrence King Publishing, 2008.

Purse, Lisa. *Contemporary Action Cinema*. Edinburgh: Edinburgh University Press, 2011.

Ramao, Tico. 'Guns and Gas: Investigating the 1970s Car Chase Film'. In *Action and Adventure Cinema*, Yvonne Tasker ed., 130–52. New York: Routledge, 2004.

Ray, Robert B. *A Certain Tendency of the Hollywood Cinema, 1930–1980*. Princeton, NJ: Princeton University Press, 1985.

—*How a Film Theory Got Lost: And Other Mysteries in Cultural Studies.*
    Bloomington: Indiana University Press, 2001.
Ressner, Jeffrey. 'The Traditionalist: An Interview With Christopher Nolan'.
    Director's Guild of America Interviews, Spring 2012, http://www.dga.org/Craft/
    DGAQ/All-Articles/1202-Spring–2012/DGA-Interview-Christopher-Nolan.aspx.
Rodowick, David Norman. *Gilles Deleuze's Time Machine.* Durham, NC: Duke
    University Press, 1997.
—'An Elegy for Theory'. *October* 122 (Fall, 2007), 91–109.
—*Reading the Figural, or, Philosophy After New Media.* Durham: Duke
    University Press, 2001.
—*The Virtual Life of Film.* Cambridge, MA: Harvard University Press, 2007.
Rombes, Nicholas. 'Introduction'. In *New Punk Cinema*, Nicholas Rombes ed.,
    1–18. Edinburgh: Edinburgh University Press, 2005.
—*Cinema in the Digital Age.* London: Wallflower Press, 2009.
Ronettes, The. 'Be My Baby' (single). Goldstar Studios, 1963.
Rosenstone, Robert. 'History in Images/History in Words: Reflections on the
    Possibility of Really Putting History onto Film'. *The American Historical
    Review* 93, no. 5 (1988), 1173–85.
Ross, Allison. 'Michelangelo Antonioni: The Aestheticization of Time and
    Experience in *The Passenger*'. In *Cinematic Thinking: Philosophical
    Approaches to the New Cinema*, James Phillips ed., 40–51. Stanford: Stanford
    University Press, 2008.
Ross, Miriam. 'Spectacular Dimensions: 3D Dance Films'. *Senses of
    Cinema* 61 (2011), http://sensesofcinema.com/2011/feature-articles/
    spectacular-dimensions–3d-dance-films/#b7.
Røssaak, Eivind. 'Figures of Sensation: Between Still and Moving Images'. In *The
    Cinema of Attractions Reloaded*, Wanda Strauven ed., 321–36. Amsterdam:
    Amsterdam University Press, 2006.
Rothman, William. 'Vertigo: The Unknown Woman in Hitchcock'. In *The 'I' of the
    Camera: Essays in Film Criticism, History and Aesthetics*, 2nd edn, 221–40.
    Cambridge: Cambridge University Press, 2004.
Rubin, Michael. *Droidmaker: George Lucas and the Digital Revolution.*
    Gainesville: Triad Publishing Company, 2006.
Ruiz, Raùl. *Poetics of Cinema.* Brian Holmes (trans.). Paris: Dis Voir, 2005.
Rutherford, Anne. *What Makes a Film Tick?: Cinematic Affect, Materiality and
    Mimetic Innervation.* New York: Peter Lang, 2011.
Said, Edward. *Orientalism.* London: Penguin, 1991.
Salewicz, Chris. *Oliver Stone: The Making of his Movies.* London: Orion Media, 1997.
Salt, Barry. *Film Style and Technology: History and Analysis.* 2nd edn. London:
    Starword, 1992.
Sarris, Andrew. 'Notes on the Auteur Theory in 1962'. In *Film Theory and
    Criticism: Introductory Readings*, Leo Braudy and Marshall Cohen (eds),
    561–4. Oxford: Oxford University Press, 2004.
Schatz, Thomas. 'The New Hollywood'. In *Film Theory Goes to the Movies*,
    Jim Collins, Hilary Radner and Ava Preacher Collins (eds), 8–36. New York:
    Routledge, 1993.
—'The Whole Equation of Pictures'. In *The Film and Authorship*, Virginia Wright-
    Wexman ed., 89–95. New Brunswick: Rutgers University Press, 2003.

—'The Studio System and Conglomerate Hollywood'. In *The Contemporary Hollywood Film Industry*, Paul McDonald and Janet Wasko (eds), 13–42. Malden, MA: Blackwell Publishing, 2008.

—*The Genius of the System: Hollywood Filmmaking in the Studio Era*. Minneapolis: University of Minnesota Press, 2010.

Sconce, Jeffrey. 'Irony, Nihilism and the New American "Smart" Film'. *Screen* 43, no. 4 (2002), 349–69.

Scott, A. O. 'A Video From Tehran: It's Not What It Isn't, but What It Is'. *The New York Times*, 28 February 2012, http://movies.nytimes.com/2012/02/29/movies/hes-jafar-panahi-but-this-is-not-a-film.html.

ScreenTeamShow. 'I Am Optimus Prime' (2007). YouTube Video (2:46min.), 2 February 2011, http://www.youtube.com/watch?v=rEwoY52Kw3I.

Shaviro, Steven. 'Straight From the Cerebral Cortex: Vision and Affect in *Strange Days*'. In *The Cinema of Kathryn Bigelow: Hollywood Transgressor*, Deborah Jermyn and Sean Redmond (eds), 159–77. London and New York: Wallflower Press, 2003.

—*Post-Cinematic Affect*. New York: Zero Books, 2010.

—'Post-Continuity'. SCMS Paper Presentation, Boston, 2012. *The Pinocchio Theory* (blog), http://www.shaviro.com/Blog/?p=1034.

Short, Sue. *Cyborg Cinema and Contemporary Subjectivity*. New York: Palgrave, 2005.

Siegel, Tatiana. 'Fade-Out on Final-Cut Privileges?'. *Variety*, 22 January 2010, http://www.variety.com/article/VR1118014187?refCatId=13.

Silverman, Kaja. *The Acoustic Mirror: The Female Voice in Psychoanalysis and Cinema*. Bloomington: Indiana University Press, 1988.

Smith, Thomas G. *Industrial Light and Magic*. London: Columbus Books, 1986.

Sobchack, Vivian. *The Address of the Eye: A Phenomenology of Film Experience*. Princeton: Princeton University Press, 1992.

—'Nostalgia for a Digital Object'. *Millenium Film Journal* 34 (1999): 4–23.

—*Carnal Thoughts: Embodiment and Moving Image Culture*. Berkeley and Los Angeles: University of California Press, 2004.

Sobol, John. 'Demoscene and Digital Culture'. In *The Sharpest Point: Animation at the End of Cinema*, Chris Gehman and Steve Reinke (eds), 206–26. Toronto: YYZ Books, 2005.

Sperb, Jason. 'Internal *Sunshine*: Illuminating Being-Memory in *Eternal Sunshine of the Spotless Mind*'. *Kriticos* 2 (2005).

Stork, Matthias. 'Chaos Cinema: The Decline and Fall of Action Filmmaking'. *Indiewire*, 22 August 2011, http://blogs.indiewire.com/pressplay/video_essay_matthias_stork_calls_out_the_chaos_cinema.

Sutton, Damian. *Photography, Cinema, Memory: The Crystal Image of Time*. Minneapolis: University of Minnesota Press, 2009.

Tafler, David. 'When Analogue Cinema Becomes Digital Memory ...'. *Wide Angle* 21, no. 1 (1999): 181–204.

Tarantino, Quentin. 'Chapter 2'. In *Kill Bill, Volumes 1 and 2* (Shooting Script). Internet Moviescript Database, http://www.imsdb.com/scripts/Kill-Bill-Volume–1-&2.html.

Tarkovsky, Andrei. *Sculpting in Time: Reflections on the Cinema*. Kitty Hunter-Blair (trans.). London: Faber, 1989.

Thompson, Kristin. *Breaking the Glass Armor: Neoformalist Film Analysis*. Princeton: Princeton University Press, 1988.

—*Storytelling in the New Hollywood: Understanding Classical Narrative Technique*. Cambridge, Mass.: Harvard University Press, 1999.

—'The Concept of Cinematic Excess'. In *Film Theory and Criticism: Introductory Readings*, Leo Braudy and Marshall Cohen (eds), 513–24. Oxford: Oxford University Press, 2004.

Thompson, Kristin and David Bordwell. *Film History: An Introduction*. 3rd edn. New York: McGraw-Hill Higher Education, 2010.

Thomson, David. 'Who Killed the Movies?'. *Esquire* 126, no. 6 (1996), 56–63.

—'The Decade When Movies Mattered'. In *The Last Great American Picture Show: New Hollywood in the 1970s*, Thomas Elsaesser, Alexander Horwath and Noel King (eds), 73–82. Amsterdam: Amsterdam University Press, 2004.

Tomasovic, Dick. 'The Hollywood Cobweb: New Laws of Attraction'. In *The Cinema of Attractions Reloaded*, Wanda Strauven ed., 309–20. Amsterdam: Amsterdam University Press, 2006.

Trezzini, Marco and Danica Gianola. 'When Cinema Meets VR – John Gaeta Talks About *Speed Racer*'. *VRMAG* 30 (2008), http://www.vrmag.org/speedracer/.

Trifonova, Temenuga. 'Time and Point of View in Contemporary Cinema'. *CineAction* 58 (2002), 11–31.

Truffaut, François. *Hitchcock*. London: Paladin, 1986.

Trumbull, Douglas. 'Statement by Douglas Trumbull'. *DouglasTrumbull.com*, 11 January 2012, http://douglastrumbull.com/.

Tuck, Greg. 'When More is Less: CGI, Spectacle and the Capitalist Sublime'. *Science Fiction Film and Television* 1, no 2 (2008), 249–73.

Turner, Dennis. 'The Subject of *The Conversation*'. *Cinema Journal* 24, no. 4 (1985), 4–22.

Turnock, Julie. 'Before Industrial Light and Magic: The Independent Hollywood Special Effects Business, 1968–1975'. *New Review of Film and Television Studies* 7, no. 2 (2009), 133–56.

Turvey, Malcolm. 'Philosophical Problems Concerning the Concept of Pleasure in Psychoanalytic Theories of (the Horror) Film'. In *Horror Film and Psychoanalysis: Freud's Worst Nightmare*, Steven Jay Schneider ed., 68–83. Cambridge: Cambridge University Press, 2004.

U2. 'Zooropa'. *Zooropa* (album). Island Records, 1993.

Viera, Maria. 'The Work of John Cassavetes: Script, Performance, Style, and Improvisation'. *Journal of Film and Video* 43, no. 3 (1990), 34–40.

Virilio, Paul. *The Vision Machine*. Julie Rose (trans.). Bloomington: Indiana University Press, 1994.

Walsh, Michael. 'Jameson and Global Aesthetics'. In *Post-Theory: Reconstructing Film Studies*, David Bordwell and Noël Carroll (eds), 481–500. Madison, WI: University of Wisconsin Press, 1996.

Wasko, Janet. 'Financing and Production: Creating the Hollywood Film Commodity'. In *The Contemporary Hollywood Film Industry*, Paul McDonald and Janet Wasko (eds), 43–62. Malden, MA: Blackwell Publishing, 2008.

Welsh, James M., Gene D. Phillips and Rodney F. Hill. *The Francis Ford Coppola Encyclopedia*. Plymouth: Scarecrow Press, 2010.

White, Hayden. 'Historiography and Historiophoty'. *The American Historical Review* 93, no. 5 (1988), 1193–9.

Wood, Aylish. *Digital Encounters*. New York: Routledge, 2007.

Wood, Robin. 'Papering the Cracks: Fantasy and Ideology in the Reagan Era'. In *Movies and Mass Culture*, John Belton ed., 203–28. New Brunswick: Rutgers University Press, 1996.

Wyatt, Justin. *High Concept: Movies and Marketing in Hollywood*. Austin: University of Texas Press, 1994.

—'From Roadshowing to Saturation Release: Majors, Independents, and Marketing/Distribution Innovations'. In *The New American Cinema*, Jon Lewis ed., 64–86. Durham: Duke University Press, 1998.

Zalewski, Daniel. 'The Hours: How Christian Marclay Created the Ultimate Digital Mosaic'. *The New Yorker*, 12 March 2012, http://www.newyorker.com/reporting/2012/03/12/120312fa_fact_zalewski.

Žižek, Slavoj. 'Passions of the Real, Passions of Semblance'. In *Welcome to the Desert of the Real!: Five essays on 11 September and Related Dates*, 5–32. London: Verso, 2002.

—'*Vertigo*: The Drama of a Deceived Platonist'. *Hitchcock Annual* (2003–2004): 67–82.

Zone, Ray. *Stereoscopic Cinema and the Origins of 3-D Film*. Lexington: University of Kentucky Press, 2007.

Filmography

À Bout de Souffle [*Breathless*]. Dir. Jean Luc Godard. 1959.
Abyss, The. Dir. James Cameron. 1989.
Adaptation. Dir. Spike Jonze. 2002.
Adventures of Tintin, The. Dir. Steven Spielberg. 2011.
A.I.: Artificial Intelligence. Dir. Steven Spielberg. 2000.
Alien. Dir. Ridley Scott. 1979.
Aliens. Dir. James Cameron. 1986.
Alien: Resurrection. Dir. Jean-Pierre Jeunet. 1997.
American Graffiti. Dir. George Lucas. 1973.
L'Année dernière à Marienbad [*Last Year at Marienbad*]. Dir. Alain Resnais. 1962.
Apocalypse Now. Dir. Francis Ford Coppola. 1979.
Apocalypto. Dir. Mel Gibson. 2006.
Amistad. Dir. Steven Spielberg. 1997.
L'arrivée d'un Train en Gare de La Ciotat [*Arrival of a Train at a Station*]. Dir. Auguste Lumière. 1895.
Artist, The. Dir. Michel Hazanavicius. 2011.
Australia. Dir. Baz Luhrmann. 2008.
Avatar. Dir. James Cameron. 2009.
Avengers, The. Dir. Joss Whedon. 2012.
L'Avventura [*The Adventure*]. Dir. Michelangelo Antonioni. 1960.
Back to the Future. Dir. Robert Zemeckis. 1985.
Back to the Future Part II. Dir. Robert Zemeckis. 1989.
Barry Lyndon. Dir. Stanley Kubrick. 1975.
Batman. Dir. Tim Burton. 1989.
Beetlejuice. Dir. Tim Burton. 1988.
Being John Malkovich. Dir. Spike Jonze. 1999.
Bicycle Thieves, The. Dir. Vittorio De Sica. 1948.
Birds, The. Dir Alfred Hitchcock. 1963.
Blade Runner. Dir. Ridley Scott. 1982.
Blade Runner: Director's Cut. Dir. Ridley Scott. 1991.
Blade Runner: Final Cut. Dir. Ridley Scott. 2007.
Blow Up. Dir. Michelangelo Antonioni. 1966.
Boarding Gate. Dir. Olivier Assayas. 2007.
Body Double. Dir. Brian De Palma. 1984.
Bonnie and Clyde. Dir. Arthur Penn. 1968.
Born on the Fourth of July. Dir. Oliver Stone. 1989.
Bourne Supremacy, The. Dir. Paul Greengrass. 2004.
Bourne Ultimatum, The. Dir. Paul Greengrass. 2007.
Breathless. Dir. Jean Luc Godard. 1959

Bringing Up Baby. Dir. Howard Hawks. 1938.
Buono, il Brutto, il Cattivo, Il. Dir. Sergio Leone. 1966.
Bullitt. Dir. Peter Yates. 1968.
Bwana Devil. Dir. Arch Oboler. 1952.
Caché [*Hidden*]. Dir. Michael Haneke. 2005.
Carrie. Dir. Brian De Palma. 1976.
Casablanca. Dir. Michael Curtiz. 1942.
C'era una volta il West. Dir. Sergio Leone. 1968.
Che. Dir. Steven Soderberg. 2008.
Children of Men. Dir. Alfonso Cuarón. 2006.
Chinatown. Dir. Roman Polanski. 1974.
Citizen Kane. Dir. Orson Welles. 1941.
Clock, The. Video installation created by Christian Marclay. 2011.
Close Encounters of the Third Kind. Steven Spielberg. 1977.
Cloverfield. Dir. Matt Reeves. 2008.
Color Purple, The. Dir. Steven Spielberg. 1985.
Conformista, il [*The Conformist*]. Dir. Bernardo Bertolucci. 1971.
Conversation, The. Dir. Francis Ford Coppola. 1974.
Crash. Dir. David Cronenberg. 1996.
Cruisin'. Dir. William Friedkin. 1980.
Crying Game, The. Dir. Neil Jordan. 1992.
Dark Knight, The. Dir. Christopher Nolan. 2008.
Dark Knight Rises, The. Dir. Christopher Nolan. 2012.
Day the Earth Stood Still, The. Dir. Robert Wise. 1951.
Days of Heaven. Dir. Terrence Malick. 1978.
Days of Thunder. Dir. Tony Scott. 1990.
Deer Hunter, The. Dir. Michael Cimino. 1978.
Deliverance. Dir. John Boorman. 1972.
Descendants, The. Dir. Alexander Payne. 2011.
Dial M For Murder. Dir. Alfred Hitchcock. 1954.
Diamonds Are Forever. Dir. Guy Hamilton. 1971.
Die Hard. Dir. John McTiernan. 1988.
Dirty Dozen, The. Dir. Robert Aldrich. 1967.
Dirty Harry. Dir Don Siegel. 1971.
Django Unchained. Dir. Quentin Tarantino. 2012.
Dog Day Afternoon. Dir. Sidney Lumet. 1975.
Donnie Brasco. Dir. Mike Newell. 1997.
Don't Look Back. Dir. D. A. Pennebaker. 1967.
Do the Right Thing. Dir. Spike Lee. 1989.
Dressed to Kill. Dir. Brian De Palma. 1980.
Duel. Dir. Steven Spielberg. 1971.
Easy Rider. Dir. Dennis Hopper. 1969.
El Mariachi. Dir. Robert Rodriguez. 1992.
Empire of the Sun. Dir. Steven Spielberg. 1987.
Enforcer, The. Dir. James Fargo. 1976.
Enter the Dragon. Dir. Robert Clouse. 1973.
Eternal Sunshine of the Spotless Mind. Dir. Michel Gondry. 2004.
E.T.: The Extra-Terrestrial. Dir. Steven Spielberg. 1982.

Existenz. Dir. David Cronenberg. 1999.
Exorcist, The. Dir. William Friedkin. 1973.
Fahrenheit 451. Dir. François Truffaut. 1966.
Fast and the Furious, The (franchise). 2003–2013.
Fifty First Dates. Dir. Peter Segal. 2004.
Fight Club. Dir. David Fincher. 1999.
Fistful of Dollars, A [*Per un Pugno di Dollari*]. Dir. Sergio Leone. 1964.
Five Easy Pieces. Dir. Bob Rafelson. 1970.
Flashdance. Dir. Adrian Lyne. 1983.
Fly, The. Dir. David Cronenberg. 1986.
Following. Dir. Christopher Nolan. 1998.
Forbidden Planet. Dir. Fred M. Wilcox. 1956.
Freaks. Dir. Tod Browning. 1932.
French Connection, The. Dir. William Friedkin. 1971.
French Connection II, The. Dir. John Frankenheimer. 1975.
Frenzy. Dir. Alfred Hitchcock. 1972.
Gallipoli. Dir. Peter Weir. 1981.
Gattopardo, il [*The Leopard*]. Dir. Luchino Visconti. 1963.
Ghost. Dir. Jerry Zucker. 1990.
Ghostbusters. Dir. Ivan Reitman. 1984.
Girl With the Dragon Tattoo, The. Dir. David Fincher. 2011.
Godfather, The. Dir. Francis Ford Coppola. 1972.
Godfather, Part II, The. Dir. Francis Ford Coppola. 1974.
Goldfinger. Dir. Guy Hamilton. 1964.
Gold Diggers of 1933, The. Dir. Mervyn LeRoy. 1933.
Good, the Bad and the Ugly, The [*Il Buono, il Brutto, il Cattivo*]. Dir. Sergio
   Leone. 1966.
Good Will Hunting. Dir. Gus van Sant. 1997.
Graduate, The. Dir. Mike Nichols. 1967.
Grease. Dir. Randall Kleiser. 1978.
Great Gatsby, The. Dir. Baz Luhrmann. 2013.
Groundhog Day. Dir. Harold Ramis. 1993.
Hearts of Darkness: A Filmmaker's Apocalypse. Dir. Fax Bahr, George
   Hickenlooper and Eleanor Coppola. 1991.
Heat. Dir. Michael Mann. 1995.
Hidden. Dir. Michael Haneke. 2005.
High Noon. Dir. Fred Zinnerman. 1952.
Hobbit 3-D, The. Dir. Peter Jackson. 2012.
House of Wax. Dir. André de Toth. 1953.
Hugo 3-D. Dir. Martin Scorsese. 2011.
Hurt Locker, The. Dir. Kathryn Bigelow. 2008.
Inception. Dir. Christopher Nolan. 2010.
Incredibles, The. Dir. Brad Bird. 2004.
Independence Day. Dir. Roland Emmerich. 1996.
Indiana Jones and the Last Crusade. Dir. Steven Spielberg. 1989.
Indiana Jones and the Temple of Doom. Dir. Steven Spielberg. 1984.
Inglourious Basterds. Dir. Quentin Tarantino. 2009.
Insomnia. Dir. Christopher Nolan. 2002.

In the Mood For Love. Dir. Wong Kar-wai. 2000.
It Happened One Night. Dir. Frank Capra. 1934.
Irreversible. Dir. Gaspar Noé. 2002.
Jason and the Argonauts. Dir. Don Chaffey. 1963.
Jaws. Dir. Steven Spielberg. 1975.
Jaws 3-D. Dir. Joe Alves. 1983.
Jetée, La. Dir. Chris Marker. 1962.
Jurassic Park. Dir. Steven Spielberg. 1993.
Kagemusha. Dir. Akira Kurosawa. 1980.
Kelly's Heroes. Dir. Brian G. Hutton. 1970.
Kill Bill, Volume 1. Dir. Quentin Tarantino. 2003.
King Kong. Dir. Merian C. Cooper. 1933.
Ladri di Biciclette [*The Bicycle Thieves*]. Dir. Vittorio De Sica. 1948.
Lady From Shanghai, The. Dir. Orson Welles. 1948.
Last Picture Show, The. Dir. Peter Bogdanovich. 1971.
Last Year at Marienbad. Dir. Alain Resnais. 1961.
Lawrence of Arabia. Dir. David Lean. 1962.
Lion King 3-D, The. Dir. Roger Allers and Rob Minkoff. 2011.
Long Goodbye, The. Dir. Robert Altman. 1973.
Lord of the Rings: The Fellowship of the Ring, The. Dir. Peter Jackson. 2001.
Mad Max. Dir. George Miller. 1979.
Mad Max 2: The Road Warrior. Dir. George Miller. 1981.
Magnificent Ambersons, The. Dir. Orson Welles. 1942.
Magnum Force. Dir. Ted Post. 1973.
Maltese Falcon. Dir. John Huston. 1941.
Manchurian Candidate, The. Dir. John Frankenheimer. 1962.
Man With a Movie Camera. Dir. Dziga Vertov. 1929.
Marnie. Dir. Alfred Hitchcock. 1964.
Mash. Dir. Robert Altman. 1970.
Matrix, The. Dir. The Wachowskis. 1999.
Matrix Revolutions. Dir. The Wachowskis. 2003.
McCabe and Mrs Miller. Dir. Robert Altman. 1971.
Mean Streets. Dir. Martin Scorsese. 1973.
Melancholia. Dir. Lars von Trier. 2011.
Memento. Dir. Christopher Nolan. 2000.
Michael Clayton. Dir. Tony Gilroy. 2007.
Midnight Cowboy. Dir. John Schlesinger. 1969.
Minority Report. Dir. Steven Spielberg. 2002.
Modern Times. Dir. Charlie Chaplin. 1936.
Munich. Dir. Steven Spielberg. 2005.
My Brilliant Career. Dir. Gillian Armstrong. 1979.
Naked Kiss, The. Dir. Sam Fuller. 1964.
Nashville. Dir. Robert Altman. 1975.
New World, The. Dir. Terrence Malick. 2005.
Night Fishing. Dir. Park Chan-Wook. 2011.
1941. Dir. Steven Spielberg. 1971.
North by Northwest. Dir. Alfred Hitchcock. 1959.
Notte, La [*The Night*]. Dir. Michelangelo Antonioni. 1961.

Nowhere to Hide. Dir. Myung-se Lee. 1999.

Once Upon a Time in the West [*C'era una volta il West*]. Dir. Sergio Leone. 1968.

Open City [*Roma, Città Aperta*]. Dir. Roberto Rossellini. 1945.

Parallax View, The. Dir. Alan Pakula. 1974.

Passenger, The. Dir. Michelangelo Antonioni. 1975.

Passion de Jeanne d'Arc, La [*The Passion of Joan of Arc*]. Dir. Carl Theodor Dreyer. 1927.

Per un Pugno di Dollari. Dir. Sergio Leone. 1964.

Piano, The. Dir. Jane Campion. 1993.

Picnic at Hanging Rock. Dir. Peter Weir. 1975.

Platoon. Dir. Oliver Stone. 1986.

Player, The. Dir. Robert Altman. 1992.

Point Blank. Dir. John Boorman. 1967.

Potemkin. Dir. Sergei Eisenstein. 1925.

Prestige, The. Dir. Christopher Nolan. 2006.

Psycho. Dir. Alfred Hitchcock. 1960.

Pulp Fiction. Dir. Quentin Tarantino. 1994.

Punch Drunk Love. Dir. Paul Thomas Anderson. 2002.

Raiders of the Lost Ark. Steven Spielberg. 1981.

Rain Man. Dir. Barry Levinson. 1988.

Ran. Dir. Akira Kurosawa. 1985.

Rear Window. Dir. Alfred Hitchcock. 1954.

Rebecca. Dir. Alfred Hitchcock. 1940.

Red Dead Redemption (Playstation 3/Xbox 360). Rockstar Games. 2010.

Red River. Dir. Howard Hawks. 1948.

Règle du Jeu, Le [*The Rules of the Game*]. Dir. Jean Renoir. 1939.

Repulsion. Dir. Roman Polanski. 1965.

Requiem for a Dream. Dir. Darren Aronofsky. 2000.

Reservoir Dogs. Dir. Quentin Tarantino. 1992.

Rise of the Planet of the Apes. Dir. Rupert Wyatt. 2011.

Road Warrior, The. Dir. George Miller. 1981.

Robocop. Dir. Paul Verhoeven. 1987.

Roma, Città Aperta [*Open City*]. Dir. Roberto Rossellini. 1945.

Run Lola Run. Dir. Tom Tykwer. 1998.

Saboteur. Dir. Alfred Hitchcock. 1942.

Saving Private Ryan. Dir. Steven Spielberg. 1998.

Schindler's List. Dir. Steven Spielberg. 1993.

Searchers, The. Dir. John Ford. 1956.

Seconds. Dir. John Frankenheimer. 1966.

Se7en. Dir. David Fincher. 1995.

Seven Samurai, The. Dir. Akira Kurosawa. 1954.

Shadows. Dir. John Cassavetes. 1959.

Shampoo. Dir. Hal Ashby. 1975.

Shock Corridor. Dir. Sam Fuller. 1963.

Sin City. Dir. Robert Rodriguez. 2005.

Sorcerer. Dir. William Friedkin. 1977.

Sortie des usines Lumière à Lyon, La [*Workers Leaving the Lumière Factory in Lyon*]. Dir. Auguste Lumiére. 1895.

Speed. Dir. Jan de Bont. 1994.

Stagecoach. Dir. John Ford. 1939.

Star Wars Episode II: Attack of the Clones. Dir. George Lucas. 2002.

Star Wars Episode IV: A New Hope. Dir. George Lucas. 1977.

Star Wars Episode V: The Empire Strikes Back. Dir. Irvin Kershner. 1980.

Strange Days. Dir. Kathryn Bigelow. 1995.

Stranger, The. Dir. Orson Welles. 1946.

Sudden Impact. Dir. Clint Eastwood. 1983.

Sugarland Express. Dir. Steven Spielberg. 1974.

Superman. Dir. Richard Donner. 1978.

Superman II. Dir. Richard Lester. 1982.

Taxi Driver. Dir. Martin Scorsese. 1976.

Ten Commandments, The. Dir. Cecil B. DeMille. 1956.

There Will Be Blood. Dir. Paul Thomas Anderson. 2007.

Terminator, The. Dir. James Cameron. 1984.

Terminator 2: Judgment Day. Dir. James Cameron. 1991.

T2 3-D: Battle Across Time (Multimedia 3-D Attraction). Universal Studios. 1996
    (opening date).

Thing, The. Dir. John Carpenter. 1982.

Thin Red Line, The. Dir. Terrence Malick. 1998.

Third Man, The. Dir. Carol Reed. 1949.

39 Steps, The. Dir. Alfred Hitchcock. 1935.

This Is Not a Film. Dir. Jafah Panahi. 2011.

300. Dir. Zack Snyder. 2006.

THX 1138. Dir. George Lucas. 1971.

Tight Rope. Dir. Richard Tuggle. 1984.

Time Code. Dir. Mike Figgis. 2000.

Titanic. Dir. James Cameron. 1997.

To Catch a Thief. Dir. Alfred Hitchcock. 1955.

Tom Jones. Dir. Tony Richardson. 1963.

Total Recall. Dir. Paul Verhoeven. 1990.

Touch of Evil. Dir. Orson Welles. 1958.

Transformers. Dir. Michael Bay. 2007.

Tree of Life. Dir. Terrence Malick. 2011.

Trip to the Moon, A. Dir. Georges Méliès. 1902.

Triumph des Willens [*Triumph of the Will*]. Dir. Leni Riefenstahl. 1935.

Tron. Dir. Steve Lisberger. 1982.

True Lies. Dir. James Cameron. 1994.

24 (Television). Created by Joel Surnow and Robert Cochran. 2001–2010.

21 Grams. Dir. Alejandro González Iñárritu. 2003.

2001: A Space Odyssey. Dir. Stanley Kubrick. 1968.

2012. Dir. Roland Emmerich. 2009.

Ulysses. Dir. Oscar Godoy. 2011.

Umberto D. Dir. Vittorio De Sica. 1952.

Unforgiven, The. Dir. Clint Eastwood. 1992.

United 93. Dir. Paul Greengrass. 2006.

Untouchables, The. Dir. Brian De Palma. 1986.

Usual Suspects, The. Dir. Brian Singer. 1995.

Vertigo. Dir. Alfred Hitchcock. 1958.

Videodrome. Dir. David Cronenberg. 1983.

Voyage dans la Lune, Le [*A Trip to the Moon*]. Dir. Georges Méliès. 1902.

Wait Until Dark. Dir. Terence Young. 1967.

War Horse. Dir. Steven Spielberg. 2011.

War of the Worlds. Dir. Steven Spielberg. 2004.

Waterworld. Dir. Kevin Reynolds. 1995.

Wavelength. Dir. Michael Snow. 1967.

Weisse Band, Das [*The White Ribbon, The*]. Dir. Michael Haneke. 2009.

Who Framed Roger Rabbit. Dir. Robert Zemeckis. 1988.

Wild at Heart. Dir. David Lynch. 1990.

Wolf Creek. Dir. Greg Mclean. 2005.

Wrong Man, The. Dir. Alfred Hitchcock. 1956.

Zabriskie Point. Dir. Michelangelo Antonioni. 1970.

DVDs

Blow Up. Warner Home Video. 2004.

Bourne Ultimatum, The. Universal Home Video. 2007.

Casablanca. Warner Home Video. 2000.

Conversation, The (Widescreen DVD Collection). Paramount Home Video. 2000.

Eternal Sunshine of the Spotless Mind (2-Disc Collector's Edition). Roadshow Home Entertainment. 2004.

Heat. Warner Home Video. 1995.

Inception (Blu-Ray/DVD 4 Disc Set). Warner Home Video. 2010.

Jaws (25th Anniversary Collector's Edition). Columbia Tristar Home Video. 2000.

Mad Max 2 (*The Road Warrior*). Warner Home Video. 2000.

Man With a Movie Camera. Blackhawk Films Collection. 1998.

Passenger, The. Sony Pictures Home Entertainment. 2006.

Rome Open City: Roberto Rossellini's War Trilogy (Rome Open City/Paisan/ Germany Year Zero). The Criterion Collection. 2010.

Saving Private Ryan (Widescreen Special Limited Edition). Dreamworks Home Entertainment. 1999.

Schindler's List (Two-Disc Special Collection). Universal Home Video. 2006.

Se7en (Deluxe Special Edition). Roadshow Home Entertainment. 1996.

Titanic. Twentieth Century Fox Home Video Entertainment. 2002.

Index

Film titles are indexed by their English name. Page references in italics denote a figure.